Design and Deploy IoT Network & Security with Microsoft Azure

Embrace Microsoft Azure for IoT Network Enhancement and Security Uplift

Puthiyavan Udayakumar
Dr. R Anandan

Apress®

Design and Deploy IoT Network & Security with Microsoft Azure:
Embrace Microsoft Azure for IoT Network Enhancement and Security Uplift

Puthiyavan Udayakumar
VISTAS, CSE-Technology
Chennai, Tamil Nadu, India

Dr. R Anandan
VISTAS, CSE-Technology
Chennai, Tamil Nadu, India

ISBN-13 (pbk): 979-8-8688-0907-1
https://doi.org/10.1007/979-8-8688-0908-8

ISBN-13 (electronic): 979-8-8688-0908-8

Copyright © 2024 by The Editor(s) (if applicable) and The Author(s), under exclusive license to APress Media, LLC, part of Springer Nature

This work is subject to copyright. All rights are reserved by the Publisher, whether the whole or part of the material is concerned, specifically the rights of translation, reprinting, reuse of illustrations, recitation, broadcasting, reproduction on microfilms or in any other physical way, and transmission or information storage and retrieval, electronic adaptation, computer software, or by similar or dissimilar methodology now known or hereafter developed.

Trademarked names, logos, and images may appear in this book. Rather than use a trademark symbol with every occurrence of a trademarked name, logo, or image we use the names, logos, and images only in an editorial fashion and to the benefit of the trademark owner, with no intention of infringement of the trademark.

The use in this publication of trade names, trademarks, service marks, and similar terms, even if they are not identified as such, is not to be taken as an expression of opinion as to whether or not they are subject to proprietary rights.

While the advice and information in this book are believed to be true and accurate at the date of publication, neither the authors nor the editors nor the publisher can accept any legal responsibility for any errors or omissions that may be made. The publisher makes no warranty, express or implied, with respect to the material contained herein.

 Managing Director, Apress Media LLC: Welmoed Spahr
 Acquisitions Editor: Smriti Srivastava
 Desk Editor: Laura Berendson
 Editorial Project Manager: Kripa Joseph

Cover designed by eStudioCalamar

Cover image designed by Unsplash

Distributed to the book trade worldwide by Springer Science+Business Media New York, 1 New York Plaza, Suite 4600, New York, NY 10004-1562, USA. Phone 1-800-SPRINGER, fax (201) 348-4505, e-mail orders-ny@springer-sbm.com, or visit www.springeronline.com. Apress Media, LLC is a California LLC and the sole member (owner) is Springer Science + Business Media Finance Inc (SSBM Finance Inc). SSBM Finance Inc is a **Delaware** corporation.

For information on translations, please e-mail booktranslations@springernature.com; for reprint, paperback, or audio rights, please e-mail bookpermissions@springernature.com.

Apress titles may be purchased in bulk for academic, corporate, or promotional use. eBook versions and licenses are also available for most titles. For more information, reference our Print and eBook Bulk Sales web page at http://www.apress.com/bulk-sales.

Any source code or other supplementary material referenced by the author in this book is available to readers on GitHub. For more detailed information, please visit https://www.apress.com/gp/services/source-code.

If disposing of this product, please recycle the paper

Table of Contents

About the Authors ix

About the Technical Reviewer xi

Acknowledgments xiii

Introduction xv

Chapter 1: Get Started with IoT Network and Security 1

    Get Started with IoT Network and Security 2

        IoT Network 4

        IoT Definitions and Terminologies 14

        Building Blocks of IoT/IIoT 17

        Use Case of IoT/IIoT 23

        Importance, Challenges, and Future Opportunities 34

        Importance of IoT Network and Security 39

        Challenges in IoT Network and Security 44

        Future Opportunities 62

    IoT Architecture 67

        Microsoft's IoT Reference Architecture 76

    Summary 94

Chapter 2: Design and Deploy Azure Edge Services 97

    IoT Network Protocol 98

        Importance of IoT Developers Knowing About IoT Network Protocols and IoT Network Architecture 106

        IoT Network Protocols 108

TABLE OF CONTENTS

IoT Network Architecture 119
IoT Network – Application Layer 122
    Constrained Application Protocol (CoAP) 124
IoT Network – Transport Layer 143
    Transmission Control Protocol (TCP) 146
    User Datagram Protocol (UDP) 155
IoT Network – Network Layer 163
    IPv6 166
    6LoWPAN 173
IoT Network – Physical Layer 182
    Bluetooth 185
    IOT Networking Deployment Models 192
    IoT Networking Considerations and Challenges 197
Design Azure IOT Edge 201
    Critical Capabilities of Azure IoT Edge 201
    Key Components of Azure IoT Edge 203
    Key Design Considerations of Azure IoT Edge 213
    Key Production Best Practices 218
Deploy Azure IOT Edge 220
Summary 225

Chapter 3: Design and Deploy Azure IoT Networks 227
Fundamentals of Network Topology 228
    Star Topology 231
    Bus Topology 235
    Point-to-Point Topology 240
    Ring Topology 247
    Mesh Topology 252

Tree Topology	257
Autonomous Network Architecture	262
Ubiquitous Network Architecture	265
Azure Networks for IOT	266
IoT Network Connection Patterns for IoT Devices	273
Design Azure IoT Network	273
Azure Well-Architected Framework	275
Manageability	277
Reliability	277
Security	277
Cost Optimization	279
Performance Efficiency	280
Azure Network Topology	280
Azure Network Connectivity	296
Deploying Azure IoT Network	308
Core Layer	308
Distribution Layer	309
Access Layer	309
Integrating OT/IoT Networks	309
Purdue Networking Model	310
Deployment Overview	312
Summary	317

Chapter 4: Design and Deploy Azure IoT Security 319

Fundamentals of IoT Security	320
Level 1 Insights	323
IoT Cybersecurity Strategy	325
Know What You Are Protecting and Why	327

TABLE OF CONTENTS

    SOC/DevSecOps Front Shield of IoT 330
    SOC Framework: The Blueprint for Security 332
    SOC Functions: The Many Arms of Defense.. 334
    SOC Operations: Putting the Framework into Action 334
    IoT Defense-In-Depth 338
    IOT Zero-Trust... 358
    Core Principles of Zero Trust 359
    Contextual Authentication and Authorization... 360
    Minimizing Access Rights.. 361
    Proactive Defense Strategies 362
    Comprehensive Incident Response Plans... 363
    Implementing Zero Trust in IoT Networks.. 364
    Challenges in Adopting Zero Trust for IoT 364
    Role of Edge Computing in IoT Zero Trust.. 365
    Integration with Artificial Intelligence and Machine Learning 365
    Case Studies of IoT Zero Trust Implementation 366
    Regulatory and Compliance Considerations.. 366
    Future Trends and Developments 366
    IoT Layer of Cybersecurity.. 367
    IoT Users Security.. 372
    IoT Device Security.. 375
    IoT Gateway.. 379
    IoT Network and Connectivity... 382
    IoT Cloud and Application Security.. 386
Design Microsoft Azure-Based IoT Security.. 390
    Fundamentals of Cybersecurity 390
    Design Principles of Cybersecurity.. 392
    Foundation of Microsoft Azure IoT Offering.. 394

TABLE OF CONTENTS

    Microsoft Defender for IoT 395

    Microsoft Defender XDR (Extended Detection and Response) 396

    Microsoft Sentinel 398

Design Elements of Microsoft Defender for IoT 400

    Quick Start of Microsoft Defender for IoT 404

Design Elements of Sentinel for IoT 406

    Secure and Centralize Data Collection 407

    Enhance Security Posture 407

    Monitor and Detect Threats 408

    Automate Response and Mitigation..408

    Operational Management 409

    Maintain Visibility and Insights 409

    Key Microsoft Recommended Best Practices..410

    Quick Start Deployment of Sentinel..412

Summary...417

Chapter 5: Design and Deploy Azure IoT Monitoring and Management 419

Fundamentals of IoT Monitoring and Management 420

    Level 1 Insights 422

    IoT Lifecycle for Network and Security Management and Monitoring 425

    Planning and Design..427

    Deployment Phase..429

    Operation and Maintenance Phase..433

    Data Management Phase 437

    Decommissioning Phase 442

    IoT Monitoring 445

    IoT and SIEM...457

    IoT and SOAR 465

vii

TABLE OF CONTENTS

IoT and NDR 472

IoT and XDR 479

Design Microsoft Azure-Based IoT Monitoring and Management 489

Microsoft Recommendation 491

Deploy Microsoft Azure-Based IoT Monitoring and Management 509

Azure IoT Central 510

Azure Monitor 517

Summary 523

Design Microsoft Azure-Based IoT Monitoring and Management 523

Deploy Microsoft Azure-Based IoT Monitoring and Management 524

Glossary 525

Index 535

About the Authors

Puthiyavan Udayakumar is a seasoned infrastructure architect and senior infrastructure consultant with over 15 years of experience in the IT industry. He is a Master Certified Architect by OpenGroup and holds numerous IT certifications. Throughout his career, he has excelled as an infrastructure solution architect and senior engineer, specializing in designing, deploying, and rolling out advanced on-premises, cloud, IoT, and cybersecurity solutions. He possesses robust expertise in on-premises, cloud, IoT, and cybersecurity, including project management and Agile delivery services. He has also authored more than ten books on various topics related to information technology.

Dr. R Anandan completed his undergraduate degree, doctorate in Computer Science and Engineering, and post-doctoral degree (D.Sc.) in Computer Science and Engineering in Mexico. He is an IBMS/390 Mainframe professional and a Chartered Engineer from the Institution of Engineers in India and received a fellowship from Bose Science Society, India. He completed seven certification courses (mainly from CISCO). He has published more than 140 research papers in various international journals, such as *Scopus* and *SCI*. He has presented 90 papers at various international conferences. He received 18 awards from national and international agencies. He authored and edited 27 books. He is also an editor for companies such as Springer, Wiley, World Scientific Press, and Nova Publishers.

About the Technical Reviewer

Kasam Shaikh is a prominent figure in India's artificial intelligence landscape, holding the distinction of being one of the country's first four Microsoft Most Valuable Professionals (MVPs) in AI. Currently serving as a Senior Architect, Kasam boasts an impressive track record as an author, having authored five best-selling books dedicated to Azure and AI technologies. Beyond his writing endeavors, Kasam is recognized as a Microsoft Certified Trainer (MCT) and influential tech YouTuber (@mekasamshaikh). He also leads the largest online Azure AI community, known as DearAzure I Azure INDIA, and is a globally renowned AI speaker. His commitment to knowledge sharing extends to contributions to Microsoft Learn, where he plays a pivotal role.

Within the realm of AI, Kasam is a respected subject matter expert (SME) in Generative AI for the Cloud, complementing his role as a Senior Cloud Architect. He actively promotes the adoption of No Code and Azure OpenAI solutions and possesses a strong foundation in Hybrid and Cross-Cloud practices. Kasam Shaikh's versatility and expertise make him an invaluable asset in the rapidly evolving landscape of technology, contributing significantly to the advancement of Azure and AI.

In summary, Kasam Shaikh is a multifaceted professional who excels in both technical expertise and knowledge dissemination. His contributions span writing, training, community leadership, public speaking, and

ABOUT THE TECHNICAL REVIEWER

architecture, establishing him as a true luminary in the world of Azure and AI. Kasam was recently awarded as the top voice in AI by LinkedIn, making him the sole exclusive Indian professional acknowledged by both Microsoft and LinkedIn for his contributions to the world of artificial intelligence!

Acknowledgments

I want to extend my heartfelt thanks to Smriti Srivastava, the Acquisitions Editor, for her invaluable insights, guidance, and steadfast support, which were crucial in shaping and refining this manuscript. Her efforts elevate Apress to new heights. I also want to express my gratitude to Shobana Srinivasan for her relentless dedication in bringing this book to fruition. My thanks go to the entire Apress production team for their contributions as well.

Introduction

The Internet of Things (IoT) is reshaping our world by connecting everyday objects to the Internet, creating a network where devices communicate and make decisions autonomously. In industrial settings, IoT drives efficiency through predictive maintenance and real-time monitoring. As IoT continues to evolve, its integration with emerging technologies like 5G and AI promises even greater advancements, offering faster connectivity, intelligent data analysis, and enhanced automation. Looking ahead, IoT's future will be defined by increased interoperability, robust security measures, and a focus on sustainability. The rise of edge computing will enable real-time data processing and reduce latency, while improved standards will ensure seamless integration across diverse platforms. As these technologies advance, they will shape a more connected and intelligent world, making IoT an integral part of our everyday lives and industrial operations.

The book *Design and Deploy IoT Network and Security with Microsoft Azure* is a valuable resource for IoT Network and Security engineers focusing on enhancing the networks and security of their IoT deployments. Its five chapters offer a structured approach to understanding, implementing, and managing IoT networks and security with Microsoft Azure offerings.

Chapter 1, "Get Started with IoT Network and Security," introduces the foundational concepts of IoT networks and their security. It begins with defining IoT, exploring key terminologies, and understanding the essential building blocks of an IoT system. Practical use cases in both consumer and industrial IoT (IIoT) are presented to highlight the real-world applications of these technologies. The chapter also delves into the significance of IoT,

INTRODUCTION

addressing the challenges it poses and exploring future opportunities. Finally, it provides an overview of the Azure IoT Reference Architecture, a critical framework for designing and implementing secure IoT solutions on the Azure platform.

Chapter 2, "Design and Deploy Azure Edge Services," covers the essentials of networking within the context of IoT, beginning with a broad overview of IoT network protocols and models. It explores various layers of the IoT network, including the application layer, where protocols like AMQP, CoAP, DDS, and MQTT operate, and the transport layer with TCP and UDP. The chapter also examines the network layer, focusing on IP and 6LoWPAN, the data link layer with standards like IEEE 802.15.4, and the physical layer encompassing technologies such as BLE, Ethernet, LTE, NFC, PLC, RFID, Wi-Fi, Z-Wave, and Zigbee. After laying this groundwork, the chapter guides the reader through the design and deployment of Azure Edge Services, tailored specifically for IoT.

Chapter 3, "Design and Deploy Azure IoT Networks," focuses on network topology and its importance in IoT networks. It starts by explaining the fundamental concepts of network topology, including various configurations like star, bus, point-to-point, hybrid, tree, ring, and mesh topologies. The chapter also discusses advanced network architectures such as autonomous and ubiquitous networks. Building on these fundamentals, the chapter then provides detailed guidance on designing and deploying Azure networks optimized for IoT applications, ensuring robust, scalable, and efficient network infrastructure.

Chapter 4, "Design and Deploy Azure IoT Security," guides you on securing IoT systems, and this chapter addresses it comprehensively. It begins by laying out the fundamentals of IoT security, including frameworks like IoT cybersecurity, defense-in-depth, and zero-trust models. The chapter examines various aspects of IoT security, covering users, devices, gateways, network and connectivity, and cloud applications. Following this foundational knowledge, the chapter introduces Azure Security Services specifically designed for IoT. Readers are then guided through developing and deploying these services to safeguard their IoT ecosystems effectively.

Chapter 5, "Design and Deploy Azure IoT Monitoring and Management," centers on the ongoing management and monitoring of IoT networks, with a focus on security. It starts with the basics of security monitoring and management, including IoT lifecycle management and continuous monitoring practices. The chapter also explores the integration of IoT with security solutions like SIEM, SOAR, NDR, and XDR. Following this, the chapter discusses the design and deployment of comprehensive security solutions for IoT environments, ensuring that these networks remain secure and well-managed throughout their operational lifespan.

This book offers IoT network and security engineers, developers, and cybersecurity architects in-depth knowledge and practical guidance for developing a robust network and security framework using Microsoft Azure solutions. It provides advanced insights and actionable strategies to strengthen the network, bolster security, and enhance the resilience of IoT Infrastructures, ensuring a fortified defense against potential threats.

CHAPTER 1

Get Started with IoT Network and Security

Welcome to the dynamic realm of IoT networks and cybersecurity. In today's interconnected world, the proliferation of IoT devices has fundamentally changed how we interact with technology. Before we embark on our exploration, it is crucial to understand the essence of IoT networks and the paramount importance of security within these interconnected systems.

Before diving into the depths, it's essential to grasp the intricacies of IoT, including its definition and the terminology that defines this rapidly evolving domain. We'll unravel the layers of complexity to gain a comprehensive understanding of what IoT truly entails. At the heart of every IoT ecosystem lie its building blocks. In this section, we dissect these foundational components, offering insights into the hardware, software, connectivity protocols, and data management systems that form the backbone of IoT infrastructures.

The power of IoT manifests through its myriad applications across industries. From smart homes to industrial automation, we explore compelling real-world use cases that demonstrate the transformative potential of IoT and its industrial counterpart, IIoT (Industrial Internet of Things). While IoT holds immense promise, it also presents unique challenges. We discuss the importance of addressing these challenges and highlight the future opportunities that await those who navigate the IoT landscape adeptly.

CHAPTER 1   GET STARTED WITH IOT NETWORK AND SECURITY

As we delve deeper into IoT networks and cybersecurity, we leverage Azure IoT as a reference architecture. Exploring its framework provides valuable insights into best practices and approaches for implementing robust IoT solutions with security at the forefront. Let us begin our journey to unravel the intricacies of IoT networks and cybersecurity, laying a solid foundation for what lies ahead.

By the end of this chapter, you should be able to understand the following:

- Get started with IoT network and security
- IoT definitions and terminologies
- Building blocks of IoT
- Use case of IoT/IIoT
- Importance, challenges, and future opportunities
- IoT architecture
- Microsoft Azure IoT references architecture

Get Started with IoT Network and Security

An IoT (Internet of Things) network refers to the interconnected web of physical devices, vehicles, appliances, and other items embedded with sensors, software, and connectivity capabilities. These devices collect and exchange data over the Internet, enabling them to interact autonomously with each other and their environments. IoT networks can range from simple setups in smart homes to complex systems in industrial settings, spanning various industries such as healthcare, agriculture, manufacturing, transportation, and more.

Did you know that farmers are utilizing sensors on their crops to optimize irrigation, monitor water levels, and determine the ideal time for harvest? This technological advancement enables farmers to maximize their produce's quality and quantity. Similarly, coal miners are employing sensors within mines to detect minute traces of hazardous gases, ultimately saving lives by providing early warnings of potential dangers. Additionally, automobile insurance companies leverage IoT technology to offer drivers reduced rates in exchange for access to their driving behavior data. This approach promotes fairer and more precise pricing, boosting profitability while cutting operational expenses.

The essence of IoT lies in its ability to harness data. By digitizing various aspects of our lives, businesses, and governance, IoT facilitates the generation of actionable insights. These insights are pivotal in saving lives, enhancing operational efficiencies, and fostering community development. Perhaps you're considering a career in IoT, where your expertise could contribute to shaping a future defined by innovation and progress.

The Internet of Things (IoT) comprises a vast network of millions of interconnected smart devices and sensors linked to the Internet. These devices and sensors gather and exchange data, serving various purposes for various entities, including businesses, municipalities, governmental bodies, healthcare facilities, and individuals. The proliferation of IoT owes much to the accessibility of inexpensive processors and wireless networks. Objects that were once static, such as doorknobs and light bulbs, can now be imbued with intelligent sensors capable of data collection and transmission to network endpoints.

Projections indicate a staggering growth in IoT adoption, with an estimated 38.6 billion connected devices anticipated by 2025, a figure set to swell to 50 billion by 2030. This translates to a remarkable monthly influx of approximately 190 million new connected devices.

Approximately one-third of these connected devices are expected to be conventional computing devices like computers, smartphones, tablets, and smart TVs. The remaining two-thirds represent a diverse array of "things," encompassing sensors, actuators, and innovative, intelligent devices engineered to monitor, regulate, analyze, and optimize various facets of our environment.

Intelligent connected sensors span a broad spectrum of applications, including smart doorbells, garage doors, thermostats, wearable fitness devices, medical implants such as pacemakers, traffic management systems, parking sensors, and an array of other innovations. The potential for objects to transition into intelligent sensors is bounded solely by the boundaries of human imagination.

IoT Network

An IoT network is a system of interconnected devices equipped with sensors that communicate and exchange data with each other. These devices can be anything from refrigerators and thermostats to industrial machines and entire buildings.

Here's a breakdown of the critical aspects of an IoT network:

- Connected devices: These everyday objects are embedded with sensors and processing abilities that allow them to collect and transmit data.

- Communication: The devices communicate with each other and with other systems via various networks, like WiFi, cellular data, or specialized IoT protocols.

- Data exchange: The data collected by the sensors is exchanged between the devices and can be sent to the cloud for analysis or used locally by the devices themselves.

There are different types of IoT networks, each suited for various purposes depending on factors like power consumption, range, and data transfer needs. Some common examples include:

- Local area networks (LANs), which are designed for connecting devices within a home or office building.

CHAPTER 1   GET STARTED WITH IOT NETWORK AND SECURITY

- Wide area networks (WANs), which are designed for connecting devices over a larger geographical area, like a city or region.

- Low-power wide area networks (LPWANs), which are designed for battery-powered devices that need to transmit data over long distances with low power consumption.

IoT networks play a significant role in enabling the Internet of Things (IoT) by providing the infrastructure for communication and data exchange between these smart devices. This has applications in various fields, including smart homes, industrial automation, and environmental monitoring.

A research study says that with 30 billion interconnected devices generating trillions of gigabytes of data, the question arises: How can this vast network collaborate to enhance decision-making and elevate our personal lives and business endeavors? At the heart of this collaboration lies our daily utilized networks, serving as the backbone of the Internet and the digitized landscape.

The evolution of communication methods has transcended the limitations of cables and plugs, propelled by groundbreaking advancements in wireless and digital technologies. These innovations have extended the reach of our interactions, paving the way for seamless connectivity and information exchange.

In their myriad sizes and complexities, networks form the bedrock of our digitized world. From modest configurations linking two computers to sprawling networks interconnecting millions of devices, their versatility knows no bounds.

In homes, simple networks facilitate Internet connectivity and resource sharing among local computers, including printers, documents, images, and music. Meanwhile, in business and large-scale organizations, networks serve as conduits for delivering products and services to customers worldwide. They also facilitate consolidation, storage, and access to vast troves of information stored on network servers. Moreover, networks foster communication and collaboration among employees through email and instant messaging while extending connectivity to industrial machinery, amplifying their value in manufacturing environments.

At the pinnacle of network infrastructure lies the Internet, a colossal interwoven web that envelops the globe like an electronic skin. Aptly named a "network of networks," the Internet interconnects many private and public networks, ranging from businesses and small office setups to individual home networks, seamlessly bridging geographical divides and fostering global connectivity.

How IoT Devices Are Connected to the Network

To ensure the gathered data from a sensor is stored and shared effectively, it must be connected to a network. This connection can be achieved through a wired Ethernet connection or a wireless link to a controller. While wireless Ethernet remains an option, practicality often favors low-power alternatives such as Bluetooth LE, Zigbee, or LoRa. Controllers play a crucial role in this setup, gathering sensor data and facilitating network or internet connectivity. These controllers may be able to make immediate decisions based on the data received, or they may relay the data to a more robust computing device for in-depth analysis. This computing device might reside within the same local area network (LAN) as the controller or may only be accessible via the Internet.

Sensors frequently collaborate with actuators, which convert electrical input into physical action. For instance, when a sensor detects elevated room temperature, it transmits the temperature data to a microcontroller. Subsequently, the microcontroller can relay this information to an actuator, triggering actions such as activating the air conditioner to regulate the temperature.

The increasing prevalence of new devices, including fitness wearables, implanted medical devices like pacemakers, air quality sensors in mine shafts, and water meters in agricultural fields, underscores the growing demand for wireless connectivity. Since many sensors operate remotely and are powered by batteries or solar panels, careful consideration must be given to power consumption. Employing low-powered connection options becomes imperative to optimize energy usage and prolong the operational lifespan of these sensors.

IoT Network Types

IoT networks form the backbone of the Internet of Things (IoT) ecosystem, enabling communication and data exchange among interconnected devices. These networks play a pivotal role in facilitating the seamless operation of IoT applications across various domains, ranging from smart homes and cities to industrial automation and healthcare.

Wireless Networks: Wireless technologies are the cornerstone of many IoT deployments due to their flexibility, scalability, and ease of deployment. Wi-Fi, Bluetooth, Zigbee, Z-Wave, and LoRaWAN are popular wireless protocols in IoT networks. Wi-Fi is prevalent in home and office environments, providing high-speed connectivity for devices within a limited range. Bluetooth Low Energy (BLE) is ideal for short-range communication between devices, making it suitable for wearables and smart home gadgets. Zigbee and Z-Wave are mesh networking protocols for low-power, low-data-rate applications, such as home automation. LoRaWAN, on the other hand, is optimized for long-range communication and is widely used in smart city deployments and industrial IoT applications.

Wired Networks: While wireless networks dominate IoT deployments, wired connections such as Ethernet are still used in specific scenarios where reliability and stability are paramount. Ethernet provides high-speed, reliable connectivity for devices within a local area network (LAN). Power over Ethernet (PoE) is often employed to power IoT devices and sensors through the Ethernet cable, simplifying installation and reducing infrastructure costs.

Cellular Networks: Cellular connectivity, including 2G, 3G, 4G LTE, and emerging 5G technologies, offers ubiquitous coverage and high bandwidth, making it suitable for IoT deployments in remote or mobile environments. Cellular IoT enables asset tracking, fleet management, and remote infrastructure monitoring applications. NB-IoT (Narrowband IoT) and LTE-M (Long-Term Evolution for Machines) are specifically designed to support IoT devices with low-power, low-data-rate requirements, extending cellular connectivity to a wide range of IoT applications.

Satellite Networks: Satellite communication provides global coverage, making it ideal for IoT deployments in remote or inaccessible locations where terrestrial networks are unavailable. Satellite IoT enables environmental monitoring, maritime tracking, and precision agriculture applications. While satellite communication offers wide-area coverage, it typically incurs higher costs and latency than terrestrial alternatives.

Edge Computing Networks: Edge computing networks bring processing and analytics capabilities closer to IoT devices, reducing latency and bandwidth usage by processing data locally. Edge computing enables real-time decision-making, enhances privacy and security, and minimizes reliance on cloud infrastructure. Fog computing, a variant of edge computing, extends these capabilities by distributing computing resources across intermediate nodes in the network, further optimizing performance and scalability for IoT applications.

Hybrid Networks: Many IoT deployments leverage a combination of wired, wireless, cellular, and satellite networks to meet diverse connectivity requirements. Hybrid networks enable seamless communication and data exchange across various environments and geographies, ensuring robustness, scalability, and flexibility for IoT applications.

Overall, IoT networks encompass diverse technologies and protocols tailored to meet the unique requirements of different use cases and environments. By selecting the appropriate network architecture and deployment strategy, organizations can harness the full potential of IoT to drive innovation, efficiency, and growth across industries. Table 1-1 lists various network types adopted across IoT/IIoT environment.

Table 1-1. *Various network types adopted across IoT/IIoT*

Network Type	Category	Description
Narrowband IoT (NB-IoT)	Cellular networks	A low-power wide-area network (LPWAN) technology standardized by the 3rd Generation Partnership Project (3GPP) for IoT applications. It provides long-range communication, deep indoor penetration, and extended battery life.
2G (GSM/GPRS/EDGE)	Cellular	2nd generation mobile network supporting voice and data.
3G (UMTS/HSPA)	Cellular	3rd generation mobile network with higher data speeds.
4G LTE	Cellular	4th generation long-term evolution with high-speed data.
5G	Cellular	5th generation network with ultra-low latency and high data rates.
LPWAN	Cellular	Low-power wide-area network optimized for IoT devices.
Private Cellular Networks	Cellular	Privately owned cellular networks for specific applications.
Ethernet	Wired	Traditional wired Ethernet connections can also be used for IoT devices in scenarios where power consumption and mobility are not significant concerns.

(continued)

Table 1-1. (*continued*)

Network Type	Category	Description
Ethernet/IP	Wired	Ethernet/IP is an industrial network protocol commonly used in manufacturing and industrial automation applications. It allows devices to communicate over Ethernet networks using standard Internet Protocol (IP).
Power over Ethernet (PoE)	Wired	Technology that allows electrical power to be transmitted over Ethernet cables.
Modbus	Wired	Modbus is a communication protocol commonly used in industrial automation systems to connect field devices such as PLCs (programmable logic controllers) and sensors to supervisory computers or SCADA systems.
PROFINET	Wired	PROFINET is an industrial Ethernet standard for real-time communication in industrial automation, offering high-speed data exchange and deterministic behavior for motion control and other critical applications.
CAN Bus	Wired	Controller area network (CAN) is a robust serial communication protocol commonly used in automotive and industrial applications for real-time data exchange between microcontrollers and devices.
RS-485	Wired	Serial communication standard commonly used in industrial applications.
Profibus	Wired	Fieldbus communication protocol used in process automation and manufacturing.

(*continued*)

Table 1-1. (*continued*)

Network Type	Category	Description
DeviceNet	Wired	Industrial network protocol used in factory automation.
OPC UA	Wired/Wireless	OPC Unified Architecture (OPC UA) is a platform-independent communication protocol for industrial automation, enabling interoperability and data exchange between different systems, devices, and software applications, regardless of the underlying network.
DNP3	Wired/Wireless	Distributed Network Protocol version 3 (DNP3) is a communication protocol used in SCADA systems for monitoring and controlling electric utility equipment, water management systems, and other critical infrastructure.
Wi-Fi	Wireless	Utilizes standard Wi-Fi protocols for IoT devices to connect to the internet or a local network. It provides high-speed data transmission but consumes more power compared to other wireless technologies.
Bluetooth	Wireless	Commonly used for short-range communication between IoT devices and smartphones or other devices. Bluetooth Low Energy (BLE) is particularly popular in IoT applications due to its low power consumption.
NFC (near field communication)	Wireless	Short-range communication technology for contactless data transfer.

(*continued*)

Table 1-1. (*continued*)

Network Type	Category	Description
Zigbee	Wireless	A low-power, low-data-rate wireless communication standard commonly used in home automation, smart lighting, and industrial control applications.
Z-Wave	Wireless	Similar to Zigbee, Z-Wave is a low-power wireless communication protocol designed for home automation and IoT applications. It operates in the sub-1 GHz frequency range and is known for its interoperability.
LoRaWAN	Wireless	LoRa (Long Range) is a wireless communication technology that enables long-range communication with low power consumption, making it suitable for IoT devices deployed over large areas, such as smart agriculture or smart cities.
Sigfox	Wireless	Another LPWAN technology that operates on unlicensed spectrum, providing long-range communication with low power consumption. Sigfox is suitable for applications like asset tracking and smart meters.
Thread	Wireless	A mesh networking protocol developed for IoT applications, particularly in smart homes and connected devices. It operates on the 6LoWPAN standard and supports IPv6 addressing.

(*continued*)

Table 1-1. (*continued*)

Network Type	Category	Description
6LoWPAN	Wireless	IPv6 over low-power wireless personal area networks (6LoWPAN) is a communication protocol that allows IPv6 packets to be transmitted over low-power wireless networks, making it suitable for IoT devices.
Wi-SUN	Wireless	Wireless Smart Utility Network (Wi-SUN) is a communication standard designed for large-scale outdoor IoT applications, particularly in smart cities and utility networks. It operates in the sub-GHz frequency band and offers long-range communication with mesh networking capabilities.
RFID	Wireless	Radio-frequency identification (RFID) is a technology that uses radio waves to identify and track objects or people automatically, commonly used in asset tracking, inventory management, and access control applications.
WirelessHART	Wireless	WirelessHART is a wireless communication standard for process automation and control in industrial environments. It provides reliable, self-organizing mesh networking with high data integrity and low power consumption for battery-operated devices.
ISA100 Wireless	Wireless	ISA100 Wireless is a standard for industrial wireless communication in process automation and control applications. It offers high reliability, scalability, and security, making it suitable for harsh industrial environments and critical applications.

Let us move forward with key IoT definitions and terminologies.

IoT Definitions and Terminologies

The Internet of Things (IoT) rapidly transforms our world, weaving a complex web of interconnected devices that collect and share data. As this technology continues to evolve and infiltrate our daily lives, understanding the language of IoT becomes increasingly essential. Whether you're a homeowner interested in smart appliances, a business owner considering automation, or simply curious about the future, familiarizing yourself with crucial IoT terminologies will empower you to navigate this exciting new landscape. By understanding the terms listed in Table 1-2 that define sensors, data exchange, and network types, you'll be better equipped to make informed decisions, troubleshoot potential issues, and grasp the vast potential of the interconnected world around you.

Table 1-2. *Terms used across IoT/IIoT*

Term	Definition
IoT	The Internet of Things (IoT) refers to the network of physical objects or "things" embedded with sensors, software, and other technologies to connect and exchange data over the Internet.
Sensor	A device that detects or measures physical properties (e.g., temperature, humidity, light, motion, etc.) and converts them into signals that can be read by other devices or systems.
Actuator	A device that is capable of moving or controlling a mechanism or system based on received commands or sensor data.
Gateway	A network device that acts as an intermediary between IoT devices and the internet or other networks, allowing data aggregation, protocol translation, and secure communication.

(continued)

Table 1-2. (*continued*)

Term	Definition
MQTT	Message Queuing Telemetry Transport (MQTT) is a lightweight messaging protocol specifically designed for IoT applications, enabling efficient communication between devices.
Zigbee	A wireless communication standard commonly used in IoT applications, particularly in low-power, low-data-rate scenarios, such as home automation and sensor networks.
LoRa	LoRa (Long Range) is a wireless communication technology designed for long-range, low-power IoT applications, often used for connecting remote devices or sensors over large distances.
BLE	Bluetooth Low Energy (BLE) is a wireless communication technology designed for short-range communication with low power consumption, commonly used in IoT devices like wearables.
Edge Computing	Edge computing refers to the practice of processing data near the source of data generation (i.e., at the edge of the network) instead of sending it to a centralized data center or cloud.
Digital Twin	A digital representation of a physical object or system, used for monitoring, analyzing, and simulating its behavior in real-time, enabling better decision-making and optimization.
RFID	Radio-Frequency Identification (RFID) is a technology that uses radio waves to identify and track objects or people automatically, commonly used in inventory management and access control.
AIoT	AIoT (Artificial Intelligence of Things) refers to the integration of artificial intelligence technologies with IoT devices and systems to improve efficiency, decision-making, and automation.

(*continued*)

Table 1-2. (*continued*)

Term	Definition
Fog Computing	Fog computing extends cloud computing to the edge of the network, bringing compute, storage, and networking resources closer to IoT devices to reduce latency and bandwidth usage.
Smart Grid	A modern electrical grid that uses digital technology, sensors, and IoT devices to monitor and manage electricity distribution more efficiently, reducing energy consumption and costs.
Wearable Device	A device that can be worn on the body, typically equipped with sensors and wireless connectivity, used for health monitoring, fitness tracking, communication, and other purposes.
SCADA	Supervisory Control and Data Acquisition (SCADA) is a system for remotely monitoring and controlling industrial processes, often used in industries like manufacturing, energy, and utilities.
Telemetry	The process of collecting and transmitting data from remote or inaccessible sources to a monitoring or control system, commonly used in IoT for monitoring and tracking purposes.
Home Automation	The automation of household activities and tasks through IoT devices and systems, enabling remote control and management of appliances, lighting, security, and climate control.
Predictive Maintenance	A maintenance strategy that uses IoT sensors and data analytics to predict when equipment or machinery is likely to fail, allowing maintenance to be performed proactively to prevent downtime.
Supply Chain Management	The management of the flow of goods and services, involving the movement and storage of raw materials, work-in-progress inventory, and finished goods, often optimized using IoT technologies.

(*continued*)

Table 1-2. (*continued*)

Term	Definition
Asset Tracking	The process of tracking the location and status of physical assets (e.g., vehicles, equipment, inventory) in real-time using IoT devices such as GPS trackers or RFID tags.
Smart City	A city that uses IoT sensors, data analytics, and other technologies to improve infrastructure, services, and quality of life for its citizens, addressing issues like traffic, waste management, etc.
Industrial IoT (IIoT)	The use of IoT technologies in industrial settings such as manufacturing, transportation, and energy to improve efficiency, productivity, and safety through data collection and analysis.
Remote Monitoring	The process of monitoring and controlling equipment, systems, or processes from a remote location using IoT devices and technology, often used in healthcare, utilities, and manufacturing.
6LoWPAN	IPv6 over low-power wireless personal area networks (6LoWPAN) is a communication protocol that allows IPv6 packets to be transmitted over low-power wireless networks, commonly used in IoT.

Table 1-2 summarizes various IoT definitions and terminologies. Let us move forward into the building blocks of IoT/IIoT.

Building Blocks of IoT/IIoT

The Internet of Things (IoT) and the Industrial Internet of Things (IIoT) encompass a complex ecosystem of interconnected devices, networks, and platforms that enable data collection, analysis, and utilization for various applications. The Internet of Things (IoT) building blocks can be customized significantly based on the detailed use case and requirements. Figure 1-1 depicts the widely accepted building blocks of the Internet of Things (IoT).

CHAPTER 1 GET STARTED WITH IOT NETWORK AND SECURITY

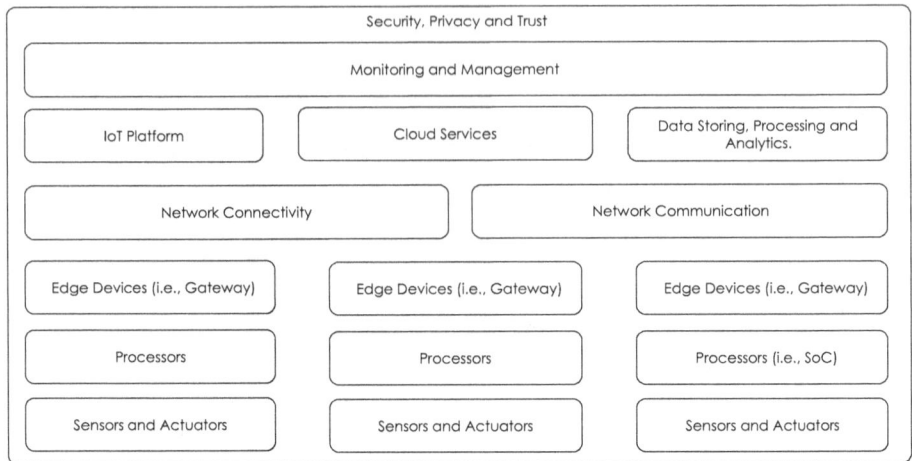

Figure 1-1. *Internet of Things – building blocks*

Here's a detailed breakdown of the building blocks for IoT/IIoT systems, each playing a crucial role in the seamless operation and communication of devices within these environments.

Sensors and Actuators: Sensors serve as the eyes and ears of IoT/IIoT systems, collecting data from the physical world. They measure parameters such as temperature, humidity, pressure, and motion. Actuators, on the other hand, enable devices to act upon the data collected by sensors. Based on the received data, they control physical processes or equipment, such as motors, valves, and switches.

Sensors: Sensors are essential components in IoT/IIoT systems, enabling data collection from the physical environment. They come in various types, including temperature sensors for monitoring thermal conditions, humidity sensors for measuring moisture levels, and pressure sensors for detecting air or liquid pressure changes. Other standard sensors include motion sensors for movement detection, proximity sensors for object detection, and light sensors for measuring illumination levels. Additionally, accelerometers capture acceleration forces, gyroscopes measure orientation, and sound sensors detect changes in sound levels. Specialized sensors like gas sensors monitor the presence and concentration of gases, while water quality sensors measure parameters like pH and dissolved oxygen in water. These sensors provide the crucial input for monitoring, analysis, and decision-making in IoT/IIoT applications across industries.

Actuators: Actuators in IoT/IIoT systems convert digital or analog signals into physical actions, allowing devices to interact with the physical world. Standard actuators include motors, which drive mechanical systems, and valves, which control the flow of liquids or gases. Relays are electromechanical switches for controlling high-power devices, while solenoids convert electrical energy into linear motion, often used in locks and hydraulic systems. LEDs are visual indicators, while pumps move fluids in water management and HVAC systems. Stepper and servo motors offer precise control of rotation and position, which is suitable for robotics and automation. Electric actuators provide controlled linear or rotary motion, and piezoelectric actuators generate mechanical motion in response to electrical signals. These actuators enable IoT/IIoT systems to effect changes in the physical world based on the data collected by sensors, facilitating automation, control, and optimization of various processes and devices.

Edge Devices/Gateways: Edge devices or gateways sit between the sensors and the central network, collecting and preprocessing data before transmission. They often perform data filtering, aggregation, and analysis locally, reducing latency and bandwidth usage. These can range from ruggedized PLCs (programmable logic controllers) to lightweight microcontrollers like Arduino or Raspberry Pi in industrial settings.

In IoT/IIoT ecosystems, edge devices and gateways are crucial intermediaries between the physical world and the cloud or central network. These devices are strategically placed at the network's edge, close to where data is generated, to perform data preprocessing and filtering before transmitting it to the cloud or local network. Edge devices typically have computing capabilities that allow them to run applications, analyze data, and make real-time localized decisions, reducing latency and bandwidth usage. They enable organizations to process and act upon data at the source, enabling faster response times and reducing the burden on centralized systems.

Conversely, gateways bridge the local network and the wider internet or cloud infrastructure. They aggregate data from multiple edge devices, perform protocol translation, and ensure secure communication with the cloud. Gateways also provide essential functions such as data encryption, device management, and network connectivity management. By consolidating and managing communication between edge devices and the cloud, gateways facilitate seamless integration of edge devices into larger IoT/IIoT architectures. Edge devices and gateways enable organizations to deploy distributed and scalable IoT solutions while ensuring efficient data processing, analysis, and communication at the network edge.

Network Connectivity: Network connectivity enables communication between devices, gateways, and backend systems. Wireless technologies like Wi-Fi, Bluetooth, Zigbee, and LoRa provide flexibility and mobility. At the same time, wired options such as Ethernet, Power over Ethernet (PoE), and various industrial protocols like Modbus and CAN ensure reliability and robustness in challenging environments.

Network connectivity is the linchpin of the Internet of Things (IoT) and the Industrial Internet of Things (IIoT), enabling seamless communication between devices, sensors, and platforms to gather, analyze, and utilize data effectively. These systems establish communication channels tailored to different use cases by utilizing protocols and standards like MQTT, Zigbee, and LoRaWAN. At the same time, wireless technologies such as Wi-Fi, cellular, and LPWAN offer flexibility in deployment. Edge computing further enhances these capabilities by bringing processing power closer to the data source, reducing latency, and enabling real-time decision-making.

Security remains a paramount concern, with encryption, authentication, and access control measures being essential to protect sensitive data and ensure the integrity of IoT/IIoT networks. Moreover, scalability, interoperability, and reliability are critical factors in the success of these systems, necessitating seamless integration, support for increasing numbers of connected devices, and robust redundancy mechanisms to minimize downtime. As technology evolves, advancements like 5G connectivity, edge AI integration, and ongoing standardization efforts promise to shape the future of IoT/IIoT network connectivity, facilitating even more efficient, secure, and sustainable deployments across various industries.

Communication Protocols: Communication protocols define the rules for data exchange between devices and networks. IoT-specific protocols like MQTT, CoAP, and AMQP are lightweight and efficient for machine-to-machine (M2M) communication. In contrast, industrial protocols such as Modbus, Profibus, and EtherCAT are optimized for real-time control and monitoring in industrial automation.

IoT communication protocols are crucial in enabling efficient data exchange and interaction between devices in the Internet of Things (IoT) ecosystem. Several protocols cater to different requirements, ranging from low power consumption to real-time communication and scalability. MQTT (Message Queuing Telemetry Transport) stands out as one of the most widely used protocols for IoT due to its lightweight nature, low bandwidth usage, and support for asynchronous messaging, making it suitable for constrained devices and unreliable networks. MQTT's publish-subscribe architecture allows devices to publish data to a central broker and subscribe to topics of interest, facilitating efficient data distribution and event-driven communication.

Another vital protocol is HTTP (Hypertext Transfer Protocol), commonly used for web-based IoT applications where interoperability with existing web infrastructure is crucial. HTTP's request-response model allows devices to communicate directly with web servers, enabling integration with cloud services and easy access to data via standard web browsers and APIs. However, HTTP's stateless nature and higher overhead than MQTT make it less suitable for resource-constrained devices or applications requiring real-time responsiveness. Additionally, CoAP (Constrained Application Protocol) addresses the limitations of HTTP in IoT by offering a lightweight alternative with support for RESTful interactions, efficient data transfer, and low overhead, making it well-suited for constrained environments and low-power devices. These protocols, along with others like AMQP (Advanced Message Queuing Protocol) and XMPP (Extensible Messaging and Presence Protocol), provide

- A diverse set of options for IoT communication
- Allowing developers to choose the most suitable protocol based on their specific use cases
- Device capabilities
- Network requirements

IoT Platforms: IoT platforms provide the infrastructure for managing, analyzing, and visualizing IoT data. They offer features such as data ingestion, device management, security, analytics, and integration with other systems. Major cloud providers like AWS IoT, Azure IoT, and Google Cloud IoT, as well as standalone platforms like IBM Watson IoT, offer comprehensive solutions for building and managing IoT applications.

Cloud Services: Cloud services store and process vast amounts of data IoT devices generate. They provide scalable storage, data processing, machine learning capabilities, and real-time analytics, enabling organizations to derive insights and make data-driven decisions. AWS, Azure, and Google Cloud platforms offer robust IoT services alongside their broader cloud offerings.

Data Processing and Analytics: Servers, cloud systems, or edge devices where data is stored, processed, and analyzed.

CHAPTER 1   GET STARTED WITH IOT NETWORK AND SECURITY

The transmitted data is sent to a central server or cloud platform. This is where the heavy processing occurs. Sophisticated algorithms and analytics tools process the raw data into actionable insights. For example, data from a temperature sensor could be analyzed to determine if a building's heating system is working efficiently.

Security Measures: Security is paramount in IoT/IIoT systems to protect against unauthorized access, data breaches, and cyber threats. Measures include authentication and authorization mechanisms, data encryption, secure bootstrapping, secure firmware updates, and intrusion detection systems to ensure data and devices' integrity, confidentiality, and availability.

Monitoring and Management: Tools and processes for managing devices, data, and the overall health and performance of the IoT system.

IoT systems usually include tools for managing the devices themselves (like updating their software) and tools for monitoring the system's health (like alerts if a device goes offline). This is critical for large-scale IoT deployments with thousands or millions of devices.

These building blocks form the backbone of IoT/IIoT systems, enabling the seamless connection, communication, and management of devices, data, and services across various industries and applications.

Use Case of IoT/IIoT

In this chapter section, we will explore real-world cases of Internet of Things use. Let us get started with the AMS use case.

AMS Use Case: The Industrial Internet of Things (IIoT) is revolutionizing industrial operations by integrating smart devices, sensors, and data analytics to optimize processes, enhance efficiency, and reduce costs. In this detailed use case, we will explore how a fictional manufacturing company, Advanced Manufacturing Solutions (AMS), leverages IIoT technologies to streamline its production processes and significantly improve efficiency and productivity.

AMS is a medium-sized manufacturing company specializing in automotive parts. With a diverse product line and a large production facility, AMS faces challenges in maintaining optimal efficiency, minimizing downtime, and ensuring product quality. To address these challenges, the company has embarked on an IIoT initiative to digitize its operations and harness data-driven insights to drive continuous improvement.

IIoT Implementation

AMS deploys a network of sensors and actuators throughout its production facility to monitor key real-time parameters such as temperature, pressure, humidity, and machine status. These sensors are connected to a central IIoT platform that collects, processes, and analyzes the data generated by the equipment and machinery on the shop floor.

Use Case Scenario 1: Predictive Maintenance

One of the primary goals of AMS's IoT implementation is to implement predictive maintenance strategies to minimize unplanned downtime and optimize equipment performance. By continuously monitoring machinery's condition and detecting early signs of wear and tear, AMS can proactively schedule maintenance activities before equipment failure occurs.

For instance, sensors installed on critical production equipment, such as CNC machines and robotic arms, collect data on factors like vibration, temperature, and energy consumption. This data is analyzed using machine learning algorithms to identify patterns indicative of potential issues. When anomalies are detected, the IIoT platform automatically generates maintenance alerts, prompting maintenance teams to conduct inspections or repairs as needed.

As a result, AMS experiences a significant reduction in unexpected equipment failures, downtime, and associated production losses. Moreover, by performing maintenance tasks only when necessary, the company optimizes resource utilization and extends the lifespan of its machinery, leading to substantial cost savings in the long run.

Use Case Scenario 2: Quality Control and Process Optimization

Another critical area where IIoT delivers tangible benefits for AMS is quality control and process optimization. The company can identify inefficiencies, defects, and deviations from production standards by leveraging real-time data insights, enabling prompt corrective actions.

For example, AMS installs vision sensors and cameras at various points along the production line to inspect parts for defects, dimensional accuracy, and surface finish. These sensors capture high-resolution images of each component, which are then analyzed using computer vision algorithms to detect imperfections or deviations from specifications.

Additionally, by correlating data from multiple sensors across different stages of the production process, AMS gains valuable insights into the root causes of quality issues and process bottlenecks. With this information, production managers can make data-driven decisions to optimize workflows, adjust machine settings, and improve product quality.

As a result of these efforts, AMS significantly reduces defective parts, rework, and scrap, leading to higher customer satisfaction and lower manufacturing costs. Moreover, the company's ability to continuously monitor and optimize its processes enables it to adapt quickly to changing market demands and maintain a competitive edge in the industry.

Use Case Scenario 3: Asset Tracking and Inventory Management

AMS implements IIoT solutions to enhance asset tracking and inventory management processes, ensuring the efficient utilization of resources and minimizing the risk of stockouts or overstocking. By leveraging real-time location tracking and inventory monitoring, AMS gains visibility into the movement and status of assets throughout its facility, enabling better decision-making and resource allocation.

To achieve this, AMS deploys RFID tags and IoT-enabled sensors on its inventory items, equipment, and vehicles. These devices transmit location data, environmental conditions, and usage information to a centralized IIoT platform, where the data is processed and analyzed in real time.

For example, AMS can track the movement of raw materials, work-in-progress components, and finished goods as they move through the production process. RFID readers installed at critical checkpoints automatically update inventory records, providing accurate and up-to-date information on stock levels, shelf life, and order fulfillment status.

Additionally, AMS utilizes geofencing and predictive analytics to optimize asset utilization and prevent loss or theft. By defining virtual boundaries and monitoring asset movements, AMS can detect unauthorized access or deviations from predefined routes, triggering alerts for immediate intervention.

As a result, AMS improves inventory accuracy, reduces the risk of stockouts or excess inventory, and enhances operational efficiency across its supply chain. Moreover, by optimizing asset utilization and minimizing losses, AMS realizes cost savings and maintains a competitive edge in the market.

Use Case Scenario 4: Energy Management and Sustainability

In addition to predictive maintenance and quality control, AMS utilizes IIoT to improve energy management and promote sustainability within its operations. By monitoring energy consumption in real time and identifying opportunities for optimization, AMS aims to reduce its environmental footprint while lowering operating costs.

AMS installs intelligent meters and energy monitoring devices to track electricity, gas, and water usage across its facility. These devices continuously collect data on energy consumption patterns, peak demand periods, and areas of inefficiency. The data is then analyzed using advanced analytics to identify energy savings and efficiency improvement opportunities.

For instance, AMS identifies equipment and processes that consume excessive energy or operate inefficiently, such as outdated machinery, air compressors, or lighting systems. By implementing energy-saving measures such as equipment upgrades, automation, and schedule optimization, AMS reduces its overall energy consumption and operating expenses while minimizing its carbon footprint.

Use Case Scenario 5: Supply Chain Optimization

In the final use case, AMS leverages IIoT to optimize its supply chain management processes, ensuring the timely delivery of raw materials and components while minimizing inventory holding costs and production delays. AMS improves efficiency and responsiveness across its entire value chain by digitizing its supply chain and enabling real-time visibility into inventory levels, production schedules, and logistics operations.

AMS integrates IoT-enabled sensors and RFID tags into its inventory management system to track the movement and status of materials throughout the supply chain. These sensors provide real-time data on inventory levels, shelf life, and storage conditions, allowing AMS to optimize inventory levels, reduce stockouts, and minimize waste.

Additionally, AMS utilizes predictive analytics and machine learning algorithms to forecast demand, identify potential supply chain disruptions, and optimize production schedules accordingly. By dynamically adjusting production plans in response to changes in demand or supply, AMS improves agility, reduces lead times, and enhances customer satisfaction.

In conclusion, AMS's detailed use case demonstrates the transformative power of IIoT in enhancing industrial efficiency, productivity, and competitiveness. By leveraging real-time data insights, predictive analytics, and proactive maintenance strategies, AMS has optimized its production processes, minimized downtime, and improved product quality. As IIoT technologies evolve, companies like AMS will have even more excellent opportunities to drive innovation, efficiency, and sustainability in the manufacturing sector.

In the context of the use cases outlined for Advanced Manufacturing Solutions (AMS), network connectivity and security play critical roles in enabling the effective implementation and operation of Industrial Internet of Things (IIoT) solutions.

Network Connectivity

Network connectivity forms the backbone of IIoT, facilitating seamless communication between devices, sensors, and the central IIoT platform. In AMS's case, a robust network infrastructure ensures that data from various sensors and devices is transmitted reliably and in real-time, allowing for timely decision-making and process optimization.

Furthermore, network connectivity enables AMS to leverage cloud-based services for data storage, analytics, and remote monitoring. By securely connecting to the cloud, AMS gains access to powerful computing resources and advanced analytics tools essential for processing the vast amounts of data generated by its IIoT deployments.

Moreover, network scalability is crucial for AMS as it expands its IoT initiatives. A scalable network infrastructure can accommodate the growing number of connected devices and support the increasing data traffic without sacrificing performance or reliability. This scalability ensures that AMS can continue to innovate and optimize its operations without being limited by network constraints.

Security

Security is paramount in IIoT deployments, especially in industrial environments where the consequences of a security breach can be severe. AMS relies on robust security measures to protect its IIoT infrastructure from cyber threats and unauthorized access.

End-to-end encryption ensures that data transmitted between devices and the IIoT platform remains confidential and cannot be intercepted by malicious actors. Authentication mechanisms, such as digital certificates and biometric identification, verify the identity of users and devices, preventing unauthorized access to sensitive systems and data.

Furthermore, AMS implements stringent access control policies to limit the privileges of users and devices based on their roles and responsibilities. This helps prevent insider threats and ensures only authorized personnel can access critical systems and data.

Additionally, AMS employs continuous monitoring and threat detection techniques to detect and respond to real-time security incidents. Intrusion detection systems, anomaly detection algorithms, and security information and event management (SIEM) tools help identify suspicious activities and potential breaches, allowing AMS to take prompt action to mitigate risks and minimize damage.

In conclusion, network connectivity and security are foundational elements of AMS's IIoT strategy. They enable the company to leverage data-driven insights for enhanced efficiency, productivity, and competitiveness while safeguarding its assets and operations against cyber threats. By investing in robust network infrastructure and comprehensive security measures, AMS ensures the reliability, scalability, and integrity of its IIoT deployments, paving the way for continued innovation and success in the digital age of manufacturing.

HTS Use Case: The application of the Internet of Things (IoT) and Industrial Internet of Things (IIoT) technologies in the healthcare industry is revolutionizing patient care, operational efficiency, and healthcare delivery. In this detailed use case, we will explore how a fictional healthcare provider, HealthTech Solutions (HTS), harnesses IIoT to improve patient outcomes, optimize resource utilization, and ensure the highest standards of care.

Overview of HealthTech Solutions (HTS): HTS is a leading healthcare provider that operates a network of hospitals, clinics, and medical facilities. Focusing on patient-centered care and innovation, HTS seeks to leverage cutting-edge technologies to enhance healthcare delivery, streamline operations, and improve patient satisfaction.

IIoT Implementation

HTS implements IIoT solutions across healthcare facilities to monitor patient health, track medical assets, and optimize clinical workflows. HTS aims to deliver personalized care, improve operational efficiency, and ensure compliance with regulatory requirements by deploying a network of connected devices, sensors, and data analytics platforms.

Use Case Scenario 1: Remote Patient Monitoring

One of the primary applications of IoT in healthcare is remote patient monitoring, which enables healthcare providers to track patients' vital signs, symptoms, and medication adherence outside of traditional clinical settings. HTS utilizes wearable devices, intelligent sensors, and mobile health applications to monitor patients with chronic conditions, such as diabetes, hypertension, and heart disease, in real time.

For example, patients with diabetes wear continuous glucose monitors (CGMs) that automatically measure their blood glucose levels and transmit the data to a centralized monitoring platform. Care teams can

CHAPTER 1   GET STARTED WITH IOT NETWORK AND SECURITY

remotely monitor patients' glucose trends, receive alerts for abnormal readings, and intervene promptly to prevent complications such as hypoglycemia or hyperglycemia.

By empowering patients to manage their conditions proactively and providing timely interventions when needed, HTS improves patient outcomes, reduces hospital readmissions, and enhances overall quality of life.

Use Case Scenario 2: Asset Tracking and Inventory Management

In addition to patient care, HTS leverages IIoT to optimize asset tracking and inventory management processes within its healthcare facilities. By tracking the location and status of medical equipment, supplies, and pharmaceuticals in real time, HTS ensures the efficient utilization of resources and minimizes the risk of stockouts or wastage.

For instance, HTS installs RFID tags and IoT sensors on medical devices, such as infusion pumps, ventilators, and defibrillators, to track their usage, maintenance history, and location. Automated inventory management systems monitor stock levels of medications and supplies, triggering alerts when inventory needs to be replenished or when expiration dates are approaching.

By streamlining asset tracking and inventory management, HTS improves operational efficiency, reduces costs associated with lost or misplaced assets, and ensures clinicians have access to the right resources when and where they are needed.

Use Case Scenario 3: Predictive Maintenance

Another critical use case for IoT in healthcare is predictive maintenance, which enables healthcare facilities to proactively monitor and maintain medical equipment to prevent breakdowns and ensure patient safety. HTS implements predictive maintenance strategies to monitor the performance of critical medical devices and addresses potential issues before they escalate.

For example, HTS equips its imaging equipment, such as MRI machines and X-ray systems, with sensors that continuously monitor key performance indicators, such as temperature, vibration, and energy consumption. Machine learning algorithms analyze the sensor data to identify patterns indicative of impending failures or maintenance needs.

When anomalies are detected, HTS's maintenance teams receive alerts and can schedule proactive maintenance activities to resolve issues before they impact patient care. HTS ensures patients receive timely and reliable diagnostic and treatment services by minimizing downtime and maximizing equipment uptime.

Use Case Scenario 4: Environmental Monitoring and Control

HTS utilizes IIoT to monitor and control environmental conditions within its healthcare facilities to ensure patients' and staff's comfort, safety, and well-being. By deploying sensors to monitor parameters such as temperature, humidity, air quality, and lighting, HTS can maintain optimal conditions for patient care and operational efficiency.

For example, HTS installs environmental sensors in patient rooms, operating theaters, and storage areas to monitor temperature and humidity levels. Automated HVAC (Heating, Ventilation, and Air Conditioning) systems adjust airflow and temperature settings based on real-time data to maintain comfortable conditions for patients and prevent the growth of harmful pathogens or mold.

Additionally, sensors monitor air quality and detect pollutants such as volatile organic compounds (VOCs) and particulate matter. When abnormal levels are detected, facility managers receive alerts, which they can use to take corrective actions, such as adjusting ventilation settings or implementing air purification measures.

By ensuring a safe and comfortable environment, HTS enhances patient satisfaction, reduces the risk of healthcare-associated infections, and creates a conducive setting for healing and recovery.

Use Case Scenario 5: Workflow Optimization and Patient Flow Management

HTS leverages IIoT to optimize clinical workflows and streamline patient flow within its healthcare facilities. By tracking the movement of patients, staff, and equipment in real time, HTS can identify bottlenecks, inefficiencies, and opportunities for improvement, leading to better resource allocation and enhanced patient experiences.

For instance, HTS deploys location-based tracking technologies, such as RFID tags or Bluetooth beacons, to monitor the movement of patients and staff throughout the hospital. This data is integrated with electronic health records (EHR) and scheduling systems to create real-time visibility into patient statuses, wait times, and room availability.

Using this information, HTS can dynamically adjust staffing levels, allocate resources more efficiently, and optimize patient appointments and procedures to minimize wait times and maximize throughput. Additionally, alerts and notifications are sent to staff when patients are ready for their appointments or when rooms need to be cleaned and prepared for the next patient.

As a result, HTS improves operational efficiency, reduces patient wait times, and enhances the overall patient experience by ensuring timely access to care and services.

Importance of Network Connectivity and Security in IIoT

In the context of these additional use cases, network connectivity and security remain crucial elements of HTS's IIoT infrastructure. A reliable network ensures that data from environmental sensors, location tracking systems, and other IoT devices can be transmitted seamlessly and in real time, enabling timely decision-making and action.

Moreover, security measures such as encryption, authentication, and access control are essential to protect sensitive data generated by these systems and ensure the integrity of HTS's IoT deployments. Implementing robust security protocols, HTS safeguards patient information, maintains regulatory compliance, and protects against potential cyber threats or data breaches.

In conclusion, HealthTech Solutions' comprehensive use case illustrates the diverse applications of IIoT in healthcare, ranging from remote patient monitoring to environmental control and workflow optimization. By leveraging IIoT technologies, healthcare providers can enhance patient care, improve operational efficiency, and ensure a safe and secure healthcare environment for all stakeholders.

Importance, Challenges, and Future Opportunities

The Internet of Things (IoT) has become increasingly vital across industries, transforming traditional operations into innovative, data-driven processes. IoT enables predictive maintenance, real-time monitoring, and supply chain optimization in manufacturing, resulting in increased efficiency and reduced downtime. For example, predictive maintenance algorithms use IoT sensors to monitor equipment health, predicting failures before they occur and allowing for proactive maintenance, preventing costly unplanned downtime.

Healthcare

In the healthcare industry, IoT technologies have the potential to revolutionize patient care, improve operational efficiency, and enhance clinical outcomes. Remote patient monitoring devices, such as wearable sensors and medical implants, enable healthcare providers to monitor patients' vital signs and health conditions in real-time, allowing for early detection of health issues and proactive interventions. These devices empower patients to take control of their health by providing continuous, personalized care outside of traditional clinical settings, leading to better management of chronic conditions and reduced hospital readmissions.

IoT also streamlines hospital operations by optimizing asset management, patient flow, and facility maintenance. Smart hospital beds equipped with sensors monitor patient movements and vital signs, automatically adjusting positions to prevent pressure ulcers and improve patient comfort. Additionally, IoT-enabled asset tracking systems ensure the availability of medical equipment and supplies, reducing inventory costs and minimizing disruptions in patient care. Overall, IoT holds great promise for transforming healthcare delivery, improving patient outcomes, and driving efficiencies across the entire healthcare ecosystem.

Finance

In the finance industry, IoT technologies offer opportunities to enhance customer experiences, optimize operations, and mitigate risks. IoT-enabled devices such as wearables and smartphones provide financial institutions with valuable data on customer behaviors, preferences, and spending patterns, allowing personalized services and targeted marketing strategies. For example, banks can use IoT data to offer real-time financial advice, customized loan offers, and fraud detection services tailored to individual customer needs.

Moreover, IoT enhances security and operational efficiency in banking operations by monitoring ATMs, branches, and critical infrastructure in real time. Smart security cameras, sensors, and access control systems detect suspicious activities and unauthorized access, enabling banks to respond quickly to security incidents and prevent financial losses. Additionally, IoT-powered predictive maintenance solutions monitor the health of banking equipment, such as ATMs and servers, predicting potential failures before they occur and minimizing downtime. By leveraging IoT technologies, financial institutions can deliver innovative services, improve customer satisfaction, and maintain a competitive edge in the digital era.

Retail

IoT is transforming the retail industry by providing retailers valuable insights into customer behavior, streamlining operations, and creating immersive shopping experiences. Retailers use IoT devices such as beacons, RFID tags, and smart shelves to track inventory levels, analyze customer traffic patterns, and optimize product placement. By collecting and analyzing data from these devices, retailers can improve inventory management, reduce stockouts, and increase sales through targeted promotions and personalized recommendations.

In addition to optimizing inventory management, IoT technologies enhance the in-store shopping experience for customers. Smart mirrors equipped with RFID technology allow customers to try on clothes virtually, view product information, and receive personalized styling recommendations. Similarly, IoT-powered interactive displays engage customers with dynamic content and enable seamless checkout experiences. By integrating IoT devices into their stores, retailers can create immersive, omnichannel shopping experiences that drive customer loyalty and increase online and offline sales.

Automotive

IoT is crucial in improving vehicle safety, enhancing driver experiences, and enabling connected car services in the automotive industry. IoT sensors in vehicles monitor various parameters such as engine performance, tire pressure, and driver behavior, providing real-time data to drivers and manufacturers. For instance, IoT-enabled telematics systems track vehicle diagnostics and notify drivers of maintenance needs, preventing breakdowns and ensuring optimal performance. IoT-based advanced driver assistance systems (ADAS) also enhance vehicle safety by providing collision avoidance, lane departure warnings, and adaptive cruise control, reducing the risk of accidents and improving road safety.

Moreover, IoT connectivity enables vehicles to communicate with each other and infrastructure through vehicle-to-vehicle (V2V) and vehicle-to-everything (V2X) communication networks. This connectivity facilitates traffic management, route optimization, and autonomous driving capabilities, leading to smoother traffic flow and reduced congestion. Furthermore, IoT-enabled connected car services such as remote diagnostics, predictive maintenance, and in-car entertainment enhance the overall driving experience, providing drivers and passengers convenience, entertainment, and peace of mind.

Education

IoT transforms education by creating intelligent learning environments, improving educational outcomes, and enhancing administrative efficiency. IoT devices such as smartboards, tablets, and wearable technology enable interactive and personalized student learning experiences. Teachers can use IoT-enabled educational tools to deliver engaging lessons, assess student progress, and provide targeted support based on individual learning needs. For example, interactive learning platforms use IoT data to adapt instructional content in real-time, catering to each student's pace and learning style, leading to improved academic performance and engagement.

Additionally, IoT technologies optimize campus operations and facilities management in educational institutions. Intelligent building systems monitor energy usage, lighting, and environmental conditions, automatically adjusting settings to conserve energy and create comfortable learning environments. IoT sensors track the occupancy of classrooms, libraries, and other facilities, enabling administrators to optimize space utilization, reduce operational costs, and improve campus safety. By leveraging IoT, educational institutions can create dynamic, technology-enabled learning environments that foster innovation, collaboration, and student success.

Energy and Utilities

IoT technologies drive efficiency, sustainability, and reliability across the entire value chain in the energy and utilities sector. Smart meters and IoT-enabled sensors monitor energy consumption, generation, and distribution in real time, providing utilities with valuable insights into grid performance and demand patterns. This data enables utilities to optimize energy production, balance supply and demand, and integrate renewable energy sources more effectively, reducing costs and environmental impact.

Moreover, IoT plays a critical role in asset management and predictive maintenance for energy infrastructure. IoT sensors monitor the condition of power plants, transformers, and distribution networks, detecting potential faults or failures before they occur. Predictive analytics and machine learning algorithms analyze this data to identify patterns and trends, enabling utilities to schedule maintenance proactively, minimize downtime, and extend the lifespan of critical assets.

Furthermore, IoT-enabled smart grid technologies enable demand response programs and grid optimization, allowing utilities to manage peak demand, reduce energy waste, and improve grid stability. By leveraging IoT, the energy and utilities industry can modernize infrastructure, increase operational efficiency, and accelerate the transition to a sustainable energy future.

Manufacturing

IoT technologies drive operational efficiency, quality control, and supply chain optimization in manufacturing. IoT sensors and connected devices monitor equipment performance, production processes, and product quality in real-time, providing manufacturers with valuable insights to improve productivity and reduce costs. For example, IoT-enabled predictive maintenance systems use sensor data to anticipate equipment failures, schedule maintenance proactively, and minimize downtime, ensuring uninterrupted production and optimizing asset utilization.

Moreover, IoT facilitates seamless integration and collaboration across the entire supply chain, from raw material suppliers to end customers. IoT sensors track the movement and condition of goods in transit, providing visibility into inventory levels, delivery status, and supply chain performance. This visibility enables manufacturers to optimize inventory management, reduce lead times, and respond quickly to changes in demand or supply, improving overall supply chain efficiency and resilience.

Furthermore, IoT enables the implementation of smart factories and Industry 4.0 initiatives, where interconnected machines and systems communicate and collaborate autonomously. This integration enables real-time data exchange, adaptive manufacturing processes, and predictive analytics, leading to greater agility, flexibility, and competitiveness in the manufacturing industry.

Importance of IoT Network and Security

IoT networks and security are paramount across various industries. In healthcare, secure IoT systems protect patient data, ensuring compliance with regulations like HIPAA and safeguarding sensitive medical records. In manufacturing, IoT security prevents disruptions to production processes, ensuring operational continuity and protecting critical infrastructure from cyber-attacks. Secure IoT networks enable efficient traffic management in transportation, enhancing safety and reducing congestion through real-time data analysis. In retail, IoT security ensures the integrity of customer data and allows personalized shopping experiences, improving customer satisfaction and loyalty. Across all sectors, robust IoT networks and security measures are essential for innovation, efficiency, and stakeholder trust.

Table 1-3 provides a detailed breakdown of the top 15 key importance areas to protect the IoT network and security domain.

Table 1-3. *Top 15 importance areas across IoT/IIoT*

No.	Importance Areas	Description	Real-World Examples
1	Protection of sensitive data	Ensuring the security of sensitive data collected, processed, and transmitted by IoT devices is crucial to prevent unauthorized access, data breaches, and privacy violations.	Healthcare IoT devices must protect patient health data to comply with regulations like HIPAA and prevent unauthorized access to sensitive medical records.
2	Safety and reliability	Secure IoT networks are essential for ensuring the safety and reliability of connected systems and devices, preventing accidents, malfunctions, or disruptions that could cause harm or financial loss.	Industrial IoT systems in manufacturing plants must be secure to prevent equipment failures or process disruptions that could lead to production downtime.
3	Protection against cyber attacks	IoT devices are prime targets for cyber attacks, and securing them is critical to prevent unauthorized access, data theft, DDoS attacks, or exploitation for malicious purposes.	The Mirai botnet launched DDoS attacks by compromising insecure IoT devices, disrupting internet services worldwide.

(continued)

Table 1-3. (*continued*)

No.	Importance Areas	Description	Real-World Examples
4	Maintaining business continuity	Secure IoT networks help maintain business continuity by preventing disruptions caused by cyber attacks, data breaches, or system failures, ensuring uninterrupted operations and service delivery.	A smart building management system ensures uninterrupted HVAC and lighting control to maintain occupant comfort and energy efficiency.
5	Regulatory compliance	Compliance with data protection regulations and industry standards is essential for avoiding legal consequences, fines, and damage to reputation resulting from non-compliance with privacy and security requirements.	Companies handling personal data must comply with GDPR, CCPA, and other regulations to protect customer privacy and avoid hefty fines.
6	Protection of critical infrastructure	Securing IoT networks that control critical infrastructure such as power grids, transportation systems, or healthcare facilities is essential to prevent disruptions that could have far-reaching consequences.	A cyber attack on a power grid could result in widespread blackouts, affecting businesses, hospitals, and public safety.

(*continued*)

Table 1-3. (*continued*)

No.	Importance Areas	Description	Real-World Examples
7	Trust and consumer confidence	Building trust and confidence among consumers and stakeholders is essential for the widespread adoption of IoT technologies, which relies on the assurance of data privacy, security, and reliability.	Smart home devices must provide robust security features to reassure consumers that their privacy and safety are protected.
8	Protection against physical threats	Physical security measures are necessary to protect IoT devices from tampering, theft, or vandalism, ensuring their integrity and functionality in various environments.	Publicly deployed IoT devices, such as surveillance cameras, must be protected from physical attacks to prevent unauthorized access or disruption.
9	Resilience to emerging threats	IoT security must be adaptive and resilient to defend against evolving cyber threats, including new attack vectors, malware, or vulnerabilities that may emerge over time.	Security measures must evolve to address emerging threats such as AI-driven attacks, supply chain compromises, or quantum computing threats.
10	Protection of intellectual property	Securing IoT networks is vital for protecting intellectual property (IP) and proprietary information from theft, reverse engineering, or unauthorized access, safeguarding business competitiveness and innovation.	Manufacturers of IoT devices must protect their firmware, software, and design secrets from theft or exploitation by competitors or hackers.

(*continued*)

Table 1-3. (*continued*)

No.	Importance Areas	Description	Real-World Examples
11	Enhancing operational efficiency	Secure IoT deployments can enhance operational efficiency by providing real-time insights, automating processes, and optimizing resource utilization, leading to cost savings and improved productivity.	IoT sensors in agriculture can monitor soil moisture levels and automate irrigation systems, optimizing water usage and improving crop yields.
12	Enabling remote monitoring and control	Secure IoT networks enable remote monitoring and control of devices and systems, allowing for proactive maintenance, troubleshooting, and remote operations management from anywhere, at any time.	Utility companies can remotely monitor and control smart meters to optimize energy distribution, detect faults, and prevent service disruptions.
13	Facilitating predictive maintenance	IoT devices can collect and analyze data to predict equipment failures or maintenance needs, enabling proactive maintenance activities that reduce downtime, extend asset lifespan, and minimize repair costs.	Industrial IoT sensors can monitor equipment vibration and temperature to detect early signs of mechanical failure, allowing for timely maintenance.

(*continued*)

Table 1-3. (*continued*)

No.	Importance Areas	Description	Real-World Examples
14	Improving decision-making	IoT data analytics provide valuable insights that support data-driven decision-making, helping organizations optimize processes, identify trends, and seize new opportunities for innovation and growth.	Smart city IoT platforms analyze traffic flow data to optimize signal timing, reduce congestion, and improve transportation infrastructure.
15	Enhancing customer experience	Secure IoT deployments can enhance the customer experience by personalizing services, improving convenience, and providing innovative features that meet evolving consumer expectations.	Retailers use IoT beacons and mobile apps to deliver personalized offers and recommendations to shoppers based on their preferences and location.

Challenges in IoT Network and Security

The widespread adoption of Internet of Things (IoT) technologies across various industries has brought about unprecedented connectivity and efficiency, but it has also introduced significant challenges in network security. As IoT devices become more pervasive in healthcare, manufacturing, transportation, and beyond, the complexity of managing and securing these networks has increased exponentially. One of the foremost challenges is the sheer scale of IoT deployments, with millions of interconnected devices creating a vast attack surface for potential cyber threats. Ensuring the security and integrity of data transmitted between these devices and protecting them from unauthorized access and manipulation has become a paramount concern for organizations worldwide.

Furthermore, the diversity of IoT devices, each with its unique operating system, communication protocols, and security features, complicates efforts to establish standardized security practices. The heterogeneity of these devices makes it challenging to implement uniform security measures across IoT ecosystems, leading to vulnerabilities that cybercriminals can exploit. Additionally, the resource constraints of many IoT devices, such as limited processing power and memory, pose challenges in implementing robust security mechanisms without sacrificing performance or energy efficiency. These challenges underscore the critical need for comprehensive strategies and innovative solutions to address the evolving threats to IoT networks and security across various industries.

Securing IoT networks presents a multitude of challenges due to the unique characteristics of IoT devices and the complex nature of network environments. Table 1-4 provides a detailed breakdown of the top 50 key challenges.

Table 1-4. Top 50 key challenges in security domain across IoT/IIoT

No.	Challenge	Description	Real-World Examples
1	Heterogeneity of devices	IoT networks comprise a wide variety of devices with different operating systems, firmware versions, and communication protocols, making security management complex.	In a smart home, devices like smart thermostats, security cameras, and smart locks may be manufactured by different companies, running different firmware versions and communicating using different protocols.
2	Limited resources	Many IoT devices have limited processing power, memory, and energy resources, making it challenging to implement robust security mechanisms without impacting device performance or battery life.	IoT sensors deployed in agriculture may have limited battery life and computational capabilities, making it challenging to implement strong encryption or security protocols without draining the battery quickly.
3	Insecure communication protocols	IoT devices often rely on various communication protocols lacking built-in security features, making them vulnerable to eavesdropping, man-in-the-middle attacks, and spoofing.	Vulnerabilities in the Zigbee protocol have been exploited to hijack smart home devices, allowing attackers to gain unauthorized access to homes.

(continued)

Table 1-4. (*continued*)

No.	Challenge	Description	Real-World Examples
4	Data privacy concerns	IoT devices collect sensitive data about users, environments, and behaviors, raising concerns about data privacy throughout their lifecycle, from collection to storage and transmission.	Wearable fitness trackers collecting health data may pose privacy risks if the data is transmitted and stored without adequate encryption or if it is shared with third parties without user consent.
5	Firmware and software vulnerabilities	IoT devices may run outdated firmware or software with known vulnerabilities, making them susceptible to exploitation for unauthorized access, denial-of-service attacks, or network compromise.	The Mirai botnet exploited vulnerabilities in the firmware of IoT devices like IP cameras and routers, using them to launch large-scale DDoS attacks.
6	Lack of standardization	The absence of universal security standards and guidelines for IoT devices leads to inconsistencies in security implementations, making it difficult to ensure adherence to best security practices.	Different smart home devices may implement security features differently, leading to varying levels of vulnerability across devices.

(*continued*)

Table 1-4. (*continued*)

No.	Challenge	Description	Real-World Examples
7	Physical security	IoT devices deployed in uncontrolled environments are vulnerable to physical tampering, theft, or vandalism, which can compromise their security and functionality.	Unsecured surveillance cameras have been hacked and used to spy on individuals or gain unauthorized access to private spaces.
8	Scalability and management	Managing security in IoT networks becomes increasingly complex as the number of devices grows, requiring scalable solutions for monitoring, updating, and patching devices regularly.	Large-scale IoT deployments in smart cities require automated systems for managing security updates and patches across thousands of devices.
9	Supply chain risks	Malicious actors can compromise IoT devices during the manufacturing process, embedding malware or backdoors that remain undetected until deployed in the field, posing supply chain risks.	The NotPetya attack was propagated through a supply chain compromise, infecting thousands of systems globally, including IoT devices.

(*continued*)

Table 1-4. (*continued*)

No.	Challenge	Description	Real-World Examples
10	Integration with legacy systems	Integrating new IoT devices with existing legacy systems may introduce security vulnerabilities or compatibility issues, requiring careful consideration of security implications.	Industrial IoT deployments may need to integrate with legacy control systems, which may lack modern security features and be vulnerable to cyber attacks.
11	Human error and insider threats	Human errors such as misconfiguration or weak password management, as well as insider threats, can compromise IoT networks by abusing privileges or leaking sensitive information.	A contractor inadvertently exposes sensitive data from a company's IoT network by misconfiguring a cloud storage bucket.
12	Regulatory compliance	Compliance with data protection regulations such as GDPR or HIPAA adds complexity to IoT security, requiring organizations to ensure that their deployments meet regulatory requirements.	Smart medical devices must comply with regulations such as HIPAA to ensure the privacy and security of patient data.

(*continued*)

Table 1-4. (*continued*)

No.	Challenge	Description	Real-World Examples
13	Interoperability issues	Ensuring seamless communication and interoperability between different IoT devices and platforms can be challenging due to disparate technologies and standards.	Smart home devices from different manufacturers may not work together seamlessly due to differences in communication protocols.
14	Distributed architecture	IoT networks often have a distributed architecture with devices spread across various locations, making centralized security management challenging.	Industrial IoT deployments may have sensors and actuators spread across multiple factory floors, requiring decentralized security solutions.
15	Real-time threat detection	Traditional security solutions may not be suitable for detecting and responding to real-time threats in IoT environments, requiring specialized threat detection mechanisms.	Anomaly detection algorithms can help identify abnormal behavior in IoT networks, indicating potential security threats.
16	Complex ecosystems	IoT deployments involve a complex ecosystem of devices, gateways, cloud services, and third-party integrations, necessitating a holistic approach to security across the entire ecosystem.	Smart cities rely on a wide range of IoT devices and services, including traffic sensors, surveillance cameras, and public Wi-Fi networks.

(*continued*)

Table 1-4. (*continued*)

No.	Challenge	Description	Real-World Examples
17	Device lifecycle management	Managing the security of IoT devices throughout their entire lifecycle, from deployment to decommissioning, requires careful consideration of security implications at each stage.	IoT devices in industrial settings must be securely decommissioned to prevent unauthorized access to sensitive systems and data.
18	Dependency on third-party services	Relying on third-party services introduces security risks, especially if proper security measures are not implemented by the service providers, compromising the security of IoT deployments.	A smart home security system relies on a cloud-based service for remote monitoring, but a security flaw in the service exposes user data.
19	Emerging threats	The evolving nature of cyber threats means that new attack vectors and vulnerabilities continually emerge, requiring proactive measures to address emerging threats in IoT networks.	Zero-day vulnerabilities in IoT devices can be exploited by attackers before security patches are available, leaving devices vulnerable to compromise.

(*continued*)

Table 1-4. (*continued*)

No.	Challenge	Description	Real-World Examples
20	Cost constraints	Implementing robust security measures in IoT devices can increase manufacturing costs, impacting the overall affordability of IoT solutions and requiring a balance between security and cost considerations.	Consumer IoT devices are often priced competitively, leading manufacturers to prioritize cost over security features.
21	User awareness and education	End users may lack awareness of IoT security risks or may not know how to properly configure and maintain devices securely, necessitating education and awareness programs.	Many users do not change the default passwords on their IoT devices, making them vulnerable to hacking.
22	Legal and liability issues	Determining liability for security breaches in IoT networks can be complicated, requiring clarification of legal responsibilities and liabilities among device manufacturers, developers, and service providers.	In the event of a data breach caused by a vulnerability in an IoT device, determining who is legally responsible can be challenging.

(*continued*)

Table 1-4. (*continued*)

No.	Challenge	Description	Real-World Examples
23	Resource-constrained environments	IoT devices deployed in resource-constrained environments face challenges related to power, network connectivity, and maintenance, requiring specialized security solutions.	IoT sensors deployed in remote areas may rely on solar power and intermittent network connectivity, making it difficult to implement continuous security monitoring.
24	Security of edge computing	Securing edge devices and ensuring the integrity of data processed at the edge is crucial in IoT deployments utilizing edge computing, requiring specialized security measures for edge devices.	Edge computing devices in a smart manufacturing facility process sensitive data locally, requiring encryption and access controls to protect against unauthorized access.
25	Security of data at rest and in transit	Securing data both at rest and in transit is essential for protecting sensitive information from unauthorized access or interception, requiring encryption and authentication mechanisms.	IoT devices transmitting data over wireless networks must use encryption to prevent eavesdropping and ensure data confidentiality.

(*continued*)

Table 1-4. (*continued*)

No.	Challenge	Description	Real-World Examples
26	Identity and access management	Establishing and managing identities for IoT devices and ensuring secure access control mechanisms is challenging due to the large number of devices and dynamic IoT environments.	Access control mechanisms must ensure that only authorized devices and users can access sensitive data or control critical systems in an IoT network.
27	IoT security awareness and training	Many organizations lack sufficient awareness and expertise in IoT security among their workforce, necessitating training and awareness programs to mitigate security risks.	Employees responsible for managing IoT devices may not be aware of the latest security threats and best practices, making the network more vulnerable to attacks.
28	Network segmentation and isolation	Segmenting IoT devices into separate network zones and isolating critical infrastructure from less secure devices can help mitigate security risks, but implementation can be challenging.	In an industrial IoT network, sensors collecting data on production lines are isolated from administrative devices to prevent unauthorized access.

(*continued*)

Table 1-4. (*continued*)

No.	Challenge	Description	Real-World Examples
29	Integration with cloud services	IoT devices often rely on cloud services for data storage and management, requiring secure data exchange mechanisms and access control mechanisms to protect sensitive information.	Smart home devices may store user data in the cloud for remote access, requiring encryption and access controls to prevent unauthorized access.
30	Overcoming vendor lock-in	Vendor lock-in can limit flexibility in implementing security measures and adapting to evolving threats, requiring careful consideration of vendor relationships and solutions.	A company may struggle to switch to a different IoT platform due to proprietary protocols and dependencies on vendor-specific features.
31	Sustainability and environmental impact	Designing sustainable IoT solutions that minimize environmental impact while maintaining security is a challenge, requiring a balance between energy efficiency, resource usage, and security requirements.	IoT devices deployed in environmental monitoring must be energy-efficient and use eco-friendly materials to minimize their carbon footprint.

(*continued*)

Table 1-4. (*continued*)

No.	Challenge	Description	Real-World Examples
32	Legacy device security	Securing legacy IoT devices that lack built-in security features or update mechanisms poses challenges in protecting these devices from vulnerabilities and attacks.	Older IoT devices may not receive security updates from manufacturers, leaving them vulnerable to known exploits and malware attacks.
33	Complex supply chains	The global supply chains involved in manufacturing IoT devices increase the risk of security breaches due to vulnerabilities introduced at various stages of production and distribution.	Compromised components in the supply chain can result in the distribution of IoT devices with pre-installed malware or backdoors.
34	Security of mesh networks	Mesh networking topologies used in IoT deployments can introduce vulnerabilities such as routing attacks and data interception, requiring specialized security measures for mesh networks.	In a smart city deployment, mesh networks of IoT devices used for street lighting may be vulnerable to attacks that disrupt communication or compromise network integrity.

(*continued*)

Table 1-4. (*continued*)

No.	Challenge	Description	Real-World Examples
35	Regulation divergence	Divergent regulations across regions and industries create compliance challenges for IoT deployments, requiring organizations to navigate and comply with different legal frameworks.	A multinational corporation deploying IoT devices globally must ensure compliance with different data protection regulations, such as GDPR in Europe and CCPA in California.
36	Resilience to physical attacks	IoT devices deployed in public spaces or critical infrastructure are susceptible to physical attacks, requiring measures to ensure their resilience against tampering, vandalism, or theft.	Publicly accessible IoT kiosks may be targeted by vandals attempting to damage or steal the devices, compromising their functionality and security.
37	Emerging technologies	The adoption of emerging technologies in IoT introduces new security challenges related to algorithmic biases, cryptographic vulnerabilities, and unpredictable threat landscapes.	The use of artificial intelligence in IoT devices introduces security risks such as adversarial attacks or biased decision-making algorithms.

(*continued*)

CHAPTER 1   GET STARTED WITH IOT NETWORK AND SECURITY

Table 1-4. (*continued*)

No.	Challenge	Description	Real-World Examples
38	Interference and spectrum management	The crowded radio frequency spectrum used by IoT devices can lead to interference and signal jamming, affecting device connectivity and security.	Wireless IoT devices operating in the 2.4 GHz band may experience interference from other devices, such as Wi-Fi routers, affecting communication reliability and security.
39	Cross-domain attacks	Attackers may exploit vulnerabilities in one IoT domain to launch attacks on another domain, posing cross-domain security risks.	A compromised IoT security camera may be used as a pivot point to launch attacks on other devices in the same network, such as smart TVs or home routers.
40	Economic incentives for security	The economic incentives for IoT manufacturers may not align with strong security practices, leading to devices being shipped with inadequate security measures.	Manufacturers may prioritize time-to-market and cost savings over security, resulting in devices with default passwords or insecure communication protocols.
41	Ethical considerations	Ethical considerations, such as the responsible use of IoT data and ensuring fairness in AI algorithms, must be addressed to prevent harm to individuals or communities.	IoT devices collecting biometric data must ensure ethical use and protection against misuse, such as discriminatory profiling or unauthorized access.

(*continued*)

Table 1-4. (*continued*)

No.	Challenge	Description	Real-World Examples
42	IoT botnets and DDoS attacks	IoT devices are often targeted for botnet recruitment to launch distributed denial-of-service (DDoS) attacks, disrupting services and networks.	The Mirai botnet, comprised of compromised IoT devices, launched massive DDoS attacks that disrupted internet services worldwide.
43	Over-the-air (OTA) updates	Secure over-the-air (OTA) updates are essential for patching vulnerabilities and updating device firmware without physical access, but they also pose security risks if not implemented properly.	IoT devices receiving OTA updates must authenticate the update source and verify the integrity of the update package to prevent installation of malicious firmware.
44	IoT device lifecycle management	Managing the entire lifecycle of IoT devices, including provisioning, configuration, monitoring, and decommissioning, poses significant security challenges.	A smart city IoT deployment must securely provision and configure devices, monitor for security threats during operation, and securely decommission devices at the end of their lifecycle.

(*continued*)

Table 1-4. (*continued*)

No.	Challenge	Description	Real-World Examples
45	Security of data at rest and in transit	Securing data both at rest and in transit is essential for protecting sensitive information from unauthorized access or interception, requiring encryption and authentication mechanisms.	IoT devices transmitting data over wireless networks must use encryption to prevent eavesdropping and ensure data confidentiality.
46	Identity and access management	Establishing and managing identities for IoT devices and ensuring secure access control mechanisms is challenging due to the large number of devices and dynamic IoT environments.	Access control mechanisms must ensure that only authorized devices and users can access sensitive data or control critical systems in an IoT network.
47	Network segmentation and isolation	Segmenting IoT devices into separate network zones and isolating critical infrastructure from less secure devices can help mitigate security risks, but implementation can be challenging.	In an industrial IoT network, sensors collecting data on production lines are isolated from administrative devices to prevent unauthorized access.

(*continued*)

Table 1-4. (continued)

No.	Challenge	Description	Real-World Examples
48	Integration with cloud services	IoT devices often rely on cloud services for data storage and management, requiring secure data exchange mechanisms and access control mechanisms to protect sensitive information.	Smart home devices may store user data in the cloud for remote access, requiring encryption and access controls to prevent unauthorized access.
49	Overcoming vendor lock-in	Vendor lock-in can limit flexibility in implementing security measures and adapting to evolving threats, requiring careful consideration of vendor relationships and solutions.	A company may struggle to switch to a different IoT platform due to proprietary protocols and dependencies on vendor-specific features.
50	Sustainability and environmental impact	Designing sustainable IoT solutions that minimize environmental impact while maintaining security is a challenge, requiring a balance between energy efficiency, resource usage, and security requirements.	IoT devices deployed in environmental monitoring must be energy-efficient and use eco-friendly materials to minimize their carbon footprint.

CHAPTER 1 GET STARTED WITH IOT NETWORK AND SECURITY

Future Opportunities

Future opportunities in IoT networks and security across various industries are promising. Advanced encryption techniques offer enhanced data protection, ensuring confidentiality in sectors like healthcare and finance. Self-healing IoT networks can automatically detect and mitigate security breaches, ensuring continuous operation in critical infrastructure such as smart cities and industrial plants. Secure hardware design with built-in security features enables tamper-resistant IoT devices, bolstering security in areas like transportation and energy. Cyber-physical system security addresses the unique challenges of interconnected systems, safeguarding smart grid deployments and autonomous vehicles. Quantum key distribution promises unconditional security for IoT communications, offering protection against quantum attacks in industries such as telecommunications and defense. Here's a detailed breakdown of Top 15 of the key future opportunities listed in Table 1-5.

Table 1-5. Top 15 key future opportunities across IoT/IIoT

No.	Future Opportunity	Description	Real-World Examples
1	AI-driven threat detection	Leveraging artificial intelligence and machine learning algorithms to detect and respond to threats in real-time, enhancing the security posture of IoT networks.	AI algorithms can analyze network traffic patterns to identify abnormal behavior indicative of a cyber attack, enabling proactive threat mitigation.
2	Blockchain for secure transactions	Implementing blockchain technology to ensure the integrity and transparency of transactions and data exchanges in IoT networks, reducing the risk of tampering and fraud.	Blockchain can be used to create tamper-proof logs of sensor data in supply chain management, ensuring data integrity and authenticity throughout the supply chain.
3	Edge computing security	Enhancing security at the edge by deploying advanced security mechanisms such as encryption, authentication, and intrusion detection directly on IoT devices or gateways.	Edge devices in industrial IoT networks can use lightweight encryption algorithms to secure data locally, reducing latency and minimizing exposure to cyber threats.

(*continued*)

Table 1-5. (*continued*)

No.	Future Opportunity	Description	Real-World Examples
4	Quantum-secure communication	Developing quantum-resistant encryption algorithms to protect IoT communications from future quantum computing threats, ensuring long-term security of sensitive data.	Post-quantum cryptography can secure IoT devices against potential threats posed by quantum computers, safeguarding data confidentiality and integrity.
5	Biometric authentication	Integrating biometric authentication methods such as fingerprint recognition or facial recognition into IoT devices to enhance security and user authentication.	Smart home devices may use biometric authentication to ensure that only authorized users can access sensitive features or data.
6	Software-defined security	Implementing software-defined security approaches that dynamically adapt to changing IoT network conditions and emerging threats, enhancing flexibility and resilience.	Software-defined perimeters can automatically adjust access controls based on device behavior, network conditions, and threat intelligence, reducing the attack surface.

(*continued*)

Table 1-5. (*continued*)

No.	Future Opportunity	Description	Real-World Examples
7	Zero-trust security architecture	Adopting a zero-trust security model that assumes all devices, users, and connections are potentially compromised and requires continuous authentication and authorization for access.	Zero-trust architectures enforce strict access controls and verification at every interaction, reducing the risk of lateral movement by attackers within IoT networks.
8	Secure firmware over-the-air updates	Implementing secure over-the-air (OTA) update mechanisms for IoT device firmware to ensure that updates are authentic, tamper-proof, and protected against interception.	IoT manufacturers can use digitally signed firmware updates delivered over encrypted channels to ensure the integrity and authenticity of updates.
9	Multi-factor authentication	Enhancing authentication mechanisms with multi-factor authentication (MFA) to provide an additional layer of security beyond traditional username and password authentication.	IoT devices may require a combination of biometric, token-based, or SMS-based authentication methods to grant access to sensitive functionalities.
10	Threat intelligence integration	Integrating threat intelligence feeds and platforms into IoT security systems to provide real-time insights into emerging threats and enable proactive threat mitigation.	Security solutions can analyze threat intelligence data to identify indicators of compromise and proactively block malicious activities in IoT networks.

(*continued*)

Table 1-5. (*continued*)

No.	Future Opportunity	Description	Real-World Examples
11	Advanced encryption techniques	Utilizing advanced encryption techniques such as homomorphic encryption or lattice-based cryptography to protect sensitive data in IoT networks, ensuring confidentiality and privacy.	Homomorphic encryption allows computation on encrypted data without decrypting it, enabling secure data processing in IoT applications such as healthcare or finance.
12	Self-healing IoT networks	Implementing self-healing capabilities in IoT networks to automatically detect and mitigate security breaches or anomalies, ensuring continuous operation and resilience against attacks.	Self-healing networks can dynamically reroute traffic or isolate compromised devices to contain security incidents and prevent further damage, improving overall network reliability and security.
13	Secure hardware design	Developing secure-by-design hardware components for IoT devices with built-in security features such as secure boot, hardware-based encryption, and tamper-resistant hardware modules.	Hardware security modules (HSMs) provide cryptographic key storage and management, protecting sensitive data and preventing unauthorized access or tampering.

(*continued*)

Table 1-5. (*continued*)

No.	Future Opportunity	Description	Real-World Examples
14	Cyber-physical system security	Addressing security challenges specific to cyber-physical systems (CPS) by integrating security mechanisms that protect both the cyber and physical components of IoT deployments.	Smart grid systems employ secure communication protocols and physical security measures to prevent unauthorized access and protect critical infrastructure from cyber attacks.
15	Quantum key distribution (QKD)	Implementing quantum key distribution (QKD) protocols to establish secure cryptographic keys for encrypting IoT communications, leveraging the principles of quantum mechanics to ensure unconditional security.	QKD enables the secure exchange of encryption keys by encoding them in quantum states, offering protection against eavesdropping and quantum attacks in IoT networks.

IoT Architecture

The architecture of IoT (Internet of Things) is structured into layers, each with specific functions and interactions within the IoT ecosystem.

IoT architecture typically consists of interconnected layers that enable data flow from devices to applications and back. At its core, IoT architecture includes the device layer, where sensors and actuators collect and transmit data, often using protocols such as MQTT or HTTP. This data is then sent to the edge layer, where edge devices or gateways process and filter the information before forwarding it to the cloud or on-premises servers. The edge layer helps reduce latency by handling data processing closer to the source, making it ideal for applications requiring real-time responses or dealing with intermittent connectivity.

On the cloud side, the data is received by IoT platforms or services that manage and analyze the incoming streams. These platforms typically offer functionalities for data storage, processing, and visualization and integration with other enterprise systems. Insights gained from data analysis can trigger actions back down to the edge or device layer, completing the feedback loop. Security measures such as encryption, access control, and monitoring are integrated throughout the architecture to safeguard data and devices from unauthorized access and potential threats. Figure 1-2 depicts the layers of Internet of Things (IoT).

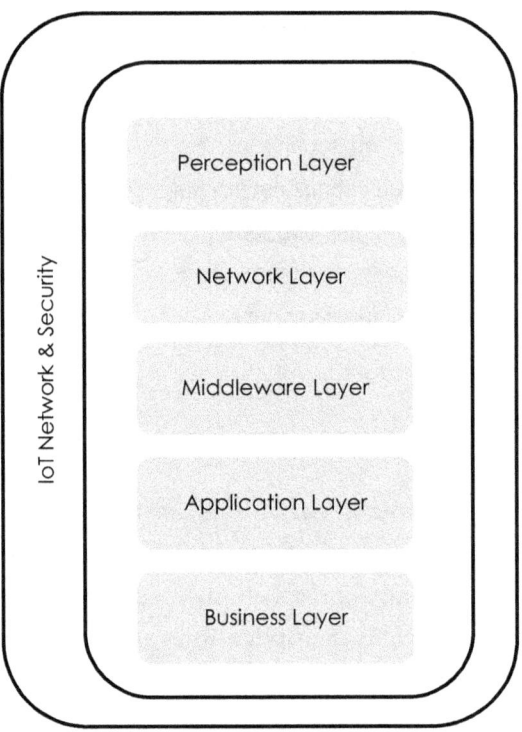

Figure 1-2. *Internet of Things – architecture layers*

At the top lies the perception layer, which encompasses physical devices like sensors and actuators. Sensors collect data from the environment, such as temperature or motion, while actuators control physical processes based on input from the IoT system.

The perception layer, the foundational tier of IoT architecture, comprises physical devices such as sensors and actuators. These devices are the "eyes and ears" of the IoT system, collecting data from the physical world and enabling interaction with it. Sensors detect various environmental parameters such as temperature, humidity, light, motion, and pressure. On the other hand, actuators allow the IoT system to influence the physical world by controlling devices such as motors, valves, or switches. The perception layer is responsible for capturing raw data from the environment and converting it into digital signals that can be processed and analyzed by higher layers of the architecture. The perception layer must ensure accurate and reliable data acquisition, considering sensor accuracy, precision, and calibration factors. Additionally, power efficiency is critical, especially for battery-operated devices, as prolonged sensor operation can drain batteries quickly. Overall, the perception layer forms the backbone of IoT systems, providing the crucial link between the physical and digital worlds.

In the perception layer of IoT architecture, sensors play a vital role in gathering data from the physical environment. These sensors come in various types and forms, tailored to specific applications. For instance, temperature sensors monitor temperature changes, while humidity sensors measure the moisture level in the air. Motion sensors detect movement, and pressure sensors gauge the force exerted on a surface. Each sensor type has unique characteristics and operating principles, requiring careful selection to ensure suitability for the intended application. Additionally, sensor fusion techniques may combine data from multiple sensors to provide more comprehensive insights or enhance accuracy.

Actuators, another component of the perception layer, enable the IoT system to act upon the environment based on the data collected. These devices can control physical processes or trigger actions in response to sensor inputs. For example, actuators can adjust the temperature in a room based on temperature sensor readings, open or close valves in an industrial process, or activate alarms in a security system. Actuators often require careful sensor integration and real-time responsiveness to ensure effective operation. Moreover, reliability, durability, and energy efficiency are essential when selecting actuators for IoT applications, especially in harsh or remote environments.

The perception layer faces various challenges, including sensor calibration, data quality assurance, and maintenance. Calibration ensures that sensors provide accurate and reliable measurements over time, accounting for factors such as drift or environmental changes. Quality assurance mechanisms are crucial for detecting and mitigating errors or anomalies in sensor data, ensuring the integrity and trustworthiness of the information collected. Regular maintenance and monitoring are also necessary to identify and address issues such as sensor degradation, malfunction, or environmental interference. Properly managing these challenges is essential to maintain the effectiveness and reliability of the perception layer, ensuring the success of IoT applications in diverse environments and use cases.

Below the perception layer is the network layer, which is responsible for connecting IoT devices to the Internet. This layer manages device connectivity through various protocols like Wi-Fi, bluetooth, or Zigbee. Gateways serve as intermediaries, aggregating data, preprocessing, and ensuring connectivity.

The network layer in IoT architecture is the backbone for connecting devices, gateways, and cloud services, facilitating seamless communication and data exchange. This layer manages device connectivity at its core using various wireless and wired communication protocols. Wireless protocols like Wi-Fi, Bluetooth, Zigbee, LoRa, and cellular networks enable devices to communicate over short or long distances, depending on the application requirements. Wired protocols such as Ethernet provide reliable, high-speed communication within local networks or industrial environments. Gateways play a crucial role in this layer, acting as intermediaries between IoT devices and the cloud, aggregating data, and ensuring connectivity.

In addition to managing device connectivity, the network layer encompasses communication protocols that define how data is transmitted between devices and services. These protocols ensure efficient and secure data transfer, addressing reliability, latency, and power consumption. For example, MQTT (Message Queuing Telemetry Transport) and CoAP (Constrained Application Protocol) are lightweight, publish-subscribe protocols commonly used in IoT for real-time communication. They enable devices to send and receive data streams efficiently, even in low-bandwidth or intermittent connectivity environments. Protocols like HTTP/HTTPS facilitate communication with web-based services and APIs, enabling integration with existing systems and platforms.

Gateways play a crucial role in the network layer by bridging local IoT networks and the cloud. These devices aggregate data from multiple sensors or devices, perform preprocessing tasks such as data filtering or aggregation, and transmit relevant information to cloud services for further analysis or storage. Edge gateways close to IoT devices reduce latency by processing data locally before forwarding it to the cloud. On the other hand, cloud gateways handle communication between IoT devices and cloud services, ensuring secure and reliable connectivity over the Internet. Gateways also manage network protocols and security, enforcing access controls and encryption to protect data in transit.

Scalability and interoperability are critical considerations in the network layer. IoT networks often consist of many devices with diverse communication capabilities and requirements. Scalable network architectures, such as those based on mesh or star topologies, accommodate varying numbers of devices and support growth over time. Interoperability standards and protocols ensure that devices from different manufacturers or ecosystems can communicate and exchange data seamlessly, enabling a cohesive IoT ecosystem that maximizes compatibility and flexibility.

The middleware layer is below the network layer and handles data processing, storage, and management. It also translates data between different protocols for interoperability and manages device provisioning, configuration, and firmware updates.

The middleware layer in IoT architecture is an intermediary between the lower-level network and perception layers and the higher-level application and business layers. It plays a crucial role in managing and processing the vast amounts of data generated by IoT devices, providing essential services such as data processing, storage, and protocol translation. One of the primary functions of the middleware layer is to process and manage data collected from sensors and other devices before it is transmitted to higher layers for further analysis or action. This includes data filtering, aggregation, and normalization to ensure consistency and quality.

Protocol translation is another critical aspect of the middleware layer. IoT devices often use different communication protocols depending on power efficiency, bandwidth, and range. The middleware layer facilitates seamless communication by translating data between various protocols, allowing devices with varying capabilities of communication to exchange information. For example, it may translate data from MQTT to CoAP or Zigbee to HTTP, enabling interoperability across heterogeneous IoT environments.

Device management is an essential function of the middleware layer, encompassing device provisioning, configuration, and firmware updates. It ensures that IoT devices are properly configured and updated with the latest firmware to maintain optimal performance and security. Device management also includes

- Monitoring device health and status
- Detecting and resolving issues
- Managing device lifecycles from deployment to decommissioning

The middleware layer also enables integration with external systems and services, such as cloud platforms, enterprise applications, and third-party APIs. This integration allows IoT data to be shared, analyzed, and acted upon in conjunction with other business processes and systems. For example, IoT data may be integrated with customer relationship management (CRM) systems to provide insights into customer behavior or with supply chain management systems to optimize inventory and logistics. APIs and standard communication protocols facilitate this integration, ensuring interoperability and compatibility across different systems and platforms.

The application layer hosts IoT applications and services that utilize data for various purposes. It includes data analytics for deriving insights, user interfaces for interaction, and integration with enterprise systems like ERP or CRM.

The application layer in IoT architecture is where the data collected from sensors and processed by middleware is utilized to derive insights, make decisions, and trigger actions. This layer hosts many applications and services that leverage IoT data to address specific use cases and business objectives. One key aspect of the application layer is data analytics and insights generation. IoT data is analyzed using various techniques such as statistical analysis, machine learning, and predictive modeling to extract meaningful insights. These insights can be used to optimize processes, improve efficiency, predict maintenance needs, and enhance decision-making.

User interfaces are another critical component of the application layer, providing end-users a means to interact with IoT systems and access information. This includes web-based dashboards, mobile applications, and voice interfaces that enable users to monitor device status, view analytics, and control connected devices remotely. User interfaces make IoT data accessible and actionable to stakeholders, whether operators, managers, or consumers.

IoT applications often require integrating enterprise systems and services to leverage existing infrastructure and workflows. The application layer facilitates this integration, enabling seamless communication and data exchange between IoT platforms and enterprise applications such as ERP (enterprise resource planning), CRM (customer relationship management), or SCM (supply chain management) systems. Integration with enterprise systems allows IoT data to be utilized with other business processes, enabling enhanced decision-making and automation.

Moreover, the application layer enables the implementation of various IoT use cases across industries and domains. These use cases span various applications, including smart cities, industrial automation, healthcare, agriculture, transportation, and consumer electronics. For example, IoT applications can be used in smart cities for intelligent traffic management, environmental monitoring, and energy efficiency. In industrial automation, IoT enables predictive maintenance, real-time monitoring of equipment, and optimization of production processes. The application layer provides the flexibility and scalability required to deploy and manage diverse IoT applications tailored to specific needs and requirements.

The business layer defines the logic and rules governing IoT system behavior based on business requirements. It integrates IoT systems with enterprise systems and establishes monetization strategies.

The business layer in IoT architecture focuses on IoT deployment's strategic and operational aspects, ensuring alignment with organizational goals, generating value, and driving innovation. At its core, the business layer defines the business logic and rules that govern IoT systems based on the organization's objectives and priorities. This includes defining use cases, defining key performance indicators (KPIs), and establishing rules for data governance, compliance, and monetization strategies.

One of the primary functions of the business layer is to define and prioritize IoT use cases that align with the organization's objectives and address specific business challenges or opportunities. This involves identifying areas where IoT technology can add value, improve efficiency, reduce costs, or create new revenue streams. Use cases may vary across industries and domains, ranging from predictive maintenance and asset tracking in manufacturing to remote patient monitoring and personalized healthcare in healthcare. The business layer ensures that these use cases are well-defined, scoped, and prioritized based on their strategic importance and potential impact on the business.

Integration with enterprise systems and processes is another key aspect of the business layer. IoT systems often need to interface with other business systems, such as ERP (enterprise resource planning), CRM (customer relationship management), or SCM (supply chain management) systems, to exchange data, trigger actions, or enable seamless workflows. The business layer facilitates this integration, ensuring IoT data and insights are integrated into existing business processes and decision-making workflows, driving operational efficiency and improving business outcomes.

Monetization and business models are critical considerations within the business layer, especially for organizations looking to capitalize on IoT investments. This involves defining how IoT products and services will be monetized through subscription models, pay-per-use pricing, value-added services, or other revenue streams. Additionally, the business layer oversees the development of strategies to maximize the return on investment (ROI) from IoT deployments, including cost optimization, revenue generation, and risk management. Organizations can leverage IoT technology to drive growth, innovation, and competitive advantage by aligning IoT initiatives with business objectives and implementing effective monetization strategies.

Security is a critical aspect that cuts across all layers. Device security ensures authentication, encryption, and secure boot mechanisms.

Network security secures communication channels, while data security and privacy protect against unauthorized access and misuse. Security monitoring and incident response ensure prompt action against security threats.

Integration and interoperability are facilitated through interlayer communication, interoperability standards, and well-defined APIs and interfaces, enabling seamless data exchange and integration with third-party systems and services.

This layered architecture allows IoT systems to be designed, deployed, and managed effectively, ensuring scalability, reliability, and security throughout the IoT ecosystem.

Microsoft's IoT Reference Architecture

Microsoft's IoT reference architecture offers a comprehensive framework for designing scalable, secure, and interoperable IoT solutions, leveraging the power of Azure's extensive services and tools. At the device layer, devices connect to Azure IoT Hub, the central messaging hub for bidirectional communication between devices and the cloud. Azure IoT Hub also provides device management capabilities, allowing for the provisioning, configuration, and monitoring of IoT devices at scale.

Azure IoT Hub is a managed service in Microsoft Azure designed to facilitate communication between IoT devices and the cloud. It is a central messaging hub, allowing devices to securely send telemetry data to the cloud for analysis and processing. It also enables cloud applications to send commands and notifications to devices for remote control and management. With built-in device management capabilities, Azure IoT Hub makes it easy to register, provision, configure, and monitor IoT devices at scale. It ensures secure communication through features like device authentication and message encryption. It also integrates Azure services such as Azure Stream Analytics, Azure Functions, and Azure Machine Learning for real-time analytics and processing. Azure IoT Hub is highly scalable and reliable, handling millions of devices and messages per second. It is essential for building scalable and secure IoT solutions in the Azure ecosystem.

Azure IoT Hub

Azure IoT Hub plays a critical role in ensuring the security and compliance of IoT solutions by providing robust security features and facilitating adherence to industry regulations and standards. It offers device authentication mechanisms to ensure that only authorized devices can connect to the IoT hub, preventing unauthorized access and data breaches. Additionally, Azure IoT Hub supports message encryption to protect data in transit, safeguarding sensitive information from interception or tampering. Integration with Azure Active Directory enables organizations to centrally manage device identities and access control policies. Moreover, Azure IoT Hub helps organizations comply with regulatory requirements such as GDPR, HIPAA, and ISO 27001 by providing data protection, privacy, and audit logging features.

Azure IoT Hub's key characteristics are scalability and reliability, making it suitable for IoT deployments of any size. The service is designed to handle millions of devices and messages per second, with built-in scalability and redundancy to ensure high availability and fault tolerance. This scalability enables IoT solutions to grow seamlessly as the number of devices and data volume increases. Azure IoT Hub also provides monitoring and diagnostic tools to help organizations track the health and performance of their IoT deployments, enabling proactive management and optimization.

Azure IoT Hub integrates seamlessly with other Azure services, allowing organizations to leverage the full capabilities of the Azure ecosystem for building end-to-end IoT solutions. For example, IoT data ingested by Azure IoT Hub can be processed and analyzed in real time using services like Azure Stream Analytics or Azure Functions.

It can also be stored and queried in Azure Cosmos DB or integrated with Azure Machine Learning for advanced analytics and predictive maintenance. This integration simplifies development, reduces complexity, and accelerates time-to-market for IoT solutions by providing a cohesive platform for building, deploying, and managing IoT applications. Overall, Azure IoT Hub is a comprehensive and versatile service that empowers organizations to unlock the full potential of their IoT initiatives with security, scalability, and seamless integration.

In the edge layer, devices can run Azure IoT Edge runtime to perform edge computing tasks such as data processing, analytics, and machine learning inference locally. Edge modules, lightweight containers running on IoT Edge devices, facilitate processing and analysis of data close to the source, reducing latency and bandwidth usage.

Azure IoT Edge

Azure IoT Edge is a platform provided by Microsoft Azure that extends cloud intelligence to edge devices, enabling them to run locally run AI, machine learning, and analytics workloads. It allows organizations to deploy and manage cloud services, such as Azure Machine Learning and Azure Stream Analytics, directly on edge devices, bringing real-time insights and actions closer to the data source. This distributed computing approach reduces latency, conserves bandwidth, and enhances privacy by processing data locally without sending it to the cloud.

At its core, Azure IoT Edge consists of three main components: IoT Edge runtime, IoT Edge modules, and IoT Edge Hub. The IoT Edge runtime enables edge devices to run containerized workloads, facilitating the deployment and execution of applications at the edge. IoT Edge modules are modular units of code packaged into containers, which can be developed using various programming languages and frameworks. These modules perform specific tasks such as data preprocessing, analytics, or control and can be easily deployed, updated, and managed independently.

CHAPTER 1   GET STARTED WITH IOT NETWORK AND SECURITY

IoT Edge Hub manages communication between IoT Edge devices and the cloud, providing secure and reliable messaging capabilities.

Azure IoT Edge offers several benefits for edge computing scenarios:

- It enables organizations to take advantage of AI and machine learning capabilities at the edge, allowing for real-time analysis and decision-making without reliance on cloud connectivity.

- It provides offline operation and resilience to network disruptions, ensuring that critical applications continue to function even when connectivity is intermittent or unavailable.

- It enhances privacy and security by processing sensitive data locally, minimizing exposure to potential security threats and regulatory compliance risks.

In addition to these benefits, Azure IoT Edge is highly scalable and flexible, supporting a wide range of edge devices, operating systems, and programming languages. It integrates seamlessly with other Azure services, enabling organizations to build end-to-end IoT solutions spanning the cloud to the edge. With Azure IoT Edge, organizations can unlock the full potential of edge computing by bringing intelligence and insights closer to where data is generated, enabling faster decision-making, improved operational efficiency, and innovative new applications in various industries and use cases.

Moving to the platform layer, Azure IoT Hub manages device-to-cloud and cloud-to-device communication, device identity, security, and integration with other Azure services. Azure IoT Central offers a fully managed SaaS solution for IoT applications, enabling rapid development and deployment without infrastructure management. Azure IoT Solution Accelerators also provide pre-built solutions and templates for common IoT scenarios, streamlining development.

Azure IoT Hub is a pivotal service within the Microsoft Azure ecosystem, providing a centralized platform for managing and communicating with Internet of Things (IoT) devices. At its core, Azure IoT Hub facilitates seamless bi-directional communication between IoT devices and the cloud, enabling devices to send telemetry data and receive commands and notifications securely. This communication is essential for monitoring device status, collecting sensor data, and controlling device behavior remotely. Azure IoT Hub is designed to handle massive volumes of device-to-cloud and cloud-to-device messages, making it suitable for IoT deployments of any scale.

Azure IoT Hub

One of Azure IoT Hub's key features is its robust device management capabilities. Organizations can use Azure IoT Hub to register, provision, configure, and monitor IoT devices at scale. This includes features such as device twin, which maintains a digital representation of each device's state and configuration, allowing for remote management and synchronization. Additionally, Azure IoT Hub provides a device provisioning service that automates the process of provisioning devices with the necessary credentials, simplifying deployment and reducing management overhead.

Security is a top priority for Azure IoT Hub, and the service includes a range of features to ensure the confidentiality, integrity, and availability of IoT data and communications. Device authentication mechanisms, including symmetric keys, X.509 certificates, and Azure Active Directory integration, ensure that only authorized devices can connect to the IoT Hub. Message encryption and TLS/SSL protocols protect data in transit, while role-based access control (RBAC) allows organizations to define fine-grained access policies for device management and data access. Azure IoT Hub also integrates with Azure Security Center to monitor and manage IoT security posture.

Azure IoT Hub integrates seamlessly with other Azure services, enabling organizations to build end-to-end IoT solutions that leverage the full capabilities of the Azure ecosystem. IoT data ingested by Azure IoT Hub can be processed and analyzed in real-time using services like Azure Stream Analytics, Azure Functions, or Azure Machine Learning. It can also be stored and queried in Azure Cosmos DB or integrated with Azure Time Series Insights for advanced analytics and visualization. This integration simplifies development, reduces complexity, and accelerates time-to-market for IoT solutions by providing a cohesive platform for building, deploying, and managing IoT applications.

In the data layer, Azure IoT Hub ingests data from devices and sends it to downstream services for processing and storage. Services like Azure Stream Analytics and Azure Cosmos DB handle real-time stream processing and storage of IoT data. At the same time, Azure Time Series Insights provides tools for visualizing and analyzing time-series data in real time.

Azure Stream Analytics

Azure Stream Analytics is a real-time data processing service provided by Microsoft Azure, designed to analyze and gain insights from streaming data in real time. It allows organizations to process and analyze high volumes of data from various sources, such as IoT devices, sensors, social media feeds, and application logs, enabling them to make informed decisions and take timely actions based on the insights derived from the data. Azure Stream Analytics is a fully managed service, eliminating the need for infrastructure management and enabling organizations to focus on building and deploying real-time analytics solutions.

At its core, Azure Stream Analytics ingests streaming data from multiple sources and processes it using SQL-like queries in real time. This allows organizations to perform transformations, aggregations, filtering, and data enrichment as it flows through the system. The service supports both temporal and spatial processing capabilities, enabling advanced analytics such as windowing, tumbling, and sliding windows for analyzing data over time as well as geospatial processing for analyzing location-based data.

Azure Stream Analytics provides seamless integration with other Azure services, allowing organizations to build end-to-end real-time analytics solutions that leverage the full capabilities of the Azure ecosystem. For example, organizations can use Azure Stream Analytics to analyze streaming data from IoT devices and then use Azure Functions or Azure Machine Learning to trigger actions or make predictions based on the analyzed data. Additionally, Azure Stream Analytics integrates with Azure Event Hubs for event ingestion, Azure Blob Storage for data storage, and Azure SQL Database or Azure Cosmos DB for data persistence, enabling organizations to store and analyze streaming data at scale.

One of the key benefits of Azure Stream Analytics is its scalability and elasticity. The service can automatically scale up or down based on the volume of incoming data and processing requirements, ensuring optimal performance and cost-effectiveness. This makes it suitable for a wide range of use cases, from simple event filtering and aggregation to complex event patterns and anomaly detection. With Azure Stream Analytics, organizations can build and deploy real-time analytics solutions quickly and easily, enabling them to gain insights from streaming data and drive actionable insights in real time.

Azure Cosmos DB

Azure Cosmos DB is a globally distributed, multi-model database service provided by Microsoft Azure, designed to meet the demands of modern, high-performance applications globally. It offers turnkey global distribution, elastic scalability, and multi-model capabilities, making it suitable for various use cases, including web, mobile, gaming, IoT, and enterprise applications. Azure Cosmos DB provides

- Guaranteed low latency

- High-throughput access to data across multiple regions

- Performance-efficient for a better user experience around the world

At its core, Azure Cosmos DB is built on a schema-agnostic data model, allowing developers to store and query data flexibly and efficiently. It supports multiple data models, including document, key-value, graph, and column family, enabling organizations to choose the most suitable model for their application requirements. This flexibility allows developers to build rich, dynamic applications that can evolve without being constrained by rigid schemas or data models.

One of Azure Cosmos DB's key features is its global distribution capabilities, which allow data to be replicated and synchronized across multiple regions worldwide. This enables organizations to achieve low-latency access to data and high availability, even in regional outages or network disruptions. Azure Cosmos DB also provides automatic failover and disaster recovery capabilities, ensuring business continuity and data resilience.

Azure Cosmos DB integrates seamlessly with other Azure services and tools, enabling organizations to build end-to-end solutions that leverage the full power of the Azure ecosystem. For example, organizations can use Azure Functions or Azure Stream Analytics to process and analyze data stored in Cosmos DB in real time, or they can use Azure Machine Learning to perform advanced analytics and predictions on the data. Additionally, Azure Cosmos DB provides native support for popular APIs and programming models, including SQL, MongoDB, Cassandra, Gremlin, and Table Storage, making it easy for developers to migrate existing applications or build new ones using familiar tools and languages. Overall, Azure Cosmos DB provides a comprehensive and flexible database solution that empowers organizations to build and scale global applications quickly while ensuring fast, reliable, and consistent access to data.

For analytics, Azure Synapse Analytics combines big data and data warehousing capabilities, allowing organizations to perform advanced analytics on IoT data. Azure Machine Learning enables the building, training, and deploying of machine learning models to analyze IoT data and derive actionable insights.

Azure Synapse Analytics

Azure Synapse Analytics, formerly known as Azure SQL Data Warehouse, is a powerful analytics service provided by Microsoft Azure that combines big data and data warehousing capabilities into a single, unified platform. It enables organizations to analyze large volumes of structured and unstructured data in real time, driving insights and decision-making across the business. Azure Synapse Analytics integrates with existing Azure services and tools, providing a comprehensive solution for building and deploying end-to-end analytics solutions.

At its core, Azure Synapse Analytics provides a massively parallel processing (MPP) architecture that enables organizations to process and analyze petabytes of data easily. It supports relational and non-relational data models, allowing users to ingest, transform, and analyze data from various sources, including SQL databases, data lakes, and streaming data. Azure Synapse Analytics uses a familiar SQL-based query language, enabling data analysts and developers to write complex queries and perform advanced analytics without requiring specialized skills or tools.

One of the key features of Azure Synapse Analytics is its seamless integration with other Azure services, enabling organizations to leverage the full power of the Azure ecosystem for building end-to-end analytics solutions. For example, organizations can use Azure Data Factory to orchestrate data pipelines, Azure Machine Learning to build and deploy machine learning models, and Power BI to visualize and share insights derived from data in Azure Synapse Analytics. Additionally, Azure Synapse Analytics integrates with Azure Active Directory for authentication and access control, ensuring data security and compliance with regulatory requirements.

Azure Synapse Analytics offers advanced analytics capabilities, including built-in machine learning, predictive analytics, and natural language processing. It enables organizations to perform complex analytics tasks such as anomaly detection, pattern recognition, and sentiment analysis on large datasets, helping them uncover valuable insights and trends hidden within their data. With Azure Synapse Analytics, organizations can accelerate time-to-insight, drive data-driven decision-making, and gain a competitive edge in today's data-driven world.

In the application layer, custom applications can be built using Azure services such as Azure App Service, Azure Functions, or Azure Logic Apps to implement business logic, workflows, and user interfaces. Power BI allows for creating interactive dashboards and reports to visualize IoT data and gain insights. Additionally, Azure IoT Central provides pre-built dashboards and visualizations for monitoring and managing IoT devices and data.

Azure App Service

Azure App Service is a fully managed platform-as-a-service (PaaS) offering provided by Microsoft Azure, enabling developers to build, deploy, and scale web applications and APIs quickly and easily. With Azure App Service, developers can focus on building their applications without worrying about infrastructure management, as Azure handles tasks such as provisioning, scaling, and maintenance automatically. It supports various programming languages and frameworks, including .NET, Java, Node.js, Python, and PHP, allowing developers to choose the technology stack that best fits their needs.

One of the key features of Azure App Service is its seamless integration with other Azure services and tools, enabling developers to extend their applications' functionality easily. For example, developers can integrate their applications with Azure Active Directory for authentication and access control, Azure SQL Database for data storage, and Azure Application

Insights for monitoring and diagnostics. Additionally, Azure App Service provides built-in support for continuous integration and deployment (CI/CD) pipelines, enabling developers to automate the deployment process and deliver updates to their applications quickly and reliably.

Azure App Service offers multiple deployment options, including Web Apps, API Apps, Mobile Apps, and Function Apps, allowing developers to choose the appropriate deployment model based on their application requirements. It also provides features such as auto-scaling, traffic routing, and SSL certificate management, ensuring high availability, performance, and security for applications deployed on the platform. With Azure App Service, developers can confidently build and deploy web applications and APIs, knowing that Azure provides a reliable and scalable platform for their applications.

Azure Functions

Azure Functions is a serverless compute service provided by Microsoft Azure. It allows developers to build and deploy event-driven, scalable, cost-effective applications without managing infrastructure. With Azure Functions, developers can write small, focused pieces of code called functions that respond to events and triggers from various sources, such as HTTP requests, message queues, timers, and database changes. This enables developers to implement business logic and automation modularly and granularly, reducing development time and complexity.

One of Azure Functions' key benefits is its pay-as-you-go pricing model, where developers only pay for the resources used by their functions during execution. This makes Azure Functions highly cost-effective, as developers can scale their applications automatically based on demand without overprovisioning resources. Additionally, Azure Functions provides built-in support for popular programming languages such as C#, JavaScript, Python, and PowerShell, as well as integration with Visual Studio Code and Azure DevOps for development and deployment.

Azure Functions seamlessly integrates with other Azure services and tools, enabling developers to extend the functionality of their applications easily. For example, developers can integrate their functions with Azure Event Grid for event-driven architectures, Azure Storage for data processing and storage, and Azure Key Vault for secure secrets management. Azure Functions also provides features such as durable functions for long-running workflows, bindings for integrating with external services, and monitoring and logging capabilities for troubleshooting and diagnostics.

With Azure Functions, developers can quickly and easily build various serverless applications, including webhooks, APIs, data processing pipelines, and IoT event handlers. The serverless architecture of Azure Functions allows developers to focus on writing code and delivering value to their users without worrying about managing servers or infrastructure.

Azure Logic Apps

Azure Logic Apps is a cloud-based workflow automation platform provided by Microsoft Azure. It enables developers to orchestrate and automate business processes and integrations across cloud services, on-premises systems, and third-party applications. With Azure Logic Apps, developers can design workflows visually using a drag-and-drop interface without complex coding or scripting. This makes it easy for developers to create and maintain workflows, reducing development time and increasing productivity.

One of Azure Logic Apps' key features is its extensive set of connectors, which allow developers to integrate with a wide range of services and systems, including Azure services, SaaS applications, on-premises data sources, and custom APIs. These connectors provide pre-built triggers and actions developers can use to build workflows that automate data ingestion, processing, transformation, and notification tasks. Additionally, Azure Logic Apps provides built-in support for error handling, retries, and scheduling, ensuring reliability and robustness for automated workflows.

Azure Logic Apps offers advanced capabilities such as conditional branching, looping, and parallel execution, enabling developers to create complex and sophisticated workflows to meet their business needs. It also provides integration with Azure Monitor and Azure Application Insights for monitoring and logging, allowing developers to track the execution of their workflows and diagnose issues quickly. With Azure Logic Apps, developers can build scalable and resilient automation solutions that streamline business processes and improve operational efficiency.

Azure Logic Apps integrates seamlessly with other Azure services and tools, allowing developers to extend the functionality of their workflows easily. For example, developers can integrate their logic apps with Azure Functions for custom processing and business logic, Azure Event Grid for event-driven architectures, and Azure DevOps for continuous integration and deployment. Azure Logic Apps also provides connectors for popular SaaS applications such as Salesforce, Office 365, and Dynamics 365, enabling organizations to automate workflows across their entire ecosystem of applications and services.

For security and compliance, Azure Security Center provides unified security management and advanced threat protection for IoT solutions deployed on Azure. The Azure IoT Hub Device Provisioning Service automates device provisioning, while Azure Key Vault safeguards cryptographic keys, certificates, and secrets used by IoT applications and devices.

Azure Security Center

Azure Security Center is a unified security management service provided by Microsoft Azure, offering advanced threat protection across hybrid cloud workloads. It gives organizations a centralized view of their security posture, helping them identify, assess, and remediate security vulnerabilities and threats across their Azure resources and on-premises environments. Azure Security Center continuously monitors for security threats and provides recommendations and best practices to help organizations improve their security posture and compliance with industry standards and regulations.

One of the key features of Azure Security Center is its ability to provide threat detection and advanced analytics using machine learning and artificial intelligence. It analyzes security telemetry from various sources, including virtual machines, containers, databases, and networks, to detect and alert suspicious activities and potential security breaches. Azure Security Center also provides security alerts and recommendations based on industry-standard security benchmarks, helping organizations prioritize and address security issues effectively.

Azure Security Center offers a range of security controls and features to help organizations protect their cloud workloads. This includes just-in-time access, network security groups, and adaptive application controls, which help organizations control resource access, limit exposure to vulnerabilities, and prevent unauthorized access. Azure Security Center also integrates with Azure Active Directory for identity and access management, Azure Key Vault for secrets management, and Azure Policy for governance and compliance.

Azure Security Center integrates seamlessly with other Azure services and tools, enabling organizations to extend their security capabilities and automate security workflows. For example, organizations can incorporate Azure Security Center with Azure Sentinel for advanced threat hunting and incident response, Azure DevOps for continuous security monitoring and compliance checks, and Azure Monitor for centralized logging and analysis of security-related events. Overall, Azure Security Center provides organizations with a comprehensive security solution for protecting their cloud workloads and reducing security risks.

CHAPTER 1   GET STARTED WITH IOT NETWORK AND SECURITY

Azure Key Vault

Azure Key Vault is a cloud service provided by Microsoft Azure that safeguards cryptographic keys, secrets, and certificates used by cloud applications and services. It offers a secure and centralized storage solution for managing sensitive information such as passwords, connection strings, API keys, and encryption keys. By securely storing and managing access to these critical resources, Azure Key Vault helps organizations maintain control over their data and ensure compliance with regulatory requirements.

One of the key features of Azure Key Vault is its ability to store keys and secrets securely. Keys stored in Key Vault can be used to encrypt and decrypt data, while secrets can be any sensitive information that an application may need, such as database connection strings or API keys. Key Vault employs industry-standard security practices, including hardware security modules (HSMs), to protect keys and secrets from unauthorized access.

Another important aspect of Azure Key Vault is its integration with other Azure services and applications. Developers can easily access keys and secrets stored in Key Vault from their Azure applications without hardcoding them into their codebase. This integration streamlines the management of sensitive information and reduces the risk of exposure, as secrets are kept separate from the application code and configuration files.

Furthermore, Azure Key Vault provides robust access control mechanisms to regulate who can access the stored keys and secrets and what actions they can perform. Access policies can be defined as granting specific permissions to users, applications, or services, ensuring that only authorized entities can retrieve or manage sensitive data. Additionally, Key Vault logs all access and operations, providing an audit trail for compliance purposes and helping organizations track usage and detect any suspicious activities. Overall, Azure Key Vault is critical for ensuring the security and compliance of cloud applications and services by offering a centralized and highly secure solution for managing cryptographic keys and secrets.

Azure Defender for IoT

Azure Defender for IoT is a security solution provided by Microsoft Azure, designed to protect IoT devices and networks from cyber threats and attacks. It provides organizations with visibility into their IoT assets, detects and alerts on suspicious activities and vulnerabilities, and helps organizations respond to and mitigate security incidents effectively. Azure Defender for IoT leverages advanced analytics and machine learning algorithms to analyze network traffic and device behavior, enabling organizations to identify and remediate security threats in real time.

One of Azure Defender for IoT's key features is its ability to provide comprehensive security coverage for IoT environments. It monitors network traffic, device configurations, and firmware updates to detect anomalies and potential security breaches, including unauthorized access, malware infections, and denial-of-service attacks. Azure Defender for IoT also provides recommendations and best practices for improving the security posture of IoT devices and networks, helping organizations implement proactive security measures to prevent future attacks.

Azure Defender for IoT integrates seamlessly with existing IoT infrastructure and devices, enabling organizations to protect their IoT deployments without disrupting operations. It supports many IoT platforms and protocols, including MQTT, OPC UA, and Modbus, and can be deployed on-premises or in the cloud. Azure Defender for IoT also integrates with Azure Security Center for centralized security management and compliance monitoring, enabling organizations to manage their security posture across hybrid cloud environments.

Azure Defender for IoT gives organizations real-time visibility and control over their IoT environments, enabling them to detect, respond to, and mitigate security threats effectively. It helps organizations reduce the risk of costly security breaches and downtime by providing proactive threat detection and automated remediation capabilities. With Azure

Defender for IoT, organizations can ensure the security and integrity of their IoT deployments, enabling them to leverage the full potential of IoT technology while minimizing security risks.

Azure API Management, Azure Event Grid, and Azure Logic Apps facilitate integration and interoperability, enabling seamless integration with third-party services and systems, event routing, and workflow automation. By following Microsoft's IoT reference architecture, organizations can accelerate IoT development, reduce complexity, and unlock the full potential of their IoT initiatives.

Now let us put all these elements together with reference architecture.

Microsoft can create custom IoT solutions by leveraging Azure PaaS (platform-as-a-service) components. The following details an overview of Azure components and services commonly used in IoT solutions, though only some solutions may utilize all of these components. Figure 1-3 depicts the Azure Reference architecture for IoT.

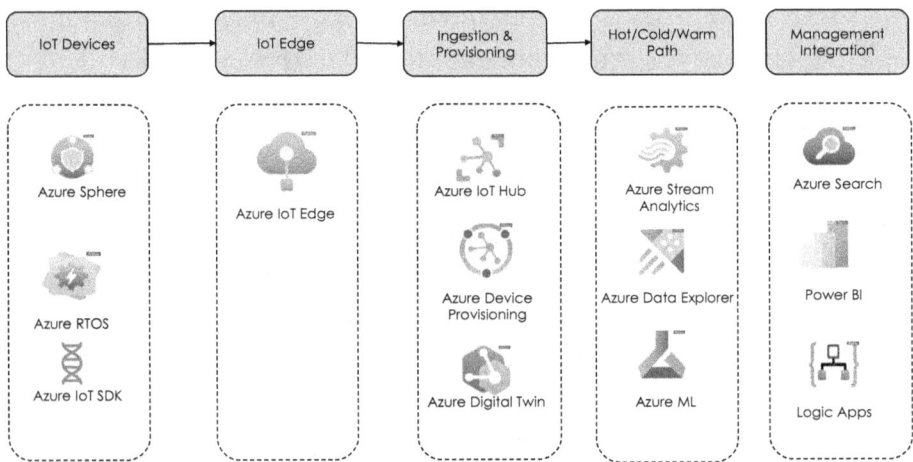

Figure 1-3. Microsoft Azure Reference Architecture for IoT

CHAPTER 1   GET STARTED WITH IOT NETWORK AND SECURITY

Figure 1-3 illustrates the architecture for IoT applications utilizing Azure PaaS components. This architecture involves the interaction between things (devices generating data), insights (formed from data analysis), and actions (taken based on insights). For instance, a motor sends temperature data, which is then analyzed to determine its performance, ultimately affecting maintenance schedules.

Devices: Azure IoT supports many devices, from microcontrollers running Azure RTOS and Azure Sphere to developer boards like MX Chip and Raspberry Pi. Devices may perform local processing through Azure IoT Edge or connect directly to Azure for data exchange.

Insights: Once devices are connected to the cloud, data processing can yield insights about their environment. Data processing can occur in three paths: hot path (near-real-time analysis), warm path (detailed processing with some delay), and cold path (batch processing). Services like Azure Stream Analytics, Azure Data Explorer, and Azure Machine Learning facilitate data processing.

Actions: Insights gathered from data can be used to manage and control environments through various actions such as storing messages, raising alarms, sending notifications, and integrating with business applications. Microsoft services like Power BI, Azure Maps, and Azure Logic Apps enable these actions to be executed seamlessly.

Considerations: The design of IoT solutions should align with the pillars of the Azure Well-Architected Framework, focusing on manageability, reliability, security, cost optimization, and performance efficiency. Microsoft provides tools and services such as Azure Digital Twins for managing connected environments, ensuring reliability through high availability and disaster recovery strategies, implementing security measures like the zero-trust model and secure communication protocols, optimizing costs, and ensuring performance efficiency across services like IoT Hub, Azure Functions, and Stream Analytics.

Manageability: Azure Digital Twins enable the control and monitoring of connected environments by providing virtual models driven by data from business systems and IoT devices. These digital twins empower businesses to gain insights and take action in various scenarios, such as predictive maintenance in manufacturing, supply chain visibility, real-time inventory tracking with smart shelves, and intelligent management of connected homes and buildings.

Reliability: Ensuring reliability is crucial for meeting customer commitments in IoT solutions. High availability (HA) and disaster recovery (DR) strategies are vital in maintaining uptime goals. Azure offers various HA/DR alternatives, each with trade-offs between the required level of resiliency, implementation complexity, and cost. Careful evaluation of these factors is necessary to select the most suitable solution.

Security: Security is paramount in IoT solutions to protect against deliberate attacks and data abuse. The zero-trust security model assumes breaches will occur and requires strong authentication, least privileged access, monitoring of device health, timely updates, and secure communication. Devices must support trustworthy communication with encryption, digital signatures, and updateable keys. Physical tamper-proofing measures are also essential to ensure the integrity and trustworthiness of the overall system.

Summary

This chapter introduces readers to the fundamental concepts of IoT network and security. The chapter begins with an overview of IoT, including its definition and terminologies, setting the stage for understanding the intricate network and security considerations in IoT systems. Readers learn about the building blocks of IoT, including sensors, actuators, connectivity, and data processing units, which form the backbone of IoT infrastructure.

CHAPTER 1   GET STARTED WITH IOT NETWORK AND SECURITY

The chapter explores various use cases of IoT and Industrial IoT (IIoT), showcasing how these technologies revolutionize manufacturing, healthcare, transportation, and agriculture industries. Additionally, it discusses the importance of IoT, its challenges, such as interoperability, scalability, and security, and the future opportunities it presents regarding innovation and efficiency.

Furthermore, the chapter delves into IoT architecture, explaining the layered approach to designing IoT systems and highlighting the role of edge computing, cloud services, and security measures. Readers are introduced to Microsoft Azure IoT Reference Architecture, which provides a comprehensive framework for building scalable, secure, and efficient IoT solutions using Azure services.

By the end of the chapter, you will have gained a solid understanding of the key concepts, challenges, and opportunities in IoT networks and security, setting the stage for deeper exploration into specific technologies and implementation strategies in subsequent chapters. In the next chapter, you will read about IoT network protocols.

CHAPTER 2

Design and Deploy Azure Edge Services

In the realm of the Internet of Things (IoT), networks play a critical role in facilitating communication between devices, enabling data exchange, and supporting various applications. This overview provides a comprehensive look at crucial aspects of IoT networks, including protocols, models, and layers, as well as the design and deployment of Azure Edge Services for IoT applications.

IoT Network Protocols Overview: This section covers the essential communication protocols within IoT ecosystems. It includes an overview of protocols like MQTT, CoAP, AMQP, and DDS, highlighting their features, use cases, and considerations for implementation. Understanding these protocols is crucial for ensuring interoperability, reliability, and security in IoT deployments.

Design Azure Edge Services for IoT: Azure Edge Services provide powerful capabilities for processing data and running services closer to IoT devices, at the network's edge. This section introduces Azure IoT Edge, discussing its architecture, components, and capabilities for deploying and managing IoT applications on edge devices. Topics include module deployment, security, and integration with Azure services.

Deploy Azure Edge Services for IoT: This section guides readers through the practical aspects of deploying Azure Edge Services for IoT applications. It covers device provisioning, managing edge modules,

CHAPTER 2   DESIGN AND DEPLOY AZURE EDGE SERVICES

monitoring and troubleshooting, and ensuring security and scalability. Readers will learn how to effectively deploy and manage IoT applications at the edge using Azure services.

Overall, this overview provides a comprehensive understanding of IoT network protocols, models, and layers, as well as the capabilities of Azure Edge Services for designing and deploying IoT solutions. It is a foundational resource for architects, developers, and engineers involved in building IoT applications and infrastructures. By the end of this chapter, you should be able to understand the following:

- IoT network protocols
- IoT network architecture
- Design Azure Edge services for IoT
- Deploy Azure Edge services for IoT

IoT Network Protocol

Let us get started fundamental of Network, A computer network is a collection of interconnected devices that can communicate with each other to share resources, data, and services. These devices can include computers, servers, routers, switches, and other hardware components. The primary purpose of a computer network is to enable efficient communication and collaboration among users and devices.

Computer networks, operating on intricate protocols and standards, define how data is transmitted, received, and processed across the network. The most prevalent protocol suite, the TCP/IP (Transmission Control Protocol/Internet Protocol) suite, governs communication on the Internet and many other networks, showcasing the depth and complexity of this field.

CHAPTER 2 DESIGN AND DEPLOY AZURE EDGE SERVICES

At a basic level, computer networks work by transmitting data in the form of packets. When a device wants to send data to another device on the network, it breaks the data into smaller packets and attaches the destination address to each packet. These packets are then sent over the network and routed to their destination through various network devices, such as routers and switches.

Routers forward packets between different networks, while switches connect devices within the same network. Each device on the network has a unique identifier called an IP address, which is used to route packets to the correct destination.

Once the packets reach their destination, the receiving device reassembles them into the original data. This process allows data to be transmitted efficiently over the network, even when the network consists of multiple interconnected devices.

Computer networks, the backbone of modern communication, enable seamless communication and data exchange between devices. They empower users to access resources and services from anywhere in the world, underscoring their crucial role in virtually all aspects of our digital lives.

A real-world example of a computer network is a company's office network. Let's say you're working in an office with multiple departments, each equipped with computers connected to the office network.

Imagine you're sending a letter to a colleague in another department. Your computer, like a diligent postman, breaks down your message into smaller, more manageable parts called packets. Each packet is then stamped with the destination address (your colleague's email address) and sent off over the office network.

As these packets journey across the network, they encounter switches and routers, the traffic controllers of the digital world. Just like a GPS, the router ensures the packets reach the correct department's network segment, while the switches within the department act like mailroom staff, ensuring the packets are delivered to the correct computer.

Once the packets reach your colleague's computer, they are reassembled into the original email message, which your colleague can read.

In this example, the office network serves as a communication medium, allowing you to send messages and share information with your colleagues across different departments. The network infrastructure, including switches, routers, and computers, ensures data is transmitted efficiently and securely between devices.

Networks can be as simple as a few connected devices in a home or office or as complex as the Internet connecting millions worldwide. Here's how a network typically operates:

- Connection Establishment: Devices connect to the network through physical or wireless connections. In wired networks, devices are connected via Ethernet cables to routers, switches, or hubs. In wireless networks, devices connect via Wi-Fi, Bluetooth, or other wireless technologies. Once connected, devices are assigned unique identifiers, such as IP addresses, to enable communication.

- Data Transmission: When a device wants to send data to another device on the network, it breaks the data into packets. Each packet contains a portion of the data and header information specifying the source and destination addresses. These packets are transmitted over the network, traveling through routers, switches, and other network devices to reach their destination.

- Routing and Forwarding: As packets travel through the network, routers and switches examine the header information to determine the best path for forwarding. Routers make decisions based on routing tables that map destination addresses to network paths, while switches forward packets based on MAC (Media Access Control) addresses. This process ensures that packets reach their destination efficiently and reliably.

- Packet Delivery: Once all packets reach their destination, the receiving device reassembles them into the original data. The device then processes the data according to the application or service it is providing. This could involve displaying a webpage, playing a video, processing a file, or any other action based on the transmitted data.

- Error Detection and Correction: Mechanisms are in place throughout the data transmission process to detect and correct errors. Error detection techniques such as checksums or CRC (Cyclic Redundancy Check) ensure the integrity of transmitted data. If errors are detected, protocols such as TCP (Transmission Control Protocol) provide mechanisms for retransmitting lost or corrupted packets.

- Security: Network security is crucial to protecting data from unauthorized access, interception, or modification. Encryption, firewalls, authentication mechanisms, and other security measures safeguard sensitive information and ensure the privacy and integrity of communication.

- Scalability and Performance: Networks must be designed to handle increasing traffic and accommodate growing numbers of devices. Scalability is achieved through load balancing, quality of service (QoS) management, and network optimization techniques to ensure optimal performance and reliability.

Networks facilitate communication and data exchange between devices, enabling individuals, businesses, and organizations to access information, collaborate, and interact in a digital world. Whether a small local network or the vast global Internet, networks play a crucial role in modern society.

The primary goal of a network is to facilitate the connection of devices for data transmission. To achieve this goal, various interconnected networks come together to form what we commonly known as the Internet.

The Internet of Things (IoT) utilizes general data networks' exact network mechanisms and processes. To understand these processes, it's essential to clarify some fundamental concepts.

Digital computers and communication systems utilize electronic, radio, and optical signals to represent data as bits. A bit, short for binary digit, can have only two values of "1" or "0." Due to their ability to be processed at extremely high speeds, bits can accurately represent any information.

- **Electronic Signals**: In wired communication systems like Ethernet networks, data is transmitted as electrical signals over copper wires. These signals can have two states: high voltage (often represented as "1") and low voltage (represented as "0"). The sequence of these voltage states represents binary digits, or bits. For example, in a digital communication system, a high voltage may represent a binary "1," while a low voltage represents a binary "0."

- **Optical Signals**: Optical communication systems, like fiber optic networks, use light signals to transmit data. In fiber optic communication, data is encoded as light pulses that travel through optical fibers. These pulses can represent binary "1"s and "0"s based on the presence or absence of light. Light pulses are generated by light sources such as lasers or light-emitting diodes (LEDs) and detected by photodetectors at the receiving end.

- **Radio Signals**: Wireless communication systems, such as Wi-Fi or cellular networks, utilize radio frequency signals to transmit data. These signals are modulated to encode digital information, with different modulation schemes representing bits. For example, in amplitude modulation (AM), the amplitude of the radio signal is varied to represent binary data. In frequency modulation (FM), the signal frequency is modified to encode binary information.

In all these communication systems, translating data into bits involves encoding the information into a format that can be transmitted over the given medium. Once transmitted, these bits are decoded at the receiving end to reconstruct the original data. This encoding and decoding process ensures that data can be accurately transmitted and received in digital communication systems.

To represent the phrase "hello world" in binary, each character must be converted into its corresponding ASCII (American Standard Code for Information Interchange) value and then into binary.

CHAPTER 2   DESIGN AND DEPLOY AZURE EDGE SERVICES

Here's how it's done:

Convert each character to ASCII:

- 'h' -> 104
- 'e' -> 101
- 'l' -> 108
- 'l' -> 108
- 'o' -> 111
- ' ' (space) -> 32
- 'w' -> 119
- 'o' -> 111
- 'r' -> 114
- 'l' -> 108
- 'd' -> 100

Convert each ASCII value to binary:

- 104 -> 01101000
- 101 -> 01100101
- 108 -> 01101100
- 108 -> 01101100
- 111 -> 01101111
- 32 -> 00100000
- 119 -> 01110111
- 111 -> 01101111
- 114 -> 01110010

CHAPTER 2　DESIGN AND DEPLOY AZURE EDGE SERVICES

- 108 -> 01101100
- 100 -> 01100100

Concatenating the binary representations of each character, we get

01101000 01100101 01101100 01101100 01101111
00100000 01110111 01101111 01110010 01101100
01100100

So, the phrase "hello world" in binary is

01101000 01100101 01101100 01101100 01101111
00100000 01110111 01101111 01110010 01101100
01100100

Each sequence of eight bits represents one character in the ASCII encoding.

Typically, eight bits are grouped to form a character known as a byte. Bytes are commonly used when discussing the capacity of computer memory and storage and the size of data files. For example,

- A 55 MB (megabyte) document file
- A 16 GB (gigabyte) memory
- A 2 TB (terabyte) hard disk drive

Data transmitted and received across a network is represented as streams of bits. A data communications link's capacity, or data rate, is measured in bits per second (bps or b/s). For instance, the bandwidth of some common connection types includes

- 56 kb/s (kilobits per second) dial-up link
- 10 Mb/s (megabits per second) ADSL link
- 1 Gb/s (gigabits per second) Gigabit Ethernet link

For human readability, groups of four and eight bits are often converted to their decimal integer equivalents. For example,

- 1010 in binary equals 10 in decimal
- 1000 1010 in binary equals 138 in decimal

The data stream is divided into datagrams in data communications and networks, each comprising many bits. These datagrams contain a header with essential information such as the destination and source addresses. A datagram is a data packet encapsulating data and labeling for routing purposes. As datagrams are transmitted, devices along the communication path inspect the header information to make switching and forwarding decisions accordingly.

Importance of IoT Developers Knowing About IoT Network Protocols and IoT Network Architecture

The Internet of Things (IoT) represents a transformative wave in technology, interconnecting many devices to streamline processes and enhance the quality of life. Understanding IoT network protocols and architecture is paramount for IoT developers in creating efficient, secure, and scalable solutions. These foundational elements dictate how devices communicate, share data, and operate within various environments, making them essential knowledge areas for any developer working in the IoT domain.

IoT network protocols are the rules and conventions for data exchange between IoT devices. Knowledge of these protocols, such as MQTT, CoAP, and Zigbee, enables developers to design systems where devices can communicate seamlessly. Efficient communication is critical in IoT environments with limited power and processing capabilities. Understanding which protocol best suits specific use cases optimizes data transmission, minimizing latency and conserving resources. Furthermore, interoperability is a significant challenge in IoT, given the diversity of devices and manufacturers. Developers proficient in various protocols can implement solutions that allow different devices to work together harmoniously, thereby expanding the scope and functionality of IoT systems.

Security is a primary concern in IoT, where numerous devices are interconnected, often transmitting sensitive data. IoT network protocols incorporate various security features, such as encryption and authentication mechanisms, to protect data as it moves across the network. Developers must be well-versed in these protocols to implement robust security measures, ensuring data integrity and preventing unauthorized access. By understanding the strengths and weaknesses of different protocols, developers can make informed decisions about which protocols to use and how to configure them to safeguard against potential threats, thereby enhancing the overall security posture of IoT deployments.

The architecture of IoT networks dictates how devices are organized and how data flows within the system. A deep understanding of IoT network architecture allows developers to design scalable and reliable systems. For instance, knowledge of centralized, decentralized, and hybrid architectures enables developers to choose the right approach based on the IoT application's scale, complexity, and specific requirements. Scalability ensures the system can grow by adding new devices without compromising performance. In contrast, reliability ensures consistent operation, even in network disruptions or device failures. Well-architected IoT networks are crucial for maintaining system integrity and delivering a seamless user experience.

IoT is rapidly evolving, with new technologies and standards emerging regularly. Developers who are knowledgeable about IoT network protocols and architecture are better equipped to integrate new advancements into existing systems. This capability fosters innovation and future-proof solutions, ensuring they remain relevant and functional as technology evolves. By staying informed about the latest developments and trends,

CHAPTER 2 DESIGN AND DEPLOY AZURE EDGE SERVICES

developers can leverage new protocols and architectural paradigms to enhance their solutions, providing more excellent value to users and staying ahead in a competitive market.

In summary, mastery of IoT network protocols and network architecture is critical for IoT developers. It underpins the efficient, secure, and scalable operation of IoT systems, facilitates interoperability among diverse devices, and enables the integration of cutting-edge innovations. This knowledge will remain a cornerstone of successful IoT development as the IoT landscape expands, creating robust and future-ready IoT solutions.

IoT Network Protocols

In the rapidly expanding Internet of Things (IoT) landscape, devices need to communicate efficiently and securely. This communication is facilitated by a variety of protocols designed to handle the unique challenges of IoT environments, such as low power consumption, limited bandwidth, and intermittent connectivity. In this section, let's explore about the IOT Protocols, including their advantages, reasons for existing, and critical characteristics.

Why IoT Network Protocols

Network protocols enable seamless communication between interconnected devices in the context of the Internet of Things (IoT). These protocols provide the rules and standards that govern how data is transmitted, received, and processed within IoT networks. With effective protocols, devices could understand each other's messages, leading to communication breakdowns and inefficiencies. Therefore, IoT network protocols are the foundation for building robust and reliable IoT systems.

One of the primary reasons for IoT network protocols is the diversity of devices and technologies within IoT ecosystems. IoT networks often consist of various manufacturers' devices, each with communication requirements and capabilities. Protocols such as MQTT, CoAP, and AMQP provide a common language that allows these heterogeneous devices to communicate effectively, regardless of their underlying hardware or software differences. This interoperability is essential for ensuring IoT solutions can scale, adapt, and integrate seamlessly with existing infrastructure.

Another key reason for the importance of IoT network protocols is the need for efficient data transmission and management. IoT devices generate vast amounts of data, often in real-time, which must be transmitted securely and reliably to other devices or cloud services for processing and analysis. With their lightweight and efficient messaging model, protocols like MQTT are designed to minimize bandwidth usage and latency, making them ideal for IoT applications. Additionally, protocols such as DDS are optimized for real-time communication, ensuring the timely delivery of critical data in applications like industrial automation and smart cities. IoT network protocols are vital in optimizing data transmission, improving system performance, and enabling innovative IoT applications across various industries.

Advantages of IoT Network Protocols

The Internet of Things (IoT) has transformed various industries, revolutionizing how we live, work, and interact with our environment. Here are some critical advantages of IoT:

Efficiency and Automation: IoT enables automation and optimization of processes, leading to increased efficiency and productivity. By connecting devices and systems, IoT solutions can automate routine tasks, monitor operations in real time, and make data-driven decisions. For example, in industrial settings, IoT sensors can monitor equipment performance, detect anomalies, and trigger maintenance activities, reducing downtime and optimizing production.

Cost Savings: IoT can result in significant cost savings by streamlining operations, reducing energy consumption, and minimizing waste. Organizations can lower operational costs and increase profitability by optimizing resource utilization and improving asset management. For instance, in intelligent buildings, IoT-enabled systems can adjust lighting, heating, and cooling based on occupancy and environmental conditions, leading to lower energy bills and maintenance costs.

Improved Decision-Making: IoT generates vast amounts of data that can be analyzed to gain valuable insights and inform decision-making. By collecting and analyzing data from sensors, devices, and systems, organizations can identify trends, predict outcomes, and make informed decisions in real time. This data-driven approach allows businesses to optimize processes, improve customer experiences, and stay ahead of competitors.

Enhanced Customer Experience: IoT enables personalized and responsive customer experiences by collecting data on user behavior, preferences, and interactions. Smart devices and applications can tailor services and recommendations to individual users, leading to higher satisfaction and loyalty. For example, in retail, IoT sensors can track customer movements, analyze shopping patterns, and deliver targeted promotions or offers in real time.

Safety and Security: IoT can enhance safety and security by monitoring and controlling various aspects of the physical environment. For example, IoT-enabled surveillance systems in smart cities can detect and respond to incidents such as accidents, crime, or natural disasters. In healthcare, wearable devices and remote monitoring solutions can track patients' vital signs and alert caregivers to potential health risks.

Innovation and New Business Models: IoT fuels innovation and opens new business opportunities to create value and disrupt traditional markets. Organizations can develop innovative solutions and business models that address evolving customer needs and market trends by connecting devices, products, and services. For example, IoT-enabled subscription services, predictive maintenance, and pay-per-use models are transforming the transportation, healthcare, and agriculture industries.

Environmental Sustainability: IoT can contribute to environmental sustainability by optimizing resource usage, reducing waste, and minimizing carbon emissions. Intelligent energy management systems, for example, can optimize energy consumption, integrate renewable energy sources, and reduce greenhouse gas emissions. Similarly, IoT-enabled agriculture solutions can maximize water usage, improve crop yields, and reduce the environmental impact of farming practices.

The advantages of IoT are far-reaching, encompassing efficiency gains, cost savings, improved decision-making, enhanced customer experiences, safety and security enhancements, innovation, and environmental sustainability. As IoT evolves and matures, its potential to transform industries and improve quality of life will only grow.

Critical Characteristics of IoT Network Protocols

IoT network protocols are essential components in the infrastructure of Internet of Things (IoT) systems, facilitating communication between devices and enabling data exchange. Understanding the key characteristics of these protocols is crucial for designing efficient and reliable IoT solutions. Here are some key factors:

- Interoperability: One of the most critical characteristics of IoT network protocols is interoperability. Devices in IoT ecosystems often come from different manufacturers and may run on other platforms or operating systems. Protocols like MQTT, CoAP, and HTTP are designed to ensure that devices can communicate seamlessly, regardless of their underlying hardware or software differences.

- Efficiency: Efficiency is paramount in IoT networks, especially considering the constraints of many IoT devices such as limited processing power, memory, and energy. IoT protocols are designed to be lightweight and efficient, minimizing bandwidth usage, latency, and power consumption. For example, MQTT is known for its low overhead and efficient message delivery, making it suitable for IoT applications with resource-constrained devices.

- Scalability: IoT networks often need to scale to accommodate many devices, from sensors and actuators to gateways and edge servers. Protocols like MQTT, CoAP, and DDS are designed to scale gracefully, supporting thousands or even millions of devices without sacrificing performance or reliability. Scalability is essential for IoT applications deployed in smart cities, industrial automation, and large-scale sensor networks.

- Reliability: Reliability is another crucial characteristic of IoT network protocols, especially in critical data integrity and delivery assurance applications. Protocols like MQTT, AMQP, and DDS provide mechanisms for reliable message delivery, ensuring that messages are delivered to their intended recipients without loss or duplication. This reliability is essential for mission-critical IoT deployments in healthcare, transportation, and manufacturing industries.

- Security: Security is a top priority in IoT networks, where sensitive data is often transmitted and processed. IoT protocols support various security mechanisms, including encryption, authentication, and access control, to protect data confidentiality, integrity, and availability. For example, MQTT supports TLS encryption and username/password authentication, while CoAP includes built-in datagram Transport Layer Security (DTLS) support. Security is essential for preventing unauthorized access, data breaches, and cyberattacks in IoT environments.

- Flexibility and Adaptability: IoT network protocols should be flexible and adaptable to accommodate diverse use cases and evolving requirements. Protocols like MQTT and CoAP support multiple communication patterns, such as publish-subscribe and request-response, allowing developers to choose the most suitable approach for their applications. Additionally, these protocols can be extended or customized to meet specific needs, ensuring compatibility with existing infrastructure and future scalability.

IoT network protocols possess vital characteristics such as interoperability, efficiency, scalability, reliability, security, flexibility, and adaptability. By understanding these characteristics and selecting the appropriate protocols for their IoT deployments, developers can build robust, efficient, and secure IoT systems that meet the demands of diverse applications and industries. Table 2-1 lists various IoT network protocols.

Table 2-1. List of various IoT network protocols

Acronym	Full Form	Description
CoAP	Constrained Application Protocol	CoAP is a lightweight protocol designed for constrained devices and low-power networks, such as those found in IoT applications. It enables communication between devices with limited resources, offering efficient data transfer and support for RESTful interactions over UDP.
DTLS	Data Transport Layer Security	DTLS is a security protocol that provides communication privacy and data integrity for applications that use UDP. It is commonly used in IoT devices to establish secure connections, ensuring that data exchanged between devices remains confidential and tamper-proof.
GSM	Global System for Mobile communications	GSM is a standard developed by the European Telecommunications Standards Institute (ETSI) for mobile communication networks. It is widely used for cellular communication and supports voice and data services, making it a foundational technology for mobile phones and IoT devices with cellular connectivity.
HTTP	Hyper Text Transfer Protocol	HTTP is the foundation of data communication for the World Wide Web. It defines how messages are formatted and transmitted between web servers and clients, enabling the retrieval of resources such as HTML documents, images, and videos. HTTP has become the primary protocol for communication in IoT applications as well.

(continued)

Table 2-1. (*continued*)

Acronym	Full Form	Description
IEEE	Institute of Electronic and Electrical Engineers	IEEE is a global professional association dedicated to advancing technology in various fields, including electrical engineering, computer science, and electronics. It establishes standards for networking protocols, hardware, and software, ensuring interoperability and compatibility across devices and networks.
IETF	Internet Engineering Task Force	IETF is an open international community of network designers, operators, vendors, and researchers concerned with the evolution of the Internet architecture and the smooth operation of the Internet. It develops and promotes voluntary Internet standards, including protocols such as HTTP, TCP/IP, and SMTP.
IP	Internet Protocol (version 4 and version 6)	IP is a core protocol that governs the routing and addressing of data packets in computer networks. IPv4 is the most widely used version, but IPv6 is increasingly being adopted to address the growing number of connected devices and the exhaustion of IPv4 addresses.
LLN	Low Power and Lossy Network	LLN refers to networks composed of low-power devices with constrained resources and operating in environments with high packet loss and variable latency. These networks are common in IoT deployments, such as smart grids, industrial automation, and environmental monitoring systems.

(*continued*)

Table 2-1. (*continued*)

Acronym	Full Form	Description
LPWAN	Low-Power Wide Area Network	LPWAN is a type of wireless network designed to support long-range communication with low-power consumption. It enables connectivity for IoT devices over large geographic areas, making it suitable for applications such as smart cities, agriculture, and asset tracking.
LTE	Long-Term Evolution protocol	LTE is a standard for wireless broadband communication, commonly known as 4G LTE. It offers high-speed data transmission, low latency, and improved spectral efficiency, making it well-suited for high-bandwidth applications like video streaming and IoT deployments requiring reliable cellular connectivity.
MQTT	Message Queuing Telemetry Transport	MQTT is a lightweight messaging protocol designed for efficient communication between devices in unreliable or low-bandwidth networks. It follows a publish-subscribe messaging model, allowing devices to subscribe to topics and receive messages asynchronously, making it popular in IoT applications.
QoS	Quality of Service	QoS refers to the ability of a network to deliver data with predictable performance, such as low latency, high bandwidth, and minimal packet loss. It is essential for ensuring the reliability and efficiency of communication in real-time applications and services, including voice over IP (VoIP) and video streaming.

(*continued*)

Table 2-1. (*continued*)

Acronym	Full Form	Description
REST	Representational State Transfer	REST is an architectural style for designing networked applications based on simple and scalable principles. It relies on stateless communication and standard HTTP methods (GET, POST, PUT, DELETE) to access and manipulate resources, making it widely used for web services and APIs, including those in IoT ecosystems.
RPL	Routing over Low power and Lossy networks	RPL is an IPv6-based routing protocol specifically designed for LLNs. It efficiently routes data packets in networks with constrained resources, variable connectivity, and high packet loss. RPL optimizes energy consumption and provides reliable communication for IoT devices in challenging environments.
SSL	Secure Sockets Layer	SSL is a cryptographic protocol that ensures secure communication over a computer network. It establishes an encrypted link between a web server and a browser, enabling the secure transmission of sensitive data such as passwords, credit card information, and personal details.

(*continued*)

Table 2-1. (*continued*)

Acronym	Full Form	Description
TCP	Transmission Control Protocol	TCP is a connection-oriented protocol responsible for reliable data transmission between devices over a network. It ensures that data packets are delivered in order and without errors, providing features such as flow control, congestion avoidance, and error detection and correction. TCP is widely used in applications like web browsing, email, and file transfer.
TLS	Transport Layer Security	TLS is an updated version of SSL and serves the same purpose: to secure communication over a computer network. It provides encryption, authentication, and data integrity, protecting sensitive information from eavesdropping, tampering, and unauthorized access. TLS is commonly used in web browsers, email clients, and IoT devices.
UDP	User Datagram Protocol	UDP is a connectionless protocol that provides unreliable data transmission between devices over a network. Unlike TCP, UDP does not establish a connection before sending data and does not guarantee delivery or order of packets. UDP is commonly used in applications such as streaming media, online gaming, and DNS.
URL	Uniform Resource Locator	URL is a string of characters that uniquely identifies the location of a resource on the Internet, such as a webpage, document, or image. It specifies the protocol (e.g., HTTP, HTTPS), domain name, and path to the resource, allowing users to access it using a web browser or other applications.

(*continued*)

Table 2-1. (*continued*)

Acronym	Full Form	Description
URI	Uniform Resource Identifier	URI is a string of characters used to identify a resource, such as a webpage, file, or service, either by location, name, or both. It encompasses URLs, as well as other identifiers such as URNs (Uniform Resource Names) and URCs (Uniform Resource Characteristics). URIs are fundamental for locating and accessing resources on the Internet.
XMPP	Extensible Messaging and Presence Protocol	XMPP is an open XML-based protocol for real-time communication, messaging, and presence information exchange over the Internet. It supports features such as instant messaging, group chat, and presence updates, making it suitable for applications like instant messaging platforms and IoT device communication.

IoT Network Architecture

The IoT (Internet of Things) network architecture is a multi-layered framework that enables communication and data exchange among interconnected devices and systems. Each layer plays a distinct role in facilitating data flow from sensors and actuators to applications and services, ensuring efficient and secure operation of IoT deployments. Figure 2-1 depicts architecture consists of four layers: application layer, transport layer, network layer, and physical layer.

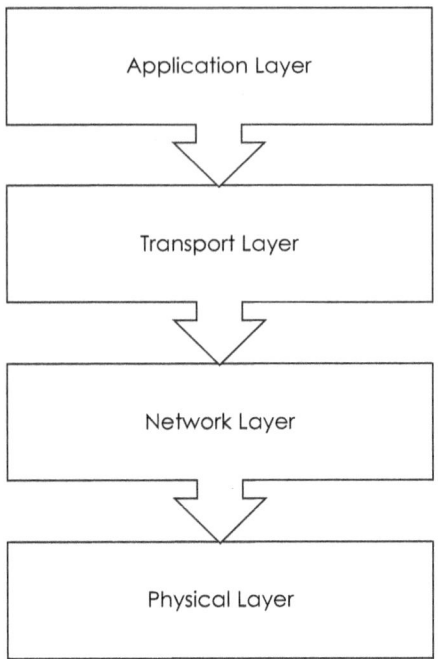

Figure 2-1. *Internet of Things – network architecture layers*

IoT architecture is structured into four distinct layers: application layer, transport layer, network layer, and physical layer. Each layer plays a critical role in ensuring seamless communication, data processing, and overall functionality of IoT systems. This layered approach allows for a modular and scalable design, making developing, managing, and integrating IoT solutions across various domains easier.

Application Layer: The application layer, the topmost layer in the IoT architecture, is a versatile powerhouse. It focuses on the end-user applications and services that utilize IoT data, providing interfaces and protocols that enable users to interact with IoT devices and analyze the collected data. This layer supports a wide array of applications, from smart homes to industrial automation, healthcare monitoring to environmental sensing. Its key functionalities, including data visualization, device management, analytics, and application-specific protocols, ensure the usability and accessibility of IoT services, often through web-based dashboards, mobile apps, or other user interfaces. Your work here directly impacts the user experience and the success of IoT solutions in various domains.

Transport Layer: The transport layer bridges the application layer and the lower layers, ensuring reliable data transmission across the network. It employs various protocols to facilitate secure and efficient communication between IoT devices and the cloud or other devices. Standard transport protocols include MQTT (Message Queuing Telemetry Transport), CoAP (Constrained Application Protocol), and HTTP/HTTPS. This layer handles the packaging, transmission, and error-checking of data packets, ensuring the information reaches its destination accurately and promptly. The transport layer is crucial for maintaining data integrity and enabling real-time communication in IoT systems.

Network Layer: The network layer establishes and maintains communication pathways between IoT devices, gateways, and the cloud. It manages the routing of data packets through various network topologies, ensuring that data can be efficiently transmitted across potentially vast and diverse IoT networks. This layer supports IPv4 and IPv6 protocols and employs various networking technologies such as Wi-Fi, Ethernet, Zigbee, and cellular networks. The network layer also handles tasks such as network addressing, data packet forwarding, and connectivity management, playing a vital role in the scalability and reliability of IoT systems.

Physical Layer: The physical layer, the bedrock of the IoT architecture, encompasses the hardware components and physical transmission media that enable data exchange. This layer, which includes sensors, actuators, transceivers, and the physical communication mediums (e.g., radio frequencies and wired connections) that link IoT devices, is where your work begins. It is responsible for transmitting and receiving raw data signals and converting them into a form that higher layers can process. The physical layer also deals with aspects like signal modulation, data encoding, and transmission power. Its efficiency and robustness are critical for the effective functioning of IoT systems, as it directly impacts the reliability and range of device communication. Your work at this foundational level sets the stage for the entire IoT system, making it a crucial part of the puzzle.

IoT Network – Application Layer

The application layer in the Internet of Things (IoT) architecture is crucial as it interfaces between the end-users and the IoT network. This layer provides the protocols and services enabling various IoT applications to function effectively. It is responsible for interpreting data, facilitating communication between devices, and ensuring the collected data is processed and presented meaningfully. The application layer is where user interaction with the IoT system happens, making it a vital component in realizing the full potential of IoT solutions.

The application layer's pivotal role in managing data from IoT devices cannot be overstated. It not only collects and stores data but also processes it to extract valuable insights. For instance, in a smart home application, sensors gather data on temperature, humidity, and light levels. The application layer then processes this data to automatically adjust heating, cooling, and lighting systems, thereby enhancing comfort and energy efficiency for the residents. This layer's ability to convert raw data into actionable information is what drives intelligent decision-making, making it a crucial component of IoT architecture.

The application layer also significantly facilitates communication and interoperability between IoT devices and systems. In an IoT ecosystem, devices often come from various manufacturers and use different communication protocols. The application layer uses standardized protocols and APIs to ensure these devices can communicate and work together seamlessly. For instance, in a smart city scenario, traffic sensors, public transport systems, and environmental monitoring stations must interoperate to provide integrated services. The application layer acts as the mediator, enabling these diverse systems to collaborate and share data efficiently.

The application layer's role in managing security in IoT networks is of utmost importance. It implements security protocols to safeguard data during transmission and processing. This includes encryption, authentication, and authorization mechanisms that ensure only authorized devices and users can access the IoT network. For example, in a healthcare IoT application, sensitive patient data must be securely transmitted from wearable health monitors to healthcare providers. The application layer ensures that this data is encrypted and that only authorized medical personnel can access it, thereby maintaining patient privacy and data integrity.

The application layer's influence on user interface design is a key aspect that directly affects how end-users interact with IoT systems. A well-designed user interface simplifies the control and monitoring of IoT devices for users. For instance, a mobile app that manages a smart home system must be intuitive and user-friendly, enabling residents to adjust settings and receive alerts with ease. The application layer ensures that the interface is responsive and provides real-time feedback, thereby enhancing user experience and satisfaction.

Scalability is another essential factor managed by the application layer. As IoT deployments grow, the application layer must handle increasing data and more connected devices without compromising performance. This involves optimizing data processing algorithms and ensuring the system can scale horizontally. For example, as more sensors and machines are added to the network in an industrial IoT application, the application layer must efficiently manage the increased data flow and maintain system responsiveness. This scalability is crucial for the sustainable growth of IoT ecosystems.

Lastly, the application layer supports various IoT applications across industries, from smart homes and healthcare to agriculture and manufacturing. Each application has specific requirements and challenges that the application layer addresses. In agriculture, for instance, the application layer might process data from soil moisture sensors and weather stations to optimize irrigation schedules, improving crop yields and resource management. By providing tailored solutions for diverse applications, the application layer enables the practical implementation of IoT technologies across multiple domains, driving innovation and efficiency in everyday life and industry.

Traditional application protocols like HTTP and XMPP are resource-intensive, making them unsuitable for IoT environments with numerous connected devices and limited resources. To address this challenge, the IoT industry has adopted more lightweight protocols. The Constrained Application Protocol (CoAP) and Message Queuing Telemetry Transport (MQTT) are the two most popular protocols designed for efficient communication in IoT applications.

Constrained Application Protocol (CoAP)

Constrained Application Protocol (CoAP) is a specialized web transfer protocol optimized for the unique demands of the Internet of Things (IoT). CoAP operates on a client-server model, where devices, typically sensors or actuators, communicate using a request-response mechanism over the User Datagram Protocol (UDP). This approach is chosen for its low overhead, crucial for constrained devices with limited resources.

CoAP's adherence to a RESTful architecture, similar to HTTP, is a key feature that makes it a breeze to integrate with existing web technologies. Just like HTTP, a URI identifies each resource on a server, and clients interact with these resources using standard methods such as GET, POST,

PUT, and DELETE. This RESTful design, combined with its lightweight nature, ensures that CoAP can function effectively on devices with minimal processing power and memory, a crucial aspect for IoT applications.

Messages in CoAP are exchanged in a compact binary format to minimize transmission size, further conserving bandwidth and energy. CoAP messages can be of four types: Confirmable (CON), which requires an acknowledgment to ensure reliable delivery; Non-Confirmable (NON), which does not require an acknowledgment and is used for non-critical transmissions; Acknowledgment (ACK), sent in response to a Confirmable message; and Reset (RST), used to indicate that a message was received but could not be processed. This structure supports reliable and efficient communication, catering to the needs of different IoT applications.

CoAP takes security seriously, employing Datagram Transport Layer Security (DTLS) to provide encryption, data integrity, and authentication. This robust security measure ensures that the data exchanged between devices is protected from eavesdropping, tampering, and forgery, common threats in IoT networks. When CoAP is used over DTLS, it is often referred to as CoAPS, indicating a secure implementation, a testament to its comprehensive functionality.

In summary, CoAP provides a lightweight, efficient, and secure communication protocol tailored for the IoT. It uses a RESTful approach over UDP, with a binary message format and built-in reliability and security features. It is well-suited for the constrained environments typical of IoT applications.

Key Features of CoAP

Lightweight and Efficient: CoAP is designed to be simple and compact, making it ideal for devices with limited memory and computational power. The protocol uses a small binary header and a simple message format to minimize communication overhead.

- UDP-Based Transport: CoAP primarily uses the User Datagram Protocol (UDP) for transport, which is simpler and more efficient than the Transmission Control Protocol (TCP) used by traditional web protocols like HTTP. This choice helps reduce latency and improves performance in low power and lossy networks.

- Request/Response Model: CoAP follows a client-server model similar to HTTP, where clients send requests to servers, and servers respond with the requested information. This model includes methods like GET, POST, PUT, and DELETE, which are analogous to HTTP methods and facilitate easy mapping of RESTful web services to IoT environments.

- Message Types and Reliability: CoAP defines four types of messages: Confirmable (CON), Non-Confirmable (NON), Acknowledgment (ACK), and Reset (RST). Confirmable messages require an acknowledgment to ensure reliable delivery, while non-confirmable messages do not, allowing for flexibility based on the application's reliability needs.

- Resource Discovery and URI-Based Addressing: CoAP supports resource discovery, allowing clients to discover resources on a server using well-defined mechanisms. Resources are identified and accessed using URI (Uniform Resource Identifier) paths, similar to web URLs, enabling intuitive and hierarchical organization of resources.

- Built-in Support for Multicast: CoAP includes native support for IP multicast, which allows a single message to be sent to multiple devices simultaneously. This feature is handy for scenarios like firmware updates or broadcasting sensor readings to various nodes.

- Asynchronous Communication: CoAP supports asynchronous communication, allowing devices to operate efficiently by sending data only when necessary. This feature is critical for battery-powered devices that need to conserve energy.

Advantages of CoAP

CoAP (Constrained Application Protocol) offers several advantages that make it well-suited for the Internet of Things (IoT). Table 2-2 provides a high-level overview of CoAP.

Table 2-2. List of various advantages of CoAP

Advantage	Description
Lightweight and efficient	CoAP is designed for devices with limited resources, featuring a compact binary message format to minimize overhead, making it ideal for constrained environments.
Low power consumption	Operating over UDP with support for asynchronous messaging, CoAP reduces the need for continuous connections, conserving power – essential for battery-operated devices.
RESTful architecture	CoAP uses a RESTful design similar to HTTP, allowing developers to utilize familiar concepts like resources and standard methods (GET, POST, PUT, DELETE).

(continued)

Table 2-2. (*continued*)

Advantage	Description
Interoperability	The RESTful approach and simple message structure facilitate interoperability between different devices and systems, ensuring seamless integration in diverse IoT ecosystems.
Reliability	CoAP supports four message types (Confirmable, Non-Confirmable, Acknowledgment, Reset), providing mechanisms for both reliable and non-reliable communication.
Scalability	With low overhead and efficient message handling, CoAP can effectively support a large number of devices without overwhelming the network infrastructure.
Security	CoAP uses datagram transport layer security (DTLS) to ensure data confidentiality, integrity, and authentication, protecting communications from threats like eavesdropping and tampering.
Multicast support	CoAP's support for IP multicast allows a single message to be delivered to multiple devices simultaneously, improving efficiency for group updates or commands.
Flexibility	Adaptable to various application requirements, CoAP can handle simple sensor data collection to more complex device management tasks, making it suitable for a wide range of IoT applications.
Simplicity	Prioritizing simplicity in its design, CoAP is easier to implement on devices with limited resources, simplifying deployment and maintenance of IoT solutions.

CoAP Architecture and Components

The Constrained Application Protocol (CoAP) is a specialized web transfer protocol used in constrained nodes and networks in the Internet of Things (IoT). CoAP is tailored to meet the needs of IoT applications that operate in environments with limited resources, such as low power, limited processing capabilities, and low bandwidth. Developed by the Internet Engineering Task Force (IETF), CoAP is documented in RFC 7252.

CoAP is a lightweight and efficient communication protocol that facilitates seamless data exchange in constrained environments. Its technical underpinnings encompass a range of features that make it an ideal choice for Internet of Things (IoT) applications. Figure 2-2 depicts CoAP architecture.

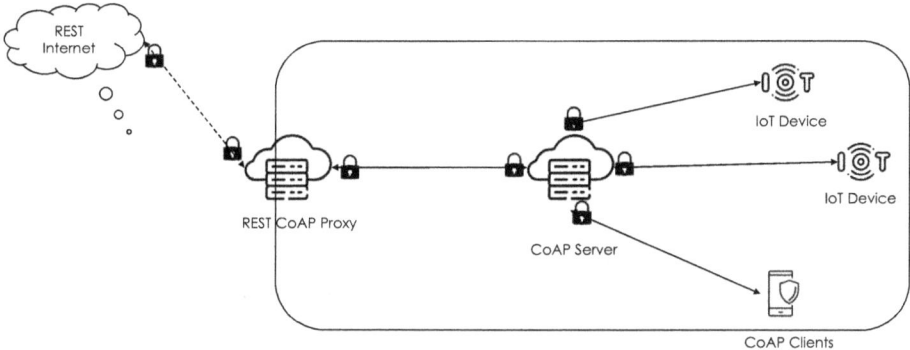

Figure 2-2. CoAP – architecture

Let's delve into the technical intricacies of how CoAP operates:

Request-Response Model:

Like its counterpart, HTTP, CoAP operates on a request-response communication model. In this model, a client sends a CoAP request to a server, and the server responds with the requested data or action. CoAP's request methods mirror those of HTTP, including GET, PUT, POST, and DELETE. This familiar model simplifies resource interaction, making it suitable for IoT device-to-server communication and machine-to-machine interactions.

Use of UDP (User Datagram Protocol):

One of CoAP's distinguishing features is its use of UDP, a lightweight and connectionless transport protocol. This design choice is crucial in constrained environments where resources are scarce. Unlike TCP, which ensures reliable data delivery through a connection-oriented approach, UDP is connectionless and requires less overhead. While CoAP doesn't guarantee reliability by default, it offers three levels of reliability (Confirmable, Non-Confirmable, and Acknowledgment) to cater to various use cases.

- Multicast Support: CoAP incorporates support for multicast communication, enabling a single CoAP message to be sent to multiple recipients simultaneously. This is especially beneficial when devices share common interests and need to receive the same information. Multicast communication reduces network traffic and efficiently disseminates data, a feature that aligns well with resource-constrained environments.

- Observe Mechanism: CoAP's observation mechanism adds a layer of efficiency to resource monitoring. With observation, a client can request to "observe" a resource's state. The server then sends periodic updates to the client whenever the resource changes. This approach eliminates the need for frequent polling, reduces unnecessary communication, and conserves energy and network resources.

- Tokenization and Message ID: CoAP employs tokenization to track stateful interactions, allowing clients and servers to match requests with responses. Additionally, CoAP uses a Message ID to identify and correlate requests and responses, ensuring that the intended communication is correctly processed.

- Proxying and Caching: CoAP supports proxying, allowing intermediary devices to forward requests between clients and servers. It also incorporates caching mechanisms to enhance performance and reduce network traffic. These features are valuable in scenarios where scalability and optimization are essential.

Layers of CoAP:

CoAP operates through a structured layering approach, ensuring efficient communication within constrained environments. These layers collectively enable seamless interaction and data exchange between IoT devices and applications. The layers of CoAP include:

- Application Layer: This layer defines the methods and interactions between clients and servers. It encompasses the request-response model and methods like GET, PUT, POST, and DELETE, handling resource identification, manipulation, and data exchange.

- Message Layer: This layer is responsible for constructing and parsing CoAP messages. It encapsulates information for communication, such as message type, method, token, and options, ensuring data is appropriately packaged for transmission.

- Transport Layer: This layer handles the actual movement of CoAP messages across the network. Primarily using UDP, this layer provides a lightweight, connectionless mechanism suitable for constrained environments, ensuring message delivery through optional reliability mechanisms.

- Observation Layer: Enables a client to "subscribe" to a resource and receive updates whenever the resource changes, enhancing efficiency by eliminating the need for continuous polling.

- Proxying and Caching Layer: This layer supports proxying and caching to optimize communication. The proxying layer allows intermediary devices to forward messages, enhancing scalability. The caching layer stores frequently accessed resources, reducing redundant communication.

Message Formats in CoAP:

CoAP employs structured message formats to facilitate efficient communication between IoT devices and applications. These formats encapsulate the necessary information for transmitting requests, responses, and control messages. There are four primary types of CoAP messages:

- CON (Confirmable) Message: This message is used for reliable communication, ensuring the recipient sends an acknowledgment. The sender retransmits the message until an ACK is received.

- NON (Non-Confirmable) Message: This message is used for faster communication without acknowledgment and is suitable for real-time communication where reliability is less critical.

- ACK (Acknowledgment) Message: Sent in response to CON messages to acknowledge their receipt, indicating successful processing.

- RST (Reset) Message: Used to cancel a pending CON message that hasn't been acknowledged, typically when the receiver cannot process the awaiting message.

The Role of Methods in CoAP:

In CoAP, methods play a pivotal role in defining the actions that can be performed on resources. Methods indicate the type of interaction a client wants to have with a resource on the server. CoAP supports four methods, similar to HTTP:

- GET: Retrieves a resource's current state or value from the server, a safe method that doesn't modify the server.

- PUT: Updates or creates a resource on the server with the provided data, replacing the current state of the resource.

- POST: This method submits data to the server for processing. It is used to create a new resource or trigger an action.

- DELETE: This command requests removing a resource from the server, indicating the intent to remove the specified resource.

By offering these methods, CoAP provides a standardized way for clients to interact with resources, enabling actions such as retrieving data, updating information, triggering actions, and removing resources. These methods align with CoAP's resource-oriented architecture and provide efficient and consistent communication within IoT ecosystems.

Message Queuing Telemetry Transport (MQTT)

Message Queuing Telemetry Transport (MQTT) is not just a lightweight messaging protocol but a highly efficient one, designed specifically for constrained devices and low-bandwidth, high-latency, or unreliable networks. This efficiency, coupled with its publish-subscribe model, simplifies communication by decoupling message producers (publishers) from consumers (subscribers). This model allows for efficient and scalable

CHAPTER 2   DESIGN AND DEPLOY AZURE EDGE SERVICES

data distribution, as devices can publish information to a central broker, distributing the messages to all interested subscribers. The protocol's minimal header size and low network overhead are crucial for IoT applications, where devices often have limited processing power, memory, and battery life.

From a security perspective, MQTT includes several features to ensure secure data transmission and protect against common threats. One of the primary security mechanisms is Transport Layer Security (TLS), which encrypts communication between clients and brokers. This encryption ensures that data remains confidential and is protected from eavesdropping and man-in-the-middle attacks. Additionally, MQTT supports various authentication methods, including username and password authentication and token-based authentication, which verify the identity of clients before allowing them to connect to the broker. MQTT provides a robust framework for secure IoT communications by implementing these security measures.

MQTT also addresses the reliability needs of IoT networks through its Quality of Service (QoS) levels. These levels define the assurance of message delivery between clients and the broker. QoS 0, or "at most once," ensures the message is delivered without acknowledgment, suitable for non-critical data. QoS 1, or "at least once," guarantees that the message is delivered at least once but may be duplicated. QoS 2, or "exactly once," ensures that each message is delivered exactly once, preventing duplicates and ensuring data integrity. These QoS levels provide flexibility in balancing the trade-offs between reliability and network resource usage, making MQTT adaptable to various IoT scenarios.

Furthermore, MQTT's lightweight nature and efficient operation make it highly suitable for real-time monitoring and control applications. Its ability to handle intermittent connectivity is precious for IoT devices deployed in remote or mobile environments, where network stability can be an issue. MQTT brokers can retain messages with the "last will" feature, which ensures that if a client disconnects unexpectedly, a predefined message is sent to alert other clients. This feature enhances the resilience and robustness of IoT systems by providing mechanisms to handle unexpected disconnections and ensuring continuous monitoring and control capabilities. MQTT's efficient communication, robust security features, and adaptability to varying QoS requirements make it a cornerstone protocol for modern IoT networks.

Key Features of MQTT

Message Queuing Telemetry Transport (MQTT) is a protocol designed for efficient, reliable communication in constrained environments, making it particularly well-suited for Internet of Things (IoT) applications. Its key features include the following.

Publish-Subscribe Model

MQTT employs a publish-subscribe messaging model, which decouples the producer of the data (publisher) from the consumer of the data (subscriber). In this model, publishers send messages to a central broker, which then distributes the messages to all interested subscribers. This architecture allows for scalable, flexible, and efficient communication, reducing the complexity of direct device-to-device communication.

Quality of Service (QoS) Levels

MQTT offers three Quality of Service (QoS) levels to ensure reliable message delivery:

- **QoS 0 (At most once)**: Messages are delivered according to the best efforts of the underlying network, with no acknowledgment required. This level is suitable for applications where occasional message loss is acceptable.

- **QoS 1 (At least once)**: Messages are assured to arrive but may be delivered more than once. This level ensures the message reaches its destination, albeit with possible duplicates.
- **QoS 2 (Exactly once)**: This highest level of service ensures that each message is delivered exactly once, with no duplicates. It involves a handshake mechanism to guarantee precise delivery.

Lightweight and Efficient

MQTT is designed to be lightweight, with a minimal packet overhead, which makes it ideal for devices with limited processing power, memory, and battery life. Its simplicity allows it to function efficiently over networks with low bandwidth, high latency, or intermittent connectivity, such as those often found in IoT environments.

Security Features

MQTT incorporates several security features to protect data and ensure secure communication:

- **Transport Layer Security (TLS)**: Provides encryption for data in transit, ensuring confidentiality and protection against eavesdropping and man-in-the-middle attacks.
- **Authentication**: Supports username and password authentication, as well as more advanced methods like token-based authentication, to verify the identity of clients before allowing them to connect to the broker.

- **Access Control**: Brokers can implement access control policies to manage permissions and restrict client access to specific topics.

Retained Messages and Last Will and Testament (LWT)

- **Retained Messages**: MQTT allows publishers to send retained messages, which are stored by the broker and delivered to any future subscribers of the topic. This ensures that new subscribers immediately receive the last known value of a topic.

- **Last Will and Testament (LWT):** Clients can specify a previous will message that the broker sends if the client disconnects unexpectedly. This feature provides a way to detect and respond to sudden client failures, enhancing the robustness and reliability of the system.

Scalability and Flexibility

MQTT's design supports many IoT applications, from simple sensor networks to complex, large-scale systems. Its publish-subscribe model, flexible QoS levels, and efficient message handling allow it to scale effectively and adapt to different requirements and use cases.

Persistent Sessions

MQTT supports persistent sessions, which means that the broker preserves the client's state (such as subscriptions and missed messages) even if the client disconnects. When the client reconnects, it can resume from where it left off, ensuring seamless communication continuity.

Small Code Footprint

MQTT clients and brokers can be implemented with a small code footprint, making deploying on devices with limited resources feasible. This feature is crucial for IoT devices, which often have stringent memory and processing power constraints.

These key features make MQTT a robust, flexible, and efficient protocol that is well-suited for the diverse and demanding requirements of IoT applications.

Advantages of MQTT

CoAP (Constrained Application Protocol) offers several advantages that make it well-suited for the Internet of Things (IoT). Table 2-3 provides a high-level overview of MQTT.

Table 2-3. List of various advantages of MQTT

Advantage	Description
Lightweight and efficient	Designed with a minimal packet overhead, MQTT is suitable for devices with limited processing power, memory, and battery life, ensuring efficient data transmission.
Publish-subscribe model	Decouples message producers from consumers via a central broker, facilitating scalable, flexible, and efficient communication among numerous devices.
Quality of service (QoS) levels	Provides three QoS levels (0, 1, 2) to ensure reliable message delivery tailored to specific application needs, balancing reliability and network resource usage.
Security features	Supports TLS for encrypted communication and various authentication methods to ensure data confidentiality, integrity, and secure client verification.

(continued)

Table 2-3. (*continued*)

Advantage	Description
Retained messages	Allows the broker to store the last known message on a topic and deliver it to new subscribers, ensuring they receive the latest information immediately.
Last will and testament (LWT)	Enables clients to specify a message to be sent by the broker if they disconnect unexpectedly, enhancing system reliability and failure detection.
Scalability	Supports efficient communication in both small sensor networks and large-scale systems, adapting to different IoT application requirements and scales.
Persistent sessions	Maintains the state of client sessions (including subscriptions and missed messages) even after disconnection, ensuring seamless continuity upon reconnection.
Small code footprint	Can be implemented with minimal code, making it feasible for deployment on resource-constrained devices typical in IoT environments.
Flexible and extensible	Can be easily integrated with various applications and extended with custom functionality, making it versatile for different IoT use cases.
Low bandwidth usage	Optimized for networks with low bandwidth, high latency, or intermittent connectivity, ensuring reliable communication under challenging conditions.

CHAPTER 2   DESIGN AND DEPLOY AZURE EDGE SERVICES

MQTT Architecture and Components

MQTT (Message Queuing Telemetry Transport) is a lightweight, publish-subscribe network protocol designed for constrained devices and low-bandwidth, high-latency, or unreliable networks. The architecture of MQTT is built around several key components that work together to facilitate efficient communication in IoT (Internet of Things) environments. These components include messages, clients, servers or brokers, and topics.

Message

In MQTT, messages are the fundamental units of communication, carrying data between clients via the broker. Each MQTT message has a specific structure, which includes

- Header: This section contains control information such as the message type, flags, and QoS (Quality of Service) level.
- Payload: The actual data being transmitted. The payload can be anything from a simple text string to complex binary data.
- Topic Name: Specifies the subject or channel to which the message is published. The broker uses it to route the message to appropriate subscribers.
- Message Identifier: Used with QoS levels 1 and 2 to identify and ensure the correct delivery of messages.

The simplicity of the MQTT message format ensures minimal overhead, which is crucial for resource-constrained devices and low-bandwidth networks.

Client

An MQTT client can act as a publisher, a subscriber, or both. It is any device that runs an MQTT library and connects to an MQTT broker to send and receive messages. Clients can be a wide variety of devices, such as

- Publishers: Send messages to the broker. They generate data and publish it on specific topics. For example, a temperature sensor might publish temperature readings on a topic like home/living room/temperature.

- Subscribers: Receive messages from the broker. They subscribe to specific topics and get notified when a message is published on those topics. For example, a home automation system might subscribe to the home/living room/temperature to monitor the temperature readings.

Clients maintain a connection to the broker and communicate using various MQTT control packets, such as CONNECT, PUBLISH, SUBSCRIBE, UNSUBSCRIBE, and DISCONNECT.

Server or Broker

The MQTT broker is the central hub in the MQTT architecture. It is responsible for managing all message routing, maintaining client connections, and ensuring the correct delivery of messages. Critical functions of the broker include:

- Message Routing: Receives publishers' messages and forwards them to subscribers based on topic subscriptions.

- Session Management: This function tracks client sessions, including persistent sessions, which store subscription information and undelivered messages for clients who reconnect.

- QoS Handling: Implements the three QoS levels (0, 1, and 2) to ensure messages are delivered according to the specified reliability requirements.

- Security: Manages client authentication and authorization, ensuring only authorized clients can publish or subscribe to topics. Brokers often use Transport Layer Security (TLS) to encrypt data transmissions.

- Retained Messages: Stores the last published message on a topic and delivers it to new subscribers immediately upon subscription.

MQTT brokers can be hosted on various platforms, from cloud-based services to local servers.

Topic

Topics are routing information in MQTT and organizing messages in a hierarchical structure that resembles a file system. Clients use them to specify the subjects or channels for message publication and subscription. Critical features of topics include:

- Hierarchical Structure: Topics are structured with levels separated by slashes (/). For example, home/living room/temperature indicates a topic related to the temperature in the living room.

- Wildcard Subscriptions: MQTT supports two types of wildcards for flexible subscription patterns:

  - Single-level wildcard (+): Matches any single level in a topic. For example, home/+/temperature matches home/livingroom/temperature and home/kitchen/temperature.

  - Multi-level wildcard (#): Matches any number of levels at the end of a topic. For example, home/# matches home/living room/temperature, home/kitchen/humidity, etc.

- Retained Messages: A particular type of message stored by the broker and delivered to any new topic subscribers. This ensures that new subscribers receive the most recent message immediately.

Topics provide a flexible and efficient way to manage and route messages within the MQTT architecture, enabling effective communication in diverse IoT applications.

The MQTT architecture's components – messages, clients, servers or brokers, and topics – provide a robust, efficient, and scalable communication framework for IoT applications. Messages carry the data, clients generate and consume these messages, brokers manage and route them, and topics organize and direct the flow of information. This architecture ensures that MQTT can meet the demands of diverse IoT scenarios, from simple sensor networks to complex, large-scale systems.

IoT Network – Transport Layer

The transport layer in an IoT network plays a crucial role in managing the communication between devices, ensuring data is transmitted reliably and efficiently. This layer is responsible for end-to-end communication and provides essential services like data segmentation, error detection, and flow control. In the context of IoT, the transport layer must handle diverse and often constrained environments, making its design and implementation critical for the overall performance and reliability of IoT systems.

Several protocols operate at the transport layer in IoT networks, each with unique characteristics suited to different application requirements. Transmission Control Protocol (TCP) and User Datagram Protocol (UDP) are the most commonly used transport layer protocols. TCP provides reliable, connection-oriented communication with error correction and flow control, ensuring data integrity and order. On the other hand, UDP offers a connectionless, low-latency communication method, which is helpful for applications where speed is more critical than reliability, such as real-time video streaming or gaming.

Given the constraints of many IoT devices – such as limited processing power, memory, and battery life – lightweight transport protocols are often preferred. MQTT (Message Queuing Telemetry Transport) and CoAP (Constrained Application Protocol) are widely adopted protocols explicitly designed for resource-constrained environments. MQTT operates over TCP, providing reliable message delivery with minimal overhead, while CoAP is built on UDP, offering low-latency communication with mechanisms to ensure message reliability when needed. These protocols are optimized for many IoT applications' low-power, low-bandwidth nature.

The transport layer is responsible for ensuring the reliability of data transmission. In TCP, this is achieved through mechanisms like retransmissions, acknowledgments, and sequence numbers. These features are essential for IoT applications that require guaranteed message delivery, such as remote monitoring and control systems. MQTT further enhances reliability with its Quality of Service (QoS) levels, which define the guarantee of message delivery: at most once (QoS 0), at least once (QoS 1), and exactly once (QoS 2). These options allow developers to balance reliability and resource consumption based on the application's specific needs.

Security at the transport layer is vital to protect data integrity and confidentiality in IoT networks. Protocols like TLS (Transport et al.) provide encryption and authentication, ensuring that data is protected from eavesdropping and tampering during transmission. However, implementing TLS in IoT environments can be challenging due to the computational overhead. Therefore, lightweight implementations of TLS, such as DTLS (Datagram et al.) for UDP, are often used to balance security and performance.

IoT networks can face significant network congestion, especially those involving numerous devices or operating in high-traffic environments. The transport layer is crucial in managing congestion through flow control and control mechanisms. TCP includes built-in algorithms like Slow Start, Congestion Avoidance, and Fast Recovery to manage network congestion. These mechanisms adjust the rate of data transmission based on network conditions, helping to maintain efficient and stable communication even under varying loads.

The transport layer in IoT networks must integrate seamlessly with application layer protocols to support a wide range of IoT services. HTTP, MQTT, CoAP, and AMQP (Advanced et al.) rely on the underlying transport layer to ensure data is delivered accurately and efficiently. The choice of transport layer protocol can significantly impact the performance and reliability of these application protocols, influencing factors like latency, throughput, and resource utilization. Therefore, selecting the appropriate transport protocol is crucial for optimizing the performance of IoT applications.

In summary, the transport layer in IoT networks is a foundational component that ensures reliable and efficient communication between devices. With protocols like TCP and UDP, along with specialized IoT protocols like MQTT and CoAP, the transport layer addresses the unique challenges of IoT environments. Key considerations include balancing reliability, performance, and security while managing network congestion

CHAPTER 2   DESIGN AND DEPLOY AZURE EDGE SERVICES

and integrating with application layer protocols. As IoT continues to evolve, the transport layer's role in facilitating robust, scalable, and secure communication will remain pivotal in the success of IoT deployments.

In the world of the Internet of Things (IoT), where an array of devices exchange data seamlessly, the choice between Transmission Control Protocol (TCP) and User Datagram Protocol (UDP) becomes paramount. TCP, known for its reliability, establishes connections with a handshake mechanism, ensuring data integrity and delivery through acknowledgment and retransmission procedures. This reliability comes at the cost of increased overhead due to acknowledgments and error correction, making TCP suitable for IoT applications where data integrity and order are critical, such as in industrial automation or healthcare monitoring systems. However, in scenarios where real-time responsiveness or low latency is prioritized over reliability, UDP emerges as the preferred choice.

User Datagram Protocol (UDP) operates with a connectionless paradigm, offering minimal overhead and lower latency than TCP. While UDP lacks the built-in mechanisms for reliability and flow control in TCP, its lightweight nature makes it ideal for time-sensitive IoT applications, including real-time sensor data streaming, video surveillance, or voice communication. In these contexts, where occasional data loss can be tolerated in exchange for faster transmission speeds and reduced network congestion, UDP empowers IoT devices to communicate efficiently, enabling swift decision-making and responsiveness in dynamic environments. Thus, TCP and UDP serve as versatile tools within the TCP/IP protocol suite, catering to diverse IoT requirements by balancing reliability and performance considerations at the transport layer.

Transmission Control Protocol (TCP)

In the intricate web of the Internet of Things (IoT), where countless devices exchange sensitive data, the Transmission Control Protocol (TCP) is a pillar of reliability and security. From an IoT network perspective,

TCP plays a pivotal role in ensuring seamless communication between devices while mitigating the risks associated with data transmission.

Establishing Reliable Connections: TCP employs a connection-oriented approach, initiating communication sessions through a three-way handshake mechanism. This handshake ensures that both sender and receiver acknowledge each other's presence, laying the foundation for reliable data exchange. In the context of IoT, where mission-critical data flows between devices, this meticulous connection establishment process minimizes the risk of unauthorized access or data interception.

Ensuring Data Integrity: Data integrity is paramount in IoT applications, especially in healthcare, smart grids, and industrial automation sectors. TCP achieves this by implementing error-checking mechanisms such as checksums and sequence numbers. These safeguards detect and rectify data corruption or loss during transmission, maintaining the integrity of vital information transferred across IoT networks.

Flow Control for Optimal Performance: IoT environments often face fluctuating network conditions and varying device capabilities. TCP's flow control mechanisms regulate the pace of data transmission, ensuring that receivers can handle incoming data without overwhelming their processing capacities. By dynamically adjusting data flow based on network feedback, TCP optimizes performance and minimizes the risk of congestion or packet loss in IoT networks.

Mitigating Threats Through Authentication: Security breaches pose a significant threat to IoT ecosystems, potentially compromising sensitive data or disrupting critical operations. TCP addresses this concern by incorporating authentication mechanisms into its connection establishment process. Through cryptographic protocols like Transport Layer Security (TLS), TCP verifies the identities of communicating devices, thwarting unauthorized access attempts and safeguarding IoT networks against malicious actors.

Encryption for Confidentiality: Confidentiality is essential in IoT applications dealing with private or proprietary information. TCP facilitates secure data transmission by supporting encryption protocols that encode sensitive data during transit. By encrypting communication channels, TCP shields IoT networks from eavesdropping and data tampering, preserving the confidentiality of transmitted information and maintaining the trust of stakeholders.

Resilience Against Network Failures: IoT deployments often span vast geographical areas, exposing them to diverse network challenges such as latency, packet loss, or link failures. TCP's robust error recovery mechanisms, including retransmission and timeout handling, bolster network resilience by swiftly recovering from communication disruptions. This resilience ensures uninterrupted connectivity and data exchange in IoT environments, even amidst adverse network conditions.

Regulating Access Through Firewalls and Proxies: In IoT deployments involving interconnected devices across public and private networks, TCP regulates access through firewalls and proxies. By adhering to established communication protocols and port numbers, TCP enables network administrators to define access policies, filter incoming traffic, and enforce security measures to safeguard IoT assets from external threats.

In conclusion, Transmission Control Protocol (TCP) is a cornerstone of IoT networking, providing a robust framework for reliable and secure data transmission. By leveraging TCP's features and capabilities, IoT ecosystems can foster trust, resilience, and efficiency, laying the groundwork for seamless connectivity and innovation in the digital era.

Key Features of TCP

Transmission Control Protocol (TCP) stands as a protocol meticulously crafted for efficient and dependable communication, especially in resource-constrained environments, rendering it exceptionally fitting for Internet of Things (IoT) applications. Its key features include the following.

Connection Establishment and Maintenance: One of the critical features of TCP in IoT networks is its ability to establish and maintain reliable connections between devices. TCP utilizes a three-way handshake mechanism to initiate communication sessions, ensuring the sender and receiver acknowledge each other's presence. This meticulous connection establishment process lays the foundation for secure data exchange and helps mitigate the risks associated with unauthorized access or data interception in IoT environments.

Error Detection and Correction: Data integrity is paramount in IoT applications, where accurate information exchange is crucial for effective decision-making. TCP addresses this requirement by implementing robust error detection and correction mechanisms. Through techniques such as checksums and sequence numbers, TCP detects and rectifies data corruption or loss during transmission. By ensuring the integrity of transmitted data, TCP enhances the reliability of IoT networks, reducing the likelihood of errors or inconsistencies in critical information.

Flow Control for Optimal Performance: In dynamic IoT environments characterized by fluctuating network conditions and diverse device capabilities, TCP's flow control mechanisms are vital in optimizing performance. By regulating the pace of data transmission based on network feedback, TCP prevents congestion and minimizes the risk of packet loss. This adaptive flow control mechanism ensures receivers can handle incoming data efficiently, promoting seamless communication and enhancing the overall performance of IoT networks.

Secure Authentication and Encryption: Security is a top priority in IoT deployments, where sensitive data flows between interconnected devices. TCP addresses security concerns by incorporating authentication and encryption mechanisms into its communication protocols. Through techniques such as Transport Layer Security (TLS), TCP verifies the identities of communicating devices and encrypts data during transit. By safeguarding communication channels against unauthorized access and data tampering, TCP enhances the confidentiality and integrity of information exchanged in IoT networks.

Robust Error Recovery Mechanisms: TCP's error recovery mechanisms ensure the resilience of IoT networks in the face of network failures or disruptions. TCP implements strategies such as retransmission and timeout handling to recover from communication disruptions swiftly. These robust error recovery mechanisms enable IoT devices to maintain uninterrupted connectivity and data exchange, even in adverse network conditions. By mitigating the impact of network failures, TCP enhances the reliability and availability of IoT applications, ensuring continuous operation and a seamless user experience.

Compatibility with Network Infrastructure: TCP's compatibility with existing network infrastructure is another critical feature that makes it well-suited for IoT deployments. TCP adheres to established communication protocols and port numbers, enabling seamless integration with firewalls, proxies, and other network security devices. This compatibility facilitates the implementation of access control policies and security measures to safeguard IoT assets from external threats. By leveraging TCP's compatibility with network infrastructure, IoT deployments can enhance their security posture and mitigate risks associated with unauthorized access or malicious attacks.

Support for Scalability and Interoperability: As IoT ecosystems expand and evolve, scalability and interoperability become essential considerations. TCP's support for scalable communication architectures and interoperable protocols makes it ideal for accommodating growing IoT deployments. TCP facilitates seamless communication between devices from different manufacturers or operating environments, promoting interoperability and compatibility across heterogeneous IoT ecosystems. By supporting scalability and interoperability, TCP enables IoT deployments to adapt to changing requirements and embrace emerging technologies, ensuring long-term viability and flexibility in a rapidly evolving digital landscape.

Advantages of TCP

Transmission Control Protocol (TCP) offers several advantages that make it well-suited for the Internet of Things (IoT). Table 2-4 provides a high-level overview of TCP.

Table 2-4. Lists of various advantages of TCP

Advantage	Description
Reliable	TCP ensures reliable data transmission by implementing error detection, retransmission, and acknowledgment mechanisms.
Ordered delivery	Data packets are delivered to the receiver in the same order they were sent, ensuring integrity and consistency.
Flow control	TCP regulates the flow of data to prevent congestion and optimize performance, particularly in dynamic IoT environments.
Error recovery	Robust error recovery mechanisms, such as retransmission and timeout handling, ensure resilience against network failures.
Secure communication	TCP supports encryption and authentication mechanisms, enhancing the security of data exchanged in IoT networks.
Compatibility	TCP seamlessly integrates with existing network infrastructure, facilitating interoperability and scalability in IoT deployments.
Congestion control	TCP dynamically adjusts transmission rates based on network conditions, mitigating congestion and ensuring efficient data transfer.

TCP Architecture and Components

Transmission Control Protocol (TCP) serves as the backbone of reliable communication in Internet of Things (IoT) networks. It offers a robust architecture comprising various components tailored to address the unique requirements of IoT environments while ensuring data integrity and security.

CHAPTER 2 DESIGN AND DEPLOY AZURE EDGE SERVICES

For example, when a user requests a web page online, a server somewhere in the world processes this request and sends back an HTML page. The server utilizes the HTTP protocol to facilitate this communication. HTTP, in turn, requests the TCP layer to establish the necessary connection and transmit the HTML file.

The TCP layer then breaks the data into small packets and forwards them to the Internet Protocol (IP) layer. These packets travel to their destination via various routes.

On the user's system, the TCP layer waits for the complete transmission and acknowledges receipt once all packets have been received. Figure 2-3 depicts TCP architecture.

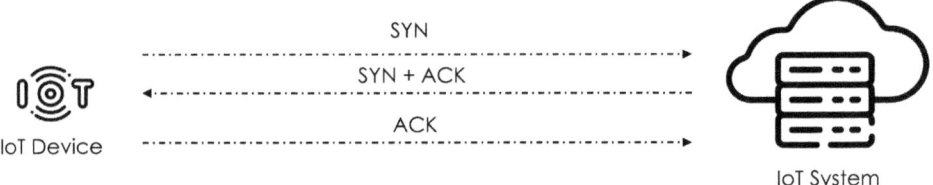

Figure 2-3. *TCP – architecture*

Connection Establishment

At the core of TCP's architecture lies the connection establishment process, which is vital for initiating secure communication sessions between IoT devices. This process involves a three-way handshake mechanism, where devices exchange synchronization (SYN) and Acknowledgment (ACK) messages to establish a reliable connection. From an IoT network and security standpoint, this ensures that data transmission begins only after both parties authenticate each other, mitigating the risk of unauthorized access or data interception.

Segmentation and Reassembly

TCP segments data into manageable units known as segments for efficient transmission across IoT networks. Each segment contains a sequence number, enabling the receiver to reconstruct the data in the correct order upon arrival. In the context of IoT security, this segmentation and reassembly process facilitates detecting and correcting data corruption or loss, ensuring the integrity of transmitted information.

Flow Control and Congestion Management

TCP incorporates flow control mechanisms to regulate the data transmission rate based on network conditions and receiver capabilities. Through sliding window algorithms, TCP ensures that data flows smoothly between IoT devices, preventing congestion and optimizing network performance. From a security perspective, this mitigates the risk of denial-of-service (DoS) attacks and enhances the resilience of IoT networks against malicious traffic.

Error Detection and Recovery

Error detection and recovery form integral components of TCP's architecture, which is crucial for maintaining reliability in IoT environments. TCP utilizes checksums to detect errors in transmitted data, while acknowledgment and retransmission mechanisms enable the recovery of lost or corrupted packets. This robust error-handling mechanism ensures that IoT devices can recover from communication disruptions swiftly, enhancing IoT networks' overall resilience and availability.

Security Enhancements

TCP incorporates security enhancements to protect data exchanged within IoT networks from unauthorized access and tampering. Through protocols like Transport Layer Security (TLS), TCP enables encrypted communication channels, safeguarding sensitive information from eavesdropping and interception. Authentication mechanisms further validate the identities of communicating devices, ensuring secure and trusted communication in IoT deployments.

Interoperability and Compatibility

TCP's architecture is designed to emphasize interoperability and compatibility. This allows IoT devices from different manufacturers and operating environments to communicate seamlessly. By adhering to standardized communication protocols and port numbers, TCP enables integration with existing network infrastructure. This, in turn, allows IoT deployments to effectively leverage security features such as firewalls and intrusion detection systems, demonstrating the practical advantages of using TCP in IoT deployments.

Resource Optimization

TCP is instrumental in optimizing resource utilization in IoT networks. It achieves this through efficient packet management and transmission strategies. By minimizing overhead and maximizing throughput, TCP ensures IoT devices can transmit data reliably and efficiently while conserving network resources. This resource optimization is a testament to the efficiency and effectiveness of TCP in IoT deployments, supporting the growth of interconnected devices without compromising performance or security.

In conclusion, TCP's architecture and components are pivotal in enhancing reliability, security, and performance in IoT networks. By addressing essential requirements such as connection establishment, error

CHAPTER 2   DESIGN AND DEPLOY AZURE EDGE SERVICES

handling, and security enhancements, TCP empowers IoT deployments to achieve seamless communication, robust data exchange, and trusted connectivity in diverse and dynamic environments.

User Datagram Protocol (UDP)

User Datagram Protocol (UDP) is a critical component in the Internet of Things (IoT) landscape, providing a lightweight and efficient means of data transmission. Given the unique demands of IoT devices – often characterized by limited power, processing capabilities, and the need for real-time communication – UDP's simplicity and speed make it an attractive choice. This protocol's design focuses on minimal overhead and rapid data transfer, aligning well with the operational needs of IoT environments.

UDP sends data in discrete packets, known as datagrams, without establishing a connection beforehand. This connectionless nature eliminates the handshake process required by protocols like TCP, resulting in faster communication. Each datagram is sent independently, allowing data to be transmitted quickly and efficiently. This is particularly useful in IoT applications where speed and low latency are critical.

A UDP datagram consists of a simple header and a data payload. The header contains four fields: source port, destination port, length, and checksum. These fields are crucial for directing the datagram to the correct application and ensuring fundamental error checking. The small size of the header minimizes overhead, which is beneficial for resource-constrained IoT devices. The payload carries the transmitted data, such as sensor readings or control commands.

The primary benefit of UDP in IoT networks is its low latency. The absence of a connection setup phase allows for near-instantaneous data transmission, which is essential for real-time applications like sensor networks, smart home devices, and industrial automation. Additionally, UDP's simplicity reduces the processing load on IoT devices, conserving their limited computational resources and extending battery life.

CHAPTER 2 DESIGN AND DEPLOY AZURE EDGE SERVICES

While UDP does not guarantee delivery, order, or integrity of packets, this flexibility can be an advantage in IoT. Applications that use UDP can implement their reliability mechanisms tailored to specific needs. For example, an IoT system can employ application-layer protocols like the Constrained Application Protocol (CoAP) to add reliability features such as acknowledgments and retransmissions, ensuring critical data is delivered even in unreliable network conditions.

UDP's lack of inherent security features presents challenges in IoT networks, often targeted by cyberattacks. Due to its connectionless nature and minimal error checking, the protocol is susceptible to spoofing, flooding, and other types of attacks. To mitigate these risks, IoT systems must implement additional security measures such as encryption, device authentication, and robust firewall rules. These measures help secure the data transmitted over UDP and protect the IoT infrastructure from malicious activities.

UDP is widely used in various IoT applications, and its speed and efficiency are crucial. For instance, it is ideal for transmitting periodic sensor data, where occasional packet loss can be tolerated. UDP is also used in applications requiring multicast or broadcast capabilities, such as firmware updates or system-wide alerts in intelligent cities. In these scenarios, the protocol's ability to handle large volumes of data with minimal delay enhances the performance and reliability of IoT networks.

In IoT networks, UDP stands out for its efficiency, low latency, and minimal resource requirements. While it lacks built-in reliability and security features, its flexibility allows IoT developers to implement custom solutions tailored to specific application needs. By leveraging additional protocols and security measures, UDP can effectively meet the demands of diverse IoT applications, ensuring rapid and reliable data transmission in even the most resource-constrained environments.

Key Features of UDP

User Datagram Protocol (UDP) is widely used in Internet of Things (IoT) networks due to its efficiency and simplicity. While it lacks some reliability features of other protocols, its speed and resource usage benefits make it a popular choice for many IoT applications. Here are some key features of UDP from an IoT network and security perspective.

Low Latency: UDP's connectionless nature means that data can be sent without a handshake process, significantly reducing latency. This is particularly beneficial for real-time IoT applications such as live video streaming, remote device control, and sensor data collection, where quick data transmission is crucial.

Resource Efficiency: IoT devices often have limited processing power and memory. UDP's simplicity requires fewer resources compared to more complex protocols like TCP. This makes UDP a suitable choice for battery-operated or low-power IoT devices that need to maximize their operational efficiency.

Scalability: UDP's minimal overhead allows for high scalability in IoT networks. It can handle a large number of devices transmitting data simultaneously without significant performance degradation, making it ideal for large-scale IoT deployments such as smart cities, industrial IoT, and extensive sensor networks.

Flexibility: The protocol's lack of built-in reliability features allows developers to implement custom reliability mechanisms as needed. This flexibility is beneficial in IoT applications where certain data types may require different levels of reliability and verification, allowing for tailored solutions that best meet specific application needs.

Security Considerations: While UDP inherently lacks security features, additional security layers can safeguard its use in IoT networks. Encryption, authentication, and firewall protections can be employed to secure data transmitted via UDP. Implementing these measures helps protect against common vulnerabilities such as spoofing and Denial of Service (DoS) attacks.

Protocol Compatibility: UDP is compatible with a variety of higher-level protocols designed for IoT. For instance, the Constrained Application Protocol (CoAP) uses UDP to provide a lightweight, reliable communication option for resource-constrained IoT devices. This compatibility extends UDP's usefulness in diverse IoT applications by leveraging existing standards and technologies.

Robust Performance in Lossy Networks: UDP can offer robust performance in IoT environments where network conditions are less predictable, such as remote or mobile deployments. Its ability to handle packet loss without significantly impacting communication makes it suitable for such challenging environments.

UDP's key features, including low latency, resource efficiency, scalability, flexibility, enhanced security measures, protocol compatibility, and robust performance in lossy networks, make it a valuable protocol for IoT networks. By understanding these benefits, IoT developers can effectively leverage UDP to meet the demands of various applications while addressing security and reliability challenges.

Advantages of UDP

The Transmission Control Protocol (TCP) is fundamental in the Internet Protocol (IP) suite, known for its reliability and robust communication capabilities. Table 2-5 highlights the key advantages of UDP and their descriptions.

Table 2-5. *List of various advantages of TCP*

Advantages	Description
Reliability	TCP ensures data is delivered accurately and in the correct order, using acknowledgments and retransmissions to handle lost or corrupted packets.
Error detection and recovery	TCP includes mechanisms for error detection and automatic recovery, ensuring that any errors in transmission are corrected without manual intervention.
Flow control	TCP manages the rate of data transmission between sender and receiver, preventing network congestion and ensuring efficient use of available bandwidth.
Congestion control	TCP dynamically adjusts the rate of data flow based on network conditions, reducing the risk of congestion and optimizing network performance.
Connection-oriented	TCP establishes a connection before data transmission, ensuring that both sender and receiver are ready and able to handle the data exchange reliably.
Ordered data transfer	TCP guarantees that packets are delivered in the order they were sent, which is critical for applications that require data to be processed in sequence.
Compatibility	TCP is widely supported across different devices and operating systems, making it a versatile and reliable choice for various network applications.
Robustness	TCP can handle various network conditions and is resilient to packet loss, duplication, and network changes, maintaining stable and reliable communication.

UDP Architecture and Components

User Datagram Protocol (UDP) is a fundamental protocol within the Internet Protocol (IP) suite that facilitates efficient, low-latency communication. Its architecture and components are designed for simplicity and speed, making it ideal for applications where quick data transmission is critical. Below, we delve into the detailed architecture and components of UDP.

Basic Architecture of UDP: UDP operates on a connectionless communication model, meaning it does not establish a dedicated end-to-end connection before transmitting data. Instead, it sends data in discrete packets called datagrams. This architecture contrasts sharply with the connection-oriented Transmission Control Protocol (TCP), which requires a handshake to set up a connection before data transfer begins. The connectionless nature of UDP reduces overhead, allowing for faster communication. Figure 2-4 depicts UDP architecture.

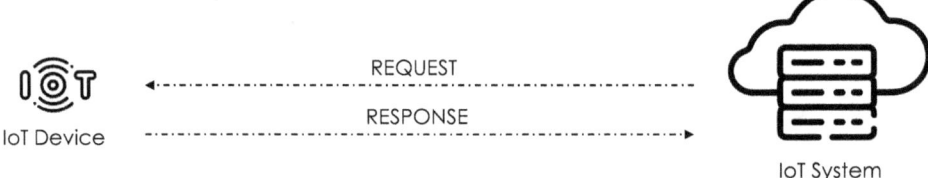

Figure 2-4. *UDP – architecture*

UDP Datagram Structure: A UDP datagram consists of two main parts: the header and the payload. The header is minimalistic, comprising four fields:

- Source Port: This 16-bit field identifies the port of the sending application. It helps the recipient understand which application or service sent the data.

- Destination Port: This is another 16-bit field that specifies the port of the receiving application. It ensures the data is delivered correctly to the destination device.

- Length: This 16-bit field indicates the total length of the UDP datagram, including both the header and the data. The length field allows the receiver to understand how much data was sent.

- Checksum: The 16-bit checksum field provides fundamental error checking. It covers both the header and the data, allowing the recipient to verify the integrity of the received datagram. Although the checksum is optional in IPv4, it is mandatory in IPv6.

The payload follows the header and contains the actual data being transmitted. This can include anything from simple sensor readings in IoT devices to more complex data structures.

Components of UDP Communication

The UDP communication model involves several key components:

- Applications: The software applications that use UDP for data transmission. These applications create and process the data sent and received via UDP. Examples include streaming services, online games, and DNS queries.

- Ports: Ports serve as communication endpoints for applications using UDP. Each application on a device is associated with a unique port number, which allows the operating system to direct incoming data to the correct application.

CHAPTER 2   DESIGN AND DEPLOY AZURE EDGE SERVICES

- Sockets: A socket is an endpoint for sending or receiving data across a network. In the context of UDP, a socket is defined by an IP address and a port number. Applications create and use sockets to handle data transmission.

- IP Layer: The Internet Protocol (IP) layer is responsible for routing the UDP datagrams between the source and destination devices across the network. It provides the underlying delivery mechanism for the datagrams.

UDP Communication Process

The communication process in UDP involves several steps:

- Datagram Creation: The sending application creates a datagram, encapsulating the data and the necessary header information (source port, destination port, length, and checksum).

- Transmission: The datagram is passed to the IP layer, which routes it to the destination address. Because UDP is connectionless, there is no guarantee of delivery, order, or duplicate protection.

- Reception: Upon reaching the destination, the IP layer hands the datagram to the UDP layer, directing it to the appropriate application based on the destination port.

- Processing: The receiving application processes the data. The receiver will verify the data's integrity if the checksum is used. Any necessary error handling, such as dealing with lost or out-of-order packets, is managed by the application itself, not the UDP protocol.

Advantages and Trade-Offs

The primary advantage of UDP is its low latency and minimal overhead, making it ideal for applications requiring fast communication and where occasional data loss is acceptable. This includes real-time applications like video streaming, VoIP, and online gaming. However, the trade-off is that UDP needs to provide TCP's reliability, ordering, and error correction features. Applications using UDP must implement their mechanisms to handle these aspects if required.

UDP's architecture and components are designed to facilitate fast and efficient communication with minimal overhead. Its simplicity makes it suitable for a wide range of applications, especially those where speed and low latency are more critical than guaranteed delivery and order. By understanding UDP's structure and operation, developers can effectively leverage its benefits while addressing its limitations through application-level controls and protocols.

IoT Network – Network Layer

The network layer in Internet of Things (IoT) networks is a critical component that facilitates communication among many interconnected devices, enabling seamless data exchange and network management. As IoT ecosystems expand and diversify, encompassing a vast array of devices ranging from sensors and actuators to gateways and cloud servers, the network layer plays a pivotal role in orchestrating data flow across heterogeneous network infrastructures. This layer operates at the heart of the IoT architecture, bridging the gap between physical devices and higher-level applications while addressing challenges related to scalability, interoperability, and resource constraints.

CHAPTER 2   DESIGN AND DEPLOY AZURE EDGE SERVICES

At its core, the network layer in IoT networks addresses and routes data packets between source and destination devices, regardless of their underlying communication technologies or protocols. In essence, it provides

- The essential framework for establishing end-to-end communication paths
- Optimizing network performance
- Ensuring efficient utilization of network resources

With the proliferation of wireless connectivity technologies such as Wi-Fi, Bluetooth, Zigbee, LoRaWAN, and cellular networks, the network layer must accommodate diverse networking paradigms and adapt to dynamic network conditions to meet the demands of IoT applications spanning various domains, including smart cities, healthcare, agriculture, manufacturing, and transportation.

One of the fundamental challenges in designing the network layer for IoT lies in addressing the heterogeneity and scale of IoT deployments, where devices may vary in terms of communication capabilities, power constraints, and network topologies. Consequently, the network layer must support flexible addressing schemes, routing protocols, and network management mechanisms to accommodate the diverse requirements of IoT devices and applications. Moreover, the proliferation of edge computing and fog computing paradigms introduces new complexities to the network layer, requiring intelligent routing and decision-making capabilities to optimize data processing and minimize latency at the network edge.

Another critical consideration in IoT network layer design is the efficient utilization of network bandwidth and resources, particularly in resource-constrained environments. IoT devices often operate with limited computational power, memory, and energy resources, necessitating the network layer's lightweight and efficient communication protocols. In this context, protocols such as the Constrained Application Protocol (CoAP) and the Message Queuing Telemetry Transport (MQTT) protocol have emerged as popular choices for IoT communication, offering lightweight messaging frameworks tailored to the constraints of IoT devices while ensuring reliable and scalable communication over IP networks.

Furthermore, security and privacy are paramount concerns in IoT networks, given the sensitive nature of the data exchanged and the potential impact of security breaches on critical infrastructure and personal privacy. The network layer is crucial in implementing security mechanisms such as encryption, authentication, access control, and intrusion detection to safeguard IoT communications against various threats, including eavesdropping, data tampering, and denial-of-service attacks. Protocols like Datagram Transport Layer Security (DTLS) and IPsec provide end-to-end encryption and integrity protection for IoT data transmitted over insecure networks, ensuring confidentiality and data integrity.

In conclusion, the network layer is the backbone of IoT networks, providing the essential infrastructure for connecting and coordinating many devices in diverse IoT deployments. By addressing scalability, interoperability, resource constraints, and security challenges, the network layer enables seamless communication and data exchange in IoT ecosystems, driving innovation and transforming industries across the globe. As IoT continues to evolve and expand, the network layer will play an increasingly pivotal role in shaping the future of connected devices and intelligent systems.

IpV6 and 6LoWPAN are the main protocol parts of the network layer. IPv6 (Internet Protocol version 6) is a foundational protocol in the IoT network layer, offering a vastly expanded address space compared to its predecessor, IPv4. With the proliferation of IoT devices expected to reach tens of billions in the coming years, IPv6 provides the necessary scalability to accommodate the immense growth of connected devices and address the looming exhaustion of IPv4 addresses. In IoT deployments, where each

CHAPTER 2   DESIGN AND DEPLOY AZURE EDGE SERVICES

device requires a unique IP address for identification and communication, IPv6's 128-bit addressing scheme ensures an abundant supply of addresses, allowing for the seamless integration of billions of devices into the global Internet ecosystem. Moreover, IPv6 introduces several enhancements over IPv4, including simplified header formats, built-in support for multicast communication, and improved security features, making it well-suited for the diverse requirements of IoT applications spanning intelligent cities, industrial automation, healthcare, and beyond.

6LoWPAN (IPv6 over low-power wireless personal area networks) emerges as a crucial IoT network layer protocol tailored to address the unique challenges posed by resource-constrained IoT devices operating in low-power wireless networks. By adapting IPv6 packets to fit within the constraints of low-power wireless technologies such as IEEE 802.15.4, 6LoWPAN enables seamless integration of IPv6 connectivity into battery-powered sensors, actuators, and other IoT devices with limited processing power and memory. 6LoWPAN achieves this optimization through header compression, fragmentation, and routing mechanisms, allowing IoT devices to communicate directly with IPv6-enabled routers and gateways while minimizing overhead and conserving energy. This protocol plays a pivotal role in extending the reach of IPv6 to the edge of the IoT network, enabling ubiquitous connectivity and interoperability across a diverse range of IoT devices and applications, from smart homes and wearables to industrial sensor networks and environmental monitoring systems.

IPv6

IPv6, or Internet Protocol version 6, represents the next generation of the Internet Protocol, succeeding IPv4. It was developed to address the limitations of IPv4, particularly the scarcity of available IP addresses. IPv6 employs a 128-bit address scheme, providing a virtually unlimited pool of unique addresses compared to the 32-bit address space of IPv4, which has been exhausted in many regions. This expanded address space is crucial

CHAPTER 2   DESIGN AND DEPLOY AZURE EDGE SERVICES

for accommodating the proliferation of IoT devices, as each connected device requires a unique identifier to communicate over the Internet. With IPv6, the address space is so vast that it can support trillions upon trillions of devices, ensuring scalability for the growing IoT ecosystem.

IPv6 operates on the same basic principles as IPv4 but introduces several improvements and enhancements. One notable improvement is the simplified header format, which reduces overhead and improves packet processing efficiency. IPv6 also integrates features such as built-in support for multicast communication, enabling efficient one-to-many and many-to-many communication patterns often used in IoT deployments. Additionally, IPv6 enhances security by mandating the use of IPsec (Internet Protocol Security) for securing communication between devices, thereby providing authentication, integrity, and confidentiality at the network layer.

In IoT networks, IPv6 is pivotal in enabling seamless connectivity and interoperability among diverse IoT devices and systems. The abundance of IPv6 addresses ensures that every IoT device can be uniquely identified and addressed, regardless of its type or location. This universal addressing scheme simplifies device management and facilitates end-to-end communication across the IoT ecosystem, from edge devices to cloud servers. Moreover, IPv6's support for multicast communication is particularly beneficial for IoT applications that involve sensor networks, where data needs to be efficiently disseminated to multiple recipients in real-time.

Security is a paramount concern in IoT networks, given the potential risks associated with compromised devices and data breaches. IPv6 enhances security in IoT deployments by incorporating IPsec as a mandatory component of the protocol suite. IPsec provides cryptographic security services at the network layer, including encryption, authentication, and integrity protection, to safeguard communication between IoT devices and mitigate the risk of eavesdropping, tampering, and impersonation attacks. By encrypting data traffic and authenticating communicating parties, IPv6 helps ensure the confidentiality and integrity of IoT data, even in untrusted network environments.

Furthermore, IPv6 enables the adoption of secure network architectures, such as end-to-end security and secure overlay networks, essential for protecting IoT deployments from external threats and vulnerabilities. With IPv6, IoT devices can establish secure connections directly with authorized servers and services, reducing the reliance on intermediary gateways and minimizing the attack surface. Additionally, IPv6's support for IPsec tunneling allows organizations to create encrypted communication tunnels over untrusted networks, such as the Internet, ensuring secure data transmission between geographically distributed IoT devices and centralized servers.

In conclusion, IPv6 is instrumental in shaping the future of IoT networks, providing the scalability, interoperability, and security required for the seamless integration and operation of billions of connected devices. By offering an expansive address space, simplified header format, and built-in support for multicast communication, IPv6 addresses the unique challenges posed by IoT deployments, enabling efficient communication and data exchange across diverse IoT ecosystems. Moreover, IPv6's integration of IPsec enhances the security posture of IoT networks, ensuring the confidentiality, integrity, and authenticity of data transmitted between IoT devices and systems. As IoT continues to evolve and expand, IPv6 will remain a cornerstone of the network infrastructure, driving innovation and enabling transformative IoT applications across various industries and domains.

Key Feature of Ipv6

IPv6, the successor to IPv4, boasts several key features that distinguish it as a foundational protocol for modern Internet communication. One of the most prominent features of IPv6 is its vastly expanded address space. While IPv4 addresses are 32 bits long, allowing for approximately 4.3 billion unique addresses, IPv6 addresses are 128, resulting in an astronomically larger pool of available addresses. This abundance of addresses is essential for accommodating the exponential growth of connected devices in the Internet of Things (IoT) era, ensuring that every device can be uniquely identified and addressed on the Internet without the limitations of address exhaustion experienced with IPv4.

Another significant feature of IPv6 is its simplified header format. Compared to IPv4, which includes various fields for options and headers, IPv6 streamlines the header structure to minimize overhead and improve packet processing efficiency. This simplified header format reduces the burden on networking equipment and enables faster routing and forwarding of packets, contributing to improved network performance and scalability. Additionally, IPv6 introduces support for extension headers, which include optional information such as routing, fragmentation, and authentication without increasing the size of the base header.

IPv6 also integrates built-in support for multicast communication, enabling efficient one-to-many and many-to-many communication patterns. Multicast allows a single packet to be sent from one sender to multiple recipients simultaneously, conserving bandwidth and reducing network traffic. This feature particularly benefits multimedia streaming, content distribution, and IoT sensor networks, where data must be disseminated to multiple recipients in real time. By leveraging multicast, IPv6 facilitates efficient and scalable communication across diverse network topologies and deployment scenarios.

Moreover, IPv6 enhances security by mandating IPsec (Internet Protocol Security) to secure communication between devices. IPsec provides cryptographic security services at the network layer, including encryption, authentication, and integrity protection, to safeguard data transmitted over IPv6 networks. With IPsec integration, IPv6 ensures that communication between devices is protected from eavesdropping, tampering, and impersonation attacks, thereby enhancing the confidentiality, integrity, and authenticity of data exchanged over the Internet. This built-in security feature makes IPv6 a compelling choice for organizations seeking to deploy secure and resilient network infrastructures in the face of evolving cyber threats.

In summary, IPv6 encompasses several vital features that make it a foundational protocol for modern Internet communication. Its expanded address space, simplified header format, multicast communication support, and IPsec security integration contribute to improved scalability, efficiency, and security in network deployments. As the Internet continues to evolve and accommodate the proliferation of connected devices and emerging technologies, IPv6 will remain a critical enabler of innovation, driving the development of resilient, scalable, and secure network infrastructures for the digital age.

Advantages of Ipv6

IPv6 brings several advantages to IoT networks and enhances security, scalability, and efficiency in IoT deployments. The expanded address space of IPv6 accommodates the proliferation of IoT devices seamlessly, while the simplified header format reduces packet overhead and improves network performance. IPv6's support for multicast communication also enables efficient one-to-many and many-to-many data transmission, which is ideal for IoT applications such as sensor networks and content distribution. Moreover, IPv6 mandates using IPsec to secure communication between devices, providing robust cryptographic security services to protect IoT deployments against cyber threats. Table 2-6 highlights the key advantages of Ipv6 and their descriptions.

Table 2-6. List of various advantages of Ipv6

Advantage	Description
Expanded address space	IPv6 offers a significantly larger address space compared to IPv4, accommodating the growing number of IoT devices seamlessly. With 128-bit addresses, IPv6 can provide unique identifiers to trillions of devices, ensuring scalability and eliminating address exhaustion.
Simplified header format	IPv6 simplifies the header format, reducing packet overhead and improving network performance. With a streamlined structure, IPv6 headers require less processing by networking equipment, enabling faster routing and forwarding of packets in IoT deployments.
Support for multicast communication	IPv6 integrates native support for multicast communication, allowing efficient one-to-many and many-to-many data transmission. Multicast conserves bandwidth and reduces network traffic, making it ideal for IoT applications such as sensor networks and content distribution.
Built-in IPsec security	IPv6 mandates the use of IPsec for securing communication between devices, enhancing data confidentiality, integrity, and authenticity. By integrating IPsec at the network layer, IPv6 protects IoT deployments against various security threats and vulnerabilities effectively.

IPv6 Architecture and Its Components

IPv6, the Internet Protocol version 6, is not just a successor to IPv4, but a revolutionary step forward in Internet protocol. It was designed to overcome the limitations of IPv4, notably the depletion of IP addresses

CHAPTER 2   DESIGN AND DEPLOY AZURE EDGE SERVICES

due to the rapid growth of Internet-connected devices. IPv6 brings a host of improvements, including a vastly expanded address space, advanced security features, and enhanced support for multimedia applications.

The core of the IPv6 architecture is its expanded address space, a feature that sets it apart from IPv4. While IPv4 offers 32-bit addresses, allowing for about 4.3 billion unique addresses, IPv6 takes a giant leap with 128-bit addresses, providing an unimaginably large pool of addresses, roughly 340 undecillion (3.4×10^{38}) unique addresses. This colossal address space ensures that every device can have its own globally unique IP address, paving the way for a future with an unlimited number of Internet-connected devices.

IPv6 addresses are typically represented in hexadecimal notation and are divided into eight groups of four hexadecimal digits separated by colons, such as 2001:0db8:85a3:0000:0000:8a2e:0370:7334. Additionally, IPv6 supports address assignment methods such as stateless autoconfiguration (SLAAC) and DHCPv6, simplifying network configuration and management.

IPv6 architecture doesn't just stop at addressing the IP address exhaustion issue. It also brings significant improvements in supporting quality of service (QoS) and multimedia applications. IPv6 incorporates flow labeling and traffic class features, enabling more efficient packet prioritization and handling. This is particularly crucial for real-time applications like voice and video streaming, where maintaining consistent network performance is a make-or-break factor.

IPv6 also includes built-in support for IPsec (Internet Protocol Security), providing a standardized framework for securing communication over IP networks. IPsec in IPv6 offers authentication, encryption, and integrity protection, ensuring the confidentiality and integrity of data transmitted over IPv6 networks.

Furthermore, IPv6 architecture introduces improvements in routing and network management. With IPv6, hierarchical addressing and routing are emphasized, facilitating efficient routing table aggregation and reducing the size of routing tables in Internet backbone routers. Additionally, IPv6 incorporates features such as neighbor discovery and multicast listener discovery, enhancing network efficiency and scalability.

In summary, the IPv6 architecture represents a significant evolution of the Internet protocol. It addresses the limitations of IPv4 while introducing numerous enhancements in address space, security, quality of service, and network management. As the Internet expands and the number of connected devices grows exponentially, IPv6 serves as the foundation for a scalable, secure, and robust Internet infrastructure.

6LoWPAN

6LoWPAN, an acronym for "IPv6 over low-power wireless personal area networks," is a network protocol that efficiently transmits IPv6 packets over low-power, low-bandwidth wireless networks. Developed by the Internet Engineering Task Force (IETF), it is specifically designed to address the unique challenges of wireless sensor networks (WSNs) and the Internet of Things (IoT). By enabling IPv6 connectivity, 6LoWPAN facilitates the seamless integration of small, resource-constrained devices into more extensive IP networks, thus playing a crucial role in the proliferation of IoT applications.

The development of 6LoWPAN was primarily driven by the need to extend the benefits of IPv6, such as a vast address space and improved routing, to low-power devices. Traditional IPv6 was not suitable for these devices due to the relatively large size of its headers, which can lead to significant overhead on constrained networks. 6LoWPAN steps in to address this issue by employing header compression techniques that significantly reduce the size of IPv6 headers. This reduction is crucial for maintaining efficient communication over networks where bandwidth and power are limited.

The architecture of 6LoWPAN is designed to operate over IEEE 802.15.4, a standard for low-rate wireless personal area networks (LR-WPANs). IEEE 802.15.4 provides a physical and medium access control (MAC) layer optimized for low-power, low-data-rate communication, making it ideal for sensor networks and other IoT applications. 6LoWPAN builds on this by providing an adaptation layer that facilitates the transmission of IPv6 packets over the 802.15.4 network. This layer handles header compression, packet fragmentation and reassembly, and routing tasks.

Fragmentation and reassembly are significant in 6LoWPAN due to the small maximum transmission unit (MTU) size of IEEE 802.15.4, which is only 127 bytes. Since IPv6 packets can be significantly larger than this, 6LoWPAN must divide these packets into smaller fragments for transmission. The receiver then reassembles these fragments. The ability to efficiently handle fragmentation and reassembly is a critical feature that enables 6LoWPAN to support IPv6 over such constrained networks without significant performance degradation.

One of the standout features of 6LoWPAN is its support for mesh networking, a network topology where multiple devices can communicate directly or through intermediate devices. This feature enhances network reliability and coverage, which is particularly beneficial in environments where devices might be spread out over a wide area or where obstacles could interfere with direct line-of-sight communication. Mesh networking in 6LoWPAN not only improves the robustness of the network but also allows for dynamic reconfiguration as devices join or leave the network, thereby enhancing its adaptability.

Security is another critical aspect addressed by 6LoWPAN. Securing these communications is paramount because of the sensitivity of data often transmitted over IoT networks, such as personal health information or home automation data. 6LoWPAN incorporates security features that leverage existing security mechanisms in IPv6 and IEEE 802.15.4. These include link-layer encryption and authentication and higher-layer security protocols such as IPsec, which can provide end-to-end security.

In summary, 6LoWPAN plays a pivotal role in enabling the vision of a seamlessly interconnected world by bringing the power of IPv6 to low-power, low-bandwidth wireless networks. Addressing key challenges such as header overhead, fragmentation, and security allows for the efficient and secure communication of small devices within the broader Internet architecture. As the IoT grows, 6LoWPAN's importance will only increase, providing the foundational infrastructure needed to support various innovative applications and services.

Key Feature of 6LoWPAN

6LoWPAN, or IPv6 over low-power wireless personal area networks, is a pivotal protocol designed to extend the capabilities of IPv6 to resource-constrained, low-power wireless networks crucial for IoT applications. Critical features of 6LoWPAN include header compression to reduce the overhead of IPv6 headers, packet fragmentation and reassembly to handle the small MTU sizes of IEEE 802.15.4 networks, and support for mesh networking to enhance reliability and coverage. Additionally, 6LoWPAN is optimized for low power consumption, ensuring longevity for battery-powered devices, while its scalability and flexibility make it suitable for diverse applications. Interoperability with IPv6 allows seamless integration into the broader Internet, and robust security mechanisms ensure data protection across the network. The following features collectively make 6LoWPAN a crucial technology for modern IoT ecosystems' efficient and secure operation.

Header Compression: One of the most critical features of 6LoWPAN is its ability to perform header compression. IPv6 headers are typically 40 bytes long, which can be too large for low-power wireless networks with limited MTU sizes, like IEEE 802.15.4, which has an MTU of just 127. 6LoWPAN uses compression techniques to reduce the size of these headers, significantly minimizing overhead and making it feasible to transmit IPv6 packets efficiently over constrained networks. This compression allows more room for payload data and reduces the energy consumption required for transmission.

Packet Fragmentation and Reassembly: Given the small MTU size of IEEE 802.15.4, 6LoWPAN must handle packet fragmentation and reassembly. IPv6 packets, which can be much larger than 127 bytes, are divided into smaller fragments that fit within the MTU limits for transmission. The receiving end then reassembles these fragments into the original packet. This capability is essential for ensuring that large packets can be transmitted over networks with small MTUs without data loss or corruption.

Mesh Networking Support: 6LoWPAN supports mesh networking, enabling devices within the network to communicate directly with one another or through intermediate nodes. This feature enhances network coverage and reliability by allowing for multiple communication paths and dynamic routing. Mesh networking is particularly beneficial in environments with physical obstructions or where devices are distributed over a wide area. It ensures that even if a direct path between devices is unavailable, the network can still function effectively by routing data through other nodes.

Low Power Consumption: Designed for low-power devices, 6LoWPAN optimizes for minimal energy consumption. This is crucial for battery-powered sensors and IoT devices, which need to operate for extended periods without frequent battery replacements. By reducing header sizes and supporting efficient routing mechanisms, 6LoWPAN minimizes the power required for communication. This helps extend the battery life of devices, making them more practical for long-term deployments.

Scalability and Flexibility: 6LoWPAN is highly scalable, making it suitable for various applications, from small personal area networks to large-scale industrial deployments. Its architecture supports various topologies and can be adapted to different network sizes and densities. Additionally, 6LoWPAN's flexibility allows it to work with other physical and MAC layer technologies beyond IEEE 802.15.4, providing a versatile solution for diverse IoT environments.

Interoperability with IPv6: A significant advantage of 6LoWPAN is its seamless interoperability with IPv6. By enabling IPv6 connectivity over low-power networks, 6LoWPAN allows resource-constrained devices to integrate into the more prominent Internet architecture. This interoperability facilitates direct device-to-device communication and broader Internet connectivity, enabling advanced IoT applications such as remote monitoring, smart metering, and home automation. It also ensures future-proofing as IPv6 adoption continues to grow.

Security Mechanisms: Security is a fundamental aspect of 6LoWPAN, which incorporates several mechanisms to protect data transmission. Leveraging the security features of IPv6 and IEEE 802.15.4, 6LoWPAN ensures secure communication through link-layer encryption and authentication. Higher-layer security protocols, such as IPsec, can also provide end-to-end security. These measures are essential for protecting sensitive data and maintaining the integrity and confidentiality of communications in IoT networks.

In summary, 6LoWPAN's essential features, including header compression, packet fragmentation and reassembly, mesh networking support, low power consumption, scalability, interoperability with IPv6, and robust security mechanisms, make it a vital protocol for enabling efficient, reliable, and secure communication in low-power IoT networks.

Advantages of 6LoWPAN

6LoWPAN offers several significant advantages that make it an essential protocol for the efficient, reliable, and secure operation of low-power wireless networks in the IoT landscape. These advantages address key challenges such as overhead reduction, data fragmentation, network reliability, power efficiency, scalability, interoperability, and security. Table 2-7 highlights the key advantages of 6LoWPAN and their descriptions.

Table 2-7. List of various advantages of 6LoWPAN

Advantage	Description
Header compression	Reduces the size of IPv6 headers, minimizing overhead and conserving bandwidth for efficient data transmission.
Packet fragmentation and reassembly	Enables the transmission of large IPv6 packets over networks with small MTU sizes by breaking them into smaller fragments and reassembling them at the destination.
Mesh networking support	Enhances network reliability and coverage by allowing devices to communicate directly or through intermediate nodes, providing multiple communication paths.
Low power consumption	Optimizes communication protocols to minimize energy usage, extending the battery life of low-power devices crucial for long-term IoT deployments
Scalability and flexibility	Supports various network topologies and sizes, making it suitable for both small and large-scale IoT applications, and adaptable to different physical and MAC layer technologies.
Interoperability with IPv6	Facilitates seamless integration of low-power devices into the larger IPv6 Internet, enabling direct communication and broader connectivity.
Robust security mechanisms	Incorporates encryption and authentication at the link layer, as well as higher-layer security protocols like IPsec, ensuring the protection of data across the network.

6LoWPAN Architecture and Its Components

6LoWPAN, or IPv6 over low-power wireless personal area networks, is designed to efficiently transmit IPv6 packets over low-power wireless networks, particularly those conforming to the IEEE 802.15.4 standard.

CHAPTER 2 DESIGN AND DEPLOY AZURE EDGE SERVICES

The architecture of 6LoWPAN is tailored to meet the constraints of these networks, which include limited power, processing capabilities, and memory. It incorporates several layers and components to ensure seamless and efficient communication.

Adaptation Layer

The adaptation layer is at the core of the 6LoWPAN architecture, which sits between the network layer (IPv6) and the IEEE 802.15.4 MAC layer. This layer is crucial for handling the specific needs of low-power, low-bandwidth networks. The primary functions of the adaptation layer include:

- Header Compression: The adaptation layer uses header compression techniques to reduce the size of IPv6 headers, which are too large for the small frame size of IEEE 802.15.4. This significantly decreases the overhead, allowing more efficient use of the limited bandwidth.

- Packet Fragmentation and Reassembly: Since the maximum transmission unit (MTU) of IEEE 802.15.4 is only 127 bytes, much smaller than the typical IPv6 packet size, the adaptation layer splits larger packets into smaller fragments. These fragments are reassembled at the destination, ensuring that large data packets can be transmitted over the network.

Network Layer

The network layer in 6LoWPAN handles IPv6 packet forwarding and routing. This layer is responsible for:

- Routing: In a 6LoWPAN network, routing can be done using different protocols, such as RPL (routing protocol for low power and lossy networks). RPL is explicitly designed for low power and lossy networks, providing efficient and reliable routing.

- Addressing: IPv6 provides a vast address space, and 6LoWPAN uses this to identify each network device uniquely. The network layer ensures packets are directed to the correct destination using IPv6 addresses.

Link Layer

Based on IEEE 802.15.4, the link layer is responsible for the network's physical and medium access control (MAC) aspects. Critical functions of the link layer include:

- Medium Access Control (MAC): This sublayer manages access to the radio frequency channel, coordinating how and when devices transmit data to avoid collisions and ensure reliable communication.

- Error Detection and Correction: The link layer includes mechanisms for detecting and correcting errors that may occur during transmission, enhancing the reliability of the data sent over the network.

Physical Layer

The physical layer defines the hardware aspects of the network, such as the radio frequencies and modulation schemes used for wireless communication. IEEE 802.15.4 specifies the following for the physical layer:

- Frequency Bands: IEEE 802.15.4 operates in several frequency bands, including 2.4 GHz, and is widely used due to its global availability and suitable balance between range and data rate.

- Modulation Techniques: The physical layer uses various modulation techniques, such as Direct Sequence Spread Spectrum (DSSS), to provide reliable communication even in interference.

Mesh and Star Topologies

6LoWPAN supports both mesh and star network topologies, providing flexibility in network design:

- Mesh Topology: In a mesh network, multiple devices (nodes) can communicate with each other either directly or through intermediate nodes. This topology enhances network reliability and coverage, as data can be routed through multiple paths if necessary.

- Star Topology: All devices communicate directly with a central coordinator in a star network. This topology simplifies the network structure and is suitable for smaller networks with limited coverage areas.

Security Mechanisms

Security in 6LoWPAN is paramount, given the data sensitivity in IoT applications. Security mechanisms include:

- Link-Layer Security: IEEE 802.15.4 provides link-layer security features such as encryption and authentication to protect data during transmission.

- Network-Layer Security: Higher-layer security protocols, such as IPsec, can provide end-to-end security, ensuring data integrity and confidentiality from the source to the destination.

In summary, the architecture of 6LoWPAN is designed to meet the challenges of low-power wireless networks, providing efficient header compression, robust packet fragmentation and reassembly, flexible routing, and strong security measures. This architecture enables the seamless integration of low-power devices into the broader IPv6 Internet, facilitating the growth of IoT applications.

IoT Network – Physical Layer

The physical layer is the lowest in the OSI model and is fundamental to the functioning of IoT networks. It is responsible for transmitting and receiving raw data between devices over a physical medium. This layer encompasses the hardware components, such as radio transceivers and antennas, as well as the signaling techniques used to encode and transmit data. The physical layer defines the electrical, mechanical, and procedural specifications to establish, maintain, and deactivate the physical link between communicating devices.

IoT networks commonly utilize various frequency bands, including the Industrial, Scientific, and Medical (ISM) bands, which are available globally and include frequencies such as 2.4 GHz, 5.8 GHz, and sub-GHz bands like 868 MHz (Europe) and 915 MHz (North America). These bands are favored

CHAPTER 2   DESIGN AND DEPLOY AZURE EDGE SERVICES

due to their availability for unlicensed use, which reduces costs and simplifies deployment. However, the choice of frequency band impacts the range, data rate, and penetration capabilities of the wireless signal, influencing the overall network performance and suitability for different IoT applications.

The physical layer employs various modulation and coding techniques to transmit data efficiently. Modulation involves altering the properties of a carrier signal (such as its amplitude, frequency, or phase) to encode the data. Typical modulation schemes used in IoT networks include Frequency Shift Keying (FSK), Phase Shift Keying (PSK), and Quadrature Amplitude Modulation (QAM). These techniques are chosen based on the required data rate, power efficiency, and resilience to interference. Error-correcting codes, such as Forward Error Correction (FEC), are also employed to enhance data reliability by enabling the detection and correction of errors during transmission.

Energy efficiency is a critical concern in IoT networks, as many devices are battery-powered and need to operate for extended periods without frequent battery replacements. The physical layer plays a significant role in power consumption through duty cycling, where devices alternate between active and sleep modes to conserve energy. Additionally, power control mechanisms adjust the transmission power based on the distance to the receiver and the required data rate, optimizing energy usage while maintaining reliable communication.

Interference from other devices and environmental factors can significantly impact the performance of IoT networks. The physical layer must handle interference from various sources, including other wireless networks, household appliances, and industrial machinery. Techniques such as spread spectrum (e.g., Direct Sequence Spread Spectrum (DSSS) and Frequency Hopping Spread Spectrum (FHSS)) mitigate interference by spreading the signal over a wider frequency band. Understanding signal propagation characteristics, such as path loss, multipath fading, and shadowing, is crucial for designing robust IoT networks, particularly in challenging environments.

CHAPTER 2   DESIGN AND DEPLOY AZURE EDGE SERVICES

While higher layers in the network stack provide encryption and authentication, the physical layer also incorporates essential security measures to protect IoT networks from attacks. Techniques such as frequency hopping and spread spectrum mitigate interference and enhance security by making it more difficult for eavesdroppers to intercept or jam the signal. Physical layer security can include physical unclonable functions (PUFs) that exploit inherent manufacturing variations to generate unique cryptographic keys, ensuring secure device authentication and communication.

Despite its critical role, the physical layer in IoT networks faces several challenges, including the need for ultra-low power consumption, robust interference mitigation, and secure communication. As IoT deployments continue to grow, advancements in physical layer technologies are essential. Future directions include the development of more efficient modulation and coding schemes, adaptive techniques for dynamic spectrum access, and enhanced physical layer security measures. Innovations in these areas will help overcome existing limitations and support the expanding landscape of IoT applications, ranging from smart homes to industrial automation.

In conclusion, the physical layer is vital to IoT networks, providing the foundation for reliable, efficient, and secure data transmission. Its role in managing frequency bands, modulation techniques, power consumption, and security is crucial for successful IoT system deployment and operation. As technology advances, ongoing research and development in the physical layer will continue to enhance the capabilities and performance of IoT networks, addressing current challenges and enabling new possibilities.

Bluetooth and LoRaWAN are the most commonly used protocols in the physical layer. Bluetooth enables short-range wireless communication between devices, ideal for connecting peripherals like headphones and keyboards, and LoRaWAN, on the other hand, facilitates long-range, low-power communication for Internet of Things (IoT) devices, making it perfect for applications like smart agriculture and smart cities.

Bluetooth

In the IoT (Internet of Things) world, Bluetooth technology is crucial in establishing connectivity among various devices, ranging from smart home appliances to wearable gadgets. Its versatility and low power consumption make it an attractive choice for creating local networks where devices can seamlessly communicate and interact with each other. However, it's important to note that while Bluetooth offers convenience and flexibility, it also brings a set of security challenges that, if not addressed, could compromise the integrity and privacy of IoT networks.

One of the primary security concerns with Bluetooth in IoT networks is unauthorized access. Due to its short-range nature, nearby devices can intercept Bluetooth signals, potentially leading to unauthorized access to sensitive data or control over IoT devices. Therefore, robust authentication mechanisms are essential to prevent unauthorized devices from joining the network and gaining access to critical resources.

Moreover, Bluetooth devices are susceptible to various attacks, such as eavesdropping, man-in-the-middle attacks, and device impersonation. These vulnerabilities can be exploited by malicious actors to intercept communication between devices, manipulate data, or impersonate legitimate devices within the network. However, by implementing encryption protocols and regularly updating device firmware, these risks can be effectively mitigated, enhancing the overall security posture of Bluetooth-enabled IoT networks.

Another security consideration is the risk of Bluetooth device tampering or cloning. Malicious actors may attempt to tamper with or clone Bluetooth devices to gain unauthorized access to the network or compromise its integrity. Employing secure boot mechanisms and device integrity checks can help detect and prevent such tampering attempts, ensuring the authenticity and trustworthiness of devices within the IoT network.

Furthermore, Bluetooth communication channels are susceptible to interference from other wireless devices operating in the same frequency band. This interference can disrupt communication between IoT devices, leading to performance degradation or complete loss of connectivity. Employing frequency hopping techniques and signal strength monitoring can help mitigate the impact of interference and ensure reliable communication within the Bluetooth-enabled IoT network.

Additionally, the proliferation of Bluetooth-enabled IoT devices increases the attack surface for potential security breaches. Each additional device introduces new potential entry points for attackers to exploit, emphasizing the importance of implementing comprehensive security measures across the entire IoT ecosystem. This includes regular security audits, firmware updates, and adherence to industry best practices to mitigate the risk of security breaches and protect sensitive data.

Despite these security challenges, it's important to remember that Bluetooth technology is not stagnant. It continues to evolve, with newer versions incorporating enhanced security features to address existing vulnerabilities. For instance, Bluetooth Low Energy (BLE) introduces features like secure connections and privacy enhancements to improve the security of IoT devices and networks. By staying abreast of emerging security threats and leveraging advancements in Bluetooth technology, IoT stakeholders can build more resilient and secure IoT ecosystems that effectively harness the benefits of connected devices while mitigating potential risks.

Key Feature of Bluetooth

Bluetooth technology, with its wireless connectivity, offers a convenient and cable-free solution for short-range communication between devices. This feature, from personal devices to industrial IoT deployments, allows for seamless data transfer and communication within a range of typically 10 meters to 100 meters, depending on the Bluetooth version and environmental factors. This convenience is a critical factor in Bluetooth's popularity.

Bluetooth's low power consumption, especially in its Bluetooth Low Energy (BLE) variants, is a boon for battery-powered devices such as smartphones, wearables, and IoT sensors. This feature not only helps prolong battery life but also enables efficient operation without the need for frequent recharging or battery replacements. The energy efficiency of Bluetooth is a significant advantage, particularly in IoT applications where energy conservation is critical, such as in remote monitoring systems or wireless sensor networks.

Bluetooth's versatility is another standout feature, as it supports various communication profiles and protocols tailored to different use cases. For instance, Bluetooth audio profiles enable high-quality wireless audio streaming between devices like headphones and speakers. In contrast, data transfer profiles facilitate the exchange of files and information between smartphones, tablets, and computers. Additionally, Bluetooth mesh networking extends its capabilities to support large-scale IoT deployments by enabling communication among many interconnected devices over a wide area.

Bluetooth technology is not just about convenience and efficiency but also about robust security features. These features, including authentication and encryption mechanisms, ensure secure pairing and communication between Bluetooth devices, thereby mitigating the risk of eavesdropping, data tampering, and other security threats. The advancements in Bluetooth security protocols, such as secure simple pairing (SSP) and Bluetooth secure connections, enhance the overall security posture of Bluetooth-enabled devices and networks, providing a reassuring layer of protection against evolving cyber threats.

Interoperability is another crucial advantage of Bluetooth technology, as it is standardized and widely supported across various devices and platforms. This enables seamless connectivity and compatibility between brands and manufacturers, allowing users to easily connect and communicate with Bluetooth-enabled devices regardless of their brand or

CHAPTER 2   DESIGN AND DEPLOY AZURE EDGE SERVICES

operating system. Bluetooth's widespread adoption and interoperability contribute to its ubiquity in consumer electronics, automotive systems, healthcare devices, and industrial automation solutions.

Moreover, Bluetooth technology continues evolving to meet modern wireless communication's evolving needs. Successive iterations of Bluetooth standards introduce improvements in data transfer rates, range, power efficiency, and connectivity features. For instance, Bluetooth 5 introduced enhancements such as increased data throughput, extended range, and support for Bluetooth mesh networking, further expanding the capabilities and applicability of Bluetooth technology in various domains.

In summary, Bluetooth technology's key features, including wireless connectivity, low power consumption, versatility, security, interoperability, and continuous innovation, make it a ubiquitous and indispensable component of modern communication systems and IoT ecosystems. Its ability to facilitate seamless, secure, and energy-efficient wireless communication between devices has revolutionized how we interact with technology and paved the way for various innovative applications across industries.

Advantages of Bluetooth

Bluetooth technology has become integral to our daily lives, powering wireless communication between many devices, from smartphones and laptops to wearable gadgets and smart home appliances. Its versatility, reliability, and low power consumption make it a preferred choice for establishing short-range connections, enabling seamless data transfer and communication in various scenarios. In this discussion, we'll delve into the advantages of Bluetooth technology and how it enhances connectivity and convenience across different applications. Table 2-8 highlights the key advantages of Bluetooth and their descriptions.

Table 2-8. *List of various advantages of Bluetooth*

Advantage	Description
Wireless connectivity	Bluetooth enables wireless communication between devices without the need for cables or wires, providing greater flexibility and convenience in connecting peripherals, such as headphones, speakers, keyboards, and mice.
Low power consumption	Bluetooth technology, particularly in its Bluetooth Low Energy (BLE) variants, boasts low power consumption, making it ideal for battery-powered devices like smartphones, wearables, and IoT sensors, prolonging battery life and enabling efficient operation.
Versatility	Bluetooth supports various communication profiles and protocols tailored to different use cases, including audio streaming, data transfer, and device control, allowing it to cater to a wide range of applications across consumer electronics, automotive, healthcare, and industrial sectors.
Security	Bluetooth incorporates robust security features, including authentication and encryption mechanisms, to protect data privacy and prevent unauthorized access, ensuring secure pairing and communication between devices and mitigating the risk of security breaches.
Interoperability	Bluetooth technology is standardized and widely supported across different devices and platforms, facilitating seamless connectivity and compatibility between various brands and manufacturers, regardless of the operating system, enhancing user convenience and accessibility.
Continuous innovation	Bluetooth technology continues to evolve with successive iterations introducing improvements in data transfer rates, range, power efficiency, and connectivity features, ensuring its relevance and applicability in the ever-changing landscape of wireless communication.

CHAPTER 2   DESIGN AND DEPLOY AZURE EDGE SERVICES

Bluetooth – Architecture and Its Components

Bluetooth architecture is a sophisticated and intricate framework that facilitates wireless communication between devices. It comprises several layers, each with distinct responsibilities, ensuring seamless data exchange and connectivity. The architecture is structured to support various applications, from simple file transfers to complex audio streaming and IoT device interactions. The critical components of Bluetooth architecture include the radio, baseband, Link Manager Protocol (LMP), Host Controller Interface (HCI), Logical Link Control and Adaptation Protocol (L2CAP), and various higher-layer protocols and profiles. Each layer plays a critical role in the overall functioning of Bluetooth technology.

Radio and Baseband: The radio layer is at the foundation of Bluetooth architecture and is responsible for transmitting and receiving data over the 2.4 GHz ISM band. This layer handles the modulation and demodulation of signals, ensuring that data is transmitted efficiently over the air. The baseband layer works closely with the radio, managing the physical channels and links. It oversees the formation of piconets and scatternets, where multiple devices can connect and communicate within a limited range. The baseband layer also handles error correction, data whitening, and channel hopping to minimize interference and enhance communication reliability.

Link Manager Protocol (LMP): The Link Manager Protocol (LMP) operates above the baseband layer, managing link setup, authentication, encryption, and other low-level control functions. LMP is crucial for establishing and maintaining Bluetooth connections. It handles device discovery, connection establishment, and link configuration tasks. LMP ensures secure communication by supporting various security measures, including pairing, authentication, and encryption. It also manages power control and quality of service (QoS) parameters to optimize the performance of Bluetooth links.

CHAPTER 2   DESIGN AND DEPLOY AZURE EDGE SERVICES

Host Controller Interface (HCI): The Host Controller Interface (HCI) bridges the lower layers (radio, baseband, and LMP) and the higher layers of the Bluetooth stack. HCI provides a standardized interface for communication between the host device (e.g., a smartphone or computer) and the Bluetooth controller (the hardware component responsible for handling Bluetooth radio and baseband operations). This separation allows for flexibility in hardware and software implementation. HCI commands and events facilitate the control and monitoring of Bluetooth functions, enabling developers to create versatile Bluetooth applications.

Logical Link Control and Adaptation Protocol (L2CAP): Above the HCI layer lies the Logical Link Control and Adaptation Protocol (L2CAP), which plays a pivotal role in data communication. L2CAP is responsible for multiplexing data from higher-layer protocols and applications, segmenting and reassembling packets, and providing quality service (QoS) features. It supports connection-oriented and connectionless data services, making it suitable for various applications. L2CAP also manages the flow control and error detection, ensuring reliable data transfer across Bluetooth links.

Service Discovery Protocol (SDP): The Service Discovery Protocol (SDP) is essential for identifying the services available on Bluetooth devices. When a Bluetooth device connects to another device, SDP allows it to discover the types of services that the other device supports, such as audio streaming, file transfer, or keyboard input. SDP uses a client-server model, where the client requests service information, and the server responds with the details. This protocol ensures that devices can dynamically adapt to the capabilities of connected devices, enhancing interoperability and user experience.

Higher-Layer Protocols and Profiles: The Bluetooth architecture supports various higher-layer protocols and profiles that define specific applications and use cases. Profiles such as the Hands-Free Profile (HFP), Advanced Audio Distribution Profile (A2DP), and Human Interface Device Profile (HID) specify how Bluetooth devices should communicate for particular functionalities. These profiles leverage underlying protocols

CHAPTER 2   DESIGN AND DEPLOY AZURE EDGE SERVICES

like RFCOMM (Radio Frequency Communication), OBEX (Object Exchange), and ATT (Attribute Protocol) to implement their features. By adhering to standardized profiles, Bluetooth devices can achieve seamless interoperability, enabling a wide range of applications, from wireless headsets to smart home devices.

Security Mechanisms: Security is a critical aspect of Bluetooth architecture, integrated across various layers to protect data and ensure secure communication. Bluetooth employs multiple security mechanisms, including pairing, authentication, encryption, and key management. Pairing establishes a trusted relationship between devices, often requiring user interaction to confirm connections. Authentication verifies the identity of devices, while encryption ensures that data transmitted over Bluetooth links is secure from eavesdropping. Key management protocols handle the generation, distribution, and renewal of encryption keys, maintaining the integrity and confidentiality of Bluetooth communication.

Bluetooth architecture is a comprehensive framework designed to facilitate reliable and secure wireless communication between diverse devices. Its layered approach ensures that each component can be developed and optimized independently, providing flexibility and scalability for various applications. From the physical transmission of data to higher-level application protocols, each layer plays a crucial role in delivering the seamless and ubiquitous connectivity that Bluetooth technology is known for.

IOT Networking Deployment Models

Various networking architectures cater to different scales and requirements in the Internet of Things (IoT).

In general, local area networks (LANs), personal area networks (PANs), and wide area networks (WANs) are foundational components in the realm of networking, each serving distinct purposes and applications. LANs are typically used to connect devices within a limited geographical area,

CHAPTER 2   DESIGN AND DEPLOY AZURE EDGE SERVICES

such as a home, office, or campus. They enable high-speed data transfer and resource sharing among connected devices, making them ideal for environments where proximity allows for efficient communication. For instance, in a typical home automation setup, various sensors and smart devices communicate over a LAN, often Wi-Fi, to provide seamless control and monitoring capabilities.

On the other hand, PANs are designed for very short-range communication, often within a range of a few meters. These networks connect personal devices like smartphones, wearable fitness trackers, and wireless earbuds. Technologies like Bluetooth and Zigbee are prevalent in PANs, facilitating convenient and low-power communication between devices. WANs, in contrast, cover much larger areas, from city-wide networks to global communication systems. They connect multiple LANs and other types of networks, enabling data exchange over long distances. WANs connect remote sites, such as agricultural sensors spread across large farms or multinational corporate networks. Figure 2-5 Illustrates that each type of network – PAN, LAN, and WAN – plays a vital role in the interconnected world, supporting a wide array of applications and services.

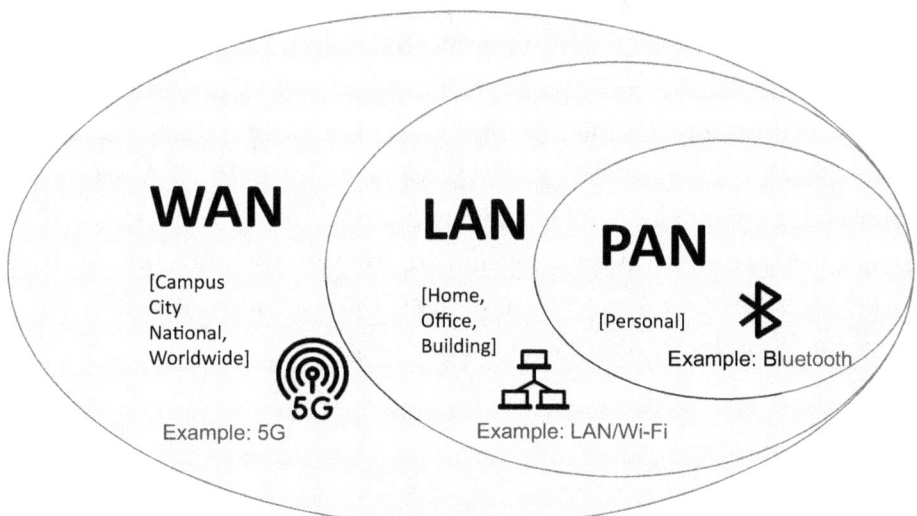

Figure 2-5. *IoT Network Model*

Starting at the most miniature scale, the personal area network (PAN) facilitates communication between devices within the immediate vicinity of an individual, typically spanning a few meters. PAN technologies like Bluetooth and Zigbee enable connecting devices such as smartphones, smartwatches, and sensors, allowing them to interact and exchange data seamlessly. PANs are commonly used in smart homes, healthcare applications, and wearable technology, enabling personalized and localized connectivity.

Moving beyond the PAN, the local area network (LAN) connects devices within a limited geographical area, such as a home, office, or campus. LANs provide higher bandwidth and more excellent coverage than PANs, allowing for the interconnection of multiple devices, including computers, printers, servers, and IoT devices. Ethernet and Wi-Fi are the most common technologies used for LAN connectivity. In IoT applications, LANs enable communication between devices within a specific environment and facilitate tasks such as data sharing, device management, and automation.

At a larger scale, the wide area network (WAN) connects devices over a broad geographical area, typically spanning multiple cities, countries, or even continents. WANs provide long-distance communication capabilities, enabling devices to connect to remote locations and access resources across vast distances. Cellular networks, satellite communications, and the Internet are the backbone for WAN connectivity. In IoT, WANs enable global connectivity for devices, allowing them to transmit data to cloud servers, access remote monitoring and control systems, and communicate worldwide with other devices and services. Table 2-9 illustrates IoT deployment model mapping with IoT protocols.

Table 2-9. *IoT deployment model with IoT protocol mapping*

Category	Acronym	Full Form	Description
PAN	BLE	Bluetooth Low Energy	Wireless communication technology designed for short-range communication with low power consumption, commonly used in IoT devices.
LAN	BW	Bandwidth	The maximum rate of data transfer across a network or communication channel, typically measured in bits per second (bps).
LAN	ISM	Industrial, scientific, and medical	Frequency bands designated for use by industrial, scientific, and medical devices, often used for wireless communication technologies.
LAN	LAN	Local area network	A network that connects devices in a limited geographical area, such as a home, office, or school.
PAN	LoWPAN	Low power wireless personal area network	A network protocol designed for low-power, short-range wireless communication between devices in a personal area network.
PAN	LPWAN	Low power wide area network	A network protocol designed for low-power, long-range communication between IoT devices over a wide area.

(*continued*)

Table 2-9. (*continued*)

Category	Acronym	Full Form	Description
PAN	NFC	Near-field communication	Short-range wireless technology that enables communication between devices when they are in close proximity.
PAN	PAN	Personal area network	A network that connects devices in the immediate vicinity of an individual, typically within a range of a few meters.
PAN	RFID	Radio frequency identification	Technology that uses radio waves to identify and track objects, commonly used in inventory management, access control, and payment systems.
WAN	VSAT	Very small aperture terminal	Satellite communication system that uses small dish antennas for two-way satellite communication.
WAN	WAN	Wide area network	A network that covers a broad geographical area, typically spanning multiple cities or countries, connecting LANs and other networks.
PAN	WPAN	Wireless personal area network	A network that connects devices within the immediate vicinity of an individual, typically using wireless technologies such as Bluetooth or Zigbee.

IoT Networking Considerations and Challenges

The Internet of Things (IoT) is revolutionizing the way devices communicate, enabling a wide array of applications, from smart homes to industrial automation. However, the deployment of IoT systems involves several critical networking considerations and challenges. Range, bandwidth, power usage, intermittent connectivity, interoperability, and security play pivotal roles in ensuring the effectiveness and reliability of IoT networks.

Range and bandwidth are fundamental aspects that determine data transmission efficiency within an IoT network. The range dictates the distance over which devices can communicate, impacting the choice of networking technologies, while bandwidth influences the volume and speed of data transfer. Power usage is another crucial factor, as many IoT devices rely on limited power sources like batteries or solar cells, necessitating energy-efficient communication protocols and power management strategies.

Moreover, intermittent connectivity and interoperability present significant challenges. IoT devices often face connectivity issues due to periodic connections or unreliable networks, which can disrupt data flow and system performance. Interoperability, or the ability of devices to work seamlessly with various other systems, is essential for creating cohesive IoT ecosystems. Finally, security is paramount, as IoT networks are vulnerable to various cyber threats, requiring robust authentication, encryption, and port protection mechanisms to safeguard data and maintain system integrity. Addressing these considerations is critical for the successful deployment and operation of IoT applications.

When selecting networking technologies for your IoT application, consider the following constraints.

Range

Networks are defined by the distances over which data is typically transmitted by the IoT devices connected to the network:

- PAN (personal area network): This type of network is suitable for short ranges, typically measured in meters. For example, a wearable fitness tracker communicates via Bluetooth Low Energy (BLE) with a smartphone app.

- LAN (local area network): Effective for short to medium ranges, up to hundreds of meters. Home automation systems or factory sensors communicate over Wi-Fi with a gateway within the same building.

- WAN (wide area network): This type of network is ideal for long distances, measured in kilometers. Agricultural sensors on a large farm monitor environmental conditions and communicate over long-range networks like LoRaWAN.

Choose a network protocol that matches the required range. For instance, BLE is unsuitable for WAN applications needing several kilometers of coverage. If range poses a challenge, consider edge computing, where data is processed locally on the device rather than transmitted to a distant data center.

Bandwidth

Bandwidth is the data transmission rate over a period. It impacts how quickly data can be collected and sent from IoT devices. Factors affecting bandwidth include

- The amount of data each device gathers and transmits
- The number of deployed devices
- Data transmission patterns (constant stream vs. intermittent bursts)
- Packet size compatibility with data volume

Wireless and cellular networks typically offer lower bandwidth, which might be better for high-volume applications. Consider whether all raw data needs to be transmitted. Reducing data capture frequency, aggregating data before transmission, and filtering insignificant data can decrease bandwidth requirements, but these methods can affect data granularity and responsiveness.

Power Usage

Data transmission consumes power, especially over long distances. Consider the power source – battery, solar cell, or capacitor – and the device's lifecycle. To extend battery life, use strategies like sleep mode during inactivity. Modeling the device's energy consumption under different loads and network conditions helps ensure the power supply matches the data transmission requirements of the chosen networking technology.

Intermittent Connectivity

Due to periodic design or unreliable networks, IoT devices may only occasionally be connected. Incorporate solutions to handle intermittent connectivity, especially if consistent service is critical. Address issues like network interference or channel contention, which can affect wireless networks using shared spectrums.

CHAPTER 2   DESIGN AND DEPLOY AZURE EDGE SERVICES

Interoperability

Interoperability refers to devices' ability to work with various other devices and systems. Standard protocols can help, but IoT standardization often needs to catch up to technological advancements. Consider the adoption rate, openness, and availability of multiple technology implementations to ensure better interoperability in your IoT network.

Security

Security is paramount. Select networking technologies that offer end-to-end security, including authentication, encryption, and port protection:

- Authentication: Use secure protocols for authenticating devices, gateways, users, services, and applications. The X.509 standard is commonly used for device authentication.

- Encryption: For Wi-Fi, employ WPA2 for network encryption. Consider a Private Pre-Shared Key (PPSK) approach. Use TLS or DTLS to encrypt application data and ensure its integrity, with DTLS adapted for unreliable connections over UDP.

- Port Protection: Ensure only necessary ports for communication remain open, and protect other ports with firewalls. Disable UPnP on routers to avoid vulnerabilities that might expose device ports.

By carefully considering these factors, you can effectively plan and implement a robust and secure IoT network tailored to your specific application requirements.

CHAPTER 2   DESIGN AND DEPLOY AZURE EDGE SERVICES

Design Azure IOT Edge

Azure IoT Edge is a robust platform combining a cloud service with a runtime environment that operates on edge devices. This runtime initiates and manages workflows on the device, consisting of a series of interconnected containers to create end-to-end solutions. Managed through Azure IoT Hub, IoT Edge enables running complex workloads at the edge, leveraging Docker-compatible containers for various applications, including artificial intelligence, third-party services, and custom business logic.

Critical Capabilities of Azure IoT Edge

The following listed elements highlight key capabilities of Azure IoT Edge.

- Near Real-Time Local Response: By processing data locally, IoT Edge reduces the need for constant cloud communication, enabling quicker responses to local changes and minimizing latency. It also allows for specialized hardware, such as field-programmable gate arrays (FPGAs), for enhanced processing.

- Edge Device Management: IoT Edge provides tools for remote management and deployment of workloads to edge devices via IoT Hub, ensuring streamlined operations and easy maintenance.

- Containerized Deployment: Using Docker-compatible containers, IoT Edge allows seamless deployment of business logic and applications at the edge.

- Secure and Certified Hardware: IoT Edge supports deployment on certified IoT Edge hardware for both Linux and Windows devices, ensuring secure and reliable operations.

- Distributed AI and Analytics: Models developed and trained in the cloud can be deployed to edge devices that process data locally and respond swiftly to events, enhancing real-time analytics capabilities.

- Leverage Existing Skills and Code: IoT Edge supports multiple programming languages, including C, C#, Java, Node.js, and Python, allowing developers to use their existing skills and codebases.

- Cost-Effective Data Management: IoT Edge enables selective data transmission to the cloud, sending only necessary or aggregated data to reduce bandwidth and storage costs, thus optimizing data management expenses.

- Reliable Offline Operation: IoT Edge ensures that devices operate seamlessly in offline or intermittent connectivity scenarios. It synchronizes the latest device state with the cloud once connectivity is restored.

- Enhanced Security: Working with IoT Hub, IoT Edge ensures secure communication between devices, corrects software installations, and integrates with Microsoft Defender for Cloud for added protection. It also supports hardware security modules for robust authenticated connections.

- Privacy Protection: IoT Edge helps safeguard personal data by processing and cleansing it locally before sending it to the cloud, ensuring compliance with privacy regulations and enhancing data confidentiality.

- Protocol Gateway Functionality: IoT Edge can act as a protocol gateway, providing connectivity and edge analytics to IoT devices that might otherwise lack these capabilities.
- Third-Party Modules: The Azure marketplace offers a variety of third-party modules that can be integrated with IoT Edge, reducing time to market and enhancing the robustness of edge solutions.

In summary, Azure IoT Edge is a versatile platform that enables efficient, secure, and cost-effective edge computing, enhancing the capabilities of IoT devices by bringing cloud functionality closer to the data source.

Key Components of Azure IoT Edge

Containerized Linux workloads can be deployed, run, and monitored using Azure IoT Edge.

The cloud is one of many places where analytics can drive business value in IoT solutions. Azure IoT Edge lets you use the analytical power of the cloud to make offline decisions and drive better business insights. For example, anomaly detection workloads can be run at the edge to respond to production line emergencies as quickly as possible. Cleaning and aggregating the data locally and sending only the insights to the cloud can reduce bandwidth costs and avoid transferring terabytes of raw data.

With Azure IoT Edge, a feature of Azure IoT Hub, you can scale out and manage an IoT solution from the cloud. With the Azure Marketplace, you can easily compose, deploy, and maintain your IoT Edge solution by packaging your business logic into standard containers and using optional prebuilt modules.

Azure IoT Edge is composed of three key components.

CHAPTER 2 DESIGN AND DEPLOY AZURE EDGE SERVICES

IoT Edge Modules

Azure IoT Edge allows you to deploy and manage business logic on the edge in modules. These modules are the smallest unit of computation managed by IoT Edge and can contain Azure services (such as Azure Stream Analytics) or your solution-specific code. Understanding how modules are developed, deployed, and maintained involves four conceptual elements:

- Module Image: A module image contains the software that defines a module.

- Module Instance: A module instance is a specific unit of computation running the module image on an IoT Edge device, started by the IoT Edge runtime.

- Module Identity: A module identity is information, including security credentials, stored in IoT Hub and associated with each module instance.

- Module Twin: A module twin is a JSON document stored in IoT Hub that contains state information for a module instance, including metadata, configurations, and conditions.

Module Images and Instances: IoT Edge module images contain applications that leverage the IoT Edge runtime's management, security, and communication features. These images can be developed by you or exported from supported Azure services, such as Azure Stream Analytics. Module images exist in the cloud and can be updated, changed, and deployed in various solutions. For example, a machine learning module predicting production line output is a different image from a computer vision module controlling a drone.

Each time a module image is deployed to a device and started by the IoT Edge runtime, a new instance of that module is created. Thus, two devices in different parts of the world can use the same module image, but each will have its module instance when the module is started on the device. Practically, module images exist as container images in a repository, and module instances run on devices.

Module Identities: The IoT Edge runtime receives a corresponding module identity when it creates a new module instance. This identity is stored in IoT Hub and serves as the addressing and security scope for all local and cloud communications for that module instance. The identity associated with a module instance depends on the identity of the device on which it runs and the name you assign to that module in your solution. For example, if you name a module "insight" that uses Azure Stream Analytics and deploy it on a device called "Hannover01," the IoT Edge runtime creates a corresponding module identity called "/devices/Hannover01/modules/insight."

If you need to deploy the same module image multiple times on the same device, you can do so with different names, ensuring each module instance has a unique identity.

Module Twins: Each module instance has a corresponding module twin used for configuration. The instance and the twin are linked through the module identity. A module twin is a JSON document that stores information and configuration properties about the module. This concept is similar to the device twin in IoT Hub, sharing the same structure and APIs for interaction. The primary difference is the identity used to instantiate the client SDK.

IoT Edge Cloud Interface

The cloud interface allows for remote monitoring and management of IoT Edge devices. It supports scalable solutions by enabling the creation and configuration of workloads tailored to specific device types. These workloads can then be deployed across multiple devices, regardless of their geographic location. The interface facilitates centralized monitoring, ensuring efficient lifecycle management for various devices.

CHAPTER 2   DESIGN AND DEPLOY AZURE EDGE SERVICES

IoT Edge Runtime

The IoT Edge runtime is a suite of programs designed to transform a device into an IoT Edge device. These components work together to enable the device to receive and execute code at the edge and to communicate the results. The IoT Edge runtime is responsible for several critical functions on IoT Edge devices:

- Installing and updating workloads
- Maintaining Azure IoT Edge security standards
- Ensuring the continuous operation of IoT Edge modules
- Reporting module health to the cloud for remote monitoring

Additionally, it manages communication between downstream devices and IoT Edge devices, between modules on an IoT Edge device, between an IoT Edge device and the cloud, and between IoT Edge devices themselves.

The IoT Edge runtime's responsibilities are divided into two categories: communication and module management, handled by two core components. The IoT Edge agent is tasked with deploying and monitoring modules, while the IoT Edge hub manages communication. The IoT Edge agent and IoT Edge hub are modules themselves, often called runtime modules, just like any other module running on an IoT Edge device.

IoT Edge Agent: At the heart of the Azure IoT Edge runtime is the IoT Edge agent, one of the two modules that constitute it. The IoT Edge agent's role is multi-faceted, including the instantiation of modules, ensuring their continuous operation, and reporting their status back to IoT Hub. This status is recorded as a property of the IoT Edge agent module twin. Upon device startup, the IoT Edge security daemon triggers the initiation of the IoT Edge agent. The agent then retrieves its module twin from IoT

CHAPTER 2   DESIGN AND DEPLOY AZURE EDGE SERVICES

Hub and scrutinizes the deployment manifest, a JSON file that specifies the modules to be started and provides detailed information for managing each module's lifecycle. The IoT Edge agent communicates runtime responses to IoT Hub, which can encompass statuses such as 200 (OK), 400 (malformed or invalid deployment configuration), 417 (no deployment configuration set), 412 (invalid schema version), 406 (device offline or not sending status reports), and 500 (runtime error).

IoT Edge Hub: The IoT Edge hub is the other core module that constitutes the Azure IoT Edge runtime. It functions as a local proxy for IoT Hub by providing the same protocol endpoints, allowing clients to connect to the IoT Edge runtime just as they would to IoT Hub. However, the IoT Edge Hub is a partial local version of the IoT Hub; it delegates specific tasks to the IoT Hub. For instance, on its first connection, the IoT Edge hub automatically downloads authorization information from the IoT Hub to enable the device to connect. This authorization information is then cached locally, allowing future connections from the device to be authorized without needing to re-download the information from the cloud.

To reduce the bandwidth usage of your IoT Edge solution, the IoT Edge hub optimizes the number of actual connections made to the cloud by consolidating logical connections from modules or downstream devices into a single physical connection. This process is transparent to the rest of the solution, so clients believe they have their connection to the cloud, even though they share the same connection. The IoT Edge hub can communicate upstream with the cloud using either the AMQP or MQTT protocol, independently of the protocols used by downstream devices. However, it supports combining logical connections into a single physical connection only through AMQP and its multiplexing capabilities, with AMQP being the default upstream protocol. The IoT Edge hub can detect its connection status with IoT Hub and will cache messages or twin updates locally if the connection is lost. Once reconnected, it syncs all the cached data. The cache location is specified by a property of the IoT Edge hub's module twin and will grow as needed, limited only by the device's storage capacity.

207

The IoT Edge hub also facilitates local communication by brokering messages for device-to-module and module-to-module interactions, keeping them independent. This brokering mechanism uses the same routing features as IoT Hub to define how messages are passed between devices or modules. Devices or modules specify the inputs where they accept messages and the outputs where they write messages. A solution developer can route messages between these sources and destinations with potential filters. Routing is supported for devices or modules built with the Azure IoT Device SDKs using the AMQP protocol, and it supports all IoT Hub messaging primitives such as telemetry, direct methods, C2D, and twins. Still, it does not support communication over user-defined topics.

The IoT Edge hub accepts connections from device or module clients using the MQTT or AMQP protocol. When a client connects to the IoT Edge hub, the following steps occur:

- Secure Connections (TLS): By default, the IoT Edge hub only accepts connections secured with Transport Layer Security (TLS), ensuring encrypted communication that third parties cannot decrypt. If a client connects on port 8883 (MQTTS) or 5671 (AMQPS), a TLS channel must be established. During the TLS handshake, the IoT Edge hub sends its certificate chain, which the client must validate using the root certificate installed as a trusted certificate on the client. If the root certificate is not trusted, the connection will be rejected with a certificate verification error.

- Authentication: The IoT Edge hub only accepts connections from devices or modules with an IoT Hub identity, which can be authenticated using symmetric keys, X.509 self-signed certificates, or X.509 CA-signed certificates. The IoT Edge hub verifies these identities

CHAPTER 2   DESIGN AND DEPLOY AZURE EDGE SERVICES

locally, allowing connections to be made even when offline. IoT Edge modules currently only support symmetric key authentication.

- Authorization: The IoT Edge hub verifies that a client belongs to its set of trusted clients as defined in IoT Hub. This is done by setting up parent/child or device/module relationships in IoT Hub. When a module is created in IoT Edge, a trust relationship is automatically established between it and its IoT Edge device, the only authorization model supported by the routing brokering mechanism.

The cloud fully controls the IoT Edge hub and gets its configuration from the IoT Hub via its module twin. The twin contains a desired property called routes that declares how messages are passed within a deployment. Additional configurations can be set up using environment variables on the IoT Edge hub.

The following are the other key components added to Azure IoT Edge services

Provisioning: Each IoT Edge device needs to be provisioned, a two-step process. The first step involves registering the device in an IoT hub and creating a cloud identity that the device uses to establish a connection to its hub. The second step is configuring the device with this cloud identity. Provisioning can be done manually for each device or at scale using the IoT Hub Device Provisioning Service, simplifying the extensive deployment process.

Authentication: IoT Edge devices must verify their identity when connecting to IoT Hub. Several authentication methods are available, including symmetric vital passwords, certificate thumbprints, and trusted platform modules (TPMs). The choice of authentication method can depend on the security requirements and the scale of the deployment.

209

Platform Options: The container and host operating systems define platform options for IoT Edge. The container operating system runs inside the IoT Edge runtime and module containers, while the host operating system is the OS of the device running these containers and modules.

There are three primary platform choices for IoT Edge devices:

- Linux Containers on Linux Hosts: This option involves running Linux-based IoT Edge containers directly on a Linux host. It is a straightforward setup for environments that are already using Linux.

- Linux Containers on Windows Hosts: Here, Linux-based IoT Edge containers run in a Linux virtual machine on a Windows host. This configuration is often referred to as IoT Edge for Linux on Windows or EFLOW.

- Windows Containers on Windows Hosts: This setup runs Windows-based IoT Edge containers directly on a Windows host. However, it is essential to note that IoT Edge version 1.2 or later does not support Windows containers; only versions up to 1.1 do.

Linux Containers on Linux

The IoT Edge runtime is installed directly on Linux host devices. IoT Edge supports various Linux devices, including X64, ARM32, and ARM64 architectures. Microsoft provides official installation packages for different operating systems, ensuring broad compatibility and ease of deployment.

Linux Containers on Windows

IoT Edge for Linux on Windows hosts a Linux virtual machine on a Windows device. This virtual machine comes prebuilt with the IoT Edge runtime, and updates are managed through Microsoft Update.

CHAPTER 2　DESIGN AND DEPLOY AZURE EDGE SERVICES

This configuration is recommended for running IoT Edge on Windows devices due to its seamless integration and update management.

Windows Containers on Windows

Starting with IoT Edge version 1.2, support for Windows containers has been discontinued. Therefore, only versions up to 1.1 support running Windows-based containers directly on Windows hosts. For newer versions, other platform options should be considered.

Provisioning Devices

Provisioning IoT Edge devices can be done individually or at scale, depending on the needs of the deployment. Single-device provisioning involves manually setting up each IoT Edge device without the assistance of the IoT Hub Device Provisioning Service (DPS). This process requires entering provisioning information, such as a connection string, directly into each device. While this method is quick and easy for a few devices, it becomes cumbersome as the number of devices increases. It supports symmetric keys and X.509 self-signed authentication methods.

Authentication Methods

- X.509 Certificate Attestation: X.509 certificates as an attestation mechanism are recommended for scaling production and simplifying device provisioning. Typically, X.509 certificates form a chain of trust, from a root certificate to the device certificate. When creating a new device identity in IoT Hub, thumbprints from the certificates are provided for verification. The device presents one certificate during authentication, which IoT Hub verifies against its thumbprint. The keys should be stored in a Hardware Security Module (HSM) for enhanced security.

- Trusted Platform Module (TPM) Attestation: TPM attestation leverages both software and hardware features for device provisioning. Each TPM chip uses a unique endorsement key for authentication. This method is available only for provisioning at scale with DPS and supports individual enrollments due to the device-specific nature of TPM. TPM attestation is more secure than symmetric keys and is recommended for production scenarios.

- Symmetric Keys Attestation: Symmetric key attestation is a more straightforward approach to device authentication, ideal for initial development and scenarios with less stringent security requirements. When a new device identity is created in the IoT Hub, two keys are generated. One of these keys is placed on the device for authentication. While this method allows for quick setup, it is less secure than X.509 certificates or TPM attestation. More robust methods should be used for solutions requiring higher security.

Managing IoT Devices at Scale

Managing the software lifecycle for millions of varied IoT devices across different locations is a significant challenge. IoT Edge addresses this by enabling the creation, configuration, deployment, and monitoring of workloads for specific device types at scale. This approach is essential for complex event processing or edge-device machine learning applications.

For instance, implementing machine learning involves:

- Training the Model in the Cloud: Models are initially developed and trained in the cloud environment.

- Deploying to Edge Devices: The trained models are encapsulated in Docker-compatible containers and deployed to various edge devices across multiple locations.

- Running and Updating Locally: Once deployed, these models operate locally, often in offline modes, and require periodic updates.

IoT Edge facilitates this end-to-end deployment cycle, with the runtime and cloud interface continuously monitoring the status of the machine learning modules.

Azure IoT Edge provides a comprehensive framework for deploying, managing, and monitoring edge computing solutions, enabling efficient and secure operations across many IoT devices.

Key Design Considerations of Azure IoT Edge

Designing an effective Azure IoT Edge solution involves several key considerations to ensure robust, scalable, and secure deployments. According to Microsoft's guidelines, here are the main factors to focus on.

Architecture and Topology

- Edge Devices: Select appropriate edge devices based on processing power, storage capacity, and connectivity options. Ensure they can handle the workloads and have the necessary hardware accelerators.

- Modules and Containerization: Use Docker containers for deploying IoT Edge modules, enabling modular, isolated, and consistent runtime environments.

- Deployment Models: For hierarchical management, consider different deployment models, such as single-device deployments, tiered deployments (gateway and edge devices), and nested edge deployments.

Security

- Device Security: To protect edge devices, implement strong security measures, including secure boot, TPM (Trusted Platform Module), and regular firmware updates.

- Communication Security: Ensure all data transmission between IoT Edge devices and the cloud or other devices is encrypted using protocols like TLS.

- Module Security: Utilize secure coding practices and container security, ensuring that modules run with the least privilege and are regularly scanned for vulnerabilities.

Scalability and Reliability

- Scalability: Plan for scaling your IoT solution by considering the ability to manage numerous devices and data streams. Use Azure IoT Hub to handle device provisioning, management, and communication at scale.

- Reliability: Implement failover mechanisms and redundant edge devices to ensure high availability and resilience. Consider the edge device's capacity to operate autonomously during cloud connectivity disruptions.

Data Management and Analytics

- Local Data Processing: Perform data processing and analytics at the edge to reduce latency, bandwidth usage, and reliance on cloud connectivity. Utilize AI and machine learning models within edge modules.

- Data Storage: Decide on temporary or permanent data storage at the edge, ensuring compliance with data retention policies and efficient synchronization with cloud storage when needed.

Connectivity and Networking

- Network Topology: Design network topology to support reliable and efficient communication between devices, gateways, and the cloud. Consider the use of protocols like MQTT, AMQP, and HTTP.

- Offline Capabilities: Ensure edge devices can function independently during network outages, buffering data locally and syncing with the cloud once connectivity is restored.

Management and Monitoring

- Device Management: Use Azure IoT Hub and Azure IoT Central for device provisioning, configuration, and management. Implement automated deployment and update strategies for edge modules.

- Monitoring and Diagnostics: Utilize Azure Monitor, Azure Log Analytics, and Azure Security Center to monitor the health, performance, and security of IoT Edge devices and modules. Implement logging and alerting mechanisms to address issues promptly.

Cost Management

- Resource Utilization: Optimize resource utilization on edge devices to balance performance and cost. Monitor and manage the usage of compute, storage, and network resources.

- Cost-effective Architecture: Design the solution to minimize cloud costs by leveraging edge computing for local processing and reducing data transmission to the cloud.

Compliance and Regulatory Requirements

- Data Privacy: Ensure that data handling at the edge complies with relevant data privacy regulations such as GDPR. Implement measures for data anonymization and encryption.

- Regulatory Standards: Adhere to industry-specific standards and regulations that may dictate specific security, data management, and operational practices.

By focusing on these key design considerations, you can create robust and efficient Azure IoT Edge solutions that meet the specific needs of your applications while ensuring security, scalability, and cost-effectiveness.

CHAPTER 2   DESIGN AND DEPLOY AZURE EDGE SERVICES

Key decision for large enterprise planning for IoT Deployment.

- Near Real-Time Response to Local Changes: Does your application need to react quickly to local changes in near real time? IoT Edge can run modules locally on devices, enabling faster response to these changes.

- Deployment and Management Using Containers: Does your application need to be deployed on IoT Edge devices in Docker-compatible containers? IoT Edge supports containerization, allowing you to manage software dependencies such as runtimes and libraries, ensuring consistent application performance across different environments.

- Security for IoT Edge Deployments: Security is a critical concern for IoT deployments. IoT Edge enhances security by integrating with Microsoft Defender for Cloud and utilizing hardware security modules, ensuring strong authentication and secure connections for confidential computing.

- Offline or Intermittent Mode Operation: Does your application need to operate with intermittent or offline connectivity? Once reconnected, IoT Edge devices can automatically synchronize their state with the cloud, ensuring seamless operations.

- AI and Analytics Workloads on IoT Edge: Do you need to run machine learning algorithms on IoT Edge devices? IoT Edge allows you to deploy and run models built and trained in the cloud on local devices.

- Optimize Data Costs: Managing cloud deployment costs is essential. By pre-processing data on IoT Edge devices, you can reduce the data sent to the cloud, optimizing data transfer and storage costs.

- Privacy for IoT Edge Deployments: Do you need to ensure compliance with privacy regulations? IoT Edge can protect personally identifiable information by keeping data on-premise, enhancing compliance with privacy standards.

Key Production Best Practices

Table 2-10 outlines essential configurations and best practices for setting up IoT Edge devices. These devices range from simple Raspberry Pi units to powerful laptops and virtual servers running on servers. Proper configuration ensures optimal performance and security if you have physical or virtual access to these devices or if they are isolated for extended periods. The table categorizes various aspects of device configuration, deployment, networking, solution management, and security considerations, providing detailed actions and guidelines for each area. Table 2-10 lists key best practices to be considered during the deployment.

Table 2-10. Key best practices

Category	Configuration
Device configuration	
Devices	IoT Edge devices can be anything from a Raspberry Pi to a laptop to a virtual machine running on a server.
Install production certificates	Ensure production certificates are installed.
Device management plan	Have a plan for managing devices.
Container engine	Use Moby as the container engine.
Protocol choice	Choose a consistent upstream protocol.
Deployment	
Consistency	Be consistent with the chosen upstream protocol.
Host storage	Set up host storage for system modules.
Memory usage	Reduce the memory space used by the IoT Edge hub.
Module images	Use correct module images in deployment manifests.
Twin size limits	Be mindful of twin size limits when using custom modules.
Update configuration	Configure how updates to modules are applied.
Networking	
Outbound/inbound	Review outbound/inbound configuration.
Device connections	Allow connections from IoT Edge devices.
Proxy communication	Configure communication through a proxy.
DNS server	Set DNS server in container engine settings.

(continued)

Table 2-10. (*continued*)

Category	Configuration
Solution management	
Logs and diagnostics	Set up logs and diagnostics.
Logging driver	Set up default logging driver.
Testing and CI/CD	Consider tests and CI/CD pipelines.
Security considerations	
Container registry	Manage access to your container registry.
Host resource access	Limit container access to host resources.

Deploy Azure IOT Edge

Deploying Azure IoT Edge involves systematically setting up and managing your IoT infrastructure. This guide is divided into four key phases, ensuring a comprehensive understanding of the deployment process. First, we will guide you through setting up an IoT Hub, which acts as the central communication hub for your IoT devices, enabling efficient data exchange and device management. Following this, you will learn how to register an IoT Edge device with your IoT Hub, a crucial step that allows the device to connect and communicate effectively with the hub.

Next, we will walk you through installing and starting the IoT Edge runtime on your chosen virtual device. This step is essential as it establishes the foundational framework required for deploying and managing modules on your IoT Edge device. Finally, we will demonstrate how to deploy a module to your IoT Edge device, empowering you to distribute and execute containerized code seamlessly on your edge devices. By following these phases, you can harness the full potential of Azure IoT Edge, enabling robust and scalable edge computing solutions.

CHAPTER 2   DESIGN AND DEPLOY AZURE EDGE SERVICES

In this section, let's delve into the four processes for deploying Azure IoT Edge:

- Setting Up IoT Hub: First, we'll guide you through creating an IoT Hub, which serves as the central communication hub for your IoT devices.

- Registering an IoT Edge Device: Next, you'll learn how to register an IoT Edge device to your IoT Hub. This step allows the device to establish a connection and communicate with the hub effectively.

- Installing and Starting IoT Edge Runtime: You'll be walked through the process of installing and initializing the IoT Edge runtime on your chosen virtual device. This step provides the foundational framework required for deploying and managing modules.

- Module Deployment: Lastly, we'll demonstrate how to deploy a module to your IoT Edge device. This capability empowers you to seamlessly distribute and execute containerized code on your edge devices.

Step 1: Setting Up IoT Hub

The provided code snippet creates a free F1 hub within the resource group IoTEdgeResources. Replace {hub_name} with a unique name for your IoT Hub. It may take a few minutes for the IoT Hub to be created.

Key Note: Use the Bash environment in Azure Cloud Shell.

```
az iot hub create --resource-group IoTEdgeResources --name {hub_name} --sku F1 --partition-count 2
```

If you encounter an error due to an existing free hub in your subscription, the solution is to change the SKU to S1. Remember, each subscription can only have one free IoT Hub. Similarly, if you receive an error indicating that the IoT Hub name is unavailable, it means that someone else is already using the specified name. In such cases, please try a different name to resolve the issue.

Spte 2: Registering an IoT Edge Device

Generate a device identity for your IoT Edge device to facilitate communication with your IoT Hub. This identity resides in the cloud, and you'll utilize a distinct device connection string to link a physical device to its corresponding identity.

Given that IoT Edge devices possess unique behaviors and management requirements compared to conventional IoT devices, specify this identity as being intended for an IoT Edge device by including the --edge-enabled flag.

Azure Cloud Shell, execute the following command to create a device named myEdgeDevice in your hub:

```
az iot hub device-identity create --device-id myEdgeDevice --edge-enabled --hub-name {hub_name}
```

If you encounter an error regarding iothubowner policy keys, ensure that your Cloud Shell runs the latest version of the Azure-iot extension.

To retrieve the connection string for your device, which links your physical device with its identity in IoT Hub, use the following Azure CLI command:

```
az iot hub device-identity connection-string show --device-id myEdgeDevice --hub-name {hub_name}
```

Step 3: Installing and Starting IoT Edge Runtime: Create a virtual machine with the Azure IoT Edge runtime. The IoT Edge runtime, which is deployed on all IoT Edge devices, consists of three components:

- IoT Edge Security Daemon: This component starts each time the IoT Edge device boots, bootstrapping the device by initiating the IoT Edge agent.

- IoT Edge Agent: This agent facilitates the deployment and monitoring of modules on the IoT Edge device, including the IoT Edge hub.

- IoT Edge Hub: This hub manages communications between modules on the IoT Edge device and between the device and the IoT Hub.

During the runtime configuration, you will provide a device connection string. This string, which you retrieved from the Azure CLI, links your physical device to the IoT Edge device identity in Azure.

Step 4: Module Deployment: Manage your Azure IoT Edge device from the cloud to deploy a module that sends telemetry data to IoT Hub. One of the key features of Azure IoT Edge is the ability to deploy code to your IoT Edge devices from the cloud. IoT Edge modules are executable packages implemented as containers. Following is the procedure for you to deploy a pre-built module from Azure Marketplace's IoT Edge Modules section directly from Azure IoT Hub.

Steps to Deploy a Module from Azure Marketplace

Sign in to Azure Portal: Go to your IoT Hub in the Azure portal.

1. Access Device Management: From the menu on the left, under Device Management, select Devices.

2. Select Target Device: Choose the device ID of the target IoT Edge device from the list.

CHAPTER 2   DESIGN AND DEPLOY AZURE EDGE SERVICES

3. Set Modules: If the status code 417 appears (the device's deployment configuration is not set), the device is ready for module deployment and Select Set Modules on the upper bar.

4. Choose Modules: Choose from existing modules, Azure Marketplace modules, or custom-built modules. For this example, deploy a module from Azure Marketplace and Under IoT Edge Modules, open the Add drop-down menu, and select Marketplace Module.

5. Add Simulated Temperature Sensor: Search for and select the Simulated Temperature Sensor module in the IoT Edge Module Marketplace. The module is added with the desired running status.

6. Configure Routes: In the Routes, you configure how messages flow between the modules and the IoT Hub. Messages are built using name/value pairs. When a device is deployed for the first time, a default route named "route" is included, specified as FROM /messages/* INTO $upstream. This setup ensures that any messages generated by the modules are directed to the IoT Hub.

7. Select Next: Routes to configure routes and A route named SimulatedTemperatureSensorToIoTHub is created automatically, sending all messages from the simulated temperature module to the IoT Hub.

8. Review and Create Deployment: Select Next: Review + create and Review the JSON file and then select Create. This file defines the modules deployed to your IoT Edge device.

CHAPTER 2   DESIGN AND DEPLOY AZURE EDGE SERVICES

Key Note: When you submit a new deployment, rest assured that the device queries the IoT Hub regularly for new instructions. If it finds an updated deployment manifest, it pulls the module images from the cloud and starts running them locally. This reliable process may take a few minutes, but you can trust that it's working in the background to ensure a smooth deployment.

After creating the module deployment details, you'll return to the device details page. You can view the deployment status on the Modules tab. You should see three modules: $edgeAgent, $edgeHub, and SimulatedTemperatureSensor. If some modules show "Yes" under Specified in Deployment but not under Reported by Device, the IoT Edge device is still starting them. Wait a few minutes and refresh the page.

Summary

This chapter introduces readers to the fundamental concepts of IoT network and security. The chapter begins with IoT network protocols. IoT network protocols are essential for communication between devices and systems in the Internet of Things (IoT) ecosystem. Standard protocols include MQTT, CoAP, and HTTP, each with specific use cases and advantages. MQTT, for instance, is lightweight and ideal for devices with limited bandwidth, while CoAP is suited for constrained environments. Understanding these protocols' characteristics and applications is crucial for designing efficient IoT solutions.

IoT network architecture is not just a layout but a crucial structure of devices, gateways, and cloud services that facilitate data flow and management in an IoT system. Key components include edge devices, which collect data; gateways, which process and transmit data; and cloud platforms, which provide storage, analytics, and application support. Your role in effective architecture design ensures the IoT network's scalability, security, and reliability, making you a crucial part of the IoT system.

CHAPTER 2 DESIGN AND DEPLOY AZURE EDGE SERVICES

Azure Network for IoT is a platform and gateway to a world of possibilities. It leverages Microsoft Azure's robust cloud services to create, manage, and monitor IoT solutions. It offers various tools and services like Azure IoT Hub for device connectivity, Azure Digital Twins for modeling physical environments, and Azure IoT Central for simplified device management. Azure's extensive network services enable seamless integration, real-time analytics, and enhanced security for IoT applications, opening up exciting opportunities for innovation.

Designing Azure Edge Services for IoT focuses on bringing cloud capabilities to the network's edge, closer to the data source. This approach reduces latency, enhances response times, and ensures continuous operation even with intermittent cloud connectivity. Key components include Azure IoT Edge, which allows for the deployment of containerized applications on edge devices, and Azure Stack Edge, which provides hardware-accelerated AI and edge computing capabilities.

Deploying Azure Edge Services for IoT involves setting up and configuring the necessary infrastructure to run IoT applications at the edge. This process includes provisioning edge devices, installing and managing IoT Edge runtime, and deploying edge modules. Proper deployment ensures that IoT solutions are efficient, scalable, and can handle real-time processing requirements. Azure provides comprehensive tools and guidelines for smooth deployment and integration with IoT ecosystems.

This chapter provides a foundational understanding of IoT network protocols and architecture, highlights the capabilities of Azure's IoT network services, and outlines the design and deployment processes for Azure edge services. With these insights, you can build robust, scalable, and efficient IoT solutions leveraging Azure's robust cloud and edge computing resources.

CHAPTER 3

Design and Deploy Azure IoT Networks

Network topology serves as the backbone upon which innovative solutions are built. This subsection delves into the fundamental principles that govern network structures, providing a comprehensive understanding of how data flows and devices communicate within an IoT ecosystem. By grasping the intricacies of network topology, readers will gain the insights necessary to design resilient and scalable architectures tailored for Azure environments.

Different network topologies exist, each with its way of connecting devices. All devices are connected to a star topology central hub, simplifying management. Bus topology is like a straight line where devices share the same communication line, which can be a simple and affordable setup. Point-to-point topology connects devices directly for fast, dedicated connections. Hybrid topology mixes different types, giving flexibility. Tree topology is like branches of a tree, with levels of connections. Ring topology forms a circle of connections, ensuring data can flow continuously. Mesh topology offers many ways for devices to connect, which is suitable for reliability. Autonomous network architecture lets devices make decisions independently, while ubiquitous network architecture aims for seamless connections everywhere.

CHAPTER 3   DESIGN AND DEPLOY AZURE IOT NETWORKS

Designing Azure networks for IoT requires a nuanced approach that considers various factors, including scalability, security, and performance. This chapter delves into the intricacies of Azure's network services and provides guidance on architecting networks optimized for IoT workloads. From defining virtual networks and subnets to implementing secure communication protocols, readers will learn how to leverage Azure's suite of tools to create robust infrastructures that support the diverse requirements of IoT applications.

Deploying Azure networks for IoT entails translating design blueprints into tangible implementations. This subsection guides readers through the deployment process through step-by-step instructions and best practices, ensuring smooth integration with existing Azure environments. From provisioning resources to configuring network security policies, readers will gain the practical skills needed to bring their Azure IoT networks to life, empowering them to embark on their journey towards building innovative IoT solutions.

By the end of this chapter, you should be able to understand the following:

- Fundamentals of network topology
- Design Azure Networks for IoT
- Deploy Azure Networks for IoT

Fundamentals of Network Topology

IoT (Internet of Things) network topology refers to the arrangement and interconnection of devices within an IoT ecosystem. In IoT systems, various devices, sensors, and actuators communicate, and centralized systems collect processes and act upon data. The network topology defines how these devices are connected and how data flows between them.

CHAPTER 3   DESIGN AND DEPLOY AZURE IOT NETWORKS

Given the diverse nature of IoT applications, there is no one-size-fits-all approach to network topology. Instead, a topology is chosen based on the number and type of devices, communication requirements, power constraints, and scalability and reliability requirements.

Common IoT network topologies include a star topology, where devices connect to a central hub or gateway; a mesh topology, where devices are interconnected, providing redundant paths for communication; and a hybrid topology, which combines elements of different topologies to meet specific requirements.

An IoT network topology design is concerned more with efficient data transmission and energy conservation. It's a crucial factor in enhancing overall system reliability and security. As IoT deployments expand in scope and scale, the choice of network topology becomes increasingly critical in enabling seamless and robust communication among interconnected devices and systems. Your decisions in network topology design can significantly impact the reliability and security of the entire IoT system, underscoring the gravity of your role as a network professional.

It describes how devices and connections are arranged within a computer network, which makes network topology an essential concept for network professionals. Knowing the intricacies of different network topologies when designing, implementing, and managing efficient communication systems is critical. Besides the star topology, several topologies are commonly used, which connect all devices to a central hub or switch. This setup simplifies troubleshooting and allows easy scalability by adding or removing devices without disrupting the network. On the other hand, a bus topology is cost-effective and straightforward to set up with its linear arrangement and shared communication line, but if the main line fails, the entire network can be halted.

Another prevalent topology is the point-to-point topology, where devices establish direct connections. This topology is often used in telecommunications and provides dedicated communication channels between endpoints. Hybrid topology combines elements of various topologies to suit specific organizational needs. For instance, a network might incorporate Star and Bus topologies to leverage their advantages. Tree topologies are hierarchical structures with multiple levels of interconnected devices. They are commonly used in large networks to maximize scalability and efficiency.

Devices are connected in a closed-loop network with the ring topology to create a continuous data transmission pathway. By providing redundant paths between devices, mesh topologies enhance fault tolerance and reliability and ensure equal access to resources. In mesh networks, each device can communicate directly with any other device, minimizing network downtime. Failures in any one device can disrupt the entire network.

Autonomous networks focus on decentralized control and allow individual devices to make decisions based on local information. On the other hand, ubiquitous network architecture emphasizes seamless connectivity across multiple devices and environments. It provides ubiquitous access to services and resources, which fosters ubiquitous computing.

To meet the evolving needs of modern communication systems, new network topologies and architectures emerge as technology advances. As a network engineer, administrator, or architect, staying up to date with these developments is more than just a professional obligation; it's a strategic advantage that can boost your career significantly. By selecting the appropriate topology for a given scenario, organizations can optimize performance, scalability, and reliability, ultimately enhancing productivity and driving innovation in the digital age. This underscores the importance of understanding network topologies as a continuous learning process for professionals in the field.

CHAPTER 3   DESIGN AND DEPLOY AZURE IOT NETWORKS

Star Topology

In the star topology, each device (node) is connected to a central hub or switch. This central node plays a crucial role as a conduit, facilitating the transmission of messages between the nodes. All peripheral nodes communicate through this central hub, making it a pivotal point for network management and communication. Figure 3-1 provides a high-level view of the star topology.

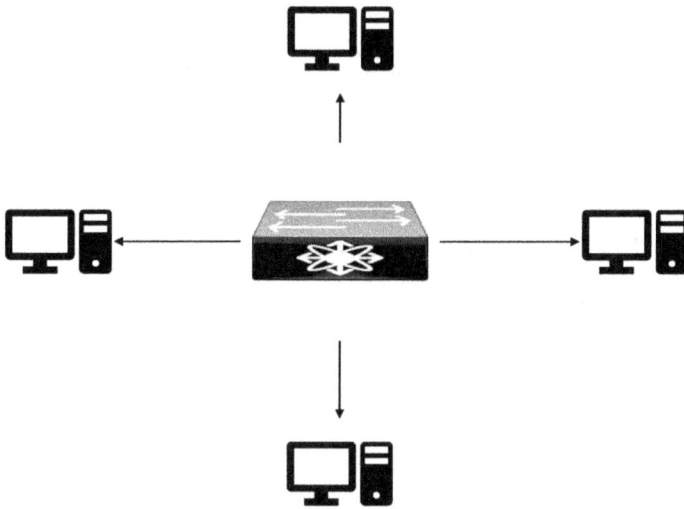

Figure 3-1. Star topology

Relevance to IoT/IIoT Networks

As a result of its straightforward and efficient approach to managing numerous devices, star topology is highly effective in the context of the Internet of Things (IoT) networks. Various sensors and devices communicate with a central system in IoT networks. With a centralized structure, the star topology simplifies the integration and management of these devices, ensuring efficient data transmission and network management.

CHAPTER 3　DESIGN AND DEPLOY AZURE IOT NETWORKS

For IoT devices to generate large amounts of data, the central hub in a star topology can be equipped with advanced processing capabilities. For IIoT applications, real-time data processing and decision-making are crucial for operational efficiency and safety.

Moreover, star topology's centralized nature supports the scalability required in IoT/IIoT networks. As more devices are added, they can be connected to the central hub without extensive reconfiguration of the network, making it easier to expand and adapt to growing needs.

Security is a crucial aspect of IoT/IIoT networks, and star topology offers significant benefits in this area. The central hub can implement robust security measures to monitor and control data flow, protecting the network from unauthorized access and cyber threats. This centralized control is particularly vital in industrial environments where security breaches can lead to significant disruptions and hazards, providing a strong case for the use of star topology in such settings.

However, the dependency on a central hub means that if the hub fails, the entire network can go down. In critical IoT/IIoT applications, this potential single point of failure necessitates the implementation of redundant hubs or backup systems to ensure network reliability and continuity.

Despite this, star topology's ease of troubleshooting and maintenance makes it a preferred choice for many IoT/IIoT deployments. Network issues can be quickly identified and isolated at the central hub, reducing downtime and facilitating efficient network management.

Key Features

Star topology, centralized control, ease of management, and scalability are highly effective network configurations, particularly in IoT and IIoT. Its troubleshooting, security, and modularity advantages make it an appealing choice for managing large, dynamic networks. Despite its potential drawbacks, such as the single point of failure and higher initial costs, its network efficiency and reliability benefits often make it a preferred choice for many applications. Knowing how it works and its key features can help organizations implement and maintain robust and scalable networks effectively. Table 3-1 highlights the key features of star topology.

Table 3-1. Key features of star topology

Feature	Description
Centralized control	A single hub manages data traffic, simplifying network management and security implementation.
Ease of troubleshooting	Network issues can be quickly identified and isolated at the hub, facilitating efficient maintenance.
Scalability	New devices can be easily added to the network by connecting them to the hub, supporting network growth.
Security	Centralized monitoring and control at the hub enhance network security, protecting against unauthorized access.
Redundancy needs	The hub represents a single point of failure, necessitating backup solutions to ensure network reliability.
Installation simplicity	Direct connections between devices and the hub simplify network setup and configuration.
Higher initial costs	The need for a robust central hub and extensive cabling can increase initial setup costs.

Advantages and Disadvantages

One significant advantage of star topology is its simplicity and ease of installation. Since each node is directly connected to the central hub, setting up and managing the network becomes straightforward. This simplicity also extends to troubleshooting; network problems can often be traced back to the hub, simplifying diagnosis and repair.

Another advantage is centralized control, which enhances the network's management and security. Administrators can easily monitor and manage data traffic through the central hub, implementing security protocols and ensuring efficient data flow. This centralized management is particularly beneficial in large networks with many devices, as it allows for better coordination and control.

IoT/IIoT networks, where the number of connected devices can grow rapidly, benefit from scalability as well. Adding new devices to the network requires no significant changes to the existing setup.

However, star topology has disadvantages. The central hub represents a single point of failure. If the hub goes down, all connected devices lose communication capability, leading to a complete network outage. This vulnerability necessitates robust backup and redundancy solutions, especially in critical applications.

Due to the need for a central hub and extensive cabling, setting up a star topology can also be more expensive in the beginning. Although these initial costs are high, the advantages of management, scalability, and security often outweigh them, making it a worthwhile investment for many applications.

How It Works

In a star topology network, each device connects to a central hub using individual cables. This hub acts as a central point for data transmission and reception. The hub forwards data from a device to another device when it wants to send data.

The central hub operates using switching or routing logic to manage data traffic. In simple terms, when a data packet arrives at the hub, the hub determines its destination based on the packet's address and sends it to the appropriate connected device. This process ensures that data is efficiently routed to its intended target without unnecessary delays.

CHAPTER 3   DESIGN AND DEPLOY AZURE IOT NETWORKS

In more advanced implementations, the central hub can include additional features like data processing, traffic monitoring, and security controls. These capabilities are particularly important in IoT/IIoT networks, where the hub may need to handle large volumes of data from various sensors and devices, ensuring that critical information is processed and transmitted promptly.

The hub's ability to centralize network control and management is crucial in maintaining network performance and reliability. By having a single point where data flows converge, network administrators can more easily monitor and optimize network performance, identify potential issues, and implement necessary adjustments.

Moreover, the centralized nature of the star topology simplifies network configuration and management. Network changes, such as adding or removing devices, can be done at the hub without affecting the rest of the network. This modularity is a significant advantage in dynamic environments like IoT/IIoT, where network configurations may frequently change.

Bus Topology

An example of a bus topology is that all devices (nodes) are connected to a single central cable, or backbone, through which data is shared between nodes. This central cable serves as a shared communication medium. The bus topology is depicted in Figure 3-2, which represents a high-topology view of the bus topology in which each device is directly connected to the central cable.

235

CHAPTER 3 DESIGN AND DEPLOY AZURE IOT NETWORKS

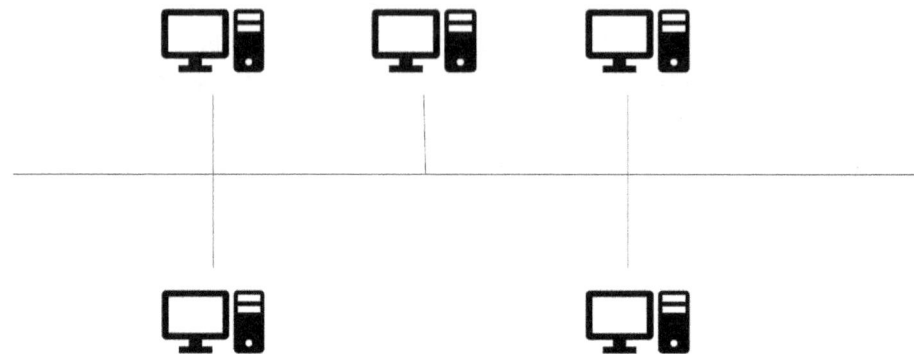

Figure 3-2. BUS topology

Relevance to IoT/IIoT Networks

Bus topology is less commonly used in modern IoT (Internet of Things) and IIoT (Industrial Internet of Things) networks than other topologies like star or mesh. However, it is still relevant, particularly in small-scale or specific industrial applications where simplicity and cost-effectiveness are priorities.

Bus topology, while less prevalent in modern IoT/IIoT networks, offers unique benefits in specific scenarios. It's a viable choice when a limited number of devices need to communicate over short distances. This simplicity is particularly advantageous in linear device arrangements, such as along a production line or within a facility section. The straightforward nature of bus topology allows for seamless integration of new devices without extensive reconfiguration, a key advantage in dynamic environments.

One advantage of bus topology in IoT/IIoT networks is the reduced cabling needed compared to a star topology. Since all devices share a single communication line, the overall cabling requirements are minimized, which can be beneficial in environments where cabling is difficult or expensive.

However, it's important to consider the limitations of bus topology in high-traffic IoT/IIoT networks. As the number of devices and data transmission volume increase, the risk of data collisions on the bus also rises. This can contribute to network congestion and decreased performance, a significant drawback that should be carefully weighed against the benefits in such scenarios.

One key concern with bus topology in IoT/IIoT networks is its vulnerability to a "single point of failure." If the central bus cable malfunctions, the entire network is disrupted, cutting off communication between all connected devices. This is a significant drawback in critical industrial applications where uninterrupted operation is crucial, underscoring the need for robust backup systems or alternative network topologies.

Despite these limitations, bus topology can still be relevant in specific IoT/IIoT use cases where its simplicity and cost-effectiveness outweigh the drawbacks. For example, bus topology can be an efficient and straightforward solution in a small-scale environmental monitoring system with sensors connected along a single pathway.

Key Features

Bus topology, characterized by its simplicity and cost-effectiveness, connects all devices to a single central cable, making it easy to install and maintain. While it has specific advantages, such as flexible device placement and lower setup costs, it also has notable drawbacks, including scalability issues and a single point of failure. Despite these limitations, bus topology can still be relevant in specific IoT/IIoT applications where its simplicity and cost benefits align with the network's requirements. Understanding its operation and critical features helps assess its suitability for various networking needs. Table 3-2 highlights the key features of bus topology.

Table 3-2. Key features of bus topology

Feature	Description
Simplicity	Easy to set up and understand due to the single central cable connection.
Cost-effectiveness	Lower initial setup costs due to minimal cabling and no need for a central hub or switch.
Flexible device placement	Devices can be positioned along the central cable as needed.
Scalability issues	Performance can degrade as the number of devices increases, leading to data collisions.
Single point of failure	The central bus cable is a critical component; if it fails, the entire network goes down.
Collision management	Uses CSMA/CD to manage data collisions, ensuring efficient communication.
Maintenance and troubleshooting	Network issues can often be traced to the bus or its connections, simplifying troubleshooting.

Advantages and Disadvantages

One significant advantage of bus topology is its simplicity and ease of implementation. Since all devices are connected to a single central cable, the setup process is straightforward, making installing and expanding the network easy. This simplicity also extends to network maintenance and troubleshooting, as any issues will likely involve the central bus or its connections.

One of the key advantages of bus topology is its cost-effectiveness. The reduced amount of cabling and the absence of a central hub or switch can significantly reduce the initial setup costs, making bus topology an appealing choice for small networks or applications with budget constraints.

Bus topology offers the advantage of flexible device placement along the central cable. This feature is particularly beneficial in industrial environments where devices often must be positioned at specific points along a production line or within a particular area.

However, bus topology has significant disadvantages, particularly regarding scalability and performance. As the number of devices on the network increases, the likelihood of data collisions also increases, leading to network congestion and reduced performance. This makes bus topology less suitable for large or high-traffic networks.

Reliability is another critical drawback. The central bus cable is a single point of failure; if it becomes damaged or fails, the entire network goes down. This vulnerability is a significant concern in industrial applications where network reliability is crucial for continuous operation.

How It Works

In a bus topology network, each device is connected to a single central cable called the bus. This cable is the shared communication medium through which all data is transmitted. When a device sends data, the data travels along the bus and is received by all connected devices.

Data packets are sent to each device on the bus based on its unique address, which identifies the intended recipient. When a device sends data, the packet includes the destination device's address. As the packet travels along the bus, each device checks the address, and only the intended recipient processes the data, while other devices ignore it.

Data collisions can occur in bus topology when two devices attempt to send data simultaneously. Bus networks often use carrier sense multiple access with collision detection (CSMA/CD) to manage this. In this protocol, a device listens to the bus before transmitting to ensure no other device is sending data. Following a collision, the devices attempt to retransmit after a random period.

Bus topologies often utilize coaxial cables to ensure bandwidth and durability. Terminators are placed along the bus to prevent signals from reflecting. This prevents interference and data loss.

Maintenance and troubleshooting in bus topology involve checking the central bus and the connections of each device. Since all devices share the same communication medium, issues often manifest as network-wide problems rather than isolated incidents, making identifying and addressing faults in the bus or its connections easier.

Point-to-Point Topology

A point-to-point topology is a simple network configuration with a direct link between two nodes. This topology connects two network devices, creating a dedicated communication path. Unlike more complex topologies, point-to-point networks involve only two nodes and a single communication channel, making them straightforward to set up and manage. Figure 3-3 provides a view of point-to-point topology.

Figure 3-3. *Point-to-point topology*

Relevance to IoT/IIoT Networks

Due to its simplicity and reliability, point-to-point topology is particularly relevant to IoT (Internet of Things) and IIoT (Industrial Internet of Things) networks. In these contexts, it is often used to establish direct communication between two specific devices. For instance, it can connect a sensor directly to a controller or machine to a monitoring system, ensuring a dedicated and uninterrupted data path.

In IoT applications, where numerous devices must communicate efficiently, point-to-point topology can be used for critical connections requiring high reliability and minimal interference. This is crucial in scenarios where timely and accurate data transmission is essential, such as in medical devices or critical infrastructure monitoring systems.

For IIoT, point-to-point topology provides robust and reliable connections in industrial settings where machines and sensors must communicate directly. This topology minimizes latency and maximizes data integrity, which is vital for real-time monitoring and control systems in manufacturing processes.

The simplicity of point-to-point connections also facilitates secure communication channels. Since the data path is dedicated and direct, unauthorized access and data breaches can be reduced, making it ideal for security-sensitive applications.

However, point-to-point topology could be more robust in scalability. While it is excellent for connecting two devices, expanding the network to include more devices requires additional point-to-point links, which can become cumbersome and inefficient for more extensive networks. This limitation makes it more suitable for small-scale or highly specific applications than large, complex IoT/IIoT deployments.

Despite its limitations, point-to-point topology can be highly effective in hybrid network designs. It can be combined with other topologies to provide dedicated connections for critical device pairs within a more extensive network, ensuring reliability and performance where it matters most.

Advantages and Disadvantages

One significant advantage of point-to-point topology is its simplicity. With only two nodes involved, the setup and configuration are straightforward, making it easy to implement and maintain. This simplicity also reduces the chances of network errors and simplifies troubleshooting, as any issues are confined to the direct link between the two nodes.

Another advantage is the high reliability and performance of point-to-point connections. Data transmission is consistent and predictable since there is no contention or interference from other devices. This makes point-to-point topology ideal for applications requiring real-time data transfer and high reliability, such as industrial automation and critical monitoring systems.

Security is also a significant advantage. By isolating the communication channel from other network traffic, point-to-point connections reduce the likelihood of data interception and enhance data security.

However, a key disadvantage of point-to-point topology is its need for scalability. Each new device requires a new point-to-point connection, which can quickly become impractical and inefficient for more extensive networks. This limitation makes it unsuitable for environments where many devices must be interconnected.

Another disadvantage is the potential for high cabling costs and complexity in environments where devices are spread out over large areas. While the simplicity of a single connection is beneficial, it can lead to extensive cabling requirements when multiple point-to-point links are needed, increasing installation and maintenance costs.

How It Works

Two network devices are connected directly by a single communication channel in a point-to-point topology. The communication channel can be a physical cable, such as an Ethernet cable, or a wireless link, such as a direct radio frequency link. In order to ensure that data transmission between these two devices isn't interfering with or being interrupted by other network traffic, the communication path is dedicated exclusively to these two devices.

When one device sends data, it transmits it directly to the other device over this dedicated link. Since no intermediate devices or routing processes are involved, data transfer is typically faster and more reliable than in more complex network topologies. This direct transmission reduces latency. A point-to-point topology is a simple network configuration with a direct link between two nodes. This topology connects two network devices, creating a dedicated communication path. Unlike more complex topologies, point-to-point networks involve only two nodes and a single communication channel, making setting up and managing straightforwardly.

Relevance to IoT/IIoT Networks

Due to its simplicity and reliability, point-to-point topology is particularly relevant to IoT (Internet of Things) and IIoT (Industrial Internet of Things) networks. In these contexts, it is often used to establish direct communication between two specific devices. For instance, it can connect a sensor directly to a controller or machine to a monitoring system, ensuring a dedicated and uninterrupted data path.

In IoT applications, where numerous devices must communicate efficiently, point-to-point topology can be used for critical connections requiring high reliability and minimal interference. This is crucial in scenarios where timely and accurate data transmission is essential, such as in medical devices or critical infrastructure monitoring systems.

For IIoT, point-to-point topology provides robust and reliable connections in industrial settings where machines and sensors must communicate directly. This topology minimizes latency and maximizes data integrity, which is vital for real-time monitoring and control systems in manufacturing processes.

The simplicity of point-to-point connections also facilitates secure communication channels. Since the data path is dedicated and direct, it reduces the risk of data breaches and unauthorized access, making it suitable for applications requiring stringent security measures.

However, point-to-point topology could be more robust in scalability. While it is excellent for connecting two devices, expanding the network to include more devices requires additional point-to-point links, which can become cumbersome and inefficient for more extensive networks. This limitation makes it more suitable for small-scale or highly specific applications than large, complex IoT/IIoT deployments.

Despite its limitations, point-to-point topology can be highly effective in hybrid network designs. It can be combined with other topologies to provide dedicated connections for critical device pairs within a more extensive network, ensuring reliability and performance where it matters most.

Key Features

Point-to-point topology is a straightforward and efficient network configuration that connects two devices directly. Its simplicity, reliability, and security make it suitable for critical IoT and IIoT applications where direct communication is essential. However, its limited scalability and potential high cabling costs restrict its use to specific scenarios rather than large-scale networks. In hybrid network designs, where dedicated connections are needed, understanding its working and its key features is crucial to determining its suitability. Table 3-3 highlights the key features of point-to-point topology.

Table 3-3. *Key features of point-to-point topology*

Feature	Description
Simplicity	Involves only two nodes with a direct connection, making setup and maintenance straightforward.
High reliability	Dedicated communication path ensures consistent and reliable data transfer.
Low latency	Direct connection minimizes data transmission delays, suitable for real-time applications.
Enhanced security	Isolated communication channel reduces the risk of data breaches and unauthorized access.
Limited scalability	Each new connection requires a separate point-to-point link, making it impractical for large networks.
High cabling costs	Extensive cabling can be required for multiple connections, increasing installation and maintenance costs.
Versatile communication	Can use wired or wireless links depending on the application and environmental conditions.

Advantages and Disadvantages

One significant advantage of point-to-point topology is its simplicity. With only two nodes involved, the setup and configuration are straightforward, making it easy to implement and maintain. This simplicity also reduces the chances of network errors and simplifies troubleshooting, as any issues are confined to the direct link between the two nodes.

Another advantage is the high reliability and performance of point-to-point connections. Data transmission is consistent and predictable since there is no contention or interference from other devices. This makes point-to-point topology ideal for applications requiring real-time data transfer and high reliability, such as industrial automation and critical monitoring systems.

Security is also a significant advantage. As point-to-point connections are direct and dedicated, they reduce the risk of data interception and enhance the overall security of data transmission.

However, a key disadvantage of point-to-point topology is its need for scalability. Each new device requires a new point-to-point connection, which can quickly become impractical and inefficient for more extensive networks. This limitation makes it unsuitable for environments where many devices must be interconnected.

Another disadvantage is the potential for high cabling costs and complexity in environments where devices are spread out over large areas. While the simplicity of a single connection is beneficial, it can lead to extensive cabling requirements when multiple point-to-point links are needed, increasing installation and maintenance costs.

How It Works

In a point-to-point topology, two network devices are connected directly by a single communication channel. The channel can take the form of a physical cable, such as an Ethernet cable, or a wireless link, such as a radio frequency link. In order to prevent other network traffic from interfering with or interrupting the transmission of data between these two devices, the communication path has been dedicated exclusively to them.

When one device sends data, it transmits it directly to the other device over this dedicated link. Since no intermediate devices or routing processes are involved, data transfer is typically faster and more reliable than in more complex network topologies. This direct transmission reduces latency and minimizes data loss or corruption.

Depending on the devices and the application, point-to-point connections can use a variety of communication protocols. A direct, exclusive path of communication between two nodes remains the fundamental principle regardless of the protocol. Standard protocols include TCP/IP for wired connections and wireless communication standards for wireless links.

As a result of physical medium, such as fiber optic cables or twisted pair cables, wired point-to-point connections are determined by their speed and reliability. A variety of factors are taken into account when choosing a medium, including distance, data transfer rate, and environmental conditions.

Wireless point-to-point connections rely on Wi-Fi, Bluetooth, or dedicated radio frequencies. These connections are beneficial in situations where physical cabling is impractical or impossible. Wireless point-to-point links can span large distances, making them suitable for remote monitoring and control in industrial environments. They also minimize the chances of data loss or corruption.

Depending on the devices and the application, the communication protocol used in a point-to-point connection can vary. Standard protocols include TCP/IP for wired connections and wireless communication standards for wireless networks. In any case, a direct and exclusive communication path between two nodes remains the fundamental principle.

It is the physical medium that determines the speed and reliability of wired point-to-point connections, such as fiber optic cables or twisted pair cables. Distance, data transfer rate, and environmental conditions all play a role in the choice of medium.

Wireless point-to-point connections rely on Wi-Fi, Bluetooth, or dedicated radio frequencies. These connections are beneficial in situations where physical cabling is impractical or impossible. Wireless point-to-point links can span large distances, making them suitable for remote monitoring and control in industrial environments.

Ring Topology

In a ring topology, each node (node) is connected to exactly two other nodes, forming a closed circuit. Data travels unidirectionally or bidirectionally around the ring until it reaches its destination in this

CHAPTER 3 DESIGN AND DEPLOY AZURE IOT NETWORKS

topology. The simplicity and structure of ring topology set it apart from other network topologies. Figure 3-4 shows a high-level view of Ring topology.

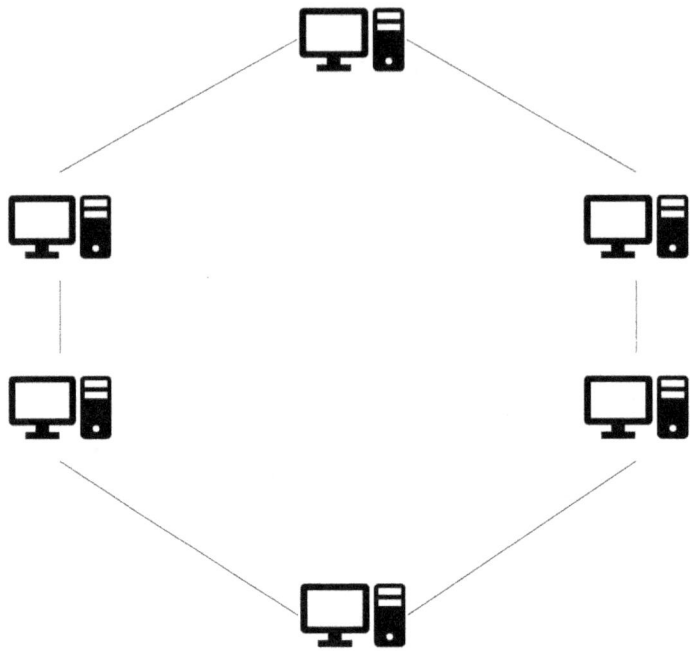

Figure 3-4. *Ring topology*

Relevance to IoT/IIoT Networks

In ring topology, IoT (Internet of Things) and IIoT (Industrial Internet of Things) networks where data flow is predictable and communication is reliable. Ring topology allows each device to have a direct path to its neighbors, reducing the chance of collisions and network congestion, which can be critical in industrial environments.

In IIoT applications, ring topology is often used to connect machines and sensors in a linear yet closed-loop configuration. It is particularly beneficial in industrial settings, where network reliability is a concern since the data can be rerouted in the opposite direction if a network segment fails.

For IoT networks, ring topology offers a structured and organized approach to connecting smart devices in a home or office environment. While it may not be as commonly used as star or mesh topologies for consumer IoT, it can still offer advantages in specific applications, such as building automation systems where devices are laid out linearly.

The deterministic nature of data transmission in ring topology is a key factor that can enhance the performance of IoT/IIoT networks. For applications requiring real-time processing and low-latency communications, the assurance that data travels along a defined path reduces the uncertainty in data delivery times, providing a reliable performance.

However, ring topology does have its limitations in IoT/IIoT contexts. Scalability can be a concern as adding or removing devices requires network reconfiguration, which can be cumbersome in large-scale deployments. Additionally, if the network grows too large, the data travel time around the ring can become significant, potentially affecting performance.

Despite these challenges, ring topology's inherent redundancy and reliability suit specific IoT/IIoT applications. Its use in hybrid network designs can also provide dedicated paths for critical communication, enhancing overall network resilience and performance.

Key Features

Ring topology is a structured and reliable network configuration where each device is connected in a closed loop. Its relevance to IoT and IIoT networks lies in its simplicity, inherent redundancy, and equal access for all devices, making it suitable for applications requiring reliable and predictable data transmission. However, scalability and potential latency issues limit its use in more extensive networks. Understanding how ring topology works and its key features helps assess its suitability for specific networking needs, particularly in industrial environments where reliability and fault tolerance are paramount. Table 3-4 highlights the key features of ring topology.

Table 3-4. *Key features of ring topology*

Feature	Description
Structured layout	Devices are connected in a closed loop, providing a predictable path for data transmission.
Redundancy	The network can reroute data in the opposite direction if a connection fails, ensuring continuous operation.
Equal access	All devices have equal access to the network, eliminating dependency on a central hub.
Token passing protocol	Prevents data collisions by allowing only the device with the token to transmit data.
Fault tolerance	Can maintain operation despite individual node or connection failures, enhancing reliability.
Scalability issues	Adding or removing devices requires network reconfiguration, making scalability a challenge.
Potential latency	Larger networks can experience increased data travel time around the ring, affecting performance.

Advantages and Disadvantages

As a result of its simplicity and structured layout, ring topology is easy to understand and implement, especially in environments where devices are arranged in a linear pattern. As a result of the predictable path for data transmission, collisions and congestion are reduced because the data flow is efficient and organized.

Another significant advantage is the inherent redundancy provided by the ring structure. If a single node or connection fails, the network can still operate by rerouting data in the opposite direction. This fault tolerance is crucial for maintaining continuous operation in critical applications, making ring topology a reliable choice for IoT networks.

Ring topology also offers equal access to the network for all devices. Since each node has a dedicated connection to its neighbors, there is no dependency on a central hub or switch, which can eliminate potential bottlenecks and improve overall network performance.

However, ring topology has its disadvantages. One major drawback is the difficulty in adding or removing devices. Each time a node is added or removed, the network must be temporarily disrupted to reconfigure the connections, which can be impractical for dynamic or large-scale networks.

Another disadvantage is the potential for network latency in large rings. As the number of devices increases, the data must travel a longer distance around the ring to reach its destination. Especially in real-time communication applications, this can result in increased latency and performance degradation.

How It Works

In a ring topology network, each device is connected to two other devices, forming a continuous loop. Data travels around the ring in a unidirectional or bidirectional manner. In unidirectional rings, data flows in one direction, whereas in bidirectional rings, it can travel in both directions, enhancing fault tolerance and data delivery speed.

When a device sends data, it is transmitted to its neighboring device along the ring. Each device in the network acts as a repeater, forwarding the data to the next device until it reaches its intended recipient. This method ensures the data circulates the ring, making it eventually accessible to the destination node.

Ring topology often employs a token-passing protocol to manage data collisions and ensure orderly communication. In this protocol, a token, a small data packet, circulates the ring. A device can only send data when it possesses the token, preventing simultaneous data transmissions and collisions.

Fault tolerance is a critical feature of ring topology. If a connection between two devices fails, the network can continue functioning by rerouting data in the opposite direction. This redundancy is significant in industrial settings, where continuous operation is essential.

In terms of hardware, ring topology can use various physical media, including coaxial cables, fiber optics, or wireless links. The choice of medium depends on the network's specific requirements, such as distance, data rate, and environmental conditions.

Mesh Topology

Mesh topology is a type of network configuration where each device (node) is interconnected with multiple other devices, forming a web-like structure. In an entire mesh topology, every node is connected to every other node, whereas in a partial mesh topology, nodes are connected to some but not all other nodes. This design ensures multiple paths for data to travel, enhancing the reliability and robustness of the network. Figure 3-5 provides a high-level topology view of mesh topology.

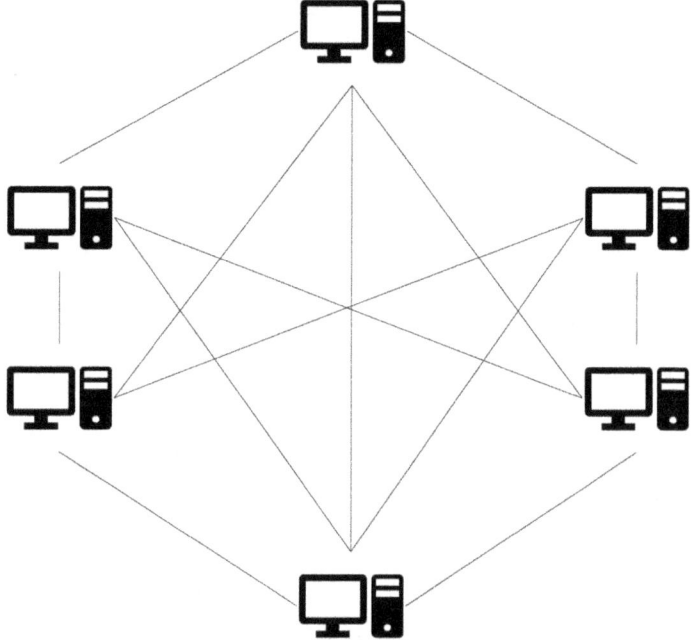

Figure 3-5. *Mesh topology*

Relevance to IoT/IIoT Networks

Mesh topology is highly relevant to IoT and IIoT networks due to its reliability, redundancy, and scalability. In IoT/IoT environments, devices often must communicate efficiently and reliably, even if some connections fail. Mesh topology provides these capabilities by allowing multiple paths for data to traverse the network.

In IoT applications, mesh topology is especially beneficial for smart home systems, environmental monitoring, and connected city infrastructures. Devices such as bright lights, thermostats, and sensors can communicate directly with each other, ensuring that data can be rerouted in case of failure, thus maintaining network integrity and functionality.

For IIoT applications, mesh topology is ideal for industrial automation, asset tracking, and remote monitoring systems. In these scenarios, sustaining communication despite individual node failures is crucial. Mesh networks can provide the robustness and fault tolerance necessary for maintaining operational efficiency in industrial settings.

Moreover, mesh topology supports scalability, essential for expanding IoT/IIoT networks. As new devices are added, they can seamlessly integrate into the existing mesh, automatically finding the best paths for data transmission. This flexibility makes mesh topology suitable for dynamic environments where the number of connected devices continues to grow.

Security is another critical aspect of mesh topology in IoT/IIoT networks. With multiple communication paths, data can be encrypted and transmitted through different routes, reducing the risk of interception and enhancing overall network security. This is particularly important for protecting sensitive data in industrial applications.

Despite its advantages, mesh topology can be complex to implement and manage due to the large number of connections and the potential for network congestion. Additionally, the cost of deploying a complete mesh network can be high because of the extensive hardware requirements. Therefore, careful planning and management are necessary to balance the benefits and challenges.

Key Features

Mesh topology is a robust and scalable network configuration that interconnects multiple devices, forming a web-like structure. Its relevance to IoT and IIoT networks lies in its high reliability, fault tolerance, and scalability, making it suitable for critical applications requiring uninterrupted communication. However, the complexity and cost of implementing and maintaining mesh topology can be significant challenges. Understanding how mesh topology works and its key features helps evaluate its suitability for various networking needs, particularly in environments where reliability and dynamic scalability are paramount. Table 3-5 highlights the key features of mesh topology.

Table 3-5. Key features of mesh topology

Feature	Description
High reliability	Multiple redundant paths ensure continuous communication even if some connections fail.
Scalability	New devices can be easily added to the network without major reconfiguration.
Load balancing	Data transmission is distributed across multiple paths, avoiding congestion and maintaining high-speed communication.
Complex setup and maintenance	Requires sophisticated algorithms and network management tools to manage numerous connections and efficient data routing.
High cost	Implementing a full mesh network can be expensive due to extensive hardware requirements.
Dynamic routing	Routing algorithms dynamically determine the best path for data transmission based on factors like hop count and load.
Wireless mesh networks	Use wireless communication technologies to create adaptable and robust networks, particularly useful for IoT applications.

Advantages and Disadvantages

One significant advantage of mesh topology is its high reliability. With multiple redundant paths for data to travel, the network can maintain communication even if one or more connections fail. This fault tolerance is essential for critical applications in IoT and IIoT environments where uninterrupted communication is vital.

Another advantage is the scalability of mesh topology. New devices can be added to the network without significant reconfiguration. Each new node automatically connects to the existing nodes, finding optimal paths for data transmission. This scalability supports the dynamic and growing nature of IoT/IIoT networks.

Mesh topology also enhances network performance through load balancing. The network can avoid congestion and maintain high-speed communication by distributing data transmission across multiple paths. When several devices are transmitting data simultaneously in a high-traffic environment, this feature is particularly useful.

However, mesh topology has its disadvantages. One major drawback is the complexity of setup and maintenance. Managing numerous connections and ensuring efficient data routing requires sophisticated algorithms and network management tools, which can be challenging and resource-intensive.

Another disadvantage is the cost associated with implementing a complete mesh network. The extensive hardware requirements, including multiple network interfaces for each device, can make the initial setup expensive. This cost factor can be a limiting factor for smaller organizations or applications with budget constraints.

How It Works

In a mesh topology network, each node is connected to multiple other nodes, creating a web-like structure. Data can travel along various paths to reach its destination, ensuring that even if some nodes or connections fail, it can be rerouted through alternative paths. This redundancy is a crucial feature of mesh topology.

In order to determine the best path to send data, a node uses routing algorithms. These algorithms consider the number of hops (intermediate nodes) and the current load on each path to ensure efficient and reliable data transmission. Standard routing protocols used in mesh networks include DSR (Dynamic Source Routing) and AODV (Adhoc On-Demand Distance Vector).

In an entire mesh topology, every node is directly connected to every other node, providing the highest level of redundancy and fault tolerance. However, this configuration requires many connections, which can be impractical for more extensive networks due to the high cost and complexity of maintaining such a network.

Partial mesh topology offers a more practical solution by connecting each node to only some other nodes. This approach balances the benefits of redundancy and fault tolerance with reduced complexity and cost. Partial mesh is often used in more extensive networks where full mesh would be too expensive or complicated to implement.

Wireless mesh networks, commonly used in IoT applications, leverage wireless communication technologies such as Wi-Fi, Zigbee, or Bluetooth. These networks are beneficial in environments where wiring is impractical or impossible. Wireless mesh networks can dynamically adjust to changes in the network, such as node movement or failure, maintaining robust and reliable communication.

Tree Topology

Tree topology is a hierarchical network configuration that combines elements of both star and bus topologies. In a tree topology, nodes are arranged in a parent-child hierarchy, with a central root node branching out to intermediate nodes, which branch out to peripheral nodes. This structure resembles a tree, hence the name. Each level of the hierarchy can have multiple nodes connected in a star-like fashion, creating a layered, organized network. Figure 3-6 provides a high-level topology view of tree topology.

CHAPTER 3   DESIGN AND DEPLOY AZURE IOT NETWORKS

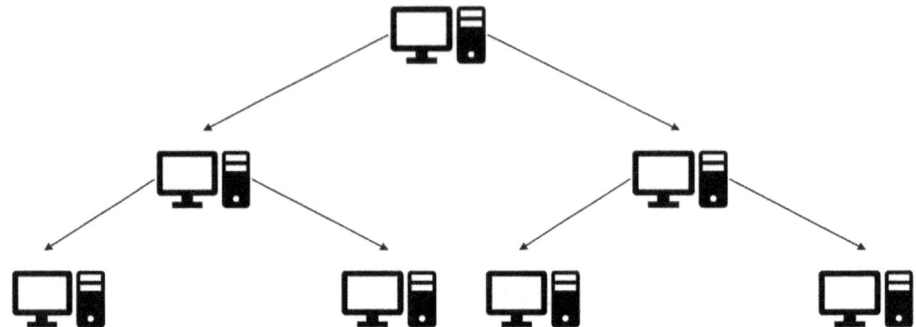

Figure 3-6. *Tree topology*

Relevance to IoT/IIoT Networks

Tree topology is particularly relevant to IoT (Internet of Things) and IIoT (Industrial Internet of Things) networks because of its hierarchical nature, which allows for efficient management and scalability. In IoT applications, where devices must communicate and transfer data to central hubs or cloud services, tree topology facilitates organized data flow and centralized management. This makes it suitable for smart homes, building automation, and extensive sensor networks.

In IIoT environments, tree topology can efficiently handle large-scale industrial systems where devices are grouped into different levels based on their functions and locations. This hierarchical arrangement ensures that data from numerous devices can be aggregated and processed efficiently. This is crucial for factory automation, energy management systems, and large-scale monitoring setups.

The hierarchical structure of tree topology simplifies network management and troubleshooting. Administrators can easily segment the network into manageable parts, isolating and addressing issues at specific levels without affecting the entire network. This is particularly useful in complex IoT/IIoT deployments with critical uptime and reliability.

CHAPTER 3   DESIGN AND DEPLOY AZURE IOT NETWORKS

Moreover, tree topology supports scalability, adding new nodes at various levels of the hierarchy without disrupting existing network operations. This feature is essential for growing IoT/IIoT networks, where the number of connected devices continually increases. As the infrastructure continues to evolve, it is able to expand seamlessly.

However, tree topology has its limitations, especially regarding network redundancy and fault tolerance. The hierarchical nature means that if a higher-level node fails, it can disrupt the communication for all connected lower-level nodes. This single point of failure can be a significant drawback in environments where continuous operation is crucial.

Despite these challenges, tree topology remains a viable option for many IoT/IoT applications due to its structured approach and ease of management. Combining the strengths of star and bus topologies provides a balanced solution that can handle the demands of modern connected environments.

Key Feature

Tree topology is a hierarchical network configuration combining star and bus topology elements, making it relevant to IoT and IIoT networks. Its structured hierarchy simplifies management and troubleshooting, supports scalability, and facilitates efficient data aggregation and centralized management. However, the single point of failure and the complexity of setup and maintenance can be significant challenges. Understanding how tree topology works and its key features helps assess its suitability for various networking needs, particularly in environments requiring organized and scalable data communication. Table 3-6 highlights the key features of tree topology.

Table 3-6. Key features of tree topology

Feature	Description
Hierarchical structure	Nodes are arranged in a parent-child hierarchy, simplifying management and troubleshooting.
Scalability	New nodes can be easily added at different levels, supporting network growth.
Efficient data aggregation	Data from peripheral nodes is collected and forwarded through intermediate nodes to the root node, optimizing data flow.
Centralized management	The root node serves as the central hub for data processing and network control, enabling organized data management.
Single point of failure	Failure of a higher-level node can disrupt communication for all dependent lower-level nodes, compromising reliability.
Complex setup	Setting up and maintaining the hierarchical structure requires careful planning and management.
Flexible connectivity	Supports various physical media, including wired and wireless connections, making it adaptable to different environments.

Advantages and Disadvantages

One significant advantage of tree topology is its structured hierarchy, which simplifies network management and troubleshooting. Each network level can be managed independently, allowing administrators to isolate and address issues effectively without affecting the entire system. This organized approach is particularly beneficial in large-scale deployments.

Another advantage is the scalability of tree topology. New nodes can be added at different levels of the hierarchy without major reconfiguration, ensuring the network can grow seamlessly. This feature is essential for IoT/IIoT networks, which often need to accommodate increasing numbers of devices.

Tree topology also facilitates efficient data aggregation and processing. Data from peripheral nodes can be collected and forwarded through intermediate nodes to the central root node, enabling centralized data management. This hierarchical data flow is ideal for structured data collection and analysis applications.

However, tree topology has disadvantages, primarily concerning redundancy and fault tolerance. The hierarchical structure means that if a higher-level node or connection fails, it can disrupt communication for all dependent lower-level nodes. This single point of failure can compromise the network's reliability.

Additionally, the complexity of tree topology can be a drawback. Setting up and maintaining the hierarchical structure requires careful planning and management. Ensuring that each level of the hierarchy is correctly configured and connected can be resource-intensive, particularly in large networks.

How It Works

In a tree topology network, the structure begins with a central root node, which serves as the primary hub for the network. This root node connects to intermediate nodes, which act as secondary hubs. These intermediate nodes then connect to peripheral nodes, creating a multi-level hierarchy that resembles a tree.

Data transmission in tree topology follows hierarchical paths. Peripheral nodes send data to their intermediate nodes, which aggregate it and forward it to the root node. The root node processes the data or routes it to other parts of the network as needed. This organized data flow ensures efficient communication and centralized data management.

The hierarchical nature of tree topology allows for efficient data aggregation. For example, in an IoT network, sensors at the peripheral level can send their readings to intermediate nodes, which then aggregate the data and send it to the central hub for processing. This hierarchical data collection minimizes data traffic and optimizes network performance.

Tree topology can connect with various physical media, including wired options like Ethernet cables and wireless technologies like Wi-Fi or Zigbee. The choice of medium depends on factors such as the network's scale, required data transfer rates, and environmental conditions. This flexibility makes tree topology adaptable to different IoT/IIoT scenarios.

Tree topology often employs protocols supporting hierarchical data routing and management to ensure efficient communication and network traffic management. These protocols facilitate the organized flow of data and help maintain the network's structure, ensuring that each node communicates effectively within its hierarchical level.

Autonomous Network Architecture

Autonomous Network Architecture makes use of artificial intelligence, machine learning, automation, and advanced analytics to operate with little human intervention. These networks are capable of self-configuration, self-healing, self-optimization, and self-protection, ensuring high efficiency, reliability, and security. Autonomous networks are particularly relevant in modern, complex network environments where traditional manual management methods are becoming increasingly impractical.

Autonomous Network Architecture is a sophisticated network design paradigm that creates self-managing networks. This architecture integrates AI and ML to enable networks to monitor their operations, detect anomalies, and take corrective actions autonomously. The primary goal is to reduce the need for human intervention, thereby minimizing errors, improving response times, and enhancing overall network performance. In an autonomous network, various network elements, such as routers, switches, and servers, are equipped with intelligent software to communicate and coordinate. These elements use real-time data and analytics to make informed decisions, ensuring the network can adapt efficiently to changing conditions and demands.

CHAPTER 3   DESIGN AND DEPLOY AZURE IOT NETWORKS

Autonomous network architecture is becoming increasingly relevant as network complexity and data traffic grow exponentially. Traditional network management approaches, which rely heavily on manual configurations and interventions, must be revised to deal with the scale and speed required in modern networks. Autonomous networks address these challenges by offering scalable, agile, and resilient solutions to handle large volumes of data and many connected devices. In telecommunications, autonomous networks are essential for managing the growing demand for high-speed internet, supporting the proliferation of IoT devices, and facilitating the deployment of 5G networks. In enterprise environments, these networks enhance the efficiency and security of IT infrastructure, supporting digital transformation initiatives and enabling businesses to operate more dynamically.

Autonomous network architecture comprises several vital components that work together to achieve self-management capabilities. Machine learning algorithms and artificial intelligence are at the core of autonomous networks, which allow them to predict potential issues while making decisions without human intervention. Automation and orchestration tools manage routine network tasks such as configuration, provisioning, and maintenance, while orchestration platforms coordinate these automated tasks across different network components to ensure seamless operation. Advanced analytics provide insights into network performance, security threats, and user behavior, which are crucial for the network to make informed decisions and optimize its operations continuously. By virtualizing network functions and running them on standard hardware, network functions can be scaled and adapted dynamically. By separating the control plane from the data plane, software-defined networking improves network adaptability and programmability by enabling network administrators to manage network services through abstractions and centralized control.

CHAPTER 3   DESIGN AND DEPLOY AZURE IOT NETWORKS

The adoption of autonomous network architecture brings several significant benefits. Reduced operational costs are achieved by minimizing the need for manual intervention, thus reducing expenses associated with network management and maintenance. Improved network performance is attained as autonomous networks can optimize performance by dynamically adjusting network parameters in response to real-time data, ensuring efficient resource utilization and minimal downtime. Enhanced security is another key benefit, as autonomous networks can detect and respond to security threats in real time, providing a higher level of protection against cyberattacks and unauthorized access. Scalability and flexibility are notable advantages, as autonomous networks can quickly scale to accommodate growing numbers of devices and data traffic, making them ideal for dynamic and expanding environments. Additionally, automation and AI enable quicker deployment of new services and technologies, fostering innovation and allowing organizations to stay competitive.

Despite its advantages, implementing autonomous network architecture also presents challenges. Integrating AI, ML, automation, and other advanced technologies requires expertise and careful planning, adding complexity to the setup. The initial investment for deploying autonomous network technologies can be significant, although long-term savings and efficiency gains often offset these costs. Security and privacy also present challenges, as while autonomous networks enhance security, they introduce new risks, such as vulnerabilities in AI algorithms and the need to protect vast amounts of data used for training and decision-making. Additionally, organizations must ensure that autonomous network operations comply with relevant regulations and standards, which vary from region to region.

Autonomous network architecture represents the future of network management, offering a robust solution to the growing complexity and demands of modern networks. By leveraging AI, ML, automation, and advanced analytics, autonomous networks promise to deliver improved performance, enhanced security, and significant operational efficiencies. As technology evolves, adopting autonomous networks will likely become essential for organizations seeking to maintain competitive advantage and operational excellence in an increasingly connected world.

Ubiquitous Network Architecture

Pervasive or ubiquitous computing, also known as ubiquitous network architecture, represents a paradigm shift in how network infrastructure is conceived and deployed. The goal is to create an environment where computing resources are seamlessly integrated into everyday objects and surroundings, making them ubiquitous and omnipresent. This concept aims to embed intelligence into the fabric of our surroundings, allowing for continuous and effortless interaction between users and their environment.

Ubiquitous network architecture, at its core, envisions a world where computing is seamlessly integrated into every aspect of daily life. This integration extends beyond personal devices and household appliances to include public infrastructure and urban spaces. The result is a network environment that facilitates a seamless flow of information, with devices communicating with each other and with users, anticipating their needs, and providing context-aware services.

One of the fundamental principles of ubiquitous network architecture is invisibility. In a ubiquitous network, computing devices are integrated into the environment so that they become virtually invisible to the user. Instead of interacting with traditional computers or devices, users interact directly with the environment, using everyday objects as interfaces to access information and services.

Ubiquitous network architecture relies on various technologies to achieve its goals, including wireless communication protocols, sensor networks, Internet of Things (IoT) devices, artificial intelligence, and cloud computing. These technologies create a networked ecosystem where devices can communicate and collaborate seamlessly, regardless of location or form factor.

CHAPTER 3   DESIGN AND DEPLOY AZURE IOT NETWORKS

One of the key benefits of ubiquitous network architecture is its ability to enhance efficiency and convenience in various domains. In smart homes, for example, ubiquitous computing enables automated control of lighting, heating, and appliances based on user preferences and environmental conditions. It facilitates real-time monitoring of traffic, pollution, and public services in urban environments, leading to more sustainable and responsive cities.

It is possible to revolutionize the way we interact with technology with a ubiquitous network architecture. By embedding computing capabilities in everyday objects such as clothing, furniture, and vehicles, we create experiences previously associated with science fiction.

In addition to offering many benefits, ubiquitous networks pose significant challenges and concerns. The integration of computing into our surroundings raises privacy, security, and ethical concerns. In light of ubiquitous surveillance and data collection, questions arise about data ownership, consent, and autonomy, which emphasize the need for careful regulation.

In conclusion, ubiquitous network architecture represents a transformative future vision where computing is seamlessly integrated into every aspect of our lives. By creating a networked ecosystem of intelligent devices and environments, ubiquitous computing has the potential to enhance efficiency, convenience, and quality of life in various domains. However, realizing this vision requires addressing complex technical, social, and ethical challenges to ensure ubiquitous computing benefits society.

Azure Networks for IOT

Providing everything from basic connectivity to advanced security, load balancing, and management capabilities, Microsoft Azure has a range of networking services designed to meet the changing needs of modern cloud environments.

CHAPTER 3 DESIGN AND DEPLOY AZURE IOT NETWORKS

Azure's network offerings for Operational Technology (OT) and Industrial Internet of Things (IIoT) are designed to provide robust, secure, and scalable solutions for industrial environments. These services facilitate the seamless integration of traditional industrial systems with modern cloud-based technologies, enabling improved efficiency, predictive maintenance, and enhanced operational insights. Table 3-7 highlights the key offering of Microsoft Azure Network for IOT mapping with possible IoT use cases, which may not be feasible for all requirements.

Table 3-7. Key offering of Microsoft for IoT with integrated networks

Azure Service Name	Description	Possible IoT Use Cases
Azure Virtual Network	Establish comprehensive connections from virtual machines to incoming VPN connections, enabling seamless communication and network management within Azure.	Connect IoT devices securely within a virtual network for centralized management and data aggregation.
Azure Load Balancer	Distribute inbound and outbound network traffic across multiple servers to ensure high availability and reliability for your applications.	Ensure high availability and balanced load for IoT applications and data processing services.
Azure DDoS Protection	Shield your applications from Distributed Denial of Service (DDoS) attacks, ensuring continuous and secure service availability.	Protect IoT infrastructure from DDoS attacks, ensuring uninterrupted operation of critical IoT services.

(*continued*)

Table 3-7. (*continued*)

Azure Service Name	Description	Possible IoT Use Cases
Azure Firewall	Utilize a fully integrated firewall service with built-in high availability and zero maintenance to protect your network resources from unauthorized access and threats.	Secure IoT devices and data with robust firewall policies, preventing unauthorized access and threats.
Azure Firewall Manager	Centrally manage and enforce your network security policies and routing rules across multiple Azure Firewall instances for streamlined and consistent security management.	Manage and enforce security policies for large-scale IoT deployments across multiple locations.
Azure Bastion	Securely connect to your virtual machines using private and fully managed RDP and SSH access without exposing your VM to public internet.	Provide secure remote access to IoT devices and management servers without exposing them to the internet.
Azure Private Link	Enable private and secure access to Azure services, ensuring that your data remains within the Azure network and is not exposed to the public internet.	Enable private and secure access to IoT services and data, avoiding public internet exposure.

(*continued*)

Table 3-7. (*continued*)

Azure Service Name	Description	Possible IoT Use Cases
Traffic Manager	Optimize the performance and availability of your applications by intelligently routing incoming traffic to the best performing and closest endpoints.	Optimize routing for IoT data, ensuring low latency and high availability for critical applications.
Network Watcher	Monitor and diagnose network issues in real-time with comprehensive tools to analyze, troubleshoot, and visualize your network health and performance.	Monitor and diagnose connectivity and performance issues within IoT networks.
Azure Network Function Manager	Deploy and manage 5G and SD-WAN network functions on edge devices, extending Azure's management capabilities to support advanced networking needs at the edge.	Manage and deploy advanced networking functions to support IoT edge devices with 5G connectivity.
Azure ExpressRoute	Establish high-speed, private network connections between your on-premises infrastructure and Azure, bypassing the public internet for improved security and performance.	Enable high-speed, secure connectivity for transferring large volumes of IoT data between on-premises systems and Azure.

(*continued*)

Table 3-7. (*continued*)

Azure Service Name	Description	Possible IoT Use Cases
Azure Virtual WAN	Securely connect multiple business locations, including offices and retail sites, through a unified, global networking architecture using a centralized management portal.	Connect IoT devices across multiple locations securely and manage them through a centralized portal.
Azure VPN Gateway	Use secure, encrypted tunnels over the internet to connect your on-premises networks or individual devices to Azure Virtual Networks, ensuring safe data transmission.	Securely connect dispersed IoT devices to Azure, ensuring encrypted data transmission over the internet.
Routing Preference	Choose how your network traffic routes between Azure and the internet, optimizing for either performance or cost based on your specific needs.	Optimize routing paths for IoT data to ensure the best performance or cost-efficiency.
Azure Public MEC, Azure Private MEC	Deliver ultra-low-latency compute capabilities at the edge to provide real-time experiences for your customers, whether through public or private mobile edge computing solutions.	Enable real-time data processing and analytics for IoT applications at the edge with ultra-low latency.
Azure Private 5G Core	Simplify the deployment and management of private 5G networks, providing secure, high-performance wireless connectivity tailored to your enterprise needs.	Deploy and manage private 5G networks to support high-performance, low-latency IoT applications.

(*continued*)

Table 3-7. (*continued*)

Azure Service Name	Description	Possible IoT Use Cases
Azure CDN	Accelerate the distribution of high-bandwidth content, such as videos and large files, to users around the world by caching content at strategically placed edge locations.	Efficiently deliver firmware updates and high-bandwidth content to IoT devices worldwide.
Azure Front Door	Enhance the delivery and security of your global, microservice-based web applications with a scalable, high-performance content delivery network.	Secure and accelerate access to IoT application interfaces and APIs on a global scale.
Azure Application Gateway	Efficiently manage and distribute web traffic to your applications using a web traffic load balancer, optimizing performance and resource utilization.	Load balance traffic to IoT web applications, ensuring efficient resource use and high availability.
Azure Web Application Firewall	Improve the security of your web applications by deploying a firewall service designed to protect against common web vulnerabilities and attacks.	Protect IoT web applications from common vulnerabilities and security threats.
Azure DNS	Ensure your domain names resolve quickly and reliably with an ultra-fast, globally distributed DNS service, providing high availability for your applications.	Ensure fast and reliable DNS resolution for IoT services, improving response times and availability.

(*continued*)

Table 3-7. (*continued*)

Azure Service Name	Description	Possible IoT Use Cases
Internet Analyzer	Evaluate how changes to your network infrastructure will impact performance, allowing you to make informed decisions to optimize user experience.	Assess the impact of network changes on IoT device performance and connectivity.
Azure NAT Gateway	Ensure scalable, resilient, and secure outbound internet connectivity for your virtual networks, simplifying network address translation management.	Provide scalable and secure internet connectivity for large numbers of IoT devices within virtual networks.
Azure Programmable Connectivity	Develop applications that leverage advanced networking features, enabling intelligent interaction between cloud and edge resources.	Create intelligent IoT applications that can dynamically interact with network resources and optimize connectivity.
Azure Operator 5G Core	Modernize your mobile network infrastructure with a flexible, scalable 5G technology core, enhancing your ability to deliver advanced mobile services.	Upgrade your mobile network to support advanced IoT use cases with flexible and scalable 5G technology.

These Azure networking services collectively provide a robust, highly scalable, and end-to-end secured environment for deploying and managing cloud applications. They support various networking needs, from basic connectivity and security to advanced load balancing, monitoring, and content delivery, enabling organizations to build efficient and resilient cloud infrastructures.

IoT Network Connection Patterns for IoT Devices

IoT devices typically use two main types of connection patterns to connect to the cloud:

- **Persistent Connections**

    It is essential to maintain persistent connections in scenarios involving command and control. Your IoT solution can control devices in near real-time when you send commands to them. A persistent connection to an IoT hub is established using the MQTT and AMQP protocols, which are supported by IoT device SDKs. These connections maintain a continuous network connection to the cloud and automatically reconnect if the network is interrupted.

- **Ephemeral Connections**

    Ephemeral connections are short-lived and primarily used to send telemetry data to your IoT hub. After transmitting the data, the connection is closed, and the device reconnects only when it has more telemetry to send. Ephemeral connections are not suitable for command and control scenarios. Devices that only need to send telemetry can use the HTTP API for these brief connections.

Design Azure IoT Network

Let us start with an overview of the Azure network landscape. The Azure network architecture ensures seamless connectivity from the Internet to Azure data centers. Any workload deployed on Azure, whether its Infrastructure as a Service (IaaS), Platform as a Service (PaaS), or Software as a Service (SaaS), utilizes the robust Azure datacenter network.

CHAPTER 3   DESIGN AND DEPLOY AZURE IOT NETWORKS

Azure's data center network architecture comprises several key components: the edge network, wide area network (WAN), regional gateways network, and datacenter network. The edge network is the demarcation point between Microsoft's and external networks, such as the Internet and enterprise networks. It facilitates Internet and ExpressRoute peering into Azure.

The wide area network, a key component of our system, is Microsoft's intelligent global backbone network. It's designed to provide seamless connectivity between different Azure regions. The regional gateway, another critical component, acts as an aggregation point for all data centers within an Azure region, enabling extensive connectivity with multi-hundred terabit connections per data center. The center network, the third pillar of our system, ensures connectivity between servers within the data center and is designed to minimize bandwidth oversubscription.

Our network components are meticulously engineered to maximize availability and support always-on, always-available cloud services. Redundancy is not just a feature but a fundamental principle built into every layer of the network, from the physical infrastructure to control protocols. This ensures high reliability and performance, even in the face of unexpected events.

The data center network exemplifies resiliency through its modified Clos network design, which ensures high bi-sectional bandwidth for large-scale cloud traffic. This network uses numerous commodity devices strategically placed in different physical locations, each with independent power and cooling systems. This strategic placement reduces the impact of environmental events and individual hardware failures.

On the control plane, all network devices operate in OSI Layer 3 routing mode to prevent traffic loops. The network employs equal-cost multi-path (ECMP) routing, with all paths between different tiers active to ensure high redundancy and bandwidth. This design is illustrated by the network's tiered structure, where each tier represents groups of network devices that provide redundancy and high bandwidth connectivity.

Azure Well-Architected Framework

The new era of digital disruption has fundamentally changed business methodologies due to cloud computing. Besides shifting workloads and reshaping how security frameworks are built and deployed, this innovation has also evolved the role of the solution architect. Today, architects are also responsible for translating business needs into application functionalities. Furthermore, the solution must be scalable, resilient, efficient, and secure and fulfill its primary function.

A robust and comprehensive framework becomes imperative as we move into the Internet of Things (IoT). An ideal IoT solution is expected to be a paragon of service provision, ensuring availability, flexibility, recoverability, and performance that cater to the nuanced needs of cloud consumers. The IoT design process requires adhering to certain design principles when crafting such solutions.

Architectural tasks encompass various activities, from planning and designing to implementing and refining technological systems. A system's architecture is like a well-oiled machine – it seamlessly integrates business needs with technical prowess. For every system component to harmoniously align with the others, a reasonable balance must be struck between risk, cost, and capability during this intricate design process.

Figure 3-7 illustrates the well-architected framework for the Internet of Things – Azure that must be adopted when designing an IoT solution.

CHAPTER 3   DESIGN AND DEPLOY AZURE IOT NETWORKS

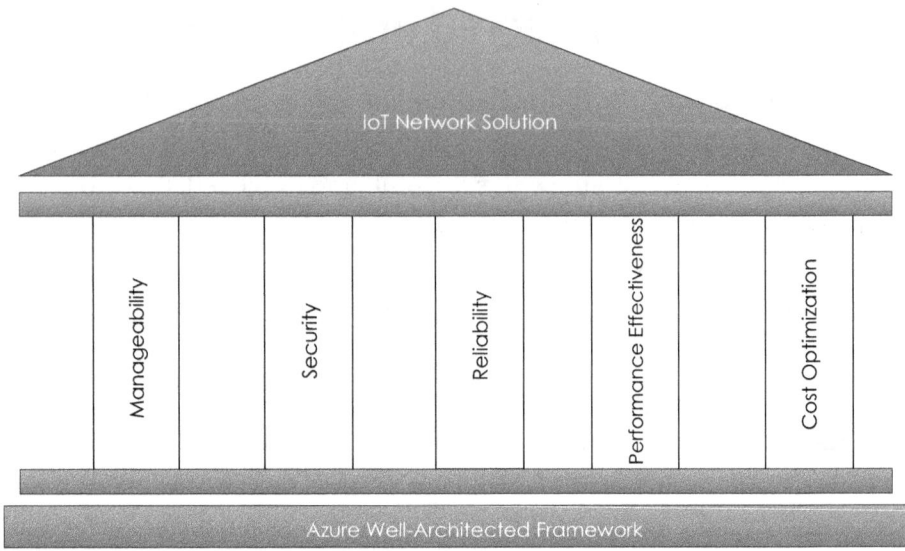

Figure 3-7. *Internet of Things – Azure Well-Architected Framework*

It is essential to understand that architecture is a one-size-fits-all template; each solution is unique and tailored to solve specific problems. Azure's Well-Architected Framework simplifies the process of creating top-tier solutions. The overarching principles, however, are universally applicable regardless of the cloud provider, architecture, or technology used. Despite not being exhaustive, these concepts are essential for IoT solution architects to build a solid foundation for the future.

Architects and engineers in the IoT focus on the principles of reliability, availability, flexibility, recoverability, and performance. Each layer of the IoT solution adheres to these guiding principles, resulting in a robust and enduring solution that adheres to these characteristics throughout the design process.

Manageability

A digital twin represents a physical environment based on data from business systems and IoT devices. These models provide businesses with actionable insights. Digital twin solutions can benefit industries for various purposes, including predictive maintenance, supply chain transparency, real-time inventory management, and developing connected homes and intelligent buildings.

Reliability

IoT solutions emphasize business continuity and disaster recovery as the cornerstones of reliability. To achieve the desired uptime, it is essential to design with high availability (HA) and disaster recovery (DR) in mind. Azure offers various services with unique redundancy and failover options to meet specific uptime goals. To decide which HA/DR option is most appropriate, evaluating the level of resiliency, implementation complexities, maintenance requirements, and the impact on the cost of goods sold (COGS) is essential.

Security

Protecting valuable data and systems from intentional attacks and misuse is paramount. Zero trust is today's leading security model, which considers every access attempt malicious and assumes breaches are inevitable. Implementing zero trust involves

- Ensuring strong device authentication
- Adhering to the principle of least privilege
- Monitoring device health
- Regularly updating devices
- Remaining vigilant against emerging threats

CHAPTER 3 DESIGN AND DEPLOY AZURE IOT NETWORKS

In addition to communication security, firmware and application software should be updated regularly to address vulnerabilities. All device interactions must be trustworthy, encrypted, and supported by robust cryptographic capabilities. It adds an extra layer of security to physically tamper-proof devices, for example, by using trusted platform modules and intrusion detection sensors.

According to the zero-trust model, security breaches are a given. Every network access attempt is treated with caution, assuming an unsecured origin. Using this approach, identity protection is robust, access is restricted, users are verified, and device visibility is maintained. Based on real-time risk assessments, dynamic access decisions can be made. IoT solutions should use robust authentication methods, limit access to essential functions, monitor device health continuously, deliver regular updates, and monitor threats vigilantly.

Keeping communication secure is crucial. Every bit of information a device sends or receives must be inherently trustworthy. Devices without cryptographic capabilities should communicate only across the local network. Data encryption, digital signatures using reliable symmetric-key encryption algorithms, support for specific communication protocols like TLS 1.2 or DTLS 1.2, and certificate handling are all essential cryptographic capabilities. A unique identifier should be stored securely and updated regularly or during an emergency.

Field gateways facilitate secure device-to-cloud communication for devices that must meet security standards. Devices must be able to receive firmware and software updates to resolve vulnerabilities. Physical security should also be considered. Microcontrollers and hardware containing secure cryptographic keys integrated with trusted platforms such as TPM are recommended to prevent physical tampering of devices. As a result, boot-up and software loading will be safe. Sensors in devices should detect unauthorized intrusions or manipulations, alerting the system and possibly initiating a "digital self-destruction" to safeguard data.

Cost Optimization

Cost optimization tools like the Azure Pricing Calculator are crucial in managing and reducing unnecessary expenditures in cloud environments. These tools provide detailed cost estimates based on specific usage patterns and configurations, allowing businesses to forecast expenses accurately. This granular visibility helps organizations identify potential savings opportunities and make informed decisions about resource allocation. For example, companies can use the calculator to compare the costs of different services and choose the most cost-effective options that still meet their operational needs.

Beyond mere cost estimation, the Azure Pricing Calculator aids in improving operational efficiency. By simulating various scenarios, businesses can test the financial impact of scaling resources up or down, transitioning to different service plans, or optimizing their current setup. This predictive capability enables proactive financial planning and ensures that resources are utilized effectively. Consequently, organizations can avoid over-provisioning, reduce wastage, and ensure they only pay for what they need, aligning their cloud expenditures with their business requirements.

The Azure Pricing Calculator also supports continuous monitoring and adjustment, which is vital for maintaining cost efficiency over time. As business needs evolve and cloud usage patterns change, ongoing calculator use helps organizations stay agile and responsive. By regularly reviewing and adjusting their configurations, businesses can optimize costs and adapt to new demands without compromising performance. This iterative process enhances financial control and supports sustainable growth by ensuring that cloud investments align with strategic goals.

CHAPTER 3   DESIGN AND DEPLOY AZURE IOT NETWORKS

Performance Efficiency

IoT applications must be architected with distinct services that scale independently based on user demands to create globally scalable IoT solutions. It is important to consider scalability for Azure services like IoT Hub, Azure Functions, and Stream Analytics, all of which have unique scaling factors and best practices. To create globally scalable IoT solutions, IoT applications must be architected with distinct services that can scale independently depending on user demands. It is important to consider scalability for Azure services like IoT Hub, Azure Functions, and Stream Analytics, all of which have unique scaling factors and best practices.

An IoT Hub manages a device's communication. Each IoT hub has a set number of units within a specific pricing and scale tier, defining how many messages devices can relay daily. Scaling up the hub keeps ongoing operations running smoothly. Ingestion throughput, processing throughput, and daily message quota play a role in IoT Hub scalability. Messages from a specific device are automatically partitioned by IoT Hub according to its ID, allowing parallel processing.

The processing capability of Azure Functions is determined by how fast a single function instance can handle events from one partition when accessing an Azure Event Hubs endpoint. When messages are processed efficiently, batches are processed in a grouped manner.

The Stream Analytics pipeline scales best when it operates in parallel, from input to output. This configuration distributes tasks across multiple computational nodes, maximizing efficiency and performance.

Azure Network Topology

Network topology is a critical element of a landing zone architecture because it defines how applications can communicate with one another. This section explores technologies and topology approaches for Azure deployments, focusing on two core approaches: topologies based on Azure Virtual WAN and traditional topologies.

CHAPTER 3　DESIGN AND DEPLOY AZURE IOT NETWORKS

Virtual WAN Network Topology

Virtual WAN can meet large-scale interconnectivity requirements. Virtual WAN is a Microsoft-managed service that reduces overall network complexity and helps modernize an organization's network. Consider using a Virtual WAN topology if your organization has specific needs. For instance, if you intend to deploy resources across several Azure regions and require global connectivity between virtual networks in these regions and multiple on-premises locations, Virtual WAN is ideal.

It is also suitable for organizations planning to use a software-defined WAN (SD-WAN) deployment to integrate a large-scale branch network directly into Azure, especially if more than 30 branch sites need native IPSec termination. Furthermore, if your organization requires transitive routing between a virtual private network (VPN) and Azure ExpressRoute, Virtual WAN provides the necessary infrastructure. This can be useful for connecting site-to-site VPNs from remote branches or point-to-site VPNs for remote users to an ExpressRoute-connected datacenter through Azure.

When planning your Azure network architecture, leveraging Azure Virtual WAN can significantly streamline your connectivity strategies. As a Microsoft-managed solution, Azure Virtual WAN provides seamless, global transit connectivity, reducing the need for manual configuration of network elements like user-defined routes (UDR) and network virtual appliances (NVAs). This service is designed to simplify the creation of a scalable hub-and-spoke network architecture, supporting extensive connectivity needs across multiple Azure regions and on-premise locations. Understanding the key design considerations is essential to effectively harnessing the capabilities of Azure Virtual WAN and ensuring a robust, high-performance network. Table 3-8 provides insight into design considerations.

Table 3-8. Key design considerations for IoT Networks

Consideration	Details
Management	Azure Virtual WAN is a Microsoft-managed solution offering end-to-end, global, and dynamic transit connectivity, eliminating the need for manual configuration of network connectivity.
Architecture	Simplifies network connectivity in Azure and from on-premises by creating a scalable hub-and-spoke architecture supporting multiple Azure regions and on-premises locations.
Transitive connectivity	Supports paths like virtual network to virtual network, virtual network to branch, branch to virtual network, and branch to branch within the same region and across regions.
Deployment restrictions	WAN hubs can only deploy Microsoft-managed resources such as virtual network gateways, Azure Firewall via Firewall Manager, route tables, and specific NVAs for SD-WAN.
Throughput and limits	Each hub supports up to 50 Gbps aggregate throughput for VNet-to-VNet traffic, and there are limits on the number of VM workloads and connections per hub.
SD-WAN integration	Integrates with various SD-WAN providers and managed services.
User VPN gateways	Scale up to 20-Gbps aggregated throughput and 100,000 client connections per virtual hub.
Site-to-site VPN gateways	Scale up to 20-Gbps aggregated throughput.
ExpressRoute integration	Supports Local, Standard, or Premium SKU for connecting circuits to a Virtual WAN hub with specific transit capabilities depending on the location.

(*continued*)

Table 3-8. (*continued*)

Consideration	Details
Security	Azure Firewall can be deployed in the Virtual WAN hub (secured virtual hub), but hub-to-hub traffic via Azure Firewall isn't currently supported within the hub itself. Workarounds include deploying the firewall in a spoke virtual network or using NSGs.
Resource group deployment	Requires all Virtual WAN resources to deploy into the same resource group.
DDoS protection	Azure DDoS Protection plans can be shared across all VNets in a Microsoft Entra tenant to protect public IP addresses, though Virtual WAN secure hubs don't support DDoS standard plans.

Designing an optimal network architecture with Azure Virtual WAN is a strategic process that maximizes the service's benefits. Virtual WAN offers an efficient way to achieve global transit connectivity without the complexities of manual transitive routing setups for organizations embarking on large-scale or international deployments. This approach enhances scalability and performance and simplifies network management across various regions and on-premises locations. The following recommendations are tailored to help you strategically deploy and manage Virtual WAN, ensuring seamless connectivity, robust security, and efficient resource utilization. Table 3-9 provides insight into design recommendations.

Table 3-9. Key design recommendations for IoT Networks

Recommendation	Details
New deployments	Use Virtual WAN for new large or global network deployments in Azure for simplified transitive routing.
Resource group management	Deploy all Virtual WAN resources into a single resource group within the connectivity subscription, even across multiple regions.
Traffic segmentation	Utilize virtual hub routing features for traffic segmentation between VNets and branches.
On-premises connectivity	Connect Virtual WAN hubs to on-premises datacenters via ExpressRoute and branches/remote locations via site-to-site VPN or SD-WAN solutions.
User connectivity	Enable user connectivity to the Virtual WAN hub through point-to-site VPN.
Azure backbone usage	Ensure intra-Azure communication remains within the Microsoft backbone network, maintaining the principle of "traffic in Azure stays in Azure."
Security	Deploy Azure Firewall in the virtual hub for outbound protection and filtering, and consider NVA firewalls for SD-WAN connectivity and next-generation firewall capabilities.
Partner integration	Follow partner vendor guidance for deploying NVAs to avoid conflicts with Azure networking configurations.
Migration	For brownfield scenarios, follow guidelines for migrating from a hub-and-spoke network topology to Virtual WAN.
Resource management	Create Azure Virtual WAN and Azure Firewall resources within the connectivity subscription, ensuring adherence to Azure Virtual WAN limits.

(continued)

Table 3-9. (*continued*)

Recommendation	Details
Monitoring	Utilize Azure Monitor insights to oversee the end-to-end topology, status, and key metrics of your Virtual WAN deployment.
DDoS protection plan	Deploy a single Azure DDoS standard protection plan in the connectivity subscription, applying it to all landing zone and platform VNets.
Scaling limits	Avoid exceeding 500 virtual network connections per Virtual WAN hub. Deploy additional hubs within the same region if necessary.

Traditional Network Topology

A traditional hub-and-spoke network topology empowers you to manage routing and security, offering high control and flexibility. This makes it suitable for organizations with specific needs. For example, a traditional topology is appropriate if your organization plans to deploy resources across one or several Azure regions and expects some traffic across these regions but only requires a partial mesh network across some areas. This approach also fits organizations with fewer remote or branch locations in each region, requiring at most 30 IPSec site-to-site tunnels. Additionally, if your organization needs complete control and granularity to manually configure Azure network routing policies, a traditional hub-and-spoke topology provides the necessary flexibility.

By thoroughly understanding the differences and benefits of Virtual WAN and traditional topologies, organizations can make informed decisions and choose the most appropriate network architecture to

CHAPTER 3　DESIGN AND DEPLOY AZURE IOT NETWORKS

meet their specific requirements in Azure. This knowledge empowers organizations to optimize network performance and security, ensuring a smooth and efficient Azure deployment.

Creating an efficient and secure Azure network architecture requires a thorough understanding of design considerations that impact connectivity, scalability, and security. Different network topologies, such as hub-and-spoke, full-mesh, and hybrid configurations, offer unique advantages and challenges. This section explores critical factors like subscription boundaries, peering methods, transit networks, and protection plans. By examining these considerations, you can ensure that your Azure network is well-structured, resilient, and capable of supporting complex, large-scale deployments. Table 3-10 provides insight into design considerations.

Table 3-10. Key design considerations for IoT Networks

Aspect	Details
Network topologies	Various network topologies can connect multiple landing zone virtual networks, including hub-and-spoke, full-mesh, and hybrid topologies. Multiple virtual networks can be connected via multiple Azure ExpressRoute circuits or connections.
Subscription boundaries	Virtual networks can't traverse subscription boundaries, but virtual network peering, ExpressRoute circuits, or VPN gateways can achieve connectivity between virtual networks across different subscriptions.
Virtual network peering	Preferred method to connect virtual networks within the same region, across different Azure regions, and across different Microsoft Entra tenants.
Transit networks	Virtual network peering and global virtual network peering are not transitive. User-defined routes (UDRs) and network virtual appliances (NVAs) are needed to enable a transit network.

(continued)

Table 3-10. (*continued*)

Aspect	Details
DDoS protection	Azure DDoS Protection plans can be shared across all virtual networks in a single Microsoft Entra tenant to protect resources with public IP addresses. The cost covers 100 public IP addresses, with additional costs for more resources.
ExpressRoute circuits	Used to establish connectivity across virtual networks within the same geopolitical region or with a premium add-on for cross-region connectivity. Network-to-network traffic may experience latency, and the ExpressRoute gateway SKU constrains bandwidth.
VPN gateways	Transitive within Azure and on-premises networks using Border Gateway Protocol (BGP), but not with ExpressRoute by default. For transitive access with ExpressRoute, consider Azure Route Server.
Connection optimization	Multiple ExpressRoute circuits connected to the same virtual network should use connection weights and BGP techniques for optimal traffic paths.
Route server	Simplifies dynamic routing between NVAs and virtual networks, eliminating the need for manual route table configuration.
Network group isolation	Multiple network groups can isolate virtual networks, each providing regional and multi-region support for connectivity.
Security administrator rules	Centrally apply rules to deny or allow traffic flows, overriding NSG rules, to enforce company policies and create security guardrails.
BGP metrics	Changes to BGP metrics for influencing ExpressRoute routing must be configured outside of the Azure platform by the organization or connectivity provider.
ExpressRoute and VPN limits	ExpressRoute circuits have limits on connections and route identification. VPN gateways support a maximum aggregated throughput of 10 Gbps and up to 100 site-to-site tunnels.

CHAPTER 3 DESIGN AND DEPLOY AZURE IOT NETWORKS

Designing a network architecture that aligns with your organization's goals requires careful consideration of different deployment scenarios and their associated requirements. From traditional hub-and-spoke models to advanced global virtual network peering, each topology offers distinct benefits and trade-offs. This section presents a set of design recommendations tailored to various use cases, ensuring optimal connectivity, security, and manageability. By adhering to these guidelines, you can construct an Azure network that meets current demands and scales efficiently to accommodate future growth. Table 3-11 provides insight into deployment recommendations.

Table 3-11. Key deployment recommendation for IoT Networks

Scenario	Recommendation
Single region deployment	Use a hub-and-spoke network topology.
Multi-region deployment without transitive connectivity	Use a hub-and-spoke network topology with no need for transitive connectivity between regions.
Multi-region deployment with global peering	Use global virtual network peering to connect virtual networks across regions.
Main hybrid connectivity method	Use ExpressRoute primarily with less than 100 VPN connections per VPN gateway.
Regional deployments	Utilize hub-and-spoke topology with regional hubs for each spoke Azure region.
ExpressRoute cross-premises connectivity	Enable in two different peering locations for resilience. Use VPN for branch connectivity and NVAs for spoke-to-spoke connectivity.

(continued)

Table 3-11. (*continued*)

Scenario	Recommendation
Internet-outbound protection	Deploy Azure Firewall or partner NVAs in the central-hub virtual network.
High-level isolation needs	Use multiple virtual networks connected via multiple ExpressRoute circuits at different peering locations.
ExpressRoute bandwidth for business units	Dedicate specific ExpressRoute bandwidth for business units.
Firewall and traffic inspection	Deploy NVAs in the central-hub virtual network for traffic protection and filtering.
Existing network connections	Use MPLS and SD-WAN for branch connectivity to corporate headquarters.
Route server for transitivity	Use Route Server for transitivity between ExpressRoute and VPN gateways in a hub-and-spoke scenario.
Direct regional connectivity	Use global virtual network peering for hub virtual networks in different regions to ensure low latency and high throughput.
Managed global transit network	Use Azure Virtual WAN for hub-and-spoke architectures across more than two regions, ensuring minimized network management overhead.
Network insights	Use Azure Monitor network insights for end-to-end monitoring of network state on Azure.
Spoke-to-hub connectivity limits	Ensure the number of spoke virtual networks connected to the hub virtual network does not exceed virtual network peering connections and private peering prefix limits.

CHAPTER 3   DESIGN AND DEPLOY AZURE IOT NETWORKS

Adopt Virtual Network Manager to Easy Your Design

You can use Virtual Network Manager to implement Azure landing zone design principles for application migrations, modernization, and innovation at scale. The Azure landing zone conceptual architecture recommends two primary networking topologies: one based on Azure Virtual WAN and another based on a traditional hub-and-spoke architecture.

Virtual Network Manager allows you to adapt and implement networking changes as your business requirements evolve. For example, if you require hybrid connectivity to migrate on-premises applications to Azure, the Virtual Network Manager can facilitate these changes without disrupting the resources you deploy in Azure.

Both existing and new virtual networks can be configured using Virtual Network Manager in three different ways:

- Hub-and-spoke topology
- Mesh topology (preview)
- Hub-and-spoke topology with direct connectivity between spokes

In Virtual Network Manager, hubs and spokes are connected directly to each other in a hub-and-spoke topology. By using the connected group feature, virtual networks within the same network group can be connected directly. The same virtual network can be shared by two connected groups.

Using Virtual Network Manager, you can dynamically or statically add virtual networks to specific network groups, defining and creating the topology you need based on your connectivity preferences. While providing region and multi-region support for spoke-to-spoke connectivity within defined limits, you can create multiple network groups to isolate virtual networks from direct connectivity.

From a security perspective, a Virtual Network Manager offers an efficient way to centrally apply security administrator rules to deny or allow traffic flows, overriding the regulations defined in network security groups (NSGs). This central control allows network security administrators to enforce access controls while enabling application owners to manage lower-level rules in NSGs.

You can group virtual networks and apply configurations to these groups rather than individual networks, allowing you to manage connectivity, configuration, security rules, and deployment across one or more regions without losing fine-grained control. Networks can be segmented by environments, teams, locations, lines of business, or other functional criteria. Group membership can be defined statically or dynamically based on set conditions.

In a traditional hub-and-spoke deployment, you manually create and maintain virtual network peering connections. Virtual Network Manager automates this process, making managing large and complex network topologies like mesh at scale easier. The security requirements of different business functions guide the creation of network groups, which can be selected manually or through conditional statements.

When designing network groups, evaluate which parts of your network share common security characteristics. For example, creating network groups for corporate and online functions allows you to manage their connectivity and security rules at scale. Virtual Network Manager can efficiently apply security attributes to multiple virtual networks across subscriptions.

Virtual Network Manager's security administrator rules have higher priority than NSG rules applied at the subnet level, enabling network and security teams to enforce company policies and create security guardrails at scale. This feature allows product teams to maintain control of NSGs within their landing zone subscriptions.

Security administrator rules can explicitly allow or deny specific network flows independent of NSG configurations at the subnet or network interface levels. This capability ensures that critical management services network flows are always permitted, and application-controlled NSGs cannot override these rules.

To implement these design principles, define the scope of the Virtual Network Manager and apply security administrator rules that enforce organization-level policies at the root management group or tenant level. This strategy ensures the hierarchical application of laws to existing and new resources across associated management groups.

Create a Virtual Network Manager instance in the Connectivity subscription, with a scope of the intermediate root management group. Enable the security administrator feature on this instance to define rules that apply across all virtual networks and subnets in your Azure landing zone hierarchy, democratizing NSG control to application teams.

Segment networks by grouping virtual networks statically or dynamically. Enable direct connectivity between spokes that frequently communicate with low latency and high throughput. Communication across all virtual networks in different regions must be enabled for global mesh topologies. Assign priority values to security administrator rules, ensuring lower values indicate higher priority. Use these rules to control network flows and delegate NSG management to application teams.

IoT IP Planning with Azure

IP planning in IoT networks is crucial to network management and architecture. It involves strategically allocating and managing IP address spaces to ensure seamless connectivity, avoid conflicts, and maintain efficient network operations. In IoT environments, devices are often numerous and diverse, making IP planning complex but essential for maintaining communication and control over the network.

CHAPTER 3   DESIGN AND DEPLOY AZURE IOT NETWORKS

Design Considerations for IP Planning in IoT Networks

When planning IP addressing in Azure, it's vital to ensure that IP address spaces are distinct between on-premises locations and different Azure regions. Overlapping IP addresses can lead to significant connectivity issues and operational challenges. Table 3-12 provides insight about design consideration for IP planning.

Table 3-12. *Key design consideration for IoT IP planning*

Consideration	Description
Overlapping IP address spaces	Overlapping IP address spaces across on-premises and Azure regions can create major contention challenges.
NAT capability	Azure VPN Gateway can connect overlapping on-premises sites with overlapping IP address spaces through network address translation (NAT) capability. This feature is available in Azure Virtual WAN and standalone Azure VPN Gateway. {Diagram that shows how NAT works with VPN Gateway.}
Adding address space	You can add address space after creating a virtual network. This process doesn't need an outage if the virtual network is already connected to another virtual network via virtual network peering. Instead, each remote peering needs a resync operation after the network space has changed.
IP address reservations	Azure reserves five IP addresses within each subnet. Factor in these addresses when sizing virtual networks and subnets.
Dedicated subnets	Some Azure services require dedicated subnets, such as Azure Firewall and Azure VPN Gateway.
Subnet delegation	You can delegate subnets to certain services to create instances of a service within the subnet.

Design Recommendations for IP Planning in IoT Networks

Effective IP planning involves foresight and strategic allocation of IP addresses to avoid conflicts and ensure efficient network operation. Table 3-13 provides insight about design recommendation for IP planning.

Table 3-13. Key design consideration for IP planning

Recommendation	Description
Non-overlapping IP addresses	Plan for non-overlapping IP address spaces across Azure regions and on-premises locations in advance.
Private IP addresses	Use IP addresses from the private internet address space, known as RFC 1918 addresses.
Avoid certain address ranges	Don't use the following address ranges: 224.0.0.0/4 (multicast), 255.255.255.255/32 (broadcast), 127.0.0.0/8 (loopback), 169.254.0.0/16 (link-local), 168.63.129.16/32 (internal DNS).
IPv6 utilization	For environments with limited availability of private IP addresses, consider using IPv6. Virtual networks can be IPv4-only or dual stack IPv4+IPv6. {Diagram that shows IPv4 and IPv6 dual stack.}
Optimal subnet sizes	Don't create large virtual networks like /16 to ensure IP address space isn't wasted. The smallest supported IPv4 subnet is /29, and the largest is /2 when using CIDR subnet definitions. IPv6 subnets must be exactly /64 in size.

(continued)

Table 3-13. (*continued*)

Recommendation	Description
Advance planning	Don't create virtual networks without planning the required address space in advance.
Public IP addresses	Avoid using public IP addresses for virtual networks, especially if the public IP addresses don't belong to your organization.
Service-specific IPs	Consider services with reserved IPs, such as AKS with CNI networking.
Non-routable networks	Use non-routable landing zone spoke virtual networks and Azure Private Link service to prevent IPv4 exhaustion.

IPv6 Considerations

Adopting IPv6 addresses the issue of IPv4 space exhaustion and provides connectivity for IPv6-only clients. Table 3-14 provides insight about design consideration for Ipv6 planning.

Table 3-14. *Key design consideration for IPv6 planning*

Consideration	Description
Phased adoption	Implement IPv6 where needed based on business needs. IPv4 and IPv6 can coexist as long as necessary.
Native IPv6 support	Use native end-to-end IPv4 and IPv6 where possible to avoid translation complications.
Dual-stack gateways	For complex applications, consider using dual-stack IPv4/IPv6 gateways to manage translation between protocols.

IPv6 adoption is crucial for addressing IPv4 space exhaustion and ensuring connectivity for IPv6-only clients. Table 3-15 lists recommendations for effectively implementing IPv6 in your network architecture.

Table 3-15. Key deployment consideration for IPv6 planning

Recommendation	Description
Resilient deployments	Deploy NVAs in VMSS Flex for resiliency and expose them through Azure Load Balancer with a public IP address front end.
Global routing	Use Azure Front Door for global routing of web traffic and proxying IPv6 client requests to an IPv4-only backend.
IPv6 CIDR blocks	Use /64 for IPv6 subnets to ensure compatibility with routing requirements.
Route and security updates	Update route tables and security group rules to accommodate IPv6 traffic.

IP Address Management (IPAM) Tools: Employing an IP address management (IPAM) tool facilitates streamlined IP address planning in Azure by offering centralized management and visibility. IPAM helps prevent overlaps and conflicts in IP address spaces.

Azure Network Connectivity

Azure Network Connectivity encompasses services and features designed to establish robust connections within the Azure ecosystem and between Azure and on-premises environments. Organizations can create secure, reliable, and scalable network infrastructures tailored to their needs by leveraging technologies like Azure Virtual Network, VPN Gateway, ExpressRoute, and Azure Firewall. Whether setting up virtual private networks (VPNs) for remote access, establishing site-to-site connections for hybrid cloud deployments, or ensuring secure internet access for Azure resources, Azure Network Connectivity provides the tools and capabilities to build resilient network architectures. With features like network peering, load balancers, and DDoS protection, Azure Network Connectivity empowers organizations to optimize performance, enhance security, and streamline management of their network environments in the cloud.

Azure offers a range of options for network connectivity, catering to diverse needs and scenarios. These options allow organizations to design and implement robust network architectures tailored to their specific requirements. Let's explore some of the key options for Azure Network Connectivity:

- Azure Virtual Network (VNet): Azure Virtual Network is the fundamental building block for private and isolated network environments in Azure. It enables organizations to create virtual networks in the cloud, complete with subnets, route tables, and network security groups. VNets offer the flexibility to segment and isolate workloads while providing connectivity to other Azure services. With VNets, organizations can define their IP address space, establish private communication between resources, and integrate with on-premises networks using VPN or ExpressRoute connections.

- VPN Gateway: Azure VPN Gateway facilitates secure communication between Azure VNets and remote networks or devices over the public internet. It supports various VPN protocols, including Point-to-Site (P2S) VPN for individual devices and Site-to-Site (S2S) VPN for connecting on-premises networks to Azure VNets. VPN Gateway ensures data encryption and integrity, enabling organizations to securely extend their on-premises infrastructure to Azure. It's suitable for scenarios requiring secure remote access or hybrid connectivity.

- ExpressRoute: Azure ExpressRoute provides private, dedicated, high-throughput connectivity between Azure data centers and on-premises networks. Unlike VPNs, ExpressRoute connections do not traverse the public internet, offering enhanced security, reliability, and consistent network performance. ExpressRoute circuits can be provisioned with different bandwidth options, ranging from standard to premium, to meet specific workload requirements. It's ideal for mission-critical workloads, large-scale data transfer, and scenarios that demand predictable latency and bandwidth.

- Azure Firewall: Azure Firewall is a cloud-native network security service that offers stateful firewall capabilities for controlling traffic and protecting Azure resources. It provides centralized management, network traffic monitoring, and features like application rules, network rules, and threat intelligence integration. Azure Firewall can be deployed as a standalone instance or integrated with Azure Virtual Network to secure inbound and outbound traffic effectively. It's suitable for scenarios requiring network security and compliance enforcement at scale.

CHAPTER 3   DESIGN AND DEPLOY AZURE IOT NETWORKS

- Network Peering: Azure Virtual Network Peering enables seamless connectivity and communication between Azure VNets across different regions or subscriptions. It allows resources in peered VNets to communicate with each other as if they were part of the same network without the need for gateways or additional transit networks. Network peering simplifies network architecture, reduces latency, and enhances scalability by eliminating data traffic hairpinning. It suits scenarios where organizations require interconnected VNets for distributed applications or multi-tier architectures.

Azure Network Connectivity offers organizations a wide range of options. By leveraging these services in combination with each other or with other Azure services, organizations can build resilient, scalable, and secure network architectures to meet their evolving business needs in the cloud.

For optimal performance, resilience, and security, network connectivity solutions in Azure must consider a variety of factors. Whether connecting on-premises environments to Azure or establishing connectivity between Azure resources, making informed design decisions is crucial. Table 3-16 illustrates the stage for exploring the critical design considerations for Azure network connectivity solutions.

Table 3-16. *Key design consideration for Azure Network Connectivity*

Consideration	Description
Azure ExpressRoute	Offers dedicated private connectivity to Azure IaaS and PaaS services from on-premises locations.
Azure VPN (S2S) gateway	Provides Site-to-Site shared connectivity over the public internet to Azure IaaS virtual networks from on-premises locations.
Azure ExpressRoute vs. VPN (S2S)	Both options have distinct capabilities, costs, and performance metrics, necessitating a comparison.
Private links	Establish connectivity to PaaS services either over ExpressRoute with private peering or VPN S2S from on-premises connected locations.
Multi-virtual network connectivity	When multiple virtual networks connect to the same ExpressRoute circuit, they merge into the same routing domain, sharing the bandwidth.
ExpressRoute global reach	Connects on-premises locations through ExpressRoute circuits to transit traffic over the Microsoft backbone network, available in various peering locations.
ExpressRoute direct	Allows creation of multiple ExpressRoute circuits at no additional cost, with direct connection to Microsoft's ExpressRoute routers.
FastPath	Enhances data path performance between on-premises and virtual network by directing traffic directly to virtual machines, bypassing the gateway.

Table 3-17 illustrates the stage for exploring the key design recommendation for Azure network connectivity solutions.

Table 3-17. *Key design recommendation for Azure Network Connectivity*

Recommendation	Description
Prioritize ExpressRoute	Use ExpressRoute as the primary connectivity channel for linking on-premises network to Azure, with VPNs serving as backup sources for enhanced resiliency.
Deploy Dual ExpressRoute circuits	Employ dual circuits from different peering locations to ensure redundant paths and eliminate single points of failure.
Optimize ExpressRoute routing	Utilize BGP local preference and AS PATH prepending for optimizing routing with multiple ExpressRoute circuits.
Select Appropriate SKU	Choose the right SKU for ExpressRoute/VPN gateways based on bandwidth and performance requirements.
Deploy zone-redundant gateways	Enhance availability by deploying zone-redundant ExpressRoute gateways in supported Azure regions.
Utilize ExpressRoute direct	For bandwidth needs surpassing 10 Gbps, utilize ExpressRoute Direct for dedicated ports and higher throughput.
Enable FastPath	Enhance performance by enabling FastPath to bypass the ExpressRoute gateway for low-latency and high-throughput scenarios.
Use VPN gateways for branch connectivity	Connect branches or remote locations to Azure using VPN gateways, deploying zone-redundant gateways for resilience where available.
Leverage ExpressRoute global reach	Connect large offices or datacenters to Azure through ExpressRoute Global Reach for enhanced connectivity.

(*continued*)

Table 3-17. (*continued*)

Recommendation	Description
Isolate traffic with different circuits	Ensure isolated routing domains and mitigate noisy-neighbor risks by using different ExpressRoute circuits for dedicated bandwidth requirements.
Monitor ExpressRoute components	Utilize ExpressRoute network insights and Connection Monitor for effective monitoring and issue resolution of connectivity between Azure and on-premises locations.
Avoid single peering location	Minimize single points of failure by avoiding reliance on ExpressRoute circuits from a single peering location.

Prepare Your Outbound and Inbound IoT Connectivity

In recent years, the Internet of Things (IoT) has revolutionized the way we interact with technology, making it possible to collect, exchange, and analyze data through a vast network of interconnected devices. As IoT systems grow in complexity and scale, various factors must be considered to ensure they are secure, efficient, and scalable. The following tables outline key design considerations and recommendations for developing robust IoT systems, particularly within the Azure ecosystem. These guidelines aim to help organizations achieve optimal performance while maintaining high security and usability standards.

Table 3-18 illustrates the stage for exploring the key design consideration for Azure network Outbound and Inbound connectivity solutions.

Table 3-18. Key design recommendation for Azure Network Connectivity

Aspect	Details
Scalability	IoT systems must support a large number of devices and users, allowing for seamless addition and integration of new devices.
Security	Robust security measures are essential to protect data and devices from unauthorized access and cyber threats.
Interoperability	IoT devices should communicate effectively across different platforms and standards, ensuring smooth data exchange and functionality.
Data management	Efficient data handling, including collection, storage, and analysis, is critical to manage the vast amounts of data generated by IoT devices.
Power efficiency	Devices should be designed to consume minimal power, extending battery life and reducing energy consumption.
Network reliability	A reliable and stable network infrastructure is necessary to maintain continuous connectivity and data transmission.
User privacy	Implementing measures to ensure user data privacy and compliance with regulations is paramount.
Cost	Consideration of both initial setup and ongoing operational costs is important for sustainable IoT deployment.
Latency	Low latency is essential for real-time applications, requiring optimized network and device performance.
User experience	The system should be user-friendly, with intuitive interfaces and easy-to-understand functionalities.

(*continued*)

Table 3-18. (*continued*)

Aspect	Details
Network security services	Utilize managed network security services to minimize operational and management costs.
Compatibility	Ensure compatibility with both native and partner network virtual appliances (NVAs) to meet specific security requirements.
Outbound connectivity	Implement scalable and efficient outbound connectivity methods for IoT devices, such as NAT gateways.
Firewall usage	Use firewalls to govern outbound traffic, non-HTTP/S inbound connections, and east-west traffic filtering.
Advanced security features	Employ advanced firewall capabilities, such as TLS inspection and intrusion detection systems, for enhanced security.
IP management	Use IP groups in firewall rules to manage multiple IP addresses and ranges across different regions and subscriptions.
Custom routes	Utilize service tags in user-defined routes to manage outbound connectivity to platform as a service (PaaS) services.
Global security policies	Create and assign global firewall policies to maintain a consistent security posture across the network.
Role-based access control	Implement role-based access control to allow granular security policy management by regional teams.
Web application protection	Use web application firewalls (WAF) and Azure Front Door for protecting inbound HTTP/S traffic.

(*continued*)

CHAPTER 3   DESIGN AND DEPLOY AZURE IOT NETWORKS

Table 3-18. (*continued*)

Aspect	Details
Avoid default outbound access	Avoid using default internet outbound access to prevent security risks and SNAT port exhaustion.
SaaS security providers	Configure supported SaaS security providers for protecting outbound connections.
Traffic filtering	Deploy NVAs for east-west and north-south traffic protection and filtering.
VM management security	Prevent exposing VM management ports to the internet and use secure methods for management tasks.
Cloud-Native architecture	Adapt security implementations and architectures to the cloud environment rather than replicating on-premises setups.

Table 3-19 illustrates the stage for exploring the key design recommendation for Azure network Outbound and Inbound connectivity solutions.

Table 3-19. *Key design recommendation for Azure Network Outbound and Inbound Connectivity*

Aspect	Recommendations
Scalability	Utilize cloud services and distributed architectures to handle the increasing number of devices and data.
Security	Implement end-to-end encryption, regular firmware updates, and secure authentication mechanisms.
Interoperability	Adopt open standards and protocols to ensure compatibility across different devices and platforms.

(*continued*)

Table 3-19. (*continued*)

Aspect	Recommendations
Data management	Use scalable data storage solutions and employ advanced analytics to extract actionable insights.
Power efficiency	Design energy-efficient hardware and use low-power communication protocols like Zigbee or LoRaWAN.
Network reliability	Employ redundant network paths and ensure strong signal coverage to prevent connectivity issues.
User privacy	Follow best practices for data anonymization and ensure compliance with GDPR or other relevant privacy laws.
Cost	Opt for cost-effective components and consider the total cost of ownership, including maintenance and upgrades.
Latency	Optimize network configurations and edge computing to reduce latency for time-sensitive applications.
User experience	Conduct user testing and gather feedback to continuously improve the interface and usability of the system.
Network security services	Use managed services like Azure Firewall and Azure Web Application Firewall to reduce complexity and operational costs.
Compatibility	Integrate partner NVAs with Azure landing zone architecture when native services do not meet specific needs.
Outbound connectivity	Use Azure NAT Gateway as the default method for enabling scalable and efficient outbound connectivity.
Firewall usage	Deploy Azure Firewall for managing outbound traffic, non-HTTP/S inbound connections, and internal traffic filtering.

(*continued*)

Table 3-19. (*continued*)

Aspect	Recommendations
Advanced security features	Utilize Azure Firewall Premium for advanced features like TLS inspection, intrusion detection, and URL filtering.
IP management	Set up IP Groups in Azure Firewall for efficient management of IP addresses and ranges.
Custom routes	Specify service tags in custom routes to automate IP address updates and reduce management overhead.
Global security policies	Establish a global Azure Firewall policy and assign it to all firewall instances for consistent security enforcement.
Role-based access control	Use Azure role-based access control to delegate specific security policies to regional teams.
Web application protection	Implement WAF within landing-zone networks and use Azure Front Door with WAF policies for global protection.
Avoid default outbound access	Always use NAT gateways for outbound connectivity instead of default internet access to enhance security.
SaaS security providers	Configure and integrate SaaS security solutions within Firewall Manager to secure outbound connections.
Traffic filtering	Deploy NVAs in separate networks or hubs, depending on the network topology, for effective traffic protection.
VM management security	Use Azure Bastion and Azure Policy to secure VM management and prevent public IP exposure.
Cloud-Native architecture	Design security solutions tailored to cloud environments to leverage inherent cloud capabilities effectively.

CHAPTER 3   DESIGN AND DEPLOY AZURE IOT NETWORKS

Deploying Azure IoT Network

Designing Operational Technology (OT) and Internet of Things (IoT) networking layers involves creating a structured and hierarchical framework that accommodates a variety of device types and ensures seamless connectivity, security, and manageability. Your organization's network likely consists of diverse device types, divided into two categories: endpoint devices and network devices.

Endpoint devices encompass multiple sub-groups, including servers, computers, IoT devices, and other peripherals. These devices are the sources and consumers of data within the network, performing specific tasks and operations critical to the organizational workflow. On the other hand, network devices provide essential networking services that enable communication between endpoint devices. This group includes network switches, firewalls, routers, and access points, all of which play crucial roles in maintaining network integrity, security, and performance.

Most network environments adopt a hierarchical model composed of three layers: the core layer, the distribution layer, and the access layer to manage these devices and their interactions efficiently.

Core Layer

The core layer represents the network's backbone, providing high-speed and highly redundant data transport. This layer ensures reliable and swift data movement and is the foundation for data aggregation from all network parts. In OT/IoT networks, the core layer must handle significant data loads and support robust protocols to ensure minimal latency and maximum uptime. Core layer devices typically include high-performance routers and switches capable of managing large traffic volumes with low latency and high throughput.

Distribution Layer

The distribution layer, the aggregation layer, sits between the core and access layers. It aggregates data from multiple access layer devices and applies policies to control the data flow to the core layer. This layer is crucial for implementing network policies such as routing, filtering, and Quality of Service (QoS). In an OT/IoT network, the distribution layer can also host services that require processing close to the data source to reduce latency, such as edge computing applications. Devices in this layer include advanced switches and routers with security policies, traffic management, and load-balancing capabilities.

Access Layer

The access layer is where endpoint devices connect to the network. This layer provides the interface for IoT sensors, servers, computers, and other peripherals to communicate with the network. In the access layer, primary devices include network switches, access points, and routers, which grant or deny access to devices and often include security measures for protecting against unauthorized access. To accommodate various device types and ensure reliable and secure communication in OT/IoT environments, the access layer must support multiple connectivity options and protocols.

Integrating OT/IoT Networks

Integrating OT and IoT devices into this hierarchical model requires careful planning to address the unique needs of these technologies. OT/IoT devices often operate in environments with stringent latency, reliability, and security requirements. Therefore, the network design must ensure that these requirements are met at each layer of the hierarchy.

Core Layer: Ensure high bandwidth and low latency to handle the large volumes of data generated by IoT devices. Implement redundant pathways to maintain network availability.

Distribution Layer: Use advanced traffic management techniques to prioritize critical OT/IoT data. Implement security policies to filter and protect data as it moves towards the core.

Access Layer: Provide diverse connectivity options (e.g., wired, wireless, LPWAN) to accommodate different OT/IoT devices. Ensure robust security measures such as endpoint authentication, encryption, and network segmentation to protect the network from potential vulnerabilities introduced by various connected devices.

By structuring your network with this hierarchical model and considering the specific requirements of OT/IoT devices, you can create a scalable, secure, and efficient networking environment that supports the diverse needs of your organization's operations. This approach ensures that data flows smoothly from endpoint devices through the network infrastructure while maintaining the high levels of performance and security necessary for modern OT/IoT applications.

Purdue Networking Model

Adopting the Purdue Networking Model for Industrial Control System (ICS) security is a strategic approach to organizing and securing ICS environments. The Purdue Model, also known as the Purdue Reference Model, was meticulously developed by the esteemed Purdue University. It serves as a comprehensive framework to help understand, design and implement security measures for industrial control systems. This model segments the ICS architecture into hierarchical levels, each representing a distinct function within the control system, thus allowing for targeted and effective security strategies.

The foundation of the Purdue Model begins with Level 0, which includes process devices and physical processes. This lowest level encompasses the sensors, actuators, and other devices directly interacting with the physical environment. At this level, the focus is on real-time control and data acquisition, with devices communicating with higher levels to provide real-time data and receive control commands. This real-time interaction is crucial for the immediate and accurate functioning of the physical processes.

Moving up to Level 1, we encounter essential control functions. This level comprises programmable logic controllers (PLCs) used in discrete manufacturing and distributed control systems (DCS) used in process manufacturing. The controllers at this level interface with Level 0 devices to execute control functions by processing sensor data, making decisions, and sending commands to actuators. This layer ensures that the basic control operations are performed efficiently and accurately.

At Level 2, supervisory control systems come into play. These systems supervise and coordinate multiple control processes within a specific area. They include human-machine interfaces (HMIs), process historians, and batch management systems. Supervisory systems at this level communicate with Level 1 controllers, providing a higher-level view of the processes, interacting with operators through HMIs, and managing historical data. This level is essential for monitoring and managing the control processes to ensure they operate within desired parameters.

Level 3 focuses on manufacturing operations, representing systems responsible for managing the overall manufacturing operation within a site. This includes production scheduling, detailed reporting, and overall site-level operations management. The systems at this level integrate information from lower levels and communicate with enterprise-level systems, facilitating the coordination and optimization of manufacturing processes. This level ensures that the production operations align with the overall manufacturing goals and schedules.

CHAPTER 3   DESIGN AND DEPLOY AZURE IOT NETWORKS

At Level 4, the focus shifts to business planning and logistics. This level includes business-related systems such as enterprise resource planning (ERP), which focus on business planning, logistics, and higher-level decision-making. Systems at this level interact with Level 3 to gather production data and contribute to business-level decision-making processes, often utilizing standard IT infrastructure. This level bridges the gap between the operational side of the manufacturing processes and the strategic business planning activities.

The highest level, Level 5, involves enterprise-wide business planning and management systems. This level includes strategic decision-making and integration with corporate IT systems. Systems at this level interact with lower levels for data exchange and contribute to corporate-level decision-making processes. This level ensures that the insights and data gathered from the operational processes are utilized in strategic planning and enterprise-wide management activities.

Each level of the Purdue Model comes with its own set of security considerations. The model, emphasizing proper segmentation and security controls, is a robust tool to protect critical industrial processes from cybersecurity threats. Implementing this model in your planning helps create a structured environment for industrial control systems and ensures that each layer is adequately protected. In addition to providing a sense of security and confidence, this comprehensive approach makes the overall system resilient against cyber threats.

Deployment Overview

Deploying an Azure Network for an Azure IoT Solution involves several systematic steps to ensure the network infrastructure is robust, secure, and scalable. The first step is to meticulously plan the network architecture, which includes defining Virtual Networks (VNets) to segment and isolate network resources, organizing VNets into subnets to manage and control

CHAPTER 3 DESIGN AND DEPLOY AZURE IOT NETWORKS

traffic flow, enforcing security rules at the subnet and network interface level through network security groups (NSGs), and planning custom routes to control the traffic flow.

Now, let's put theory into practice. You'll start by creating a Virtual Network through the Azure Portal. This is where you'll see the theoretical concepts we discussed in action. You'll search for "Virtual Network," fill in the details such as the name, address space, subscription, resource group, and location, define subnets within the VNet, and then review and create the VNet. After this, you'll add subnets to the VNet by going to the "Subnets" section, clicking "+ Subnet," and configuring NSGs for each subnet to manage security. Your Azure Network will be deployed effectively with this hands-on approach.

Deploy a Virtual Network using Azure Portal

To create a new virtual network using the Azure portal, take the following steps:

Step 1: Log in to personal or business account into Azure portal (https://portal.azure.com/).

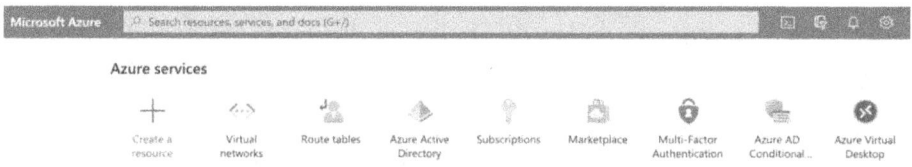

Step 2: Click the Create a resource button in the Azure portal, Enter the "virtual network" name in the search box and click on create Virtual Network.

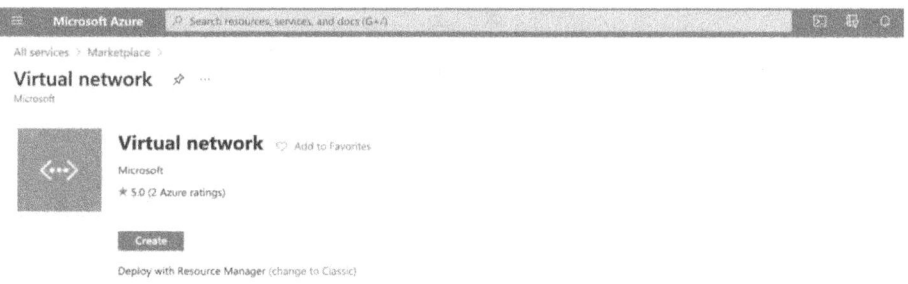

CHAPTER 3   DESIGN AND DEPLOY AZURE IOT NETWORKS

Step 3: On the basics tab, provide the inputs listed in Table 3-20.

Table 3-20. Key settings and inputs for basics tab

Setting	Inputs
Project details:	
Subscription	Select your subscription.
Resource group	Select a resource group or create a new resource group.
Instance details:	
Name	Provide IoT new VNet
Region	Select the region you want to deploy or close to your OT/IoT resource needs.

Step 4: On the IP Addresses tab provide the inputs listed in Table 3-21.

Table 3-21. Key settings and inputs for IP configuration

Setting	Inputs
Project details:	
IP addresses space	In CIDR notation, one or more address prefixes define a virtual network's address space. After creating the virtual network, you can add address spaces.
Subnet	Address range in CIDR notation for a subnet. Virtual networks must contain it within their address space. There are no special characters in subnet names except letters, numbers, underscores, periods, or hyphens.

CHAPTER 3   DESIGN AND DEPLOY AZURE IOT NETWORKS

Before you get started with IP addresses, you need to determine the first IPv4 Address space range of the subnet and Subnet.

Step 5: On the Security tab, you can choose whether to enable or disable Bastion Host, DDoS protection, and Firewall. If any of these options are allowed, you need to provide additional information for that service.

Step 6: On the Review and Create tab, wait for validation pass status before you create.

The third step involves configuring network security groups (NSGs). You'll create NSGs by searching for "network security group" in the Azure Portal, providing them with the necessary details, and then setting up inbound and outbound security rules to control traffic. These NSGs are then associated with the appropriate subnets within your VNet.

Step 1: In the search box at the top of the portal, type Network security group.

Step 2: From the search results, select Network security groups.

Step 3: Click on + Create.

On the Create network security group page, under the Basics tab, enter or select the values listed in Table 3-22.

Table 3-22. *Key settings and inputs for NSG configuration*

Setting	Inputs
Project details:	
Subscription	Select your subscription.
Resource group	Select a resource group or create a new resource group.
Instance details:	
Instance details	Enter a name for the new network security group.
Network security group name	Enter a name for the new network security group.
Region	Select the region you want to deploy or close to your OT/IoT resource needs.

CHAPTER 3   DESIGN AND DEPLOY AZURE IOT NETWORKS

Step 4: Click on Review + create.

Step 5: Once you see the Validation passed message, click Create.

Subsequently, you'll set up the Azure IoT Hub by creating it in the Azure Portal, filling in the details like name, subscription, resource group, region, and pricing tier, and configuring networking settings to connect the IoT Hub to the VNet and subnets. After creating the IoT Hub, configure its settings to include device provisioning, authentication methods, and messaging endpoints.

We will use powershell.

Step 1: Log into Azure account.

```
Login-AzAccount
```

Step 2: Deploy an IoT Hub.

```
New-AzIotHub
   -ResourceGroupName MyIoTRG1
   -Name IoTHub
   -SkuName S1 -Units 1
   -Location "East US"
```

Next, create a NAT Gateway by searching for it in the Azure Portal, providing the required details, attaching it to the necessary subnets, assigning public IP addresses or prefixes, and then reviewing and creating it. This is followed by creating an Azure Firewall in the Azure Portal, filling in the required information, configuring firewall policies and rules for inbound and outbound traffic, and associating the firewall with the relevant subnets. Define application, network, and DNAT rules to control traffic flow effectively.

The sixth step is to integrate the IoT Hub with other Azure services. This includes setting up integrations with services like Azure Stream Analytics, Azure Functions, and Azure Storage for data processing and storage. Additionally, configure diagnostics settings for the IoT Hub and network components to monitor performance and troubleshoot issues using Azure Monitor and Azure Log Analytics for comprehensive monitoring and alerting.

Next, you should test and validate the network by deploying IoT devices to connect to the IoT Hub and ensure they function correctly. You should also validate network security by testing security rules and policies, performing penetration testing, and conducting vulnerability assessments to identify and mitigate risks.

Finally, automate the deployment process using Azure Resource Manager (ARM) templates to deploy network resources and IoT components. Deploy continuous integration and continuous deployment pipelines with Azure DevOps to automate updates and deployments, ensuring a seamless and efficient deployment process.

By following these detailed steps, you can deploy a secure, scalable, and efficient Azure Network for your IoT solution. This process, meticulously designed to ensure robust connectivity and protection for your IoT devices and data, will give you the confidence that your deployment is effective and reliable.

Summary

In this chapter, we delve into the intricacies of designing and deploying an Azure IoT network, beginning with the fundamentals of network topology. This section introduces the basic concepts necessary for structuring an effective IoT network. Different network topologies such as star, mesh, and hybrid are discussed, each with advantages and disadvantages in IoT deployments. The importance of selecting an appropriate topology based on scalability, reliability, and performance is emphasized, alongside discussions on the roles of edge devices, gateways, and cloud services in creating a cohesive IoT ecosystem.

CHAPTER 3   DESIGN AND DEPLOY AZURE IOT NETWORKS

The chapter then transitions to designing networks specifically for Azure IoT, providing detailed guidance on leveraging Azure services to construct robust IoT networks. By using Azure services, you can ensure the security, performance, and scalability of your IoT networks. It covers setting up Azure Virtual Networks (VNet) to securely connect IoT devices, segmenting the network using subnets and Network security groups (NSG), and establishing secure, high-performance connections between on-premises infrastructure and Azure through VPN Gateways and ExpressRoute. Additionally, the chapter explores the use of load balancers and traffic management to ensure optimal distribution of network traffic and high availability. Best practices for network design are also discussed, such as minimizing latency, ensuring redundancy, and securing data in transit.

The final part of the chapter provides a step-by-step guide to deploying IoT networks using Azure, covering practical aspects such as configuring IoT Hub to manage device connections and communications, provisioning devices, and applying network policies to protect the network. The chapter also highlights the importance of monitoring and maintenance, detailing how to use Azure Monitor and Network Watcher to track network performance and troubleshoot issues. Real-world examples and case studies are used to illustrate the deployment process, highlighting common challenges and solutions. In the next chapter, we will delve into designing and deploying Azure IoT Security, a crucial aspect of IoT network management.

The next chapter will delve into designing and deploying Azure IoT Security. This chapter will explore critical aspects of securing IoT networks, including implementing the zero-trust model, ensuring data encryption, and protecting against cyber threats. You will learn about Azure's security services and tools and how to integrate them into your IoT solution to comprehensively safeguard your network and data.

CHAPTER 4

Design and Deploy Azure IoT Security

The fundamentals of IoT security begin with the recognition that IoT devices are particularly vulnerable to cyber threats due to their vast connectivity and data exchange capabilities. A foundational aspect of IoT security is implementing strong authentication and authorization mechanisms. By restricting access to the network to authorized devices and users, unauthorized entry can be prevented, and data breaches can be mitigated. This includes employing multifactor authentication and leveraging certificates or other cryptographic methods to verify identities. Additionally, devices and users should only receive the minimum access necessary to perform their functions according to the principle of least privilege. For devices to be protected against newly discovered threats and address known vulnerabilities, firmware, and software must be regularly updated and patched.

Another critical component of IoT security is ensuring robust data protection both in transit and at rest. Encryption prevents malicious actors from intercepting and tampering with data as it travels between devices and cloud services. Implementing secure communication protocols such as TLS (Transport Layer Security) ensures that data remains confidential and integral. By integrating these security practices, IoT networks can be fortified against a broad spectrum of cyber threats, providing data and services' integrity, confidentiality, and availability.

CHAPTER 4   DESIGN AND DEPLOY AZURE IOT SECURITY

Designing Microsoft Azure-based IoT security involves integrating Azure's comprehensive security services and tools to create a robust and resilient IoT environment. The design process starts with implementing Azure's zero-trust security model, which assumes that breaches are inevitable and requires verification of every access request as though it originates from an open network. Device authentication must be strong, the principle of least privilege must be followed, and the health of the device must be continuously monitored. Azure IoT Hub and Azure Active Directory facilitate secure device registration and management, enforcing strict access controls and policies. Encryption of data both in transit and at rest is achieved through Azure's built-in capabilities, such as Azure Security Center and Azure Key Vault, which provide advanced threat protection and secure key management. However, a key aspect of Azure's IoT security is its scalable and secure infrastructure, which ensures that businesses can deploy IoT solutions that are not only effective but also resilient to evolving cyber threats.

By the end of this chapter, you should be able to understand the following:

- Fundamentals of IoT Security
- Design Microsoft Azure-Based IoT Security
- Deploy Microsoft Azure-Based IoT Security

Fundamentals of IoT Security

The Internet of Things (IoT) is a network of interconnected devices communicating and exchanging data. As IoT devices become increasingly incorporated into our daily lives, from homes to industrial systems, we must ensure their security. IoT security involves a set of strategies and technologies designed to protect these devices and their data from unauthorized access and cyber threats.

CHAPTER 4   DESIGN AND DEPLOY AZURE IOT SECURITY

One of the core fundamentals of IoT security is device authentication. This process ensures that each device on the network is legitimate and can be trusted. Authentication mechanisms can range from simple password protection to more sophisticated methods like digital certificates and biometrics. Ensuring that devices are authenticated helps prevent unauthorized devices from joining and potentially compromising the network.

Data encryption is another crucial aspect of IoT security. Encryption converts data into a code to prevent unauthorized access. This is particularly important for IoT devices that transmit sensitive information, such as health data or financial transactions. Encrypting the data both in transit and at rest reduces the risk of data breaches. Advanced encryption standards (AES) and public critical infrastructure (PKI) are standard encryption techniques in IoT.

Securing communication channels between IoT devices is also vital. Communication protocols like HTTPS, TLS (Transport Layer Security), and DTLS (Datagram Transport Layer Security) ensure the security of data transmitted over networks. These protocols help protect against eavesdropping, tampering, and message forgery, ensuring that the integrity and confidentiality of the data are maintained.

Another critical principle is introducing robust access control measures. Access control determines who or what has access to the IoT network and its resources. Role-based access control (RBAC) or attribute-based access control (ABAC) can achieve this by assigning access permissions based on users' and devices' roles or attributes. A properly controlled access control system can help mitigate unauthorized access and potential device damage.

To maintain IoT security, manufacturers must regularly release firmware and software updates. Updates and patches are necessary to fix security vulnerabilities and bugs in their devices. IoT devices should continually be updated with the latest firmware and software. Automatic updates can streamline this process, ensuring devices remain secure without constant manual intervention.

Another crucial security strategy is dividing an IoT network into smaller, isolated segments. This can help prevent the propagation of cyberattacks. By separating critical devices from less secure or more vulnerable ones, breaches can be contained, preventing attackers from moving laterally across the network. Isolating sensitive components enhances the overall security posture.

Monitoring and logging are fundamental to detecting and responding to security incidents in IoT environments. Monitoring network traffic and device behavior can help identify anomalies and potential threats early. Logs should be maintained to record activities, which can be invaluable for forensic analysis during a security breach. Practical monitoring tools can offer real-time alerts and automated responses to mitigate threats quickly.

Physical security is often neglected but is just as important as cyber defenses. IoT devices, especially those in public or remote locations, should be protected against physical tampering and theft. Secure enclosures, tamper-evident seals, and regular physical inspections can help safeguard devices from physical threats. Physical security complements cyber measures to provide a comprehensive defense strategy.

Finally, user education and awareness are crucial to maintaining IoT security. Users must learn about the risks associated with IoT devices and how to secure them properly. This process involves configuring security settings, recognizing potential phishing attacks, and responding to security incidents appropriately. Regular training and awareness programs for users can improve IoT ecosystem security.

IoT security encompasses various strategies and technologies to protect interconnected devices and their data. Each element plays a crucial role in ensuring the security and integrity of IoT systems, from authentication and encryption to access control and network segmentation. Continuous monitoring, physical security, and user education further bolster these defenses, creating a robust framework to guard against IoT environments' myriad threats.

Level 1 Insights

One essential aspect of IoT security is the adoption of secure boot processes. A safe boot ensures that a device only runs the code the manufacturer authorizes. This involves cryptographic validation of the firmware before execution, preventing malicious or unauthorized firmware from running. By implementing a secure boot process, IoT devices can safeguard against threats like rootkits, which attempt to gain control of a device at startup.

Another important consideration is the concept of a trusted execution environment (TEE). A TEE is a secure area within a device's central processor that ensures sensitive data and code are isolated and protected from unauthorized access. By leveraging TEEs, IoT devices can securely execute sensitive operations such as cryptographic functions, secure storage, and authentication processes. This isolation helps protect against various attacks, including software-based and physical attacks.

An often overlooked yet vital aspect of IoT security is supply chain security. The security of IoT devices can be compromised at any point during their manufacturing, distribution, or deployment. Ensuring the integrity and authenticity of hardware and software components throughout the supply chain is essential. This can be achieved through rigorous supplier vetting, component traceability, and secure supply chain protocols to prevent the introduction of malicious components or firmware.

IoT security also involves managing vulnerabilities through coordinated vulnerability disclosure (CVD) programs. CVD programs enable researchers and users to report security vulnerabilities in IoT devices in a structured and responsible manner. By establishing clear policies and channels for vulnerability reporting, manufacturers can quickly address and mitigate security flaws before malicious actors can exploit them.

CHAPTER 4   DESIGN AND DEPLOY AZURE IOT SECURITY

The principle of least privilege (PoLP) is essential in IoT security architecture. PoLP only grants devices and applications the minimum access levels necessary to perform their functions. This reduces the potential attack surface by limiting the number of possible entry points for attackers. Implementing PoLP requires careful planning and continuous review of access controls to ensure that privileges are tightly controlled.

Data integrity and provenance are also vital considerations. Data integrity means verifying that data has not been altered or tampered with, while data provenance tracks the origin and history of data. Techniques such as digital signatures and blockchain can be used to maintain data integrity and provenance, providing verifiable and tamper-evident records of data exchanges. These measures are essential in applications like supply chain management and healthcare, where data accuracy and trustworthiness are paramount.

Machine learning and artificial intelligence (AI) are a growing trend in IoT security. AI and ML can improve security by enabling more sophisticated threat detection and response mechanisms. Security systems powered by AI can adapt to evolving threats better than traditional methods because they can analyze large amounts of data to detect indicators and trends that indicate security threats.

In behavioral analysis, anomalies are detected by monitoring and analyzing IoT device behavior. Security systems can identify deviations from normal behavior that may point to a security vulnerability or compromised device by establishing a baseline of normal behavior. As an additional layer of defense against unknown or zero-day threats, behavioral analysis complements signature-based detection methods.

Integrating IoT devices with edge computing introduces new security challenges and opportunities. Rather than relying on centralized cloud servers to process data, edge computing processes it closer to the source. While this reduces latency and bandwidth usage, it also requires robust security measures at the edge. Ensuring that edge devices are secure involves implementing strong access controls, data encryption, and continuous monitoring to protect against local threats.

Last but not least, IoT security is heavily influenced by regulatory compliance. Governments and industry bodies are increasingly enacting regulations and rules to ensure the safety and privacy of IoT devices. Compliance with legislation such as the General Data Protection Regulation (GDPR) in Europe, the California Consumer Privacy Act (CCPA) in the United States, and other regional laws is crucial for manufacturers and users of IoT devices. Adhering to these regulations helps protect users' data and enhances the overall security posture of IoT ecosystems.

In conclusion, the field of IoT security is vast and multifaceted, encompassing a range of practices and technologies designed to protect interconnected devices and their data. From secure boot processes and trusted execution environments to supply chain security and AI-driven threat detection, each component plays a crucial role in defending against the myriad threats facing IoT systems. By continuously evolving and adopting new security measures, stakeholders can ensure the resilience and integrity of the growing IoT landscape.

IoT Cybersecurity Strategy

With the rapid proliferation of interconnected devices that constitute the Internet of Things (IoT), the need for a robust IoT cybersecurity strategy has never been more critical. As IoT devices permeate various sectors, including healthcare, manufacturing, transportation, and smart cities, the potential attack surface for cyber threats expands exponentially. These devices, often handling sensitive data and performing critical functions, demand top-notch security. A comprehensive IoT cybersecurity strategy is the key to addressing these challenges and implementing robust measures to protect against evolving threats.

CHAPTER 4   DESIGN AND DEPLOY AZURE IOT SECURITY

IoT cybersecurity strategies are based on establishing robust security frameworks and policies. These frameworks should outline IoT devices' security requirements and guidelines throughout their entire lifecycle, from design and manufacturing to deployment and maintenance. Embedding security into every phase of IoT device management ensures that security is not an afterthought but a fundamental aspect of the process.

Another critical element is the implementation of robust authentication and authorization mechanisms. Ensuring that only authorized devices and users can access the IoT network is fundamental to preventing unauthorized access and potential breaches. This includes deploying multifactor authentication, digital certificates, and role-based access control (RBAC) to verify identities and manage permissions effectively.

Data protection is also a cornerstone of IoT cybersecurity. This involves securing data at rest and in transit through advanced encryption techniques and secure communication protocols. Data integrity and confidentiality are crucial, as IoT devices often handle sensitive information such as personal health records, financial transactions, and industrial control data. Protecting this data helps prevent breaches that could lead to significant economic and reputational damage.

Regular firmware and software updates are crucial to maintaining the security of IoT devices. Manufacturers must provide timely updates to address known vulnerabilities and enhance device security. However, the responsibility continues. Users and organizations also play a vital role in this process. By promptly applying these updates, they can significantly decrease the window of chance for attackers to exploit unpatched vulnerabilities, thereby bolstering the overall security of IoT networks.

Monitoring and threat detection are vital components of an IoT cybersecurity strategy. Continuous monitoring of network traffic and device behavior enables quick spotting of anomalies and potentially dangerous threats. Implementing advanced threat detection systems like intrusion detection systems (IDS) and machine learning-based analytics can help identify and respond to security incidents swiftly. Effective monitoring is critical to maintaining the integrity and availability of IoT networks.

Finally, fostering a culture of security awareness and education is crucial. Users, developers, and administrators must know the potential risks associated with IoT devices and understand best practices for securing them. Regular training programs and awareness campaigns can empower stakeholders to recognize and respond to security threats, enhancing the overall resilience of IoT ecosystems.

In conclusion, a comprehensive IoT cybersecurity strategy encompasses multiple layers of defense, from solid security frameworks and robust authentication to data protection, regular updates, and continuous monitoring. By addressing these key areas and fostering a culture of security awareness, organizations can effectively mitigate the risks associated with IoT devices and ensure their secure and reliable operation. As the IoT landscape evolves, so must the strategies and measures employed to protect it.

Know What You Are Protecting and Why

Understanding the "what" and "why" in IoT cybersecurity is crucial for devising effective protection strategies. This approach ensures that security measures are not just implemented for the sake of it but are tailored to the specific assets and their significance. This clarity helps allocate resources efficiently and enhances the overall security posture.

Identify Critical Assets: The first step is identifying the critical assets within the IoT ecosystem. These assets range from physical devices such as sensors and actuators to data flows, network infrastructure, and software applications. Knowing what you are protecting involves a comprehensive inventory of all IoT devices and their interconnections. Each device's role, functionality, and importance to the overall system must be documented.

For instance, medical devices like insulin pumps or heart monitors are critical assets in an intelligent healthcare system because they directly impact patient health.

Assess the Value of Assets: Once you have determined the assets, the subsequent step is to assess their value. This includes understanding the data these devices handle and the functions they perform. The value can be measured regarding the potential impact of a security breach, which could be financial, operational, reputational, or regulatory. For example, compromising an industrial control system in a manufacturing plant could lead to significant production downtime, economic losses, and safety hazards, highlighting its high value and the need for stringent security measures.

Understand Threats and Vulnerabilities: Knowing why you are protecting an asset involves understanding its specific threats and vulnerabilities. This requires a thorough threat assessment to identify potential attackers, their motivations, and the methods they might use to exploit vulnerabilities. Common threats to IoT devices include malware, denial of service (DoS) attacks, and unauthorized access. Understanding these threats helps prioritize security measures for most at-risk assets.

Protecting Sensitive Data: Data is a critical asset in any IoT ecosystem. Knowing the sensitivity and regulatory requirements surrounding data helps define the "why" of protection. For example, personal health information (PHI) in IoT healthcare devices is subject to strict regulations like HIPAA in the United States. Protecting such data is crucial to complying with legal requirements and maintaining patient trust and confidentiality. Data encryption, secure storage, and stringent access controls are vital to safeguarding sensitive information.

Ensuring Operational Continuity: For many IoT systems, ensuring operational continuity is crucial for implementing robust security measures. Disruptions in critical systems, such as those controlling infrastructure, transportation, or utilities, can have far-reaching consequences. For instance, a cyberattack on a smart grid could lead to widespread power outages, affecting millions of people. Thus, protecting these systems from cyber threats is essential to maintain public safety and operational stability.

Safeguarding Intellectual Property: In industrial and commercial IoT applications, protecting intellectual property (IP) is often a primary concern. IoT devices in these environments may handle proprietary processes, trade secrets, or other valuable IPs. Unauthorized access to these devices could result in the theft of sensitive information, leading to competitive disadvantages or financial losses. Implementing strong access controls and monitoring systems is crucial to protect IP from cyber espionage and theft.

Mitigating Financial Risks: Understanding the financial implications of a security breach underscores the importance of protecting IoT assets. A successful cyberattack can lead to direct economic losses due to system downtime, regulatory fines, and the costs connected with incident response and remediation. Additionally, there can be indirect costs related to reputational damage and loss of customer trust. Quantifying these potential financial impacts helps justify investments in robust cybersecurity measures.

Many industries have specific regulations and standards that mandate certain security practices to protect IoT assets. Complying with these standards and regulations is another crucial reason for protecting IoT assets. For example, the General Data Protection Regulation (GDPR) imposes stringent data protection requirements in Europe. Failure to follow can result in heavy fines and legal repercussions. Ensuring compliance avoids fines and demonstrates a commitment to security and privacy.

Maintaining Customer Trust: Maintaining customer trust in consumer IoT products is paramount. Security breaches can erode customer confidence and lead to loss of business. For instance, if a smart home device is compromised, it can expose users to privacy invasions and physical security risks. Protecting these devices through secure design, regular updates, and transparent privacy practices helps build and maintain customer trust.

Enabling Business Continuity and Growth: A secure IoT ecosystem supports business continuity and growth. Organizations can avoid disruptions by protecting critical assets, ensuring compliance, and focusing on innovation and expansion. A strong security posture also differentiates businesses in the market, providing a competitive edge. Customers and partners are likelier to engage with organizations that prioritize and demonstrate robust cybersecurity practices.

Understanding what you protect and why provides a clear framework for implementing effective IoT cybersecurity measures. It ensures that resources are directed toward safeguarding the most critical assets, mitigating the most significant risks, and achieving the highest levels of security and compliance. This strategic approach enhances protection and supports operational stability, regulatory compliance, and customer trust.

SOC/DevSecOps Front Shield of IoT

In IoT cybersecurity, integrating Security Operations Centers (SOC) and Development, Security, and Operations (DevSecOps) is essential for robust and comprehensive security management. These frameworks are pivotal in addressing IoT ecosystems' unique and complex challenges, ensuring continuous monitoring, rapid response, and secure development practices.

In the ever-growing digital age, organizations face constant cyber threats. To combat these threats, they rely on Security Operations Centers (SOCs). A SOC acts as a centralized command center, employing a robust framework, well-defined functions, and efficient operations to safeguard sensitive information and critical infrastructure.

Industrial IoT (IIoT) environments have been created by the convergence of Operational Technology (OT), Information Technology (IT), and the Internet of Things (IoT). While this convergence unlocks exciting possibilities for automation and efficiency, it also creates a landscape ripe for cyberattacks. Here's why Security Operations Centers (SOCs) are essential for securing these environments:

- Unique Security Challenges: OT/IoT/IIoT systems often have unique security considerations compared to traditional IT infrastructure. Legacy OT systems might need more robust security features, while resource-constrained IoT devices might need help to support complex security tools. SOCs, with their understanding of IT and OT security principles, can develop a comprehensive strategy that addresses these diverse needs.

- Expanded Attack Surface: The sheer number of interconnected devices in an IIoT environment creates a vast attack surface. Traditional security measures designed for a smaller IT footprint might need to be improved. SOCs provide continuous monitoring and threat detection capabilities, allowing them to identify suspicious activity across the IIoT network, from traditional IT systems to connected sensors and actuators.

More than reactive security measures are required in the face of constantly innovating malicious actors. Waiting for attacks to occur leaves critical infrastructure vulnerable. This is why SOCs employ proactive threat-hunting techniques to search for hidden threats and vulnerabilities within the IoT ecosystem. This proactive approach enables early detection and mitigation of potential security incidents, preventing them from disrupting operations or causing physical harm. Organizations operating in OT/IoT/IoT environments can gain a significant advantage by implementing a well-equipped SOC. The SOC's ability to bridge the gap between IT and OT security, continuously monitor a vast attack surface, and proactively hunt for threats empowers them to maintain a robust security posture and safeguard their critical infrastructure in the constantly evolving digital landscape.

CHAPTER 4   DESIGN AND DEPLOY AZURE IOT SECURITY

The escalating level of complexity of cyber threats demands a multifaceted approach to security. Security Operations Centers (SOCs) emerge as a critical response, forming a centralized command center that integrates various building blocks to achieve optimal protection. These building blocks encompass the SOC framework, which defines the core structure and processes; the SOC functions, which outline the specific activities performed within the SOC; and SOC operations, which govern the day-to-day execution of security measures. By effectively combining these elements, SOCs empower organizations to proactively identify threats, efficiently respond to incidents, and ensure a robust security strategy in the face of constantly changing digital adversaries. Figure 4-1 depicts the SOC building block.

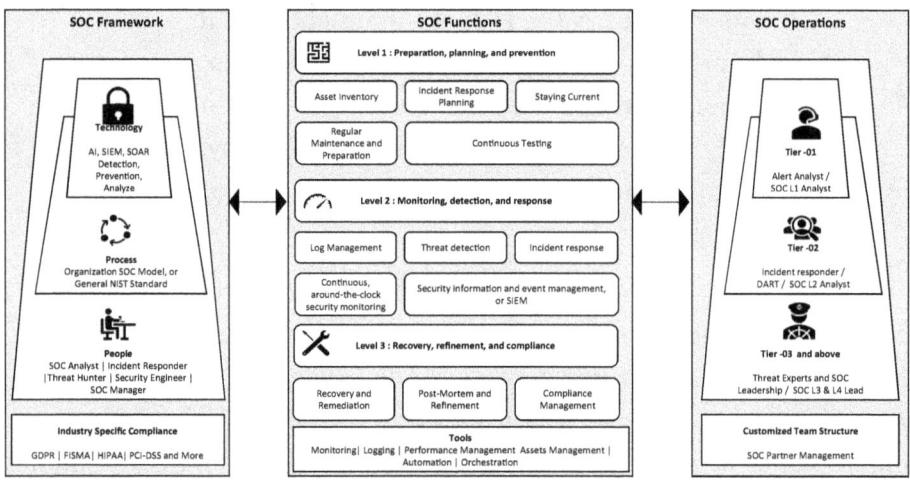

Figure 4-1. *SOC building block*

SOC Framework: The Blueprint for Security

The SOC framework serves as the architectural foundation, outlining the core components and processes that enable effective security operations. It defines

- Security Technologies: This encompasses the security tools and software for threat detection, monitoring, analysis, and response. Examples include security information and event management (SIEM) systems, firewalls, intrusion detection systems (IDS), and vulnerability scanners.

- Processes and Procedures: The framework outlines the standardized workflows for security analysts, including incident response procedures, threat intelligence gathering, vulnerability management, and security incident and event management (SIEM) log analysis protocols.

- People and Roles: The framework defines the different roles within the SOC, such as security analysts (Tier 1, 2, and 3), threat hunters, incident responders, and security engineers. It outlines the responsibilities and skillsets required for each role.

- Metrics and Reporting: The framework establishes key performance indicators (KPIs) for measuring the SOC's effectiveness. These metrics include time to detection, time to resolution, and the number of false positives.

- A well-defined SOC framework ensures a systematic approach to security, fosters collaboration between different teams, and enables efficient incident response.

SOC Functions: The Many Arms of Defense

The SOC fulfills several critical functions to maintain a robust security posture:

- Security Monitoring: SOC analysts use security tools to continuously monitor network traffic, system logs, and user activity for suspicious activity.

- Threat Detection and Analysis: Once suspicious activity is identified, analysts delve deeper to determine the nature and severity of the threat. This involves threat intelligence gathering, vulnerability analysis, and threat hunting to uncover potential security breaches proactively.

- Incident Response: During a security incident, the SOC initiates a coordinated response following established procedures. This includes containment, eradication, remediation, and recovery steps.

- Security information and event management (SIEM): Systems play a vital role by collecting and aggregating security data from various sources, enabling centralized log analysis and event correlation for faster detection and investigation.

These combined functions form the core activities of a SOC, ensuring continuous vigilance and swift response to security threats.

SOC Operations: Putting the Framework into Action

The day-to-day operations of a SOC ensure the effective execution of the framework and its defined functions. Here's a glimpse into how a SOC operates:

- Shift Management: SOCs often operate 24/7 to provide continuous security coverage. Security analysts work in shifts to monitor for threats and respond to incidents around the clock.

- Alert Triaging and Prioritization: Security tools generate a multitude of alerts. SOC analysts must prioritize these alerts based on severity and potential impact, focusing on the most critical threats first.

- Threat Hunting: Beyond reactive monitoring, security operations centers undertake proactive threat hunting to uncover hidden threats.

- Collaboration and Communication: For SOC operations to be successful, IT operations, security engineers, and incident response teams must communicate seamlessly and collaborate.

- Security Awareness and Training: Employees regularly trained on cybersecurity best practices are significantly less likely to be targeted by social engineering attacks or phishing.

Optimizing SOC operations can help organizations ensure continuous monitoring, efficient response, and proactive threat hunting, ultimately achieving a more secure digital environment.

In conclusion, with its robust framework, well-defined functions, and efficient operations, the Security Operations Center (SOC) is a vital line of defense for organizations in the ever-evolving cybersecurity landscape. By establishing a comprehensive SOC strategy, organizations can effectively safeguard their critical assets and confidently navigate the digital world.

Now, let's focus on other key elements in depth.

CHAPTER 4   DESIGN AND DEPLOY AZURE IOT SECURITY

Security Operations Centers (SOC) – Continuous Monitoring and Rapid Response: The primary role of a SOC in IoT cybersecurity is to provide continuous monitoring and rapid response capabilities. Given the sheer volume of data and the number of devices in IoT networks, it's critical to have an experienced team to oversee and analyze network traffic in real time. SOC teams use specialized tools and techniques to detect anomalies, potential breaches, and suspicious activities. This 24/7 monitoring is crucial because IoT devices often operate continuously and are integral to essential services such as healthcare, manufacturing, and utilities.

Incident Response and Mitigation: When a security incident occurs, the SOC coordinates the response. This includes finding the source of the breach, stopping the threat, eradicating the malicious elements, and recovering affected systems. In the context of IoT, timely incident response is crucial to minimize downtime and prevent cascading effects across interconnected devices. For example, a compromised sensor in an industrial setting could disrupt entire production lines, making rapid containment and recovery by the SOC essential.

Threat Intelligence and Proactive Defense: SOC teams don't just react to threats; they anticipate and defend against them. By analyzing threat data and trends, they can implement proactive measures to strengthen the security posture of IoT networks. This includes updating security policies, patching vulnerabilities, and refining monitoring tools. Threat intelligence enables SOCs to stay ahead of cybercriminals, who continually evolve their tactics to exploit IoT devices.

Development, Security, and Operations (DevSecOps) – Integrating Security into Development: DevSecOps represents integrating security practices into the software development lifecycle. This means embedding security considerations from the initial design phase to deployment and maintenance for IoT. This approach is vital because IoT devices often have unique security challenges, such as limited computational power, diverse operating environments, and the need for long-term operation without frequent human intervention.

CHAPTER 4 DESIGN AND DEPLOY AZURE IOT SECURITY

Shift-Left Security: One of the core principles of DevSecOps is "shift-left" security, which involves incorporating security testing and validation early in the development process. By identifying and addressing security vulnerabilities during the coding phase, developers can prevent potential exploits that could be much costlier and harder to fix later. This could involve rigorous testing for common vulnerabilities such as buffer overflows, improper authentication mechanisms, and insecure communication protocols for IoT devices.

Automated Security Testing and CI/CD Pipelines: DevSecOps practices emphasize automated security testing and Continuous Integration/Continuous Deployment (CI/CD) pipelines. Automated tools can perform static and dynamic IoT firmware and software analysis, identifying vulnerabilities and compliance issues before deployment. CI/CD pipelines ensure that security checks are integrated into every stage of the development process, providing consistent and repeatable security assessments. This is even more critical for IoT devices that require frequent updates to address emerging threats and vulnerabilities.

Collaboration and Culture of Security: Another critical aspect of DevSecOps is fostering a culture of collaboration between development, operations, and security teams. In the context of IoT, this means that all stakeholders work together to prioritize security, ensuring that it is not an afterthought but an integral part of the development process. This collaborative culture is the backbone of DevSecOps, helping bridge the gap between rapid development cycles and the stringent security requirements of IoT devices.

Regulatory Compliance and Secure Deployment: DevSecOps practices also help ensure regulatory compliance by embedding security controls and auditing capabilities within the development pipeline. By automating compliance checks and documentation, devSecOps can streamline processes to meet regulatory requirements and maintain secure deployment practices in regulated environments, such as healthcare and finance.

Continuous Improvement and Adaptability: Both SOC and DevSecOps frameworks emphasize continuous improvement and adaptability. In the dynamic landscape of IoT, new threats and vulnerabilities constantly emerge. A SOC provides the operational agility to respond to incidents and adapt defenses in real time. At the same time, DevSecOps ensures that the development process is continuously improving, with security integrated at every stage. This dual focus on real-time defense and secure development is the key to maintaining robust IoT security in an ever-evolving threat landscape.

In conclusion, integrating SOC and DevSecOps is crucial for comprehensive IoT cybersecurity. SOC provides continuous monitoring, rapid incident response, and threat intelligence to protect IoT ecosystems. By integrating security into the development process, from the initial design phase to deployment and maintenance, DevSecOps ensures that safety is always a priority. Together, these frameworks create a resilient security posture capable of defending against the unique and evolving threats facing IoT devices and networks.

IoT Defense-In-Depth

Defense-in-depth strategies are comprehensive approaches to securing an organization's assets that utilize multiple security measures. The idea is to create layers of protection so that if one line of defense is compromised, additional layers act as a backup to stop threats. This strategy combines end-to-end encryption with edge, network, and cloud security capabilities in IoT (Internet of Things). IoT applications will be more challenging to compromise and more accessible to detect, isolate, and remediate if compromised.

The burgeoning Internet of Things (IoT) presents exciting opportunities but also introduces unique security challenges. The potential risks are significant, with millions of interconnected devices, often with limited processing power and varying security features, creating a vast and potentially vulnerable attack surface. To combat these challenges, organizations must adopt a robust defense-in-depth strategy.

CHAPTER 4   DESIGN AND DEPLOY AZURE IOT SECURITY

The integration of Operational Technology (OT), Information Technology (IT), and the Internet of Things (IoT) has given birth to complex and interconnected Industrial IoT (IIoT) environments. While this convergence unlocks a new era of automation and efficiency, it also creates a sprawling attack surface ripe for exploitation. Traditional security measures designed for a siloed IT environment are no longer sufficient. A defense-in-depth strategy becomes essential for OT/IoT/IIoT security.

Here's why a layered approach is critical:

- Unique Security Challenges: OT/IoT/IIoT systems present unique security challenges compared to traditional IT infrastructure. Legacy OT systems might need more robust security features, while resource-constrained IoT devices might need help to support complex security tools. A defense-in-depth strategy acknowledges these differences and incorporates security measures tailored to each element within the IIoT ecosystem.

- Expanded Attack Surface: The sheer number of interconnected devices in an IIoT environment creates a vast attack surface. A single point of failure can have cascading consequences, disrupting operations and potentially causing physical harm. Defense-in-depth provides multiple layers of security, making it harder for hackers to gain a foothold and mitigating the potential damage even if a breach occurs.

- Proactive Threat Mitigation: Reactive security based solely on perimeter defenses is no longer enough. Attackers are constantly innovating, and waiting for attacks to happen leaves critical infrastructure vulnerable. A defense-in-depth strategy incorporates proactive measures like continuous monitoring,

CHAPTER 4 DESIGN AND DEPLOY AZURE IOT SECURITY

threat hunting, and user education. This proactive method authorizes early detection and mitigation of potential security incidents before they escalate. It empowers the organization to stay one step ahead of possible threats, enhancing control over security. Organizations operating in OT/IoT/IoT environments can significantly improve their security posture.

By employing a defense-in-depth strategy. The layered approach depicted in Figure 4-2 addresses the unique challenges of these environments, minimizes the attack surface, and enables proactive threat mitigation. This multifaceted approach safeguards critical infrastructure, ensures operational continuity, and fosters a more secure and resilient IIoT ecosystem.

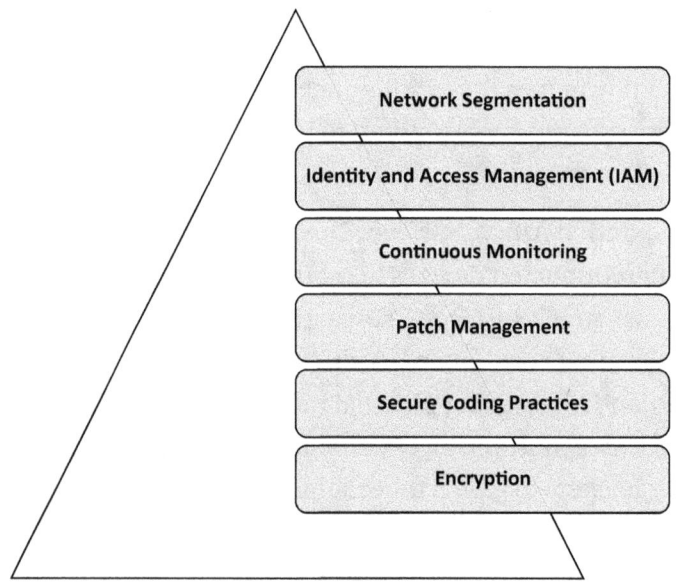

Figure 4-2. IoT defense-in-depth elements

Similar to a well-fortified castle, it utilizes multiple security measures to create a series of hurdles for attackers. Here, we'll delve into the top six cornerstones of a secure IoT defense-in-depth strategy:

- Network Segmentation: Imagine an unbarred gate leading to a treasure trove. Network segmentation acts as a series of fortified walls, isolating critical systems from less sensitive devices and the Internet. This compartmentalization limits the potential damage if an attacker breaches a single device.

- Access Management (IAM): Strong IAM ensures only authorized devices can access specific resources, just as a castle needs a strict entry protocol. This involves assigning unique identities, implementing robust authentication methods, and enforcing granular access controls.

- Continuous Monitoring: A vigilant guard is essential for castle security. Continuous monitoring fulfills this role in the digital realm. Security tools constantly monitor network activity, identifying suspicious behavior and potential breaches before they escalate.

- Patch Management: Imagine a castle with a weak, outdated drawbridge. Patch management addresses this concern, ensuring devices are updated with the latest security patches and closing vulnerabilities that attackers might exploit.

- Secure Coding Practices: A strong castle starts with a solid foundation. Secure coding practices build this foundation for IoT devices. By following secure coding principles from the outset, developers can create devices with inherent security features, minimizing vulnerabilities.

- Encryption: Sensitive messages within a castle require encryption for secure communication. Similarly, encryption safeguards data transmitted between devices in an IoT environment. This ensures that even if intercepted, the data remains unusable for attackers.

IoT deployments can be significantly enhanced by implementing these six core principles, creating a layered defense that enhances security. This proven, multifaceted approach helps to mitigate risks, minimize attack surfaces, and ensure the long-term security of the ever-expanding IoT landscape, instilling confidence in the effectiveness of the strategy.

Let us get into one more level down to understand each element's insight.

Network Segmentation: An IoT defense-in-depth strategy should treat only some devices equally. Network segmentation isolates critical systems from less sensitive ones and the Internet. This way, if a breach occurs in one segment, it won't automatically spread to others. Techniques like VLANs (virtual local area networks) can create separate networks for different device types.

Network segmentation emerges as a critical defense strategy in the ever-expanding world of IoT (Internet of Things), where countless devices connect and generate data. It goes beyond the traditional "one-size-fits-all" approach to network security by creating isolated zones for different device types. This compartmentalization offers several advantages, making it a robust cornerstone of IoT security posture.

Understanding the Why: Imagine an unsecured network where all devices, from critical industrial control systems to bare lightbulbs, share the same space. If an attacker gains a foothold on a low-security device, they can quickly pivot and launch attacks on more sensitive systems within the network. Network segmentation disrupts this by creating barriers between different device categories.

Following are key benefits of segmentation:

- Reduced Attack Surface: Malicious actors' attack surface shrinks by isolating critical systems. Even if a vulnerability exists within a segment, it prevents attackers from quickly accessing more valuable targets.

- Contained Damage: Breaches are inevitable, but segmentation helps contain the damage. If a compromised device infects a segment, it won't automatically spread to other critical systems in the network.

- Improved Security Posture: Segmentation allows for tailored security controls for each segment. High-security zones can have stricter access controls and firewalls, while lower-risk segments can have a more relaxed approach.

- Simplified Network Management: Segmenting the network makes monitoring activity in each zone easier. This allows security teams to identify suspicious behavior more quickly and efficiently.

Following are the implementation strategies:

- VLANs (Virtual Local Area Networks): These are logical subdivisions within a physical network, creating separate broadcast domains for different device types. This isolates traffic and prevents unauthorized communication between segments.

- DMZs (Demilitarized Zones): These are isolated network segments that can host devices that must communicate with the internal and Internet networks. This creates a buffer zone between the two, adding an extra layer of security.

- ACLs (Access Control Lists): These rule-based firewalls define which devices can communicate with each other and the Internet. ACLs can be implemented on routers and switches to enforce segmentation policies.
- Challenges and Considerations:
  - Complexity: Managing multiple network segments can be complex, requiring careful planning and configuration.
  - Scalability: As the number of devices grows, so does the complexity of segmentation. Designing a scalable segmentation strategy that can accommodate future growth is crucial.
  - Performance: Adding additional network segments can introduce some latency. However, the security benefits often outweigh the minimal performance impact.
  - Device Management: Segmenting the network requires managing devices within each segment. This might involve assigning static IPs or deploying tools like DHCP reservations.

Network segmentation is a powerful tool for securing IoT deployments. By creating isolated zones for different device types, organizations can significantly reduce the attack surface, minimize the impact of breaches, and improve their overall security posture. However, successful implementation requires careful planning, consideration of scalability, and ongoing management to ensure optimal security without compromising network performance.

Identity and Access Management (IAM): Strong IAM is paramount for securing any network, especially for IoT. It involves assigning unique identities to each device and implementing granular access controls. This minimizes the potential damage if an attacker gains access to a single device's credentials.

CHAPTER 4 DESIGN AND DEPLOY AZURE IOT SECURITY

The Internet of Things (IoT) revolution has brought a surge of interconnected devices, each collecting and transmitting data. While this connectivity offers exciting possibilities, it also creates a vast attack surface for malicious actors. Here's where identity and access management (IAM) steps in as a critical line of defense.

Why IAM Matters in IoT: Traditional IT systems often have well-defined user accounts and access controls. However, the sheer number and diversity of devices in an IoT environment make traditional methods impractical. Imagine millions of sensors, actuators, and smart devices vying for resource access. Without proper IAM, an attacker who compromises a single device could gain access to a vast network and wreak havoc.

The Pillars of IoT IAM:

- Device Identity: The foundation of IAM is assigning each device a unique identity. This identity can be a combination of hardware identifiers, cryptographic keys, or certificates.

- Authentication: Once a device attempts to connect, it must prove its identity. This can be achieved through preshared keys, digital certificates, or multifactor authentication.

- Authorization: Even authenticated devices shouldn't have unrestricted access. IAM defines what actions and resources each device is authorized to perform. This minimizes the damage if an attacker gains access.

Benefits of Robust IAM:

- Reduced Attack Surface: By strictly controlling device access, IAM limits the potential entry points for attackers. Even if a device is compromised, its ability to cause harm is restricted.

- Enhanced Visibility: IAM systems provide detailed logs of device activity. This allows security teams to monitor suspicious behavior and quickly identify potential breaches.

- Compliance Adherence: Many industries have regulations regarding data privacy and security. A robust IAM system helps organizations comply with these regulations by ensuring that only authorized devices can access sensitive data.

Challenges of Implementing IAM in IoT:

- Device Heterogeneity: The vast array of device types in an IoT environment can make implementing a one-size-fits-all IAM solution difficult. Different devices may have varying capabilities for authentication and authorization.

- Scalability: As the number of devices grows, managing individual identities and access controls can become challenging. Automated provisioning and lifecycle management can help address this concern.

- Resource Constraints: Some resource-constrained devices may need the processing power or memory to support complex authentication protocols. Lightweight authentication methods need to be considered for such devices.

Effective IAM is the cornerstone of securing an IoT environment. Organizations can significantly reduce the risk of unauthorized access and data breaches by establishing strong device identities, implementing robust authentication methods, and enforcing granular access controls. However, a successful IAM strategy requires careful planning to address device heterogeneity, scalability, and resource constraints.

Continuous Monitoring: Threats constantly evolve, so security shouldn't be static. Continuously monitoring network activity for suspicious behavior is crucial. Security information and event management (SIEM) systems can be deployed to aggregate logs from various sources and identify potential anomalies.

The dynamic nature of the IoT landscape demands constant vigilance. Unlike traditional IT systems, where configurations remain relatively static, IoT deployments involve many devices constantly generating and transmitting data. This necessitates shifting from reactive security measures to a proactive approach: continuous monitoring.

Why Continuous Monitoring is Essential:

- Evolving Threats: The threat landscape for IoT is constantly changing, with new vulnerabilities discovered regularly. Continuous monitoring allows for early detection of suspicious activity, enabling security teams to respond swiftly and mitigate potential breaches.

- Baseline Establishment: Understanding the standard behavior patterns of devices within the network is crucial for identifying anomalies. Continuous monitoring establishes a baseline for device activity, making detecting deviations that might indicate a compromise easier.

- Improved Efficiency: Security teams can only be expected to manually sift through mountains of data from every device. Continuous monitoring tools aggregate data from various sources, automate anomaly detection, and generate alerts, freeing up human resources for more strategic tasks.

What to Monitor:

- Device Activity: This includes monitoring metrics like device uptime, resource utilization, network traffic patterns, and communication frequency. Deviations from established baselines can indicate potential issues.

- Log Data: Devices generate logs that capture events and activities. Continuous monitoring analyzes these logs for suspicious entries, such as failed login attempts, unauthorized access attempts, or unusual data transmissions.

- Vulnerability Management: Keeping device software up-to-date is critical. Continuous monitoring can identify outdated firmware and flag devices without security patches, allowing for timely updates.

The Tools of the Trade:

- Security Information and Event Management (SIEM): These systems collect data from various sources, including network devices, security tools, and IoT devices. SIEMs correlate events and identify potential security incidents.

- Log Management Tools: These tools centralize log data from various devices and applications, enabling efficient analysis and anomaly detection.

- Network Traffic Analysis (NTA) Tools: These tools monitor network traffic for suspicious activity, such as unauthorized communication attempts or data exfiltration attempts.

Challenges of Continuous Monitoring:

- Data Overload: The sheer volume of data generated by IoT devices can overwhelm traditional monitoring tools. Scalable solutions are needed to handle the data influx efficiently.

- Alert Fatigue: Continuous monitoring can generate a high volume of alerts, leading to "alert fatigue" for security teams. Effective alert prioritization and filtering are crucial to focus on the most critical issues.

- Expertise Gap: Analyzing complex security data can require specialized skills. Organizations might need to invest in training or consider managed security services to bridge the expertise gap.

Continuous monitoring is an indispensable component of a secure IoT strategy. Organizations can proactively identify and address security threats by establishing baselines, identifying anomalies, and taking swift action before they escalate into major incidents. However, implementing a successful continuous monitoring strategy requires careful planning to address data overload, alert fatigue, and potential skill gaps within the security team.

Patch Management: Like any software, IoT devices are susceptible to vulnerabilities. Regular patching is essential to address these vulnerabilities and minimize the attack surface. Patching should be automated whenever possible to ensure timely updates.

The ever-present threat of vulnerabilities underscores the importance of robust patch management in the IoT (Internet of Things) realm. Unlike traditional computers, where users can initiate updates themselves, IoT devices often lack the user interface or processing power for manual patching. This necessitates a strategic approach to ensure these devices remain up-to-date and secure.

Why Patch Management is Critical for IoT:

- Exploiting Vulnerabilities: Unpatched devices are vulnerable to known exploits, allowing attackers to gain unauthorized access, steal data, or disrupt operations. Patching addresses these vulnerabilities, closing the door on potential attacks.

- Improved Security Posture: Regular patching ensures devices have the latest security fixes, which can significantly improve the overall security posture of the IoT ecosystem. This minimizes the attack surface and makes it harder for attackers to gain a foothold.

- Compliance Requirements: Many industries have regulations mandating the implementation of security best practices. Patch management is crucial to achieving compliance by ensuring devices are up-to-date with the latest security patches.

Challenges of Patching IoT Devices:

- Device Heterogeneity: The vast array of device types in an IoT deployment presents a challenge. Different manufacturers have varying patching processes and update mechanisms so that a one-size-fits-all approach won't work.

- Resource Constraints: Some resource-constrained devices might need more storage space or processing power, making it challenging to accommodate extensive firmware updates.

- Deployment Challenges: Patching can disrupt device operation, especially in critical applications. Organizations need to plan and schedule deployments carefully to minimize downtime.

Best Practices for Effective IoT Patch Management:

- Inventory and Classification: The first step is to have a comprehensive inventory of all devices within the network. This allows for identifying device types, firmware versions, and patching requirements.

- Automated Patching: Whenever possible, automate the patching process. This ensures timely updates and reduces the risk of human error. However, some devices might require manual intervention.

- Testing and Validation: Before deploying patches to production environments, thorough testing in a staging environment is crucial to ensure compatibility and avoid unintended consequences.

- End-of-Life (EOL) Management: Organizations need to plan to mitigate risks as devices reach their end-of-life and no longer receive security updates. This might involve replacing outdated devices with newer, more secure models.

The Tools for the Job:

- IoT Device Management Platforms: These platforms offer centralized management of various aspects of IoT devices, including firmware updates and patch deployment.

- Vulnerability Management Tools: These tools scan devices to identify known vulnerabilities and recommend corresponding security patches.

- Patch Testing Tools: These tools help test patches in a controlled environment before deployment to production devices.

Patch management is a cornerstone of a secure IoT strategy. By implementing a comprehensive approach that addresses device heterogeneity, resource constraints, and deployment challenges, organizations can ensure their devices remain up-to-date and less susceptible to cyberattacks. Leveraging automation, testing, and EOL management practices further strengthens the organization's security posture in a dynamic and ever-evolving threat landscape.

Secure Coding Practices: Security needs to be built into devices from the ground up. Secure coding practices during development can help prevent vulnerabilities that attackers can exploit. This includes practices like proper input validation and memory management.

The security of any system hinges on its foundation. In IoT (Internet of Things), where devices interact and collect sensitive data, secure coding practices become paramount. Developers can significantly reduce vulnerabilities and create a more secure foundation for IoT devices by employing these practices from the beginning of the development process.

Why Secure Coding Matters in IoT:

- Mitigating Vulnerabilities: Traditional software development methodologies overlook security considerations. Secure coding practices identify and address potential vulnerabilities early in the development lifecycle, preventing them from becoming exploitable weaknesses later.

- Reduced Attack Surface: By following secure coding principles, developers can minimize the attack surface of IoT devices. This makes it harder for attackers to find and exploit vulnerabilities, enhancing overall security.

- Long-Term Cost Savings: Security vulnerabilities discovered after deployment can be costly, requiring patches, updates, and potential product recalls. Secure coding practices from the outset help avoid these expenses and ensure long-term cost savings.

Core Principles of Secure Coding for IoT:

- Input Validation: IoT devices receive data from various sources. Secure coding practices emphasize validating all user inputs to prevent malicious code injection attacks, such as SQL injection or cross-site scripting (XSS).

- Memory Management: Memory-related vulnerabilities can allow attackers to gain unauthorized access or corrupt data. Secure coding involves using memory-safe languages and techniques to prevent buffer overflows and memory leaks.

- Cryptography: Encryption is crucial when dealing with sensitive data. Secure coding practices advocate for robust encryption algorithms and proper key management techniques to safeguard sensitive information.

- Least Privilege: The principle of least privilege dictates that devices should have only the minimum level of access required to perform their intended functions. Secure coding practices implement this principle to minimize the potential damage if an attacker gains access.

- Secure Coding Standards: Several industry-recognized secure coding standards exist, such as OWASP Top 10 and CERT secure coding standards. Following these standards provides developers with a comprehensive checklist for secure code development.

Benefits of Secure Coding:

- Reduced Development Time: Secure coding practices that proactively address security concerns during development can actually save time in the long run compared to fixing vulnerabilities after deployment.

- Improved Maintainability: Secure code is often cleaner, more modular, and easier to maintain. This translates to lower maintenance costs and faster development cycles in the future.

- Enhanced Reputation: Organizations that prioritize secure coding practices are committed to building trustworthy products, which can improve their reputation and foster trust with customers.

Challenges of Secure Coding:

- Developer Training: Secure coding requires specialized knowledge and training that developers might not possess. Organizations must invest in training programs to equip developers with the necessary skills.

- Legacy Code: Existing codebases in IoT projects might not have been written with security in mind. Refactoring these codebases to adhere to secure coding principles can be time-consuming.

- Balancing Security and Functionality: Security measures can sometimes introduce performance overhead or limit functionality. Finding the right balance between security and functionality is crucial.

Secure coding practices are essential to building safe and reliable IoT devices. By integrating these practices into the development lifecycle, organizations can significantly reduce vulnerabilities, minimize attack surfaces, and ensure the long-term security of their IoT deployments. Investing in developer training, addressing legacy code, and balancing security and functionality are all vital to achieving a robust and secure IoT ecosystem.

Encryption: Sensitive data transmitted between devices and the cloud should always be encrypted. This includes data at rest and in transit. Encryption renders the data unusable even if intercepted by attackers.

In the ever-expanding world of IoT (Internet of Things), where countless devices exchange data across networks, encryption emerges as an unyielding defender. By scrambling data using cryptographic algorithms, encryption safeguards sensitive information from prying eyes, ensuring the confidentiality and integrity of communication within the IoT landscape.

Why Encryption Matters in IoT:

- Securing Sensitive Data: IoT devices often collect and transmit sensitive data, ranging from personal information to industrial control commands. Encryption protects this data in transit, rendering it unusable even if intercepted by malicious actors.

- Ensuring Data Integrity: Data tampering can have disastrous consequences in IoT environments. Encryption ensures data remains unaltered during transmission, preventing unauthorized modifications that could disrupt operations.

- Maintaining Privacy: With growing concerns about data privacy, encryption empowers users to control who has access to their information. Organizations that encrypt data demonstrate a commitment to user privacy and regulatory compliance.

What Needs Encryption in IoT:

- Data in Transit: Any data transmitted between devices and cloud platforms or across networks should be encrypted. This includes user credentials, sensor data, and control commands.

- Data at Rest: Sensitive data stored on IoT devices, even temporarily, should be encrypted to prevent unauthorized access in case of device compromise.

- Authentication and Authorization Messages: The credentials and access control tokens used for device authentication and authorization should be encrypted to prevent eavesdropping and potential man-in-the-middle attacks.

Encryption Methods for IoT:

- Symmetric Encryption: Uses a single shared secret key for encryption and decryption. This method is efficient but requires secure key distribution and management.

- Asymmetric Encryption: Employs a public key pair for encryption and decryption. Public keys are widely distributed, while private keys are kept secret. This method offers better scalability but can be computationally expensive for resource-constrained devices.

- Elliptic Curve Cryptography (ECC): A newer approach that provides equivalent security with smaller key sizes, making it suitable for resource-limited IoT devices.

Challenges of Implementing Encryption in IoT:

- Processing Power and Memory Constraints: Encryption algorithms can be computationally intensive. Resource-constrained devices might struggle with complex encryption methods, impacting performance.

- Key Management: Secure key generation, distribution, storage, and rotation are crucial aspects of encryption. Managing keys across a vast network of devices can be challenging.

- Battery Life: Encryption can increase power consumption on battery-powered devices. Optimizing encryption methods and implementing lightweight algorithms can help mitigate this issue.

Best Practices for Secure IoT Encryption:

- Choose the Right Algorithm: Select an encryption method that balances security strength with the devices' processing power requirements.

- Implement Secure Key Management: Employ robust essential management practices to ensure the confidentiality and integrity of encryption keys.

- Use Secure Communication Protocols: Use protocols, such as HTTPS and TLS, which encrypt data at the transport layer, to ensure secure communication between devices and cloud platforms.

Encryption is a cornerstone of robust security in the IoT. Encryption empowers organizations to build trust with users and navigate the ever-evolving threat landscape by safeguarding sensitive data, ensuring data integrity, and upholding privacy. Careful consideration of processing power limitations, secure key management, and optimal encryption methods is paramount for successful implementation, fostering a secure and thriving IoT ecosystem.

- Regular Security Assessments: Regular penetration testing and vulnerability assessments help to identify weaknesses in the IoT security posture. Qualified security professionals should conduct these assessments and cover all architecture layers.

- Staying Up to Date: The IoT threat landscape is constantly evolving. Maintaining a robust defense is crucial to staying informed about the latest threats and vulnerabilities. Subscribing to security advisories and attending industry conferences are good ways to stay updated.

By implementing a comprehensive defense-in-depth strategy that addresses these areas, organizations can significantly improve the security of their IoT deployments.

IOT Zero-Trust

The Internet of Things (IoT) refers to a rapidly evolving network of interconnected devices, ranging from simple sensors to complex systems, all communicating and exchanging data over the Internet. With the proliferation of IoT devices, security concerns have escalated, leading to the adoption of more stringent security models. One such model gaining traction is Zero Trust, which fundamentally alters the approach to network security by assuming that threats can exist inside and outside the network. In the context of IoT, Zero Trust becomes even more critical due to these devices' diversity, scale, and often limited security capabilities.

Traditional security models operate on a secure perimeter, where devices and users within the network are trusted by default. However, IoT networks typically have many devices with varying levels of security, making them vulnerable to breaches. Moreover, these devices often operate in environments where physical security is not guaranteed. The Zero Trust model mitigates these risks by enforcing strict identity verification for every device and user, irrespective of their location within the network. This approach is essential for IoT, where devices' sheer volume and heterogeneity create a broad attack surface.

Core Principles of Zero Trust

Zero Trust is founded on a few essential principles forming a robust security framework. Each principle contributes uniquely to creating an environment where security is not reliant on perimeter defenses but is integrated into every aspect of the network. Figure 4-3 depicts the core principles of IoT Zero Trust.

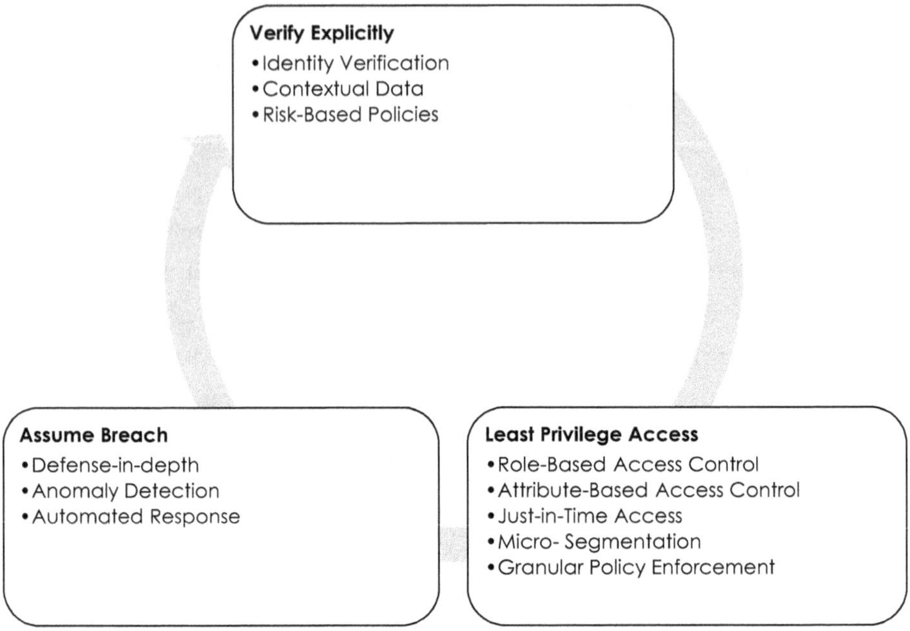

CHAPTER 4   DESIGN AND DEPLOY AZURE IOT SECURITY

Verify Explicitly
- Identity Verification
- Contextual Data
- Risk-Based Policies

Assume Breach
- Defense-in-depth
- Anomaly Detection
- Automated Response

Least Privilege Access
- Role-Based Access Control
- Attribute-Based Access Control
- Just-in-Time Access
- Micro-Segmentation
- Granular Policy Enforcement

Figure 4-3. IoT Zero Trust

Here's a closer look at these core principles:

> **Verify Explicitly:** Continuously authenticate and authorize every user and device based on all available data points, including identity, location, and device health.

Contextual Authentication and Authorization

The principle of explicit verification emphasizes the need for continuous and context-aware authentication and authorization. Every access request, whether from a user or a device, must be validated based on multiple factors:

- Identity Verification: Users and devices must prove their identity through robust multifactor authentication (MFA), which could involve passwords, biometrics, or security tokens.

- Contextual Data: Verification is not just a one-time check; it includes assessing real-time contextual data such as the user's location, the device's security posture, time of access, and more.

- Risk-Based Policies: Access decisions should be influenced by the request's risk profile. For instance, a request from a new location or an unknown device may trigger additional verification steps.

Role of Continuous Monitoring: Continuous monitoring is integral to explicit verification. It ensures that access rights are regularly re-evaluated and adjusted based on current data and behavior patterns. This real-time assessment helps detect and respond to anomalies quickly.

Least Privilege Access: Limit access to only those resources necessary for users and devices to perform their tasks, thereby reducing the risk of lateral movement within the network.

Minimizing Access Rights

The principle of least privilege stipulates that end-users and devices are granted the minimum level of access necessary to perform their tasks. This minimizes potential damage from compromised accounts or devices:

- Role-Based Access Control (RBAC): Access rights are assigned based on the user or device's role within the organization, ensuring they can only access data and systems pertinent to their duties.

- Attribute-Based Access Control (ABAC): Access decisions are also influenced by user attributes (e.g., department, project involvement) and environmental conditions (e.g., time of day, security clearance).

- Just-in-Time Access: Temporary access permissions are granted only when needed, reducing the window of opportunity for exploitation.

Assume Breach: Operate based on the notion that a breach has occurred or could occur, and design the network to contain and mitigate the impact of a potential compromise.

Proactive Defense Strategies

Assuming a breach has occurred means designing security strategies to detect, contain, and mitigate the impact of breaches:

- Defense-in-Depth: Employing multiple layers of security controls to protect data and resources, ensuring that a failure in one layer does not compromise the entire system.

- Anomaly Detection: Using machine learning and AI to identify unusual patterns in network traffic or device behavior that could indicate a breach.

- Automated Response: Implementing systems that can automatically respond to detected threats, such as isolating compromised devices or revoking access credentials.

Comprehensive Incident Response Plans

A critical aspect of assuming a breach is having a robust incident response plan:

- Preparation and Training: Regularly train staff on security protocols and ensure that everyone knows their role in the event of a breach.

- Detection and Analysis: Quickly identify and analyze incidents to understand their scope and impact.

- Containment and Eradication: Isolating affected systems prevents further spread and removes the threat from the network.

- Recovery and Learning: Restore systems to regular operation and analyze the breach to improve future defenses.

The core principles of Zero Trust – verify explicitly, use least privilege access, and assume breach – provide a comprehensive framework for securing modern networks, especially those with a significant IoT component. By continuously validating every access request, minimizing access rights, and preparing for inevitable breaches, organizations can create a robust defense against sophisticated cyber threats. Implementing these principles requires a strategic approach and ongoing commitment, but the resulting security posture is well worth the effort, providing a resilient foundation for today's interconnected world.

Implementing Zero Trust in IoT Networks

Implementing Zero Trust in IoT networks involves several strategic steps:

- Implementing Fine-Grained Controls: To enforce the least privileged access, organizations must implement fine-grained controls:

    - Micro-Segmentation: Segmenting the network into micro or smaller segments to protect critical assets and restrict lateral movement of threats.

    - Granular Policy Enforcement: Creating detailed policies that govern access to specific resources and continuously adjusting these policies based on changing conditions.

- **Identity and Access Management (IAM)**: Deploy robust IAM systems to identify and authorize users and devices before granting them access.

- **Continuous Monitoring and Analytics**: Deploy advanced monitoring tools to continuously analyze network traffic and device behavior for signs of anomalies or malicious activity.

- **Security Information and Event Management (SIEM)**: Enhancing SIEM systems to provide real-time monitoring and response capabilities.

Challenges in Adopting Zero Trust for IoT

Despite its benefits, adopting Zero Trust in IoT networks presents unique challenges:

Device Diversity: IoT devices vary widely in terms of hardware, software, and capabilities, making it challenging to implement a one-size-fits-all security solution.

Resource Constraints: Many IoT devices have limited processing power and memory, which can restrict the implementation of complex security protocols.

Legacy Devices: Older IoT devices may lack the necessary security features to support Zero Trust principles, requiring additional effort to secure or replace them.

Role of Edge Computing in IoT Zero Trust

By handling data closer to the origin, edge computing reduces latency and bandwidth usage while also adding an additional layer of security to IoT networks based on the Zero Trust model. By enforcing Zero Trust policies locally, authenticating and authorizing devices, and detecting anomalies before data is transmitted to the central network, edge devices can enhance the security of IoT networks.

Integration with Artificial Intelligence and Machine Learning

IoT networks can be enhanced by the use of artificial intelligence (AI) and machine learning (ML). A large amount of data from IoT devices can be analyzed by AI and machine learning algorithms to find patterns and detect anomalies that may indicate security threats. These systems can identify and respond more accurately to evolving threats by continuously learning from new data.

CHAPTER 4　DESIGN AND DEPLOY AZURE IOT SECURITY

Case Studies of IoT Zero Trust Implementation

Several organizations have successfully implemented Zero Trust in their IoT networks:

- **Healthcare**: Hospitals have adopted Zero Trust to secure medical devices, ensuring that only authorized personnel can access sensitive patient data and critical systems.

- **Manufacturing**: Factories use Zero Trust to protect industrial control systems (ICS) and prevent disruptions to production processes caused by cyberattacks.

- **Intelligent Cities**: Local governments implement Zero Trust to safeguard smart infrastructure, such as traffic management systems and public utilities.

Regulatory and Compliance Considerations

Adopting Zero Trust in IoT networks also involves navigating various regulatory and compliance requirements. Regulations such as the GDPR (General Data Protection Regulation) and the HIPAA (Health Insurance Portability and Accountability Act) mandate stringent security measures to protect personal and sensitive data. Zero Trust principles align well with these regulations by ensuring continuous verification, least privilege access, and comprehensive monitoring.

Future Trends and Developments

The future of IoT Zero Trust will likely see advancements in several areas:

- **Enhanced Encryption Techniques**: Innovations in encryption will provide more robust security for data in transit and at rest within IoT networks.

- **Blockchain Technology**: Blockchain can offer decentralized and tamper-proof solutions for IoT security, enhancing trust and transparency.

- **Standardization**: Industry standards for IoT security and Zero Trust will continue to evolve, providing more explicit guidelines and best practices for implementation.

Integrating Zero Trust in IoT networks represents a fundamental shift in how security is approached. By assuming that threats are ever-present and continuously verifying every interaction within the network, Zero Trust provides a robust framework to protect against the myriad of vulnerabilities inherent in IoT ecosystems. While challenges remain, adopting advanced technologies such as edge computing, AI, and blockchain, along with ongoing standardization efforts, will pave the way for more secure and resilient IoT deployments. As IoT devices grow, embracing Zero Trust will be crucial in safeguarding data and infrastructure from evolving cyber threats.

IoT Layer of Cybersecurity

As the Internet of Things (IoT) grows to become more widespread, integrating billions of devices into our daily lives and industrial operations, the importance of IoT cybersecurity has become increasingly paramount. The interconnectivity of IoT devices enhances efficiency, convenience, and innovation across various sectors, including healthcare, manufacturing, smart cities, and more.

However, this proliferation also introduces significant security challenges. Cyber threats can enter through any connected device, necessitating comprehensive security measures to protect data, privacy, and system integrity.

- **IoT Users Security**: IoT user security is a critical component of the overall cybersecurity framework. Users, whether individuals or organizations, must be protected from unauthorized access and potential data misuse. Implementing robust user authentication mechanisms, such as multifactor authentication (MFA), ensures that only authorized individuals can access sensitive information and control IoT devices. To mitigate human-related vulnerabilities, such as weak passwords and phishing attempts, it is essential to educate users about security best practices.

- **IoT Devices Security**: Securing IoT devices themselves is another crucial aspect. These devices often need more processing power and memory, making it challenging to implement traditional security measures. However, manufacturers must prioritize built-in security features, including secure boot, firmware updates, and encryption. Device security also involves continuous monitoring for any signs of tampering or unusual behavior, ensuring that any compromised device can be quickly identified and isolated. By embedding security into the device design from the outset, the risk of exploitation is significantly reduced.

- **IoT Gateway Security**: IoT gateways act as intermediaries between IoT devices and central systems, aggregating data and translating communication protocols. Given their pivotal role, gateways must be fortified with robust security measures. This includes secure communication channels, authentication and authorization mechanisms, and intrusion detection systems. Protecting the integrity of the entire IoT ecosystem by securing IoT gateways ensures that data transmitted between devices and the cloud will be confidential and tamper-proof.

- **IoT Network and Connectivity Security**: The network and connectivity layer of IoT infrastructure is a primary target for cyberattacks, making its security paramount. Deploying robust encryption protocols for data in transit and segmenting networks to isolate different types of traffic are essential strategies. Additionally, deploying firewalls, intrusion detection and prevention systems (IDPS), and regularly updating network security policies can help safeguard networks from unauthorized access and data breaches. Ensuring secure and reliable network connectivity is fundamental to maintaining seamless IoT system operation and security.

- **IoT Cloud and Application Security**: Finally, the cloud and applications that store and process IoT data must be secured against potential threats. Cloud security involves safeguarding data storage, ensuring secure APIs, and maintaining robust access controls to prevent unauthorized access. Application security focuses on securing the software that interacts with IoT devices, which includes regular security assessments, code reviews, and vulnerability management. Ensure compliance with regulatory standards, protect sensitive data, and prevent disruptions caused by cyberattacks by securing the cloud and applications.

CHAPTER 4 DESIGN AND DEPLOY AZURE IOT SECURITY

The Internet of Things (IoT) has transformed how we work with technology, bringing unprecedented connectivity and convenience. However, with this interconnectedness comes a myriad of cybersecurity challenges that must be overcome to ensure IoT systems' integrity, confidentiality, and availability. In response to these challenges, organizations increasingly adopt comprehensive IoT cybersecurity frameworks and strategies to safeguard their IoT deployments. Table 4-1 provides an overview of key focus areas in IoT cybersecurity, offering descriptions, real-world examples, and insights into Microsoft Azure's offerings designed to bolster security across various facets of IoT environments.

The IoT Cybersecurity Framework emphasizes the importance of establishing robust security measures tailored to the unique characteristics of IoT ecosystems. Real-world examples such as the NIST Cybersecurity Framework and the ISA/IEC 62443 Standard underscore the need for structured approaches to IoT security. Meanwhile, the concept of defense-in-depth highlights the necessity of deploying a variety of layers of security controls to mitigate evolving threats. Azure offerings like Azure Security Center and Azure Sentinel align with this approach, providing comprehensive security solutions for IoT environments.

Zero Trust, another critical aspect of IoT security, mandates stringent verification of devices and users accessing IoT networks. Implementing two-factor authentication and role-based access control exemplifies real-world strategies to enforce Zero Trust principles. Furthermore, ensuring the security of IoT devices themselves is paramount, with measures like secure boot mechanisms and firmware updates being instrumental in thwarting unauthorized access and manipulation. Azure's suite of IoT solutions, including Azure Sphere and Azure IoT Hub, empowers organizations to fortify device security and protect against emerging threats in the IoT landscape.

Table 4-1. *Illustrates the Azure offer mapping against focus areas of IoT cybersecurity*

Focus Area	Description and Real-World Examples	Microsoft Azure Offerings Against IoT
IoT users security	Measures to secure access and privileges for individuals interacting with IoT systems. Real-world examples include role-based access control and user authentication mechanisms.	Azure Active Directory, Azure Identity Protection
IoT devices security	Techniques to protect IoT devices from unauthorized access and manipulation. Real-world examples include secure boot mechanisms, firmware updates, and physical tamper resistance.	Azure Sphere, Azure IoT Hub, Azure Security Center
IoT gateway security	Security measures implemented at gateways to control traffic between IoT devices and networks. Examples include implementation of VPNs, access control lists (ACLs), and encryption for data in transit.	Azure IoT Hub, Azure Firewall
IoT network and connectivity Security	Security protocols and measures to safeguard communication channels between IoT devices and networks. Real-world examples include the use of secure communication protocols (e.g., TLS/SSL) for IoT devices.	Azure IoT Hub, Azure Virtual Network
IoT cloud and application	Security controls and best practices for safeguarding cloud-based IoT applications and services. Examples include implementing encryption for data at rest and in transit, access control mechanisms, and regular security audits and updates.	Azure Security Center, Azure Key Vault, Azure Sentinel, Azure Monitor

CHAPTER 4   DESIGN AND DEPLOY AZURE IOT SECURITY

In conclusion, the multifaceted approach to IoT cybersecurity – encompassing user, device, gateway, network, and cloud security – is vital in addressing the diverse and complex threats facing modern IoT ecosystems. Each module plays a distinct yet interconnected role in safeguarding the integrity, confidentiality, and availability of IoT systems, ensuring that the benefits of IoT can be realized without compromising security.

IoT Users Security

IoT user security refers to the protection mechanisms and practices designed to safeguard users of IoT systems from cyber threats. As IoT devices become increasingly integrated into personal lives and organizational operations, ensuring the security of these users is crucial. This involves implementing strong authentication, protecting personal data, educating users, and continuously monitoring potential threats. Adequate user security protects individuals and enhances the overall security posture of IoT ecosystems.

Strong Authentication Mechanisms: One primary method for securing IoT users is through robust authentication mechanisms. Traditional passwords often need to be more robust due to their vulnerability to brute-force attacks and phishing schemes. By requiring a password, a smartphone code, or biometric data along with a password, multifactor authentication (MFA) significantly enhances security. MFA reduces the likelihood of unauthorized access, even if one authentication factor is compromised. Implementing MFA across all IoT applications and devices is critical in protecting user identities and access privileges.

Role-Based Access Control: Implementing role-based access control (RBAC) is another critical security strategy for IoT users. RBAC ensures that users are provided with the minimum level of access required to perform their functions, thereby limiting the potential impact of a compromised account. By defining roles and assigning permissions based on those roles, organizations can better manage access rights and enforce the principle of least privilege. This method aims to prevent unauthorized access to sensitive data and critical system functions, enhancing the overall security of the IoT ecosystem.

Data Encryption and Privacy: Protecting the privacy of users is a fundamental aspect of IoT security. Personal data collected by IoT devices, such as health information, location data, and usage patterns, must be encrypted in transit and at rest. Encryption ensures that even if data is intercepted, unauthorized parties cannot easily read or manipulate it. Moreover, IoT systems should adhere to data protection laws, including General Data Protection Regulation (GDPR), to ensure users' privacy rights are respected. By implementing robust encryption protocols and adhering to privacy regulations, you can prevent data breaches and build user trust.

User Education and Awareness: In order to mitigate human-related vulnerabilities, it is crucial to educate users about security best practices. IoT devices present many risks, and users should be educated about how to protect their personal information. A few of the things you should do are recognize phishing attempts, create strong passwords, and stay on top of software updates. By conducting regular security awareness programs and training sessions, you can prevent user errors causing security incidents. Empowering users with knowledge and resources helps to create a proactive security culture.

Secure Device Configuration: Ensuring IoT devices are securely configured is another key aspect of protecting IoT users. Attackers often exploit default settings and credentials to gain unauthorized access. Users should be encouraged to change default passwords, disable unnecessary features, and enable security settings. Manufacturers can support this by providing user-friendly interfaces and clear instructions for configuring security options. Secure device configuration helps to close common security gaps and prevent exploitation.

CHAPTER 4   DESIGN AND DEPLOY AZURE IOT SECURITY

Continuous Monitoring and Incident Response: Monitoring user activities and device behaviors is essential for detecting and responding to security threats. Advanced monitoring tools can analyze patterns and identify anomalies that may indicate malicious activity. An incident response plan should be in place as soon as a threat is detected to minimize its impact. This includes isolating affected devices, notifying users, and restoring normal operations. Security incidents are promptly addressed via continuous monitoring and a robust incident response plan, minimizing damage and enhancing user protection.

Securing Communication Channels: Ensuring secure communication between IoT devices and users is critical. Secure communication protocols, such as Transport Layer Security (TLS), should be implemented to protect data exchanged between devices and users. This prevents eavesdropping and man-in-the-middle attacks that can compromise sensitive information. Additionally, users should be informed about the importance of using secure networks, such as avoiding public Wi-Fi for sensitive transactions. Securing communication channels is essential for maintaining the confidentiality and integrity of user data.

Regulatory Compliance and Standards: Adhering to regulatory requirements and industry standards is vital for protecting IoT users. Regulations such as GDPR and the California Consumer Privacy Act (CCPA) set stringent requirements for data protection and user privacy. By following these regulations, we ensure that user data will be handled responsibly and securely. Additionally, industry standards, such as those developed by the Internet Engineering Task Force (IETF) and the National Institute of Standards and Technology (NIST), offer best practices for securing IoT systems. By following regulatory guidelines and standards, organizations can enhance security measures and protect users more effectively.

Building Trust through Transparency: Transparency is a critical element in building trust with IoT users. Organizations should communicate their security policies, data handling practices, and any incidents of data breaches. Providing users with control over their data, such as the ability to view, modify, or delete their personal information, further enhances trust. Transparent communication helps users understand how their data is protected and reassures them that their privacy is a priority. Building trust through transparency enhances user confidence and encourages responsible behavior from organizations.

Securing IoT users involves a multifaceted approach that includes robust authentication, access control, data encryption, user education, secure device configuration, continuous monitoring, secure communication, regulatory compliance, and transparency. Each of these parts serves a vital role in protecting users from cyber threats and ensuring the integrity of the IoT ecosystem. IoT will continue to evolve, and so will the strategies and technologies to secure it, so that users can engage with the interconnected world confidently and safely.

IoT Device Security

IoT device security is a critical facet of the broader IoT cybersecurity landscape. IoT devices proliferate across various sectors, bringing unprecedented convenience and significant security challenges. It is important to note that devices like these, which range from simple sensors to complex machinery, often lack the robust security features found in traditional computing devices, making them attractive targets for cyberattackers. Ensuring the security of IoT devices involves a comprehensive approach encompassing device manufacturing, deployment, and lifecycle management.

Secure Device Design: Security should be integrated into the design phase of IoT devices. This involves adopting a security-by-design approach, where security considerations are embedded into the hardware and software from the outset. Manufacturers should implement secure boot processes to ensure devices boot only with authenticated software. Additionally, hardware-based security modules, such as trusted platform modules (TPMs), can provide a secure foundation for storing cryptographic keys and performing critical security functions. By starting with secure design principles, manufacturers can significantly reduce the attack surface of IoT devices.

Firmware and Software Updates: IoT devices should be updated regularly to maintain their security. Vulnerabilities discovered post-deployment can be exploited by attackers if not promptly addressed. Therefore, devices must support secure over-the-air (OTA) updates to ensure that patches and new security features can be delivered without physical access. This process should include cryptographic validation of updates to prevent tampering. Ensuring that devices can receive and apply updates efficiently helps mitigate emerging threats and maintain device integrity over time.

Device Authentication and Authorization: Strong authentication and authorization mechanisms are crucial for securing IoT devices. Devices should authenticate themselves to the network using unique, cryptographically secured identities. Authorization method prevents unauthorized devices from connecting the network and accessing sensitive data. Implementing mutual authentication, where the device and the network verify each other's identity, further strengthens security. Additionally, access to device functionalities should be restricted based on role-based permission, ensuring that only authorized entities can control or configure the device.

Encryption and Data Protection: Encryption is vital in protecting data generated and processed by IoT devices. Data should be encrypted at rest and in transit to prevent unauthorized access and tampering. Devices must support strong encryption standards, such as data at rest with AES and data in transit with TLS. Moreover, secure critical management practices are essential to protect encryption keys from being compromised. The confidentiality and integrity of data handled by IoT devices can be preserved by ensuring robust encryption and data protection measures.

Physical Security Measures: Physical security is commonly neglected but is critical for IoT devices, especially those deployed in public or unprotected environments. Devices should be designed to be tamper-resistant, incorporating features such as tamper-evident seals and hardened enclosures. Physical access controls must be implemented to prevent unauthorized individuals from accessing or manipulating the devices. The risk of physical tampering and related security breaches can be minimized by considering physical security in the device design and deployment phases.

Monitoring and Anomaly Detection: Continuous monitoring and anomaly detection are essential for identifying and responding to potential IoT device security incidents. Implementing real-time monitoring systems that track device behavior and network traffic can help detect anomalies indicative of malicious activity. Machine learning algorithms can examine data patterns and flag deviations from normal behavior. By integrating robust monitoring and anomaly detection capabilities, organizations can swiftly identify compromised devices and take appropriate actions to mitigate risks.

Secure Device Lifecycle Management: Securing IoT devices throughout their lifecycle is critical. This includes secure provisioning, operation, and decommissioning. Devices should be securely onboarded to the network with authenticated credentials during provisioning. Throughout their operational phase, continuous security assessments and updates should be conducted. Finally, secure decommissioning practices must be followed to ensure that all sensitive data is wiped and devices are correctly disposed of or recycled. A comprehensive lifecycle management approach ensures that security is maintained from deployment to decommissioning.

Incident Response and Recovery: An effective incident response plan is essential for addressing IoT device security breaches. Organizations should develop and regularly update incident response protocols that outline the steps to take in the event of a security incident. This includes identifying affected devices, isolating them from the network, investigating the root cause, and implementing corrective measures. Additionally, recovery procedures should be in place to restore normal operations quickly. Organizations can mitigate the consequences of security breaches and ensure business continuity by having a robust incident response and recovery plan.

Regulatory Compliance and Standards: Adhering to regulatory requirements and industry standards is crucial for IoT device security. The General Data Protection Regulation (GDPR) and the California Consumer Privacy Act (CCPA) mandate stringent security measures for protecting personal data. Compliance with these regulations ensures that IoT devices are designed and operated in a manner that respects user privacy and security. Furthermore, industry standards, such as those developed by the National Institute of Standards and Technology (NIST) and the Internet of Things Security Foundation (IoTSF), offers the best practices and methods for securing IoT devices. By following these standards, manufacturers and organizations can strengthen their own security posture and achieve required regulatory compliance.

Securing IoT devices is a multifaceted challenge that requires a holistic approach encompassing design, deployment, and lifecycle management. By incorporating secure design principles, supporting regular updates, implementing strong authentication, and ensuring data encryption, manufacturers can create resilient devices against cyber threats. Continuous monitoring, physical security, and robust incident response plans enhance device security. Adherence to regulatory requirements and industry standards ensures that devices meet security benchmarks. As IoT continues to evolve, ongoing efforts to strengthen device security will be essential in protecting users and maintaining the integrity of IoT ecosystems.

CHAPTER 4   DESIGN AND DEPLOY AZURE IOT SECURITY

IoT Gateway

Gateways play an important role in the IoT ecosystem, serving as intermediaries that bridge the communication between IoT devices and the broader network, including cloud platforms and data centers. They aggregate data from various devices, translate communication protocols, and provide centralized processing and control. Due to their pivotal role, IoT gateways are attractive targets for cyberattackers. Security is paramount to maintaining IoT systems' integrity, confidentiality, and availability. This involves implementing robust security measures at multiple levels, including hardware, software, communication, and operational practices.

Hardware Security for IoT Gateways: The foundation of IoT gateway security starts with the hardware. Secure hardware design includes tamper-resistant components and secure boot mechanisms to prevent unauthorized firmware modifications. Trusted platform modules (TPMs) or hardware security modules (HSMs) can be integrated into gateways to securely store cryptographic keys and perform critical security functions. These modules provide a hardware root of trust, ensuring the gateway's firmware and software have not been tampered with. Physical security measures, such as tamper-evident enclosures and secure physical access controls, further protect the gateway from physical attacks.

Secure Boot and Firmware Integrity: Ensuring the integrity of the gateway's firmware is crucial for preventing unauthorized modifications. Secure boot processes verify the authenticity of the firmware at startup using cryptographic signatures. This ensures that only firmware signed by trusted entities can run on the gateway. Additionally, mechanisms for secure over-the-air (OTA) updates must be in place to apply patches and updates securely. These updates should be cryptographically verified to prevent the introduction of malicious code. Regularly updating firmware to patch vulnerabilities is a critical practice in maintaining the security of IoT gateways.

Authentication and Authorization: Solid authentication and authorization mechanisms are essential for controlling access to IoT gateways. Gateways should authenticate devices and users using robust multifactor authentication (MFA) methods. This can include passwords, biometrics, and security tokens. Mutual authentication ensures that the gateway and the connecting devices verify each other's identities before establishing communication. Authorization policies should enforce the principle of least privilege, granting access only to necessary functions and data. RBAC (role-based access control) and ABAC (attribute-based access control) can help manage permissions effectively, reducing the risk of unauthorized access.

Secure Communication Protocols: IoT gateways often handle sensitive data that needs to be protected during transmission. Implementing secure communication protocols, such as TLS (Transport Layer Security) and DTLS (Datagram Transport Layer Security), ensures that data exchanged between devices, gateways, and cloud services is encrypted and protected from eavesdropping and tampering. Secure communication also includes authenticating communication endpoints to prevent man-in-the-middle attacks. Maintaining secure communications requires regularly updating and configuring these protocols according to the latest security standards.

Data Protection and Privacy: Protecting the data handled by IoT gateways is crucial for ensuring user privacy and regulatory compliance. Data encryption should be applied to data at rest and in transit. Gateways must securely store sensitive data, using encryption and secure critical management practices to protect cryptographic keys. Implementing data anonymization and pseudonymization techniques can further enhance privacy, especially when dealing with personal or sensitive information. Ensuring that data protection measures comply with relevant regulations, such as GDPR and CCPA, is essential for maintaining legal compliance and user trust.

Intrusion Detection and Prevention: Monitoring IoT gateways for signs of malicious activity is critical for early threat detection and response. Network IDS (intrusion detection systems) and IPS (intrusion prevention systems) can be implemented to analyze network traffic and gateway activities for anomalies. Machine learning algorithms can analyze patterns and detect unusual activities that may be indicative of a security breach. Automated response mechanisms can isolate the affected gateway, alert administrators, and initiate mitigation procedures when a potential threat is detected. Continuous monitoring and real-time threat detection are vital for maintaining the security of IoT gateways.

Network Segmentation and Isolation: Network segmentation and isolation are effective strategies for limiting the impact of a security breach. Organizations can control and restrict communication between different parts of the IoT ecosystem by segmenting the network into smaller, isolated segments. IoT gateways should be placed in dedicated network segments with strict access controls, limiting exposure to other network parts. Implementing virtual local area networks (VLANs) and firewall rules can further enhance network segmentation. In order to minimize the risk of lateral movement by attackers, critical systems and data should be isolated from less secure network parts.

Regular Security Audits and Penetration Testing: To detect and resolve vulnerabilities in IoT gateways, regular audits and penetration tests are essential. Security audits involve reviewing the gateway's configuration, policies, and methods to make sure compliance with security standards and best practices. Penetration testing simulates real-world attacks to identify weaknesses that attackers could exploit. Skilled security professionals should perform these tests, including automated and manual testing techniques. Regularly auditing and testing IoT gateways' security helps uncover and remediate potential security gaps.

Incident Response and Recovery: An effective incident response plan is critical for quickly addressing IoT gateway security incidents. The plan should outline the steps to take when a security breach is detected, including identifying the affected gateways, isolating them from the network, and conducting a forensic investigation to determine the root cause. Recovery procedures should focus on restoring normal operations and applying security patches to prevent future incidents. Training staff on incident response procedures and regularly updating the plan to reflect new threats and vulnerabilities ensures a swift and effective response to security incidents.

Compliance with Security Standards and Regulations: Adhering to industry security standards and regulatory requirements is essential for maintaining the security of IoT gateways. Standards such as those from the National Institute of Standards and Technology (NIST) and the Internet Engineering Task Force (IETF) provide guidelines and best practices for securing IoT systems. Compliance with regulations like GDPR, CCPA, and HIPAA ensures that data privacy and security demands are achieved. Implementing security measures that align with these standards and regulations enhances the security of IoT gateways and builds trust with users and stakeholders.

Securing IoT gateways is a multifaceted challenge that requires a comprehensive approach. From secure hardware design and firmware integrity to robust authentication, secure communication protocols, and continuous monitoring, each aspect plays a critical role in protecting these vital components of the IoT ecosystem. Network segmentation, regular security audits, and effective incident response further enhance the security posture of IoT gateways. Adhering to industry standards and regulatory requirements ensures that security measures meet the necessary benchmarks. As IoT continues to evolve, ongoing efforts to strengthen gateway security will be essential in safeguarding the interconnected world and maintaining user trust.

IoT Network and Connectivity

In the Internet of Things (IoT) ecosystem, the network and connectivity layer enables communication between devices, gateways, and cloud platforms. However, this interconnectivity also introduces significant security challenges. The network acts as the primary conduit for data transmission, making it a prime target for cyberattackers seeking to intercept, manipulate, or disrupt IoT communications. Ensuring the security of IoT networks and connectivity involves a multilayered approach that includes encryption, access control, monitoring, and incident response measures to protect data integrity, confidentiality, and availability.

Secure Communication Protocols: Secure communication protocols protect data as it travels across IoT networks. Deploying encryption protocols such as TLS (Transport Layer Security) and Datagram Transport Layer Security (DTLS) ensures that data in transit is encrypted and protected from eavesdropping and tampering. These protocols provide end-to-end encryption, securing the communication channels between IoT devices, gateways, and cloud services. Regularly updating and configuring these protocols to adhere to the latest security standards is crucial for maintaining secure and reliable communication.

Network Segmentation and Isolation: Network segmentation and isolation are effective strategies for enhancing IoT network security. Organizations can limit the spread of potential security breaches by classifying the network into smaller, isolated segments. IoT devices, gateways, and other critical components should be placed in dedicated network segments with strict access controls. Virtual local area networks (VLANs) and software-defined networking (SDN) can be used to implement segmentation, ensuring that different types of traffic are separated and monitored. In order to decrease the risk of unintended movement by attackers, critical systems and data should be isolated from less secure network parts.

Access Control and Identity Management: Robust access control and identity management are essential for securing IoT networks. Implementing role-based access control (RBAC) and attribute-based access control (ABAC) ensures that users and devices are given the minimum access necessary to accomplish their tasks. Network access control (NAC) solutions can enforce policies that grant or deny network

CHAPTER 4   DESIGN AND DEPLOY AZURE IOT SECURITY

access based on devices' identity and security posture. Multi-factor authentication (MFA) is a robust authentication mechanism that can help prevent unauthorized access by integrating secure and unique identities with IoT devices.Multi-factor authentication (MFA) is a robust authentication mechanism that can help prevent unauthorized access by integrating secure and unique identities with IoT devices.

Intrusion Detection and Prevention Systems (IDPS): IDPS are critical for monitoring IoT networks and detecting potential security threats. IDPS solutions analyze network traffic for signs of malicious activity, such as unusual data patterns, unauthorized access attempts, and known attack signatures. When a threat is detected, intrusion prevention systems can automatically block or mitigate the attack, preventing it from causing further damage. Integrating IDPS with other security tools, such as security information and event management (SIEM) systems, increases threat detection and response capabilities.

Secure Network Configuration and Management: Ensuring IoT networks are securely configured and managed is vital for preventing security vulnerabilities. This includes implementing solid passwords, turning off unnecessary services and ports, and applying the principle of least privilege. Regularly updating network devices, such as routers and switches, with the latest firmware and security patches helps protect against known vulnerabilities. Network management tools should also continuously monitor and audit network configurations, ensuring compliance with security policies and best practices.

Encryption and Key Management: Effective encryption and key management are crucial for protecting data within IoT networks. Robust encryption algorithms should encrypt data in transit and at rest. Secure critical management practices, such as using hardware security modules (HSMs) and key rotation policies, ensure that encryption keys are protected and regularly updated. Properly managing encryption keys helps prevent unauthorized access to sensitive data and provides the confidentiality and integrity of communications across the IoT network.

Threat Intelligence and Monitoring: Leveraging threat intelligence and continuous monitoring is vital for staying on top of emerging threats in IoT networks. Threat intelligence services provide real-time information about new vulnerabilities, attack vectors, and threat actors. Integrating this intelligence with monitoring tools allows organizations to detect and respond to potential threats early. Monitoring network traffic, device behavior, and security events helps identify anomalies and possible security incidents early, enabling swift and effective response actions.

Implementing Firewalls and Network Security Devices: Firewalls and other network security devices protect IoT networks from external threats. Firewalls can be deployed to enforce security policies, block unauthorized access, and monitor incoming and outgoing traffic. Advanced security devices, such as next-generation firewalls (NGFWs) and unified threat management (UTM) systems, offer integrated security features, including deep packet inspection, intrusion prevention, and application control. Deploying these devices at network perimeters and critical junctions helps to fortify the network against attacks.

Incident Response and Recovery: A robust incident response plan is critical for managing security incidents in IoT networks. The plan should outline procedures for detecting, analyzing, and responding to security breaches, including roles and responsibilities, communication protocols, and escalation paths. Incident response teams should be trained and regularly exercise response scenarios to ensure preparedness. Recovery procedures should focus on restoring normal operations quickly and securely, including data recovery, system patching, and forensic analysis to understand and mitigate the incident's root cause.

Compliance with Security Standards and Regulations: Adhering to security standards and regulatory requirements is essential for ensuring the security of IoT networks. Standards from the National Institute of Standards and Technology (NIST) and the International Organization for Standardization (ISO) provide guidelines for securing IoT systems and networks. Compliance with regulations like the General Data Protection

Regulation (GDPR) and the California Consumer Privacy Act (CCPA) ensures that data privacy and security measures meet legal requirements. Implementing security practices that align with these standards and regulations helps organizations enhance their security posture and maintain trust with users and stakeholders.

Securing IoT networks and connectivity requires a comprehensive, multilayered approach that addresses the unique challenges of the IoT ecosystem. Organizations can bolster the integrity and confidentiality of data transmitted across their networks by implementing secure communication protocols, network segmentation, access control, and continuous monitoring. Additionally, robust encryption, key management, and incident response measures help to safeguard against threats and ensure rapid recovery from security incidents. Adhering to industry standards and regulatory requirements further enhances security and compliance. As IoT evolves, ongoing efforts to strengthen network and connectivity security will be crucial in protecting interconnected systems and maintaining user trust.

IoT Cloud and Application Security

IoT cloud and application security are critical aspects of the IoT ecosystem, focusing on protecting the cloud's data, applications, and services. Due to the large amount of data generated by IoT devices and processed and stored in cloud platforms, it is essential to ensure the security of these cloud environments. Security measures must address threats such as data breaches, unauthorized access, and service disruptions. Organizations can safeguard sensitive information, maintain service integrity, and comply with regulatory requirements by deploying robust security practices for IoT cloud and applications.

Data Protection and Encryption: Data protection is a cornerstone of IoT cloud and application security. Encrypting data at rest and in transit is essential. Data can be protected from cyber threats and data breaches by encrypting it throughout its lifecycle to thwart unauthorized access and ensure data confidentiality. Strong encryption standards should be employed, such as AES-256 for data storage and TLS for data transmission. Additionally, secure critical management practices must be implemented to protect cryptographic keys. Data can be protected from cyber threats and data breaches by encrypting it throughout its lifecycle.

Identity and Access Management (IAM): IAM is critical for controlling who can access IoT cloud resources and applications. Implementing robust IAM policies helps to ensure that only authorized end-users and their devices can access sensitive data and services. This includes using multifactor authentication (MFA) to verify user identities, applying role-based access control (RBAC) to limit permissions based on job roles, and frequently auditing access logs to validate and verify that there are no suspicious activities. By managing identities and access rights effectively, organizations can minimize the risk of unauthorized access and enhance overall security.

Secure Application Development: Secure application development practices are essential for creating resilient IoT applications. This involves adopting a security-by-design approach, which integrates security considerations into the development lifecycle. Developers should adhere to securing coding practices to control common vulnerabilities such as SQL injection, cross-site scripting (XSS), and buffer overflows. Organizations can create robust and secure IoT solutions by building security into applications from the ground up with regular code reviews, vulnerability assessments, and penetration testing.

Continuous Monitoring and Threat Detection: Continuous monitoring addresses the fact that threat detection is vital for maintaining the security of IoT cloud environments and applications. Deploying SIEM enables real-time analysis of security events and incidents. SIEM systems can aggregate and correlate data from various information system sources, such as pattern networks of network traffic, application and platform logs, and user activities, to detect anomalies and potential threats. Integrating machine learning and artificial intelligence (AI) can enhance threat detection capabilities by identifying patterns indicative of malicious behavior. Continuous monitoring helps organizations respond quickly to security incidents and minimize potential damage.

Secure API Management: APIs are crucial in IoT ecosystems, enabling communication between devices, cloud services, and applications. Assuring the security of these APIs is paramount to protecting the integrity and confidentiality of data. Implementing secure API management practices to control access involves strong authentication and authorization mechanisms, such as OAuth and API keys. Encrypting API communications and applying rate limiting can prevent abuse and protect against denial-of-service (DoS) attacks. Regularly auditing and testing APIs for vulnerabilities helps identify and mitigate security risks.

Compliance with Regulatory Requirements: Compliance with regulatory requirements is essential for IoT cloud and application security. Regulations such as the General Data Protection Regulation (GDPR), California Consumer Privacy Act (CCPA), and Health Insurance Portability and Accountability Act (HIPAA) set high standards and requirements for data protection and privacy. Organizations must implement security measures that comply with these regulations, including data encryption, access controls, and regular audits. Compliance helps protect sensitive data and builds trust with customers and stakeholders by demonstrating a commitment to security and privacy.

Incident Response and Disaster Recovery: An effective incident response and disaster recovery plan is critical for managing security incidents in IoT cloud environments. The plan should outline procedures for detecting, analyzing, and responding to security breaches, including roles and responsibilities, communication protocols, and escalation paths. Incident response teams should be trained and regularly exercise response scenarios to ensure preparedness. Disaster recovery plans should focus on restoring normal operations quickly and securely, including data recovery, system patching, and forensic analysis, to understand and mitigate the

CHAPTER 4   DESIGN AND DEPLOY AZURE IOT SECURITY

incident's root cause. The development of an incident response and disaster recovery plan is essential to minimizing the impact of security incidents and ensuring business continuity.

Secure Configuration and Hardening: Securing the configuration and hardening of cloud environments and applications is essential for reducing the attack surface. This incorporates implementing the principle of least privilege, turning off unnecessary services, and regularly updating software and systems with the latest security patches. Configuration management tools and automated scripts can help enforce security policies and maintain consistent configurations across environments. Regularly conducting configuration audits and vulnerability assessments helps identify and remediate security gaps. Secure configuration and hardening practices are vital for protecting IoT cloud infrastructure from cyber threats.

Data Privacy and Governance: Data privacy and governance are critical components of IoT cloud and application security. In order to comply with data protection regulations, organizations must implement policies and procedures related to handling personal and sensitive data. This includes establishing data classification schemes, defining data retention policies, and implementing access controls to restrict data access to authorized users. By prioritizing data privacy and governance, organizations can protect user data and maintain trust. Keeping data privacy and governance policies up-to-date helps ensure compliance with evolving regulatory requirements.

Security Awareness and Training: Educating employees and stakeholders about best security practices is crucial for maintaining IoT cloud and application security. Regular security awareness and training programs help individuals understand the importance of security and how to identify and respond to potential threats. Training should cover phishing awareness, secure password practices, and safe data handling procedures. Creating a culture of security understanding within the organization helps mitigate human-related security risks and reinforces the importance of maintaining robust security practices.

CHAPTER 4   DESIGN AND DEPLOY AZURE IOT SECURITY

Securing IoT cloud environments and applications is a comprehensive and ongoing effort that involves multiple layers of protection. Organizations can safeguard their IoT cloud infrastructure by implementing robust data protection, identity and access management, secure development practices, continuous monitoring, and secure API management. Compliance with regulatory requirements, effective incident response, secure configuration, data privacy, and security awareness are critical components of a holistic security strategy. As IoT continues to evolve and expand, maintaining robust cloud and application security will be essential in protecting sensitive data, ensuring service integrity, and building trust with users and stakeholders.

Design Microsoft Azure-Based IoT Security

Fundamentals of Cybersecurity

Security architecture, a crucial aspect of secure information system design and maintenance, is fortified by the principles of confidentiality, integrity, and availability, collectively known as the CIA triad. CIA principles are not just theoretical concepts but the very pillars of a robust security strategy, ensuring that information is shielded from many threats and vulnerabilities. This practical and essential framework provides a strong reassurance to any security professional.

- Confidentiality is the principle that ensures sensitive information is accessible only to those who are authorized to view it. Keeping private or sensitive data secure is essential to preventing unauthorized access. Measures to achieve confidentiality include encryption, in which data is transformed into a secure format that can be decrypted with an accurate key. Access controls are also fundamental, involving the implementation of user authentication and authorization to restrict access to data. Authentication methods include passwords, biometrics, or multifactor authentication, while authorization ensures users have the necessary permissions to access specific resources. Data masking, another technique used to protect confidentiality, involves hiding parts of data to safeguard sensitive information while still allowing certain operations to be performed.

- Integrity is the principle that ensures information remains accurate and unaltered, except by authorized individuals. Maintaining the trustworthiness of data is crucial, as any unauthorized modifications can lead to significant issues, including data corruption or fraud. Integrity is maintained through hash functions, which generate a unique fixed-size string or number from input data, making it easy to detect changes. Digital signatures also play a crucial role in verifying the authenticity and integrity of messages, software, and digital documents. In addition, checksums and cyclic redundancy checks (CRCs) verify data integrity during transmission and storage, ensuring no tampering or corruption.

- The availability principle ensures authorized users can access data and services on demand. This is vital for the smooth operation of any organization, as downtime or inaccessibility of information can lead to operational disruptions and financial loss. Ensuring availability involves implementing redundancy, such as backup systems and failover mechanisms, to protect against hardware failures or other disruptions. Regular maintenance and updates of systems and networks also play a significant role in maintaining availability, as they help prevent potential vulnerabilities that attackers could exploit. Additionally, implementing robust security measures to protect against denial-of-service (DoS) attacks is crucial for maintaining the availability of critical systems and services.

In summary, the CIA triad – confidentiality, integrity, and availability – forms the foundation of a comprehensive security architecture. Each principle addresses a critical aspect of information security, and together, they ensure that data remains protected against a wide range of threats. Information systems can be safeguarded by maintaining confidentiality, integrity, and availability, and stakeholders' trust and confidence can be maintained, instilling a sense of confidence in the overall security strategy.

Design Principles of Cybersecurity

Designing effective cybersecurity strategies involves several key principles that guide the protection of information and systems. However, in the context of the Internet of Things (IoT), where interconnected devices and systems are ubiquitous, these principles take on a new level of importance and complexity. Here are the fundamental design principles of cybersecurity, specifically tailored and applied to the unique challenges of IoT, with examples to illustrate each.

Data and systems are protected with an in-depth defense strategy that utilizes multiple defense mechanisms. In IoT, this might involve securing each layer of the device's architecture, from the physical hardware to the network, application, and data layers. For example, a smart home system might use encryption to secure data transmitted between devices, firewalls to protect the network, and regular software updates to address the devices' vulnerabilities. This multilayered approach ensures that even if one security measure is breached, others are in place to mitigate the attack.

Zero Trust is a robust security model that operates on the principle of 'never trust, always verify.' In an IoT environment, this means that devices should not automatically trust other devices or network traffic, even if they are within the same network perimeter. This approach, known as Zero Trust, is a potent tool in minimizing the risk of compromised devices being used to launch attacks within the network, as it requires each device to authenticate and verify its identity before it can access or control other devices or data within the network.

Configuring devices to operate with restricted permissions in IoT means applying the least privilege to ensure each device or user has the minimum level of access needed to perform its function. Smart thermostats should, for example, be restricted from accessing other unrelated systems, such as security cameras or personal data stored on a network, and should only have access to heating and cooling systems. In this way, if the device is compromised, there will be minimal damage.

Security by design involves integrating security measures into the development process of IoT devices and systems from the outset rather than as an afterthought. For example, manufacturers of connected medical devices, such as insulin pumps, should incorporate robust encryption protocols, secure boot processes, and regular security testing during development. By embedding security into the product design, vulnerabilities can be minimized, and devices can be more resilient against attacks.

Keep it simple emphasizes the importance of simplicity in security designs to reduce potential errors and vulnerabilities. Complex systems can be challenging to manage and secure effectively. In IoT, a simple, straightforward security mechanism might involve using standard, well-tested encryption protocols rather than developing custom, complex encryption methods that could introduce new vulnerabilities. For instance, a simple home IoT security system might use a user-friendly app to manage device security settings, ensuring that users can easily configure and maintain the security of their devices without confusion.

Obscurity refers to hiding system details to reduce the attack surface available to hackers. While not a standalone security measure, obscurity can complement other security practices. In the context of IoT, obscurity might involve hiding device and network configurations or using non-standard communication ports to make it more difficult for attackers to discover and exploit devices. For example, an IoT-enabled security camera system could use obscure network ports for data transmission, rendering it hard for potential attackers to detect and target the cameras.

In summary, the design principles of cybersecurity – defense in depth, zero trust, least privilege, security by design, keep it simple, and obscurity – are essential for protecting IoT systems. By implementing these principles, organizations can enhance the security and resilience of their interconnected devices and networks, safeguarding against a wide range of cyber threats.

Foundation of Microsoft Azure IoT Offering

As the Internet of Things (IoT) begins to spread and integrate into various industries, securing IoT deployments becomes increasingly critical. Microsoft Azure, a leading cloud computing platform, delivers a comprehensive suite of IoT security services designed to protect IoT devices, data, and applications throughout their lifecycle. Azure's IoT security solutions leverage advanced technologies and best practices to address the unique security challenges associated with IoT ecosystems, providing organizations with the tools to secure their IoT deployments effectively.

Security without compromise is possible with comprehensive IoT solutions that protect your environment while driving innovation. Using a risk-prioritized approach, you can significantly improve your IoT security posture and reduce your attack surface by gaining critical visibility and context into all your IoT assets and devices. Utilize built-in AI, automation, and expert insights to thwart malicious activities effectively. Stay ahead of sophisticated cyberattacks. Moreover, accelerating incident response with tools optimized for your security operations center (SOC) ensures faster and more efficient handling of security incidents.

Microsoft Azure IoT security services are built to provide end-to-end security for IoT deployments, encompassing device security, data protection, identity management, threat detection, and compliance. Azure's security offerings are integrated into its broader IoT platform, which includes Azure IoT Hub, Azure IoT Central, Azure Sphere, and Azure Security Center for IoT. However, essential cybersecurity products such as Microsoft Defender for IoT and Microsoft Sentinel play significant roles. Let us dive deep into it.

Microsoft Defender for IoT

Microsoft Defender for IoT is a specialized security solution that protects devices and networks from cyber threats. It provides comprehensive security capabilities, including device discovery, threat detection, and continuous monitoring, tailored to the unique requirements of IoT environments.

Key Features of Microsoft Defender for IoT:

- Device Discovery and Inventory: Microsoft Defender for IoT automatically discovers and inventories IoT devices connected to the network. This visibility helps organizations understand their IoT landscape, identify unmanaged devices, and ensure that all devices are accounted for and protected.

- Threat Detection and Response: Leveraging advanced machine learning and behavioral analytics, Microsoft Defender for IoT detects suspicious activities and potential threats. It identifies anomalies, unauthorized access attempts, and malicious behavior across the IoT network. When threats are detected, the solution provides actionable alerts and response recommendations.

- Vulnerability Management: Defender for IoT continuously scans devices for known vulnerabilities and misconfigurations. It provides detailed insights into security weaknesses and prioritizes remediation actions based on risk severity, helping organizations identify and resolve vulnerabilities before they can be exploited.

- Network Segmentation: To limit the potential consequences of a security breach, Microsoft Defender for IoT supports network segmentation strategies. It helps organizations design and implement network segmentation policies that isolate critical IoT devices and systems from the broader network, reducing the attack surface.

- Integration with Azure Sentinel: Microsoft Defender for IoT integrates seamlessly with Azure Sentinel, Microsoft's cloud-native security information and event management (SIEM) solution. With this integration, IoT security events can be monitored and managed centralized within the broader security operations center (SOC) workflow.

Microsoft Defender XDR (Extended Detection and Response)

Microsoft Defender XDR is a holistic security solution that extends detection and response capabilities across multiple domains, including endpoints, identities, emails, applications, and cloud environments. It provides unified threat protection and centralized management to enhance an organization's security posture.

Key Features of Microsoft Defender XDR:

- Unified Threat Protection: Defender XDR consolidates threat detection and response across various security vectors, including endpoints (Microsoft Defender for Endpoint), identities (Microsoft Defender for Identity), emails (Microsoft Defender for Office 365), and cloud applications (Microsoft Cloud App Security). This unified approach helps organizations detect and respond to threats more effectively.

- Automated Investigation and Remediation: Microsoft Defender XDR leverages automation to investigate and remediate threats. Automated playbooks and workflows streamline the response process, reducing the time and effort required to address security incidents. This helps security teams focus on more complex threats and strategic tasks.

- Behavioral Analytics and AI: Defender XDR uses behavioral analytics and artificial intelligence to detect advanced threats and anomalies. The solution identifies sophisticated attacks that may evade traditional security measures by analyzing user behavior, device activity, and network traffic patterns.

- Incident Correlation and Contextualization: The solution correlates security events and incidents across different domains, providing a comprehensive view of the attack chain. This contextualization helps security analysts understand an attack's full scope and impact, enabling more informed and effective response actions.

- Integration with Microsoft 365 and Azure: Defender XDR integrates seamlessly with Microsoft 365 and Azure services, providing enhanced security for cloud environments and collaboration tools. This integration ensures consistent security policies and comprehensive protection across the IT ecosystem.

Microsoft Sentinel

SIEM and SOAR solutions are offered by Microsoft Sentinel. It provides comprehensive security monitoring, threat detection, and incident response capabilities, leveraging the power of cloud scalability and artificial intelligence.

Key Features of Microsoft Sentinel:

- Centralized Security Monitoring: Microsoft Sentinel collects and analyzes security data from various sources, including on-premises, cloud environments, and third-party solutions. This centralized system offers a holistic view of the organization's security posture and enables more effective threat detection and response.

- AI-Driven Threat Detection: Sentinel uses advanced machine learning and artificial intelligence to detect threats. It identifies patterns, anomalies, and known attack techniques across vast amounts of data, enabling the detection of sophisticated threats that might otherwise go unnoticed.

- Automated Response and Orchestration: The SOAR capabilities of Sentinel allow organizations to automate response actions using playbooks and workflows. This automation reduces response times and operational overhead, helping security teams manage incidents more efficiently.

- Customizable Dashboards and Workbooks: Sentinel offers customizable dashboards and workbooks that provide visual insights into security metrics, trends, and incidents. Security teams can create tailored views and reports to monitor KPIs (key performance indicators) and track the effectiveness of security measures.

- Integration with Microsoft Ecosystem: Microsoft Sentinel integrates with various Microsoft security solutions, including Microsoft Defender products, Azure services, and Microsoft 365. This integration ensures seamless data flow and consistent security policies across the organization.

- Threat Intelligence Integration: Sentinel integrates with various threat intelligence feeds, providing up-to-date information on emerging threats and attack vectors. This integration enhances threat detection capabilities and helps security teams avoid evolving cyber threats.

Microsoft's security solutions, including Microsoft Defender for IoT, Microsoft Defender XDR, and Microsoft Sentinel, provide comprehensive protection across different IT and IoT landscape aspects. Defender for IoT focuses on securing IoT devices and networks, Defender XDR extends detection and response capabilities across multiple domains, and Sentinel offers centralized security monitoring and incident response. Together, these solutions provide a robust security framework that helps organizations protect their assets, detect and respond to threats, and maintain a strong security posture in an increasingly complex threat landscape.

CHAPTER 4　DESIGN AND DEPLOY AZURE IOT SECURITY

Design Elements of Microsoft Defender for IoT

In this section, let's delve into the critical design elements of Microsoft Defender for IoT. Microsoft Defender for IoT offers a specialized approach to securing network environments through passive, agentless monitoring. This solution discovers and protects IoT and OT devices within your business-critical networks. Unlike traditional signature-based security measures, Defender for IoT utilizes behavioral analytics and threat intelligence tailored for IoT and OT environments. This enables the detection of sophisticated threats, such as zero-day malware or stealthy "living-off-the-land" tactics that might otherwise go unnoticed.

Defender for IoT is a valuable asset for both OT and IT teams as it automatically identifies unmanaged devices, connections, and critical vulnerabilities within the network. This capability allows Defender for IoT to flag anomalous or unauthorized activities without compromising the stability or performance of your IoT and OT systems. Overall, it delivers an advanced level of security tailored to the unique challenges of interconnected environments.

To address these security gaps, Microsoft Defender for IoT offers a tailored solution to identify and protect IoT and OT devices while detecting vulnerabilities and threats. It provides a comprehensive security layer for your IoT/OT landscape, even for devices lacking built-in security features. What distinguishes Defender for IoT is its agentless approach to monitoring at the network layer, allowing seamless integration with both industrial equipment and Security Operation Center (SOC) tools. This ensures that your network remains secure without compromising operational efficiency.

Microsoft Defender for IoT is designed to monitor your network closely by aggregating data from various sources. It acts as a central hub where information from network sensors and other third-party tools converges to give you a complete picture of your IoT and operational technology (OT) security. Access to Defender for IoT is through the Azure portal, where you'll find features like device inventories, security checks, and ongoing monitoring for potential threats. The system supports cloud-based and local (on-premises) setups, accommodating large networks across different locations.

Here's a quick rundown of its main components:

- **Azure Portal**: A cloud-based dashboard where you can manage everything and connect to other Microsoft services like Microsoft Sentinel.

- **Network Sensors**: Sensors that scan your operational technology (OT) or broader enterprise IoT network to identify devices. These can be installed on virtual or physical machines, send data to the cloud, or operate locally.

- **Local Management Console**: An on-site management console for networks not connected to the Internet (air-gapped environments), allowing you to oversee your OT sensors.

Sensors for operational technology (OT) and enterprise IoT networks play a crucial role in monitoring and securing these networks. These sensors can be easily connected to a SPAN port or network TAP and provide insights into potential risks within minutes of connection. Utilizing advanced analytics engines aware of OT/IoT nuances and Layer-6 Deep Packet Inspection (DPI), these sensors can identify threats, including fileless malware, based on unusual or unauthorized network activities.

One distinctive feature of these network sensors is their capability for on-device data handling. All processes, from data collection and analysis to threat alerting, happen directly on the sensor. This benefits environments with limited bandwidth or high-latency issues, as only essential telemetry data and insights are forwarded for further management. Depending on your setup and needs, these summarized findings can be sent to the cloud-based Azure portal or a local on-premises management console.

Cloud-connected sensors and locally managed sensors in the Defender for IoT system serve similar purposes but have distinct functionalities and management approaches:

- **Cloud-Connected Sensors**: All captured data is shown in the sensor console, with alerts sent to Azure for further analysis and integration with other Azure services. They automatically receive Microsoft's threat intelligence updates, and the sensor name assigned during setup is read-only.

- **Locally Managed Sensors**: These sensors provide a more hands-on approach. All sensor data can be viewed directly from the sensor console, and a consolidated view of multiple sensors can be achieved using an on-premises management console. Manual updates for threat intelligence packages are required, and sensor names can be changed directly from the console.

Microsoft Defender for IoT employs a range of sophisticated analytics engines to scrutinize data ingested from network sensors. These engines generate alerts based on real-time and pre-recorded network traffic, incorporating machine learning, profile analytics, risk assessment, a comprehensive device database, threat intelligence, and behavioral analytics to form a robust security framework. The primary analytics engines include:

- **Protocol Violation Detection Engine**: Identifies deviations in packet structures and field values from ICS protocol specifications.

- **Policy Violation Engine**: Flags deviations from learned or manually configured baseline behaviors.

- **Industrial Malware Detection Engine**: Detects malicious activities from known malware strains.

- **Anomaly Detection Engine**: Specialized in identifying unusual machine-to-machine (M2M) communications.

- **Operational Incident Detection Engine**: Detects operational issues like intermittent connectivity, which can indicate equipment failure.

Microsoft Defender for IoT offers versatile management options for hybrid networks, including cloud-based and on-premises components. The Azure portal is a centralized dashboard for viewing all data collected by cloud-connected network sensors, enhancing raw data with features such as workbooks, connections to Microsoft Sentinel, and security recommendations. The OT sensor console allows monitoring of data specific to each OT sensor. An on-premises management console provides a centralized view of all sensor data, additional maintenance tools, and reporting features for air-gapped environments.

Defender for IoT can identify various devices across IT, OT, or IoT environments, displaying them uniquely in the Device Inventory pages by their IP and MAC addresses. Devices with multiple network interface cards (NICs) are considered individual devices, while public Internet IP addresses, multicast groups, and broadcast groups are not counted as individual devices. Devices managed by Microsoft Defender for Endpoint Plan 2 are not counted again by Defender for IoT, preventing double-counting.

Microsoft Defender for IoT offers distinct capabilities tailored for different environments. For end-user organizations in IoT/OT environments, it provides agentless, network-level monitoring with rapid deployment and seamless integration with industrial equipment and SOC tools, supporting fully on-premises or Azure-connected and hybrid environments. For IoT device builders using Azure IoT Hub, it offers a lightweight micro-agent compatible with standard IoT operating systems, ensuring security from the edge to the cloud, including source code for adaptable deployment.

Quick Start of Microsoft Defender for IoT

From a deployment perspective, Defender for IoT offers agentless, network-layer security, ensuring continuous discovery of IoT/OT assets, robust vulnerability management, and effective threat detection within operational and enterprise networks. It seamlessly integrates with Microsoft Sentinel and various third-party SOC tools like Splunk, IBM QRadar, and ServiceNow without modifying existing environments. Importantly, Defender for IoT maintains zero impact on network performance and provides the flexibility to deploy fully on-premises or in Azure-connected environments.

Explore, oversee, and safeguard devices across your operational networks, including OT (Operational Technology), ICS (Industrial Control Systems), IIoT (Industrial Internet of Things), and BMS (Building Management Systems). Gain comprehensive insight into unmanaged IoT devices within your corporate network for Enterprise IoT.

Defender for IoT empowers you to streamline security management and establish comprehensive threat detection and analysis capabilities across hybrid cloud workloads and your Azure IoT solution. The Azure Defender for IoT suite comprises several integral components:

- IoT Hub Integration: Seamlessly integrates with IoT Hub, enabling centralized management and monitoring of security aspects.

- Device Agents (Optional): Allows deployment of device agents to enhance security measures at the device level.

CHAPTER 4 DESIGN AND DEPLOY AZURE IOT SECURITY

- Send Security Message SDK: Facilitates the transmission of security messages for analysis, contributing to overall threat intelligence.

- Analytics Pipeline: Processes and analyzes security events, ensuring a robust defense mechanism.

Now, let's delve into the detailed steps for the outlined tasks:

Task 1: Enable Azure Defender for IoT

- Log in to the Azure portal using your Azure account credentials.

- Navigate to Defender for IoT and click "Getting Started" under "Defender for IoT" on the left-hand menu.

Task 2: Configure OT/ICS Security

Utilizing patented agentless technology, sensors rapidly identify and consistently monitor network devices, providing in-depth visibility into OT/ICS/IoT risks within minutes of connection. These sensors conduct on-site data collection, analysis, and alerting, making them well-suited for locations with limited bandwidth or high latency.

Defender for IoT sensors employs passive, agentless network monitoring to meticulously uncover a comprehensive inventory of your network's IoT/OT assets. The sensors analyze a diverse range of known and proprietary industrial protocols, allowing for a thorough understanding of your IoT/OT network topology and communication paths.

To safeguard your network, the Defender for IoT sensor seamlessly connects to switch SPAN (Mirror) ports and network TAPs, initiating instant collection of network traffic via passive (agentless) monitoring. Deep packet inspection (DPI) is then employed to dissect traffic exchanged between serial and Ethernet-based control network equipment. Configuration options enable secure, vendor-approved commands to gather detailed device information as needed, ensuring a robust defense mechanism.

Integrating Microsoft Threat Intelligence updates enhances Defender for IoT's protective capabilities. Leveraging data collected from tens of thousands of signals daily across Microsoft's ecosystem, including Endpoint, Cloud, Microsoft Entra ID, and Microsoft 365, alongside IoT and OT intelligence from Section 52, the threat intelligence packages provide valuable signatures, malware signatures, CVEs, and indicators of other malicious activities.

Integrating with Microsoft's ecosystem offers substantial benefits to your business. By combining Microsoft Sentinel with Defender for IoT alert detections, you gain a comprehensive view of IT/OT boundaries. Utilizing IoT/OT playbooks facilitates the automation of the response process. Additionally, integration with Microsoft Defender for Endpoint extends detection and response capabilities, forming an extended detection and response (XDR) framework to prevent attacks proactively.

Setting up OT/ICS security consists of three stages:

1. Setting up a sensor
2. Configuring the SPAN Port or TAP, and, finally
3. Registering the sensor with Microsoft Defender for IoT

Design Elements of Sentinel for IoT

In this section, let us get started by understanding key design elements of Sentinel Center for IoT.

When adopting Microsoft Sentinel in an Internet of Things (IoT) environment, several best practices can enhance your deployment's efficiency, security, and manageability. These practices focus on data collection, security posture, and operational management to ensure comprehensive monitoring and threat detection across IoT devices.

Secure and Centralize Data Collection

- Use Azure IoT Hub: Utilize Azure IoT Hub as the central point for collecting telemetry data from IoT devices. This allows for secure data ingestion and integration with Microsoft Sentinel.

- Enable Diagnostic Settings: Configure diagnostic settings on IoT Hub to send logs and metrics to a Log Analytics workspace. This ensures that all relevant data is available for analysis in Microsoft Sentinel.

- Standardize Data Formats: Ensure that data from various IoT devices is standardized in format before ingestion. This facilitates more accessible analysis and correlation of data within Microsoft Sentinel.

Enhance Security Posture

- Deploy Azure Security Center for IoT: Integrate Azure Security Center for IoT with Microsoft Sentinel to gain visibility into the security posture of your IoT devices. This integration helps identify vulnerabilities and potential threats.

- Implement Device Authentication: To prevent unauthorized access, use robust authentication mechanisms for IoT devices, such as X.509 certificates or SAS tokens.

- Network Segmentation: Isolate IoT devices on separate network segments to minimize the impact of a potential security breach.

Monitor and Detect Threats

- Create Custom Analytics Rules: Develop custom analytics rules in Microsoft Sentinel to detect anomalies and threats specific to your IoT environment. Examples include detecting unusual device behavior, unexpected communication patterns, or unauthorized access attempts.

- Leverage Machine Learning: Utilize machine learning-based detection capabilities in Microsoft Sentinel to identify complex threats that traditional rule-based detection might miss.

- Implement Threat Intelligence: Integrate threat intelligence sources with Microsoft Sentinel to enhance the detection of known IoT-related threats and vulnerabilities.

Automate Response and Mitigation

- Set Up Playbooks: Create automated playbooks using Azure Logic Apps to respond to detected threats. These playbooks can perform actions such as isolating compromised devices, alerting administrators, or initiating remediation.

- Continuous Improvement: Regularly review and update your playbooks to adapt to new threats and improve response strategies based on past incidents.

Operational Management

- Role-Based Access Control (RBAC): Implement RBAC in Microsoft Sentinel to ensure only authorized personnel can access and manage IoT data and configurations.

- Monitor Performance and Costs: Use Azure Monitor to keep track of the performance and costs associated with data ingestion and analysis in Microsoft Sentinel. Optimize data retention settings and analytics rules to balance cost and security needs.

- Regular Audits and Compliance: Conduct regular audits to ensure compliance with industry standards and regulations. Use Microsoft Sentinel's built-in capabilities to generate compliance reports and validate security controls.

Maintain Visibility and Insights

- Dashboards and Reports: Create custom dashboards in Microsoft Sentinel to provide visibility into the security status of IoT devices. These dashboards can display critical metrics, alerts, and trends for quick assessment.

- Log Retention Policies: Configure appropriate log retention policies based on your organization's requirements. Ensure that critical logs are retained for sufficient periods to support investigations and compliance.

By following these best practices, organizations can effectively leverage Microsoft Sentinel to secure and manage their IoT environments, ensuring comprehensive threat detection and robust incident response capabilities.

Key Microsoft Recommended Best Practices

When strategizing your Microsoft Sentinel workspace deployment, it's paramount to grasp the intricacies of designing your Log Analytics workspace architecture. Microsoft Sentinel is a product of business and technical requirements, and it's crucial to comprehend how these factors influence the architecture. Key considerations in these decisions encompass the number of tenants, compliance requirements, access control, and cost implications. A deep understanding of these aspects is instrumental in crafting an efficient and effective workspace architecture that caters to your organization's unique needs.

One of the pivotal aspects to consider is the tenancy setup. While managing a smaller number of workspaces simplifies administration, there are specific scenarios that might necessitate multiple tenants and workspaces. For instance, organizations often operate multiple Microsoft Entra tenants due to mergers, acquisitions, or identity separation needs. It's important to note that most Microsoft Sentinel features operate within a single workspace, which ingests all logs housed within it. The decision on your Microsoft Sentinel architecture has significant cost implications.

For organizations with multiple tenants, such as managed security service providers (MSSPs), creating at least one workspace per Microsoft Entra tenant is recommended. This supports built-in, service-to-service data connectors that operate within their respective tenants. Based on diagnostic settings, specific connectors cannot link to workspaces outside their resident tenant. Azure Lighthouse can be utilized to manage multiple Microsoft Sentinel instances efficiently across different tenants.

Compliance is a pivotal factor in your Microsoft Sentinel architecture. Once data is collected, stored, and processed, ensuring compliance with regulations becomes a top priority. Microsoft Sentinel primarily stores and processes data within the same geographical region, although some operations, like those using Microsoft's Machine Learning, might process data outside the workspace's geography. It's crucial to assess data sources and their data transmission pathways to ensure compliance with data sovereignty and security standards.

Regional considerations involve using separate Microsoft Sentinel instances for each region, which can help meet regulatory requirements and manage data segregation by team, area, or site. This strategy also helps avoid bandwidth and egress costs associated with cross-region data transfer. Bandwidth costs vary based on the source, destination region, and collection method. Templates for deploying analytics rules, custom queries, workbooks, and other resources can streamline multiregion deployments.

Access control is another crucial aspect to consider. Different teams require varied levels of access to Microsoft Sentinel data. For instance, the SOC team might need full access, while operations and applications teams might only need access to specific data subsets. Combining resource-context RBAC and table-level RBAC provides flexible access control, supporting various use cases. Resource-context RBAC allows permissions to be assigned at the resource level, facilitating controlled access across different subscriptions and resource groups. Table-level RBAC further refines access by allowing specific data types to be accessible to designated users.

In scenarios involving multiple workspaces, it is advisable to simplify incident management by consolidating incidents from each Microsoft Sentinel instance into a single location. Cross-workspace queries can reference and utilize valuable data stored in different workspaces, subscriptions, or tenants. This approach ensures efficient and comprehensive data analysis and response.

Following best practices for creating your workspace enhances performance and manageability. Naming conventions that include identifiers like "Microsoft Sentinel" help distinguish the workspace among others. Using a single workspace for both Microsoft Sentinel and Microsoft

Defender for Cloud ensures all collected logs are accessible for analysis. A dedicated workspace cluster is recommended for high data ingestion volumes, better query performance, and enhanced encryption options. Avoid applying resource locks to Log Analytics workspaces used by Microsoft Sentinel, as this can disrupt operations.

By considering these factors and following best practices, you can design a robust and efficient Microsoft Sentinel workspace architecture that meets your organization's security and operational needs.

Quick Start Deployment of Sentinel

Modernize your security operations center (SOC) with Microsoft Sentinel. Detect sophisticated threats and respond decisively using an intelligent, comprehensive security information and event management (SIEM) solution. Microsoft Sentinel offers proactive threat detection, investigation, and response, eliminating the need for security infrastructure setup and maintenance. It scales elastically to meet your security needs and can reduce costs by up to 48% compared to legacy SIEM solutions.

Key Components:

- Gather data at cloud scale across all users, devices, applications, and infrastructure, whether on-premises or across multiple clouds.

- Identify previously undetected threats and reduce false positives using advanced analytics and Microsoft's unparalleled threat intelligence.

- Harness the power of AI to delve into threats and track suspicious activities at scale, benefiting from Microsoft's vast experience in cybersecurity. Microsoft Sentinel is your trusted partner in threat investigation, backed by advanced AI capabilities and Microsoft's unparalleled cybersecurity expertise.

- Quickly respond to incidents with built-in orchestration and automation for everyday tasks.

Before you start your deployment, it's essential to understand the process. You'll need to enable Microsoft Sentinel, activate the health and audit feature, and enable the solutions and content tailored to your organization's needs. The following procedure will guide you through each of these steps.

Step 1. Enable the Microsoft Sentinel Service: In the Azure portal, enable Microsoft Sentinel to run on the Log Analytics workspace your organization planned as part of your workspace design.

First, you must add Microsoft Sentinel to an existing workspace or create a new one. Follow these steps:

1. Sign in to the Azure portal.

2. Search for and select Microsoft Sentinel:

    a. Create a Sentinel instance.

    b. Click on "Create."

    c. Choose the workspace you want to use or create a new one. Note that while you can run Microsoft Sentinel on multiple workspaces, each workspace will isolate its data.

3. Workspace selection:

    a. The default workspaces Microsoft Defender for Cloud created do not appear in the list. Microsoft Sentinel cannot be installed on these workspaces.

    b. Once Microsoft Sentinel is deployed on a workspace, that workspace cannot be moved to another resource group or subscription.

4. Finalize setup.

5. Click on "Add" to complete the setup.

Step 2. Enable Health and Audit: Enable the health and audit feature at this stage to ensure that the service's numerous components function correctly and are not subject to unauthorized actions. This feature helps maintain the service's integrity and reliability.

1. Navigate to Settings:

    a. In Microsoft Sentinel, go to the Configuration menu on the left.

    b. Select Settings from the banner.

2. Access Auditing and Health Monitoring:

    a. Please scroll down to the Auditing and Health Monitoring section and expand it.

    b. Click on Enable to activate auditing and health monitoring across all resource types. This will send the auditing and tracking data exclusively to your Microsoft Sentinel workspace.

3. Advanced Configuration (Optional):

    a. Alternatively, select the Configure diagnostic settings link to enable health monitoring specifically for the data collector and automation resources. Here, you can also configure advanced options, such as additional destinations for the data.

4. Confirmation:

    a. If you select Enable, the button will gray out and change to "Enabling..." and "Enabled." Auditing and health monitoring are active, and the appropriate diagnostic settings have been automatically added. You can view and edit them by selecting the Configure diagnostic settings link.

5. Configure Diagnostic Settings:

If you selected Configure diagnostic settings, proceed as follows:

In the Diagnostic settings screen, click + Add diagnostic setting (or select an existing setting to edit it).

In the Diagnostic setting name field, enter a meaningful name for your setting.

In the Logs column, select the appropriate categories for the resource types you want to monitor (e.g., Data Collection – Connectors). Select all logs if you're going to monitor analytics rules.

Under Destination details, choose Send to Log Analytics workspace and select your Subscription and Log Analytics workspace from the dropdown menus.

Besides the Log Analytics workspace, you may also select additional destinations to send your data.

6. Save Settings.

a. Click Save on the top banner to save your new setting.

This process ensures that auditing and health monitoring are correctly configured in Microsoft Sentinel, enabling comprehensive visibility and security for your resources.

Step 3. Enable Solutions and Content: Identify which data sources you need to ingest into Microsoft Sentinel based on your deployment plan. Then, enable the relevant solutions and content so that the necessary data can start flowing into Microsoft Sentinel.

You can install content and solutions individually or in bulk.

1. Check for Updates:

    - If a deployed solution has updates, the status column in the list view will show "Update." These solutions are also included in the "Updates" count at the top of the page.

2. Install Individual Solutions:

    - Search for and select the solution you want to install in the Content hub.

    - Select View details from the bottom right-hand side on the solution's details pane.

    - Click Create or Update.

3. Configure Solution Deployment:

    - On the Basics tab, enter the necessary details, such as subscription, resource group, and workspace. For example,

    - Click Next to proceed through the remaining tabs. These tabs provide information and configuration options for the solution's content components. Note that different solutions may have different tabs depending on the types of content they offer.

    - You might need to enter credentials for third-party services so Microsoft Sentinel can authenticate your systems. For example, with playbooks, you can configure response actions according to your system requirements.

4. Deploy the Solution:

    - In the Review + Create tab, wait for the "Validation Passed" message.

    - Select Create or Update to deploy the solution. If you want to deploy the solution as code, you can also select the Download a template for automation link.

Summary

In the chapter "Design and Deploy Azure IoT Security," we explore the fundamental principles and best practices for securing IoT (Internet of Things) environments using Azure security services.

We begin by delving into the fundamentals of IoT security, covering essential topics such as the IoT Cybersecurity Framework, defense-in-depth strategies, and zero-trust principles. We then discuss the importance of securing IoT users, devices, gateways, networks, connectivity, and cloud applications to mitigate potential risks effectively.

Next, we explore the range of Azure security services tailored for IoT deployments. These services provide comprehensive protection across the IoT ecosystem, from device to cloud.

Moving forward, we dive into designing Azure security services specifically for IoT environments. We emphasize the importance of considering scalability, interoperability, and compliance requirements during the design phase.

Finally, we offer practical, actionable guidance on deploying Azure security services for IoT. We provide clear, step-by-step instructions for implementing security measures, ensuring that your IoT deployments are resilient against cyber threats and adhere to industry standards and best practices.

CHAPTER 4 DESIGN AND DEPLOY AZURE IOT SECURITY

This chapter equips you with the relevant knowledge and essential tools necessary to design and deploy robust security architectures for Azure-based IoT solutions. This is crucial in safeguarding against emerging threats and vulnerabilities in today's interconnected world.

In the book's next chapter, you will read about the IoT network monitoring and management solutions.

CHAPTER 5

Design and Deploy Azure IoT Monitoring and Management

The Internet of Things (IoT) disrupts businesses by connecting billions of devices to the cloud. This vast network generates a wealth of data, but managing and monitoring these devices can be complex. Azure IoT provides a comprehensive solution to address this challenge.

Imagine managing millions of constantly communicating devices – that's the reality of IoT. Your role in crafting a well-designed and deployed Azure IoT solution is significant as you ensure seamless operation and prepare the way for future growth. Your design should prioritize data encryption, authentication, and authorization to protect devices and their valuable data.

Additionally, a well-planned deployment optimizes resource allocation within Azure, controlling costs. Finally, a thoughtful design with clear documentation simplifies ongoing maintenance for your team, ensuring your IoT solution thrives in the long run. By the end of this chapter, you should be able to understand the following:

CHAPTER 5 DESIGN AND DEPLOY AZURE IOT MONITORING AND MANAGEMENT

- Fundamentals of IoT monitoring and management
- Design Microsoft Azure-based IoT monitoring and management
- Deploy Microsoft Azure-based IoT monitoring and management

Fundamentals of IoT Monitoring and Management

Managing and monitoring IoT devices is critical to unlock the full benefits of IoT and ensuring its safe and reliable operation. Here's a breakdown of the fundamental aspects of IoT network and security management and monitoring:

- Network Connectivity: The foundation of any IoT system is a robust network that allows devices to communicate and exchange data. This can involve various technologies depending on your needs, such as cellular networks, Wi-Fi, Bluetooth Low Energy (BLE), or specialized industrial protocols.

- Device Management: With potentially millions of devices deployed, managing them efficiently is essential. IoT platforms like Azure IoT Hub provide device provisioning, registration, and lifecycle management features. This allows you to add new devices, update firmware, and remotely configure settings.

- Data Collection and Storage: The real value of IoT resides in the data stored by devices. Sensor data, usage statistics, and environmental readings all provide valuable insights. IoT platforms offer data ingestion, storage, and pre-processing tools, preparing the data for further analysis.

- Security Threats: The vast number of connected devices creates a large attack surface for cybercriminals. Securing your IoT network requires a multi-layered approach. This includes strong device authentication, secure communication protocols with encryption, and regular security patching for both devices and the underlying infrastructure.

- Monitoring and Analytics: Monitoring your IoT network is crucial for identifying potential issues like device failures, network outages, or suspicious activity. IoT platforms offer dashboards and real-time visualizations to monitor device health, data flow, and system performance.

- Anomaly Detection: Above essential monitoring, anomaly detection systems can identify unusual device behavior that might indicate a cyberattack or malfunction. These systems analyze data patterns and alert you to deviations from regular operation.

- Identity and Access Management (IAM): Securing authorization to devices and data is critical. IAM frameworks ensure that only authorized users and applications can interact with your IoT devices and the data they generate.

- Network Segmentation: Dividing your network into segments can limit the potential damage of a cyberattack. By isolating critical devices and data from less sensitive areas, you can prevent a breach in one segment from compromising the entire network.

- Compliance: Depending on your industry and the type of data collected, you might need to comply with specific data privacy regulations. Your IoT management and monitoring practices should be designed to ensure adherence to these regulations.

- Automation: Automating tasks like device provisioning, security updates, and anomaly response can save time and resources. IoT platforms offer tools for workflow automation, allowing you to streamline your management processes and improve efficiency.

By understanding and implementing these fundamentals, you can establish a secure and well-managed IoT network, enabling you to harness the full potential of your connected devices and create a solid foundation for future growth.

Level 1 Insights

The Internet of Things (IoT) is weaving into our lives' fabric. From smart thermostats optimizing energy use in our homes to industrial sensors monitoring critical infrastructure, billions of devices are now chattering away, collecting and transmitting data. This interconnected world offers tremendous potential for innovation and efficiency but introduces new challenges. Effectively managing and monitoring these networks and the security of their devices is no longer optional – it's essential.

CHAPTER 5   DESIGN AND DEPLOY AZURE IOT MONITORING AND MANAGEMENT

Here's why robust IoT network and security management and monitoring are critical for the success of any IoT deployment:

- Complexity at Scale: Imagine managing a network that grows exponentially, with millions of devices constantly transmitting data. Traditional IT management tools wouldn't suffice. IoT network management platforms provide the scalability and centralized control needed to effectively provision, configure, and maintain these vast networks.

- A Flood of Data: The sheer volume of data collected by IoT devices can be impossible. Insurmountable. Without proper data collection and storage strategies, valuable insights can be lost in a sea of information. IoT platforms offer tools to streamline data ingestion, filter out irrelevant data, and prepare the data for analysis, allowing you to extract the actual value from your IoT investments.

- A Vulnerable Landscape: The sheer number of connected devices creates a massive attack surface for malicious actors. A single compromised device can act as a gateway, allowing hackers to infiltrate your network and potentially access sensitive information or disrupt critical operations. Robust security protocols, encryption, and regular patching are crucial to shield your IoT network from cyber threats.

- Proactive Problem Solving: Network outages, device failures, and unexpected data patterns can all indicate trouble. These issues might go unnoticed without continuous monitoring until they snowball into major problems.

- Optimizing Performance: An IoT network can suffer from performance bottlenecks or resource constraints like any complex system. Effective monitoring empowers you to identify these bottlenecks and optimize network performance to ensure smooth operation and efficient data flow.

- Compliance and Data Privacy: In response to concerns over data privacy, the General Data Protection Regulation is putting tighter controls on the collection, storage, and use of data. You need strong data governance practices within your IoT management and monitoring framework to ensure compliance with these regulations.

- The Power of Automation: Managing a large-scale IoT network can be time-consuming. Automation tools offered by IoT platforms can streamline tasks like device provisioning, security updates, and anomaly response. This frees your IT team to focus on strategic initiatives and fosters a more efficient operation.

- Future-Proofing Your Investment: The world of IoT is constantly evolving, with new devices and applications emerging continually. A well-designed IoT network, security management, and monitoring system should be flexible and adaptable to accommodate future growth and integration with new technologies.

- Building Trust and Transparency: Trust and transparency are paramount in a world increasingly reliant on connected devices. A secure and well-managed IoT network demonstrates your commitment to protecting sensitive data and safeguarding the integrity of your systems. This builds trust with partners, customers, and stakeholders alike.

- Unlocking the True Potential of IoT: By effectively managing and monitoring your IoT network and security, you unlock the true potential of your connected devices. You gain valuable insights from data analysis, optimize operations for efficiency, and make data-driven decisions to improve your products and services.

Failing to prioritize IoT network and security management and monitoring can have severe consequences. Data breaches, operational disruptions, and reputational damage are all potential risks. Your IoT network can be transformed into a powerful asset by implementing a comprehensive and well-designed management and monitoring strategy to drive innovation, efficiency, and competitive edge.

IoT Lifecycle for Network and Security Management and Monitoring

The Internet of Things (IoT) network and security lifecycle encompasses the stages and processes necessary to ensure the security of IoT devices, networks, and security throughout their operational life.

The Internet of Things (IoT) network and security lifecycle is an organized method designed to ensure the security and functionality of IoT systems from their inception through to decommissioning. As IoT devices proliferate, integrating deeply into various sectors such as healthcare, manufacturing, and intelligent cities, securing these networks becomes paramount. This lifecycle approach encompasses five phases: planning and design, deployment, operation and maintenance, data management, and decommissioning. Each phase addresses specific aspects of security, ensuring that IoT systems are resilient against threats, compliant with regulations, and efficient in operation.

Figure 5-1 depicts the lifecycle of IoT network and security management and monitoring.

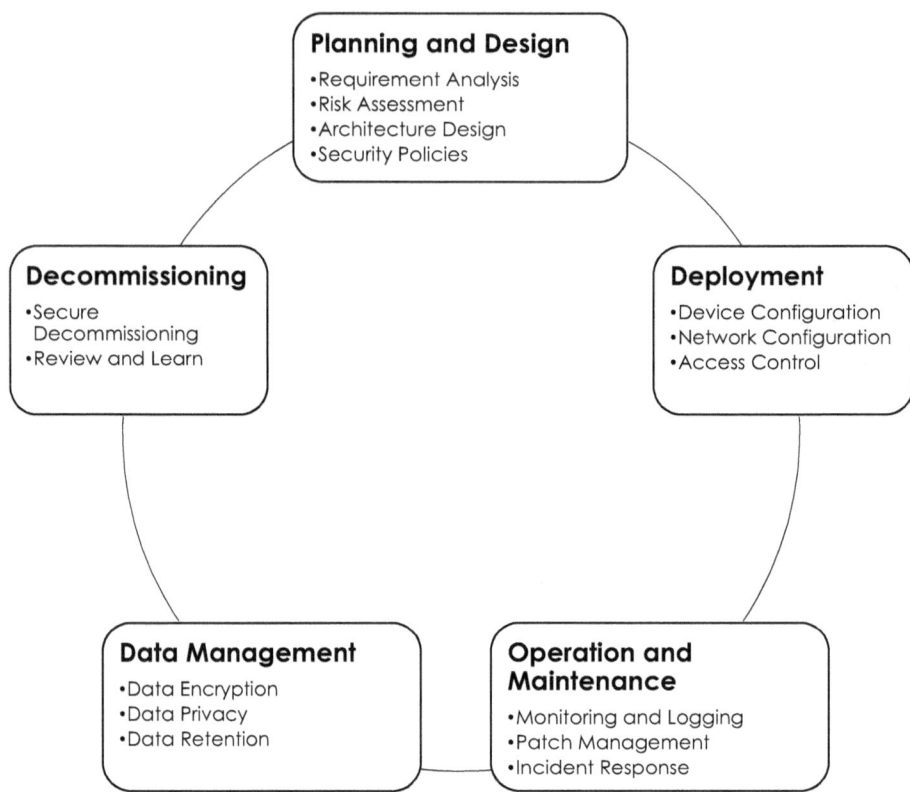

Figure 5-1. *IoT network and security lifecycle*

The lifecycle begins with the planning and design phase, where the functional and security requirements for the IoT system are defined. During this phase, a thorough risk assessment identifies potential threats, vulnerabilities, and risks. A secure architecture is designed, which includes network topology, device management, data flow, and security controls. Security policies and protocols for device authentication, data encryption, access control, and incident response are also developed at this stage.

Planning and Design

The Planning and Design phase is the foundational stage of the IoT network and security lifecycle, where the groundwork for a secure and efficient IoT system is established. This phase involves a comprehensive approach to understanding the requirements, identifying risks, designing a robust architecture, and developing security policies.

Requirement Analysis: Requirement assessment is the primary stage in planning and designing an IoT system. This involves gathering and defining the functional and non-functional requirements of the IoT deployment. Functional requirements detail what the system should do, such as specific tasks, functions, and operations of the IoT devices and network. Non-functional requirements encompass aspects like performance, reliability, scalability, and security. This step ensures that the system will meet the intended use cases and operational needs while aligning with organizational goals.

Risk Assessment: Following requirement analysis, a meticulous and thorough risk assessment is conducted to identify potential threats, vulnerabilities, and risks associated with the IoT deployment. This involves analyzing the entire ecosystem, including devices, networks, data flows, and user interactions. The risk assessment helps understand the security landscape, identify possible attack vectors, and evaluate the potential impact of security breaches. This process often involves creating a threat model, which visualizes and prioritizes risks, aiding in formulating mitigation strategies.

Architecture Design: The pivotal step after identifying the risks is the design of a secure architecture. This phase, which includes defining the network topology and data flow design, is paramount. It sets the stage for a resilient system that can withstand attacks and operational challenges. The architecture should incorporate secure device management practices, ensuring that devices can be easily monitored, updated, and managed. The data flow design is also crucial, detailing how data will be transmitted, processed, and stored securely. The architecture must include security controls, such as firewalls, intrusion detection/prevention systems, and secure communication protocols (e.g., TLS/SSL).

Security Policies: Developing robust security policies is critical to the planning and design phase. These policies offer guidance for ensuring consistent and effective security practices across the IoT ecosystem. Key security policies include:

- Device Authentication: Ensuring only authorized devices are able to access the network by using digital certificates and secure keys.

- Data Encryption: Preventing unauthorized access to and tampering with data in transit and at rest using robust encryption methods.

- Access Control: Defines who can access devices and data and under what conditions. This includes implementing role-based access control (RBAC) and least privilege principles.

- Incident Response: Establishing protocols for responding to security incidents, including detection, reporting, containment, eradication, and recovery.

All stakeholders must recognize their roles and obligations in maintaining the security of the IoT system by documenting, communicating, and enforcing these policies.

In conclusion, the Planning and Design phase sets the stage for a secure and reliable IoT deployment. By thoroughly analyzing requirements, assessing risks, designing a robust architecture, and establishing comprehensive security policies, organizations can deploy a solid baseline to support the subsequent phases of the IoT network and security lifecycle. This phase is critical for anticipating potential issues and ensuring the IoT system is resilient, compliant, and aligned with organizational objectives.

Following the planning and design phase, the deployment phase involves

- Configuring IoT devices with secure settings, such as strong passwords
- Turning off unnecessary services
- Updating firmware

Deployment Phase

The IoT network and security lifecycle deployment phase is crucial for implementing the planned system. This phase focuses on implementing the secure configurations and architectures designed during the planning stage. It involves configuring devices, setting up the network, and establishing robust access control mechanisms. Each phase step ensures the IoT deployment is secure, efficient, and ready for operation.

Device Configuration: Device configuration is the first critical step in the deployment phase. This process involves setting up IoT devices with secure settings to prevent unauthorized access and vulnerabilities. Essential activities of device configuration include

- Setting Strong Passwords: To protect against unauthorized access, all IoT devices should be configured with strong, unique passwords. Default passwords should be changed immediately after deployment.

- Disabling Unnecessary Services: Disabling unnecessary services or features not required for the device's primary function reduces the attack surface and potential vulnerabilities.

- Updating Firmware: Devices should be updated with the latest firmware to ensure they have the most recent security patches and improvements. Regular updates are essential to protect against known vulnerabilities.

- Configuring Secure Communication: Devices should use secure communication protocols, such as TLS/SSL, to encrypt data in transit and prevent eavesdropping or tampering.

- Implementing Device Authentication: Strong authentication mechanisms, such as digital certificates or secure keys, should ensure that only authorized devices can connect to the network.

Proper device configuration lays the foundation for a secure IoT deployment, reducing the risk of breaches and ensuring devices operate as intended.

Network Configuration: Network configuration is another vital aspect of the deployment phase. This involves setting up the network infrastructure to ensure secure and reliable communication among IoT devices. Critical activities in network configuration include:

- Network Segmentation: Classifies the network into different zones based on the function and security requirements of the devices. This limits the spread of potential attacks and isolates critical components from less secure areas.

- Firewalls and Intrusion Detection Systems: Deploy Network firewalls to control traffic between network segments and use intrusion detection/prevention systems (IDS/IPS) to monitor suspicious activity and block potential threats.

- Secure Communication Protocols: Ensuring all data transmitted over the network is encrypted using secure communication protocols like TLS/SSL. This protects data in transit from being intercepted or altered.

- VLANs and Subnets: Virtual Local Area Networks (VLANs) and subnets isolate traffic further and enforce security policies. This helps manage and control traffic flow, reducing the risk of attackers' lateral movement within the network.

- Quality of Service (QoS): Configuring QoS settings to prioritize critical IoT traffic and ensure reliable performance, especially for time-sensitive applications. Proper network configuration ensures that the IoT infrastructure is robust, secure, and capable of supporting the deployment's operational needs.

Access Control: Access control is critical to the deployment phase, ensuring only authorized users and devices can interact with the IoT system. Essential activities of access control include the following:

Role-Based Access Control (RBAC): By implementing RBAC, we empower users within the organization. This system assigns permissions based on user roles, ensuring that every user has the least amount of necessary access to perform their duties. This method is based on the principle of least privilege, fostering a sense of trust and responsibility among users.

- Authentication Mechanisms: We deploy robust authentication mechanisms, such as multi-factor authentication (MFA), to verify the identity of users and devices before granting access. This robustness instills a sense of security and confidence, providing our users and administrators peace of mind.

- Access Policies: We define and enforce access policies that specify who can access which resources and under what conditions. These policies, based on user roles, access time, and device location, provide a sense of control and security, ensuring that only authorized entities can interact with the system.

- Audit and Logging: Set up logging and audit trails to monitor access to the IoT system. This helps detect and respond to unauthorized access attempts and provides a record for forensic analysis in case of a security incident.

- Encryption and Key Management: Ensuring access credentials, such as passwords and encryption keys, are securely managed and stored. This minimizes unauthorized exposure to sensitive data and system components.

The integrity and confidentiality of the IoT system are protected by effective access control mechanisms, eliminating unauthorized access, and guaranteeing that only assigned users and devices can access the system's resources.

The deployment phase is not just a step; it's a critical responsibility for establishing a secure and functional IoT system. By meticulously configuring devices, setting up a secure network infrastructure, and implementing robust access control measures, we ensure that our IoT deployment is safe and ready for operation. This phase is pivotal in laying the groundwork for ongoing security and operational efficiency, supporting the overall goals of the IoT network and security lifecycle.

Once deployed, the operation and maintenance phase ensures continuous security and functionality of the IoT network. This phase includes monitoring and logging the IoT network and devices for unusual activity or security breaches. Detailed logs are maintained for audit and forensic purposes. Patches and updates are applied to IoT devices and network components regularly to address known vulnerabilities. An incident response plan is also established and maintained to address any possible security incidents quickly and effectively.

Operation and Maintenance Phase

In the IoT network and security lifecycle, the operation and maintenance phases play a crucial role in responding to security incidents, ensuring the continued security, performance, and reliability of the IoT system after deployment. Monitoring, updating, and responding to security incidents are continuous activities that are essential for maintaining the integrity and availability of the IoT deployment over time.

Monitoring and Logging: During the operation and maintenance phase, monitoring and logging are important for detecting and responding to unusual behaviors or security incidents.

- Continuous Monitoring: Implementing constant monitoring tools and systems to track IoT devices, network infrastructure performance, and security status. This includes monitoring device health, network traffic, and data flows to detect anomalies that could indicate potential security threats.

- Real-time Alerts: This is about setting up real-time alert systems that notify administrators of potential security threats, such as unauthorized access attempts, unusual data patterns, or device malfunctions. These alerts are crucial for enabling swift response to potential issues.

- Logging: Maintaining detailed logs of all activities within the IoT environment. Logs should capture device connections, data transfers, access attempts, and system changes. These logs are critical for auditing, troubleshooting, and forensic analysis during a security incident.

- Data Analysis: This is about using advanced analytics and machine learning techniques to analyze monitoring reports and identify potential security risks. It's a proactive approach that helps anticipate and mitigate potential threats before they cause harm.

- Compliance Monitoring: Ensuring the IoT system complies with relevant regulatory requirements and standards. Regular audits and compliance checks help maintain adherence to data protection and security regulations.

Effective monitoring and logging provide visibility into the IoT environment, enabling organizations to detect and address issues promptly, thereby maintaining the security and reliability of the system.

Patch Management: Patch management is a critical process in the operation and maintenance phase. IoT devices and network components are regularly updated and patched to address vulnerabilities and improve functionality.

- Vulnerability Management: Continuously scanning for vulnerabilities in IoT devices and network components. This involves using automated tools to identify outdated software, misconfigurations, and other security weaknesses.

- Patch Deployment: Regularly applying patches and updates released by device manufacturers and software vendors. Patches often address security vulnerabilities, fix bugs, and add new features. Timely deployment is essential to protect the system from known threats.

- Testing Patches: Before deploying patches to the live environment, testing them in a controlled setting is essential to ensure they do not introduce new issues or disrupt existing functionalities. This helps prevent potential downtime or adverse effects on the system.

- Automated Patch Management: Implementing automated patch management solutions to streamline identifying, testing, and deploying patches. The automation of critical updates reduces the risk of human error and ensures that they are applied in a timely manner.

- Documentation and Reporting: Tracking all patches, identifying devices affected, dates of deployment, and issues addressed. This documentation is essential for compliance and audit purposes.

Effective patch management ensures that IoT devices and systems remain up-to-date with the latest security protections and functionality improvements, reducing the risk of exploitation by malicious actors.

Incident Response: Incident response is a crucial component of the operation and maintenance phase. It involves the processes and actions taken to effectively address security incidents and breaches.

An incident response plan describes a wide range of steps to be taken in the event of a security incident. A detailed procedure for handling the incident should be included in the plan, along with roles and responsibilities, and communication protocols.

CHAPTER 5　DESIGN AND DEPLOY AZURE IOT MONITORING AND MANAGEMENT

Security incidents can be quickly detected and identified using monitoring systems and alerts. Accurate detection is essential for acting promptly and minimizing damage.

In addition to containing the outbreak, containment may include isolating and blocking malicious traffic, and deactivating compromised accounts or services to prevent further spread of the infection. In addition to containing the outbreak, containment may include isolating and blocking malicious traffic, and deactivating compromised accounts or services to prevent further spread of the infection.

The eradication process involves identifying and eliminating the root cause of the incident. This may involve removing malware, securing vulnerabilities, or applying patches and configuration changes to prevent recurrence.

- Recovery: Returning affected systems and devices to a functional, secure, and fully functional state. This includes restoring data from backups, if necessary.

- Analysis of the incident: Identify what happened, how it was handled, and what improvements can be made to prevent future incidents. To improve the incident response plan and security posture, actionable recommendations should result from this analysis.

- Analysis of the incident: Identify what happened, how it was handled, and what improvements can be made to prevent future incidents. To improve the incident response plan and security posture, actionable recommendations should result from this analysis.

If necessary, communicate effectively both internally and externally. A vital part of incident response is reporting incidents to relevant authorities and regulatory bodies, if required by law or industry standards.

Effective incident response minimizes the damage caused by security incidents, reduces recovery time, and improves the overall resilience of the IoT system.

Operating and maintaining an IoT deployment is essential to an IoT deployment's ongoing security and performance. By implementing robust monitoring and logging practices, maintaining an effective patch management process, and having a well-defined incident response plan, organizations can ensure that their IoT systems remain secure, reliable, and compliant with regulations throughout their operational life.

Data management is a critical aspect of the IoT lifecycle. Encrypting data both in transit and at rest protects it from unauthorized access. Measures are implemented to comply with data privacy regulations and protect personal information IoT devices collect. Data retention policies are defined and enforced to manage the lifecycle of the data collected, ensuring that it is retained only as long as necessary and disposed of securely when no longer needed.

Data Management Phase

The Data Management phase of the IoT network and security lifecycle is crucial and is the backbone of the entire process. It's your responsibility to handle the data generated and processed by IoT devices, ensuring data integrity, confidentiality, and availability through encryption, privacy measures, and retention policies. Your role in effective data management is not just essential; it's irreplaceable for protecting sensitive information and complying with regulatory requirements.

Data Encryption: Data encryption is fundamental; it's your tool for securing IoT data. It empowers you to protect information in transit and at rest. With data encryption, you're in control of the security of the IoT data.

- Encryption in Transit: Data transmitted between IoT devices, gateways, and central systems is vulnerable to interception and tampering. Secure IoT/OT network communication protocols such as TLS (Transport Layer Security) or SSL (Secure Sockets Layer) should be used to protect this data. These protocols encrypt data before sending it over networks, making it unreadable by unauthorized parties.

- Encryption at Rest: Data stored on IoT devices, gateways, and central servers should also be encrypted to protect it from unauthorized access. This involves using robust encryption algorithms such as Advanced Encryption Standard (AES). Encrypting data at rest ensures that the data remains protected even if physical devices are compromised or stolen.

- Key Management: Effective encryption requires robust critical management practices. Encryption keys should be generated, stored, and rotated securely. Only authorized personnel must have access to encryption keys. Automated essential systems of management can help secure critical handling throughout their lifecycle.

- End-to-end Encryption: Deploying end-to-end encryption assures that confidential data remains encrypted from the point of origin (the IoT device) to its final destination (the central server or cloud). This comprehensive approach provides a higher level of security by ensuring that data is never exposed in plaintext during transmission or storage.

Proper implementation of data encryption techniques is crucial for safeguarding confidential data against unapproved access and breaches, thus maintaining the confidentiality and integrity of IoT data.

Data Privacy: Data privacy is not just a measure; it's a responsibility. It involves implementing measures to protect the personal and sensitive information collected by IoT devices and ensuring that it is handled in compliance with privacy laws and regulations. Your role in data privacy is crucial for protecting individuals' rights and reducing the risk of legal repercussions.

Data Minimization, an essential practice in data privacy, involves collecting only the data necessary for the intended purpose. This approach significantly reduces the risk of storing excessive personal information, enhancing data privacy.

- Anonymization and Pseudonymization: Techniques such as anonymization and pseudonymization can protect personal data. Anonymization involves removing or altering personal identifiers so individuals cannot be identified. Pseudonymization involves replacing identifiable information with pseudonyms, allowing data to be processed without directly identifying individuals while enabling linkage to the original data when necessary.

- Consent Management: Obtaining informed consent from individuals before collecting and processing their data is essential for compliance with privacy regulations such as GDPR. Users need to understand what data will be collected, what it will be processed, and their rights over their data through clear and transparent consent mechanisms.

- Access Controls: Implementing strict access controls ensures only authorized personnel can access personal and sensitive data. Role-based access control (RBAC) and the principle of least privilege should be enforced to limit access to data based on job responsibilities.

- Data Privacy Policies: Developing and communicating data privacy policies to stakeholders is crucial for ensuring that data is handled appropriately. These policies should outline the organization's commitment to data privacy, the data gathered, how it is processed, and the steps to protect it.

Ensuring data privacy helps organizations build trust with users and comply with legal requirements, protecting individuals' rights and reducing the risk of legal repercussions.

Data Retention: Data retention involves defining and enforcing policies for how long data should be stored and ensuring that it is disposed of securely when no longer needed.

- Retention Policies: Establish clear data retention policies that specify the duration for which different data types should be retained. These policies should be developed on legal obligations, industry standards, and business needs. For example, certain data may need to be retained for a specific period to comply with regulatory requirements, while other data may only need to be kept for operational purposes.

- Automated Retention Management: Implementing automated systems to manage data retention can help consistently enforce retention policies. These systems can automatically delete or archive data once it reaches the end of its retention period, reducing the risk of storing outdated or unnecessary information.

- Secure Disposal: When data is no longer needed, it should be disposed of securely to prevent unauthorized access. Ensuring that deleted data cannot be recovered involves wiping, degaussing, or physically destroying storage media.

- Data Archiving: Archiving solutions can be implemented for data that must be preserved for inflated periods but is not actively used. Archiving involves moving data to a separate storage location optimized for long-term retention, reducing the burden on primary storage systems while ensuring that data is still accessible when needed.

- Compliance Audits: Regular audits should be conducted to ensure compliance with data retention policies and identify any discrepancies or areas for improvement. These audits help verify that data is retained and destroyed on demand in alignment with established policies and regulatory requirements.

Effective data retention management ensures that organizations store data only as long as necessary, reducing storage costs, minimizing the risk of data breaches, and complying with legal and regulatory requirements.

Data management phase is vital for protecting IoT data's integrity, confidentiality, and availability. Organizations can safeguard sensitive information, comply with regulatory requirements, and build user trust by implementing solid data encryption, ensuring data privacy, and managing data retention effectively. This phase is essential for maintaining the overall security and reliability of the IoT system throughout its lifecycle.

The final phase of the lifecycle is decommissioning, where IoT devices that have reached the end of their useful life are securely decommissioned. This includes wiping data, removing devices from the network, and securely disposing of hardware. A post-mortem lifecycle analysis is conducted to identify lessons learned and improve future deployment processes.

Decommissioning Phase

The Decommissioning phase of the IoT network and security lifecycle is the final stage, focusing on securely retiring IoT devices and systems that have reached the end of their useful life. This phase ensures that all data and configurations are securely removed and that lessons learned from the lifecycle are used to improve future deployments. Effective decommissioning mitigates risks associated with outdated or vulnerable devices remaining in the network and helps maintain overall security.

Secure Decommissioning: Secure decommissioning involves carefully removing IoT devices from the network and securely wiping or destroying all sensitive data.

- Data Wiping: All data stored on IoT devices must be securely erased to prevent unauthorized access or recovery. This involves using data wiping tools and techniques that overwrite the existing data multiple times, ensuring it is irretrievable. For devices with storage media such as hard drives or SSDs, certified data-wiping software should be used to meet industry standards for secure deletion.

- Configuration Removal: Any configurations, settings, or credentials stored on the devices should be reset to factory defaults or securely removed. This prevents the potential misuse of network credentials, API keys, or other sensitive information that could be exploited if the device is repurposed or accessed by unauthorized individuals.

- Physical Destruction: Physical destruction may be necessary for devices that cannot be securely wiped or are highly sensitive. This involves physically destroying the device or its storage components to ensure data cannot be recovered. Methods such as shredding, crushing, or degaussing (for magnetic storage media) can render the device inoperable and data inaccessible.

- Device Removal from Network: It is crucial to ensure that decommissioned devices are correctly removed. This involves updating network management systems to reflect the removal of the devices, revoking any associated network credentials, and ensuring that no communication attempts from the device are accepted.

- Documentation: It is essential to maintain detailed records of each device's decommissioning process. This includes documenting the steps taken to wipe or destroy data securely, the methods used for physical destruction (if applicable), and confirming the device's removal from the network.

Secure decommissioning protects against data breaches and unauthorized access by ensuring that all sensitive information is properly removed and that decommissioned devices do not pose a security risk.

Review and Learn: The Review and Learn process involves analyzing the decommissioning phase and the entire IoT lifecycle to identify lessons learned and areas for improvement.

- Post-Mortem Analysis: Conducting a thorough post-mortem analysis of the decommissioning process helps identify what went well and what could be improved. This involves reviewing the steps taken during decommissioning, any challenges encountered, and how they were addressed. The goal is to learn from the experience and make necessary adjustments to the decommissioning procedures.

- Security Incident Review: Reviewing any security incidents that occurred during the lifecycle of the IoT system provides valuable insights into potential vulnerabilities and the effectiveness of the incident response measures. Understanding the root causes of incidents and the effectiveness of mitigations can inform future security practices.

- Policy and Procedure Updates: Updating policies and procedures is essential based on the findings from the post-mortem analysis and security incident reviews. This may include revising decommissioning protocols, enhancing data-wiping techniques, or improving physical destruction methods. Regular updates ensure they remain effective and aligned with best practices.

- Training and Awareness: Sharing the lessons learned with relevant stakeholders, including IT staff, security teams, and management, helps build awareness and improve future practices. User awareness training sessions must be conducted to educate personnel on updated decommissioning processes and any new security measures.

- Feedback: Establish a feedback loop where insights from the decommissioning phase inform the planning and design of future IoT deployments. This continuous improvement ensures that the organization's IoT lifecycle management evolves based on real-world experiences and emerging threats.

Reviewing and learning from the decommissioning process ensure that the organization continuously improves its IoT security practices, reduces future risks, and enhances the overall effectiveness of its IoT deployments.

CHAPTER 5   DESIGN AND DEPLOY AZURE IOT MONITORING AND MANAGEMENT

The decommissioning phase is crucial for securely retiring IoT devices and systems while safeguarding sensitive data and maintaining network security. By implementing secure decommissioning practices and conducting thorough reviews and learning sessions, organizations can ensure that they mitigate risks associated with obsolete devices and continuously improve their IoT lifecycle management processes.

Key security considerations must be continuously addressed throughout the entire lifecycle. Threat modeling is performed regularly to identify new and emerging threats. Adherence to relevant standards and regulatory requirements, such as GDPR and HIPAA, is ensured. Ongoing training and awareness programs are provided for stakeholders to keep them informed about security best practices and emerging threats. Managing supply chain security involves assessing and mitigating risks associated with the supply chain and ensuring that all components and software come from trustworthy sources.

In summary, the IoT network and security lifecycle is a comprehensive approach to securing IoT systems from inception to decommissioning. It involves meticulous planning, robust deployment, vigilant operation, careful data management, and secure decommissioning, all while addressing security threats and ensuring compliance with standards and regulations. Implementing a structured lifecycle approach helps organizations mitigate risks and protect their IoT environments effectively.

IoT Monitoring

In IoT cybersecurity, continuous monitoring is crucial in safeguarding IoT deployments against evolving threats and vulnerabilities. Devices connected to the Internet are often deployed in dynamic and diverse environments, making them vulnerable to various security risks, including malware, unauthorized access, data breaches, and network attacks. Continuous monitoring gives organizations real-time visibility into their IoT infrastructure, enabling them to promptly detect and respond to security incidents.

Real-time Threat Detection: Continuous monitoring involves tracking device behavior, network traffic, and system activities to identify potential security threats. By analyzing incoming data streams, monitoring systems can detect anomalies, suspicious activities, and indicators of compromise, signaling potential security breaches. For example, abnormal patterns of network traffic, unexpected device behaviors, or unauthorized access attempts may indicate a security incident that requires immediate attention.

Vulnerability Management: Continuous monitoring helps organizations identify and mitigate vulnerabilities in IoT devices and systems. By continuously scanning for known vulnerabilities, monitoring systems can assess the security posture of IoT devices and prioritize patching and remediation efforts. By taking a proactive approach, organizations can avoid potential threats and reduce the risk of malicious actors exploiting their vulnerabilities.

Continuous monitoring plays a crucial role in maintaining compliance with regulatory requirements and industry standards in IoT cybersecurity. By providing detailed logs, audit trails, and reports of security activities, it ensures that organizations can demonstrate adherence to security standards and respond effectively to compliance audits. This proactive approach is essential for protecting sensitive data and mitigating legal risks.

Incident Response: Continuous monitoring is integral to effective incident response in IoT environments. When security incidents occur, monitoring systems provide real-time alerts and notifications, enabling organizations to respond swiftly and mitigate the impact of the incident. By automating incident detection and response processes, continuous monitoring helps organizations minimize downtime, prevent data loss, and contain security breaches before they escalate.

Adaptive Security Measures: Continuous monitoring enables organizations to adapt their security measures dynamically in response to emerging threats and changing conditions. By analyzing real-time data and threat intelligence, monitoring systems can adjust security policies, update access controls, and deploy additional security controls as needed. This adaptive approach can achieve a proactive security posture and resilience against evolving cyber threats.

Network Segmentation and Isolation: Continuous monitoring facilitates network segmentation and isolation in IoT environments, limiting the impact of security incidents and containing potential threats. By monitoring network traffic and device communication patterns, organizations can identify and segment vulnerable devices or compromised areas of the network, preventing lateral movement and minimizing the spread of attacks. This proactive segmentation strategy enhances the overall security of IoT deployments.

Continuous monitoring is instrumental in maintaining the privacy and integrity of data transmitted and processed by IoT devices. Detecting unauthorized data access, breaches, or data exfiltration attempts in real-time ensures that sensitive information remains protected and data integrity is preserved throughout the IoT ecosystem. This proactive monitoring approach is a key component of data protection in IoT environments.

In summary, continuous monitoring is essential for ensuring the cybersecurity of IoT deployments by providing real-time threat detection, vulnerability management, compliance monitoring, incident response capabilities, adaptive security measures, network segmentation, and data privacy and integrity protection. Organizations can enhance their IoT infrastructure's resilience, reliability, and security by implementing robust monitoring solutions in an increasingly connected and threat-prone environment.

CHAPTER 5 DESIGN AND DEPLOY AZURE IOT MONITORING AND MANAGEMENT

What Is IoT Monitoring?

IoT monitoring refers to continuously observing, measuring, and interpreting data induced by Internet of Things (IoT) devices and systems. This process involves collecting data from sensors, devices, networks, and applications to ensure the proper functioning and performance of the IoT ecosystem. Monitoring encompasses various aspects, such as device health, network performance, data integrity, and security. It utilizes specialized software and hardware tools to gather, process, and visualize data, providing insights into the real-time status and historical trends of the IoT infrastructure.

The scope of IoT monitoring can vary widely dependent on the particular application and deployment environment. For example, in industrial IoT, monitoring might include tracking machine performance, energy consumption, and production metrics. In a smart city, it could involve monitoring traffic flow, air quality, and public safety systems. Regardless of the context, the primary goal of IoT monitoring is to maintain the reliability, efficiency, and security of the interconnected devices and systems.

Implementing IoT monitoring requires a comprehensive strategy that includes selecting appropriate sensors and devices, deploying effective communication protocols, and utilizing advanced data analytics platforms. The monitoring infrastructure must be capable of handling massive volumes of data collected by myriad devices while ensuring minimal latency and high availability. This often involves leveraging cloud-based solutions and edge computing to handle data nearer to the source and reduce the burden on central servers.

Effective IoT monitoring also involves setting up alerts and notifications to inform stakeholders promptly of any anomalies or performance issues. These alerts can be activated based on predetermined thresholds or through advanced anomaly detection algorithms that identify deviations from normal behavior. By providing real-time insights and timely alerts, IoT monitoring enables proactive maintenance and swift response to potential problems.

Security is another critical aspect of IoT monitoring. As IoT devices are often deployed in diverse and sometimes vulnerable environments, continuous monitoring helps detect security breaches, unauthorized access, and other threats. Monitoring tools can analyze traffic patterns, identify suspicious activities, and take automated actions to mitigate risks, such as isolating compromised devices or blocking malicious traffic.

In summary, IoT monitoring is not just a tool for managing IoT deployments, but a key to optimizing operations. It provides the visibility and insights to ensure IoT systems operate efficiently, securely, and reliably. Through continuous observation and analysis, organizations can harness the full potential of IoT technologies while mitigating risks and enhancing operational performance, making you feel efficient and effective in your role.

Why Is IoT Monitoring Required?

IoT monitoring is required to ensure the smooth and efficient operation of IoT systems, which are increasingly integral to various industries and applications. IoT deployments' complex and distributed nature necessitates continuous oversight to maintain functionality and performance. Organizations need effective monitoring to detect issues, manage devices, and secure their networks, leading to potential system failures, security breaches, and operational inefficiencies.

One primary reason for IoT monitoring is to maintain device health and performance. IoT devices often operate in challenging environments and are subject to wear and tear. Monitoring these devices helps identify performance degradation, predict failures, and schedule maintenance activities before critical breakdowns occur. This preventative approach decreases downtime and extends the devices' lifespan, resulting in cost savings.

Another crucial aspect of IoT monitoring is ensuring data integrity and accuracy. IoT systems generate vast data that drive decision-making processes and operational strategies. Only accurate data can lead to inefficiencies and sound decisions. Monitoring helps validate data quality, identify discrepancies, and ensure the information collected from various sensors and devices is reliable and accurate.

Security is a severe concern in IoT implementations, given the rising prevalence of cyber threats directed at connected devices. IoT monitoring is essential for detecting and responding to real-time security incidents. It helps identify unauthorized access, detect malware, and prevent data breaches. By continuously analyzing network traffic and device behavior, monitoring systems can identify anomalies and take immediate action to mitigate potential threats.

IoT monitoring also plays a vital role in optimizing network performance. With numerous devices transmitting data simultaneously, network congestion and bottlenecks can occur, affecting the overall performance of the IoT system. Monitoring helps identify network issues, optimize bandwidth usage, and ensure seamless device communication. This is particularly important in applications where real-time data transmission is critical, such as healthcare or industrial automation.

Another reason IoT monitoring is necessary is compliance with regulatory requirements and industry standards. All industries, including healthcare and finance, have strict data security and privacy regulations. IoT monitoring helps organizations ensure compliance by providing detailed logs and reports of device activities, data flows, and security incidents. This documentation is crucial for audits and demonstrating adherence to regulatory standards.

Lastly, IoT monitoring enhances user experience by ensuring that IoT applications and services run smoothly. Performance issues in consumer-facing applications like smart homes and wearable devices can directly impact user satisfaction. Monitoring ensures that devices and services are always available, responsive, and functioning as expected, improving user trust and engagement.

CHAPTER 5   DESIGN AND DEPLOY AZURE IOT MONITORING AND MANAGEMENT

Where Is IoT Monitoring Required?

IoT monitoring is required across various industries and applications, wherever IoT devices are deployed to collect, process, and transmit data. Each environment has unique monitoring needs and challenges, necessitating tailored solutions to ensure adequate oversight and management.

In industrial settings, IoT monitoring is crucial for maintaining the efficiency and safety of manufacturing processes. Industrial IoT (IIoT) devices monitor machinery, track production metrics, and ensure worker safety. Monitoring systems help detect equipment malfunctions, optimize production schedules, and prevent accidents by providing real-time data on machine conditions and environmental factors.

Smart cities are another critical area where IoT monitoring is essential. In smart city deployments, IoT devices manage traffic, monitor air quality, control street lighting, and enhance public safety. Monitoring these devices ensures that city services operate smoothly and efficiently. For example, traffic monitoring systems can detect congestion and adjust traffic signals in real time to improve flow, while air quality sensors provide data to manage pollution levels.

Healthcare is a critical domain where IoT monitoring plays a vital role. IoT devices in healthcare, such as wearable fitness trackers, remote patient monitoring systems, and intelligent medical equipment, require continuous monitoring to ensure patient safety and effective care delivery. Monitoring helps track vital signs, detect anomalies in patient health data, and ensure that medical devices function correctly, enhancing patient outcomes and reducing healthcare costs.

In agriculture, IoT monitoring optimizes farming practices and improves crop yields. IoT sensors monitor soil moisture, temperature, and nutrient levels, providing data to farmers for precise irrigation and fertilization. Monitoring systems help detect environmental changes, predict pest infestations, and manage resources efficiently, leading to more sustainable and productive farming practices.

CHAPTER 5   DESIGN AND DEPLOY AZURE IOT MONITORING AND MANAGEMENT

Retail is another sector where IoT monitoring is increasingly important. Retailers use IoT devices for inventory management, customer tracking, and supply chain optimization. Monitoring these systems helps ensure that products are always in stock, reduces losses due to theft or spoilage, and enhances customer experience through personalized services. Real-time monitoring of supply chains also helps manage logistics and reduce delays.

IoT monitoring is essential for managing intelligent grids, renewable energy sources, and utility infrastructures in the energy sector. Monitoring systems track energy consumption, production, and distribution, ensuring the stability and efficiency of energy networks. For example, smart meters provide real-time data on energy usage, helping consumers and utilities manage consumption and reduce costs. Monitoring renewable energy sources like solar panels and wind turbines ensures optimal performance and timely maintenance.

Lastly, IoT monitoring is required in residential applications like smart homes. IoT devices in smart homes control lighting, heating, security systems, and appliances. Monitoring these devices ensures they operate efficiently, securely, and according to user preferences. For example, smart thermostats can be monitored to optimize energy usage, while security cameras provide real-time alerts for unusual activities, enhancing home security.

What Are the Benefits of Designing and Deploying IoT Monitoring?

Designing and deploying IoT monitoring systems enhances the overall effectiveness, security, and reliability of IoT deployments and empowers organizations and users. By implementing robust monitoring solutions, organizations can take control of their IoT technologies, unlocking their full potential and achieving significant improvements in various operational aspects.

One of the primary benefits is improved operational efficiency. IoT monitoring provides real-time insights into the performance and health of devices, networks, and applications. Detecting and addressing issues promptly reduces downtime and ensures smooth operations. For example, manufacturing monitoring systems can identify equipment malfunctions early, allowing for timely maintenance and minimizing production disruptions.

Another significant benefit is the proactive security provided by IoT monitoring. It helps detect and respond to security threats quickly, preventing unauthorized access and data breaches. By continuously analyzing network traffic and device behavior, monitoring systems can identify anomalies and potential attacks, helping organizations take preventative measures to protect their IoT infrastructure. This is particularly important given the increasing number of cyber threats targeting IoT devices.

Cost savings are also a notable advantage of deploying IoT monitoring. By preventing equipment failures and optimizing maintenance schedules, organizations can significantly reduce repair and replacement costs. Additionally, monitoring helps maximize resource usage, such as energy and materials, leading to further cost reductions. For instance, innovative energy monitoring systems can identify inefficiencies in energy consumption and suggest measures to reduce usage, leading to lower utility bills and a sense of financial prudence.

Improved data quality and integrity are critical benefits of IoT monitoring. Monitoring systems validate data collected from IoT devices, ensuring that it is accurate, complete, and reliable. This unwavering reliability is essential for making informed decisions and deriving actionable insights from IoT data. Inaccurate or corrupted data can lead to poor decision-making and operational inefficiencies, so maintaining high data quality is crucial.

Another benefit of IoT monitoring is enhanced user experience. Monitoring in consumer applications like smart homes and wearable devices ensures that services are always available, responsive, and functioning as expected. Users are more satisfied and engaged when their devices perform consistently, as they can rely on them. For example, monitoring smart home devices ensures that lighting, heating, and security systems operate seamlessly according to user preferences.

Designing and deploying IoT monitoring systems significantly benefits compliance with regulatory requirements and industry standards. Many industries, such as healthcare, finance, and utilities, are subject to strict data security, privacy, and operational standards regulations. IoT monitoring helps organizations ensure compliance by providing detailed logs, reports, and audit trails of device activities, data flows, and security incidents. Regulatory compliance documentation and industry best practices are essential to reduce the risk of legal penalties and reputational damage.

Furthermore, IoT monitoring enables organizations to optimize resource utilization and improve sustainability. By tracking energy consumption, water usage, and other resources in real-time, monitoring systems identify inefficiencies and opportunities for optimization. For example, monitoring soil moisture levels and weather conditions in agriculture helps farmers optimize irrigation schedules, reducing water usage and environmental impact. Additionally, monitoring heating, cooling, and lighting usage in intelligent buildings allows them to reduce energy consumption and greenhouse gas emissions.

Data-driven decision-making and strategic planning are also enabled by IoT monitoring. By providing insights into end-user behavior, industry trends, and operational patterns, IoT monitoring contributes to business intelligence. This is achieved through the analysis of historical data and the identification of trends. The monitoring of customer traffic and purchasing patterns in retail, for example, helps retailers maximize sales and customer satisfaction by optimizing product placement, pricing, and promotions.

Finally, IoT monitoring provides a foundation for innovation and future growth. By continuously monitoring IoT deployments, organizations gather valuable feedback and insights that inform the development of new products, services, and business models. This iterative process of learning and adaptation enables organizations to stay ahead of competitors, respond to varying industry demands, and take advantage of emerging opportunities. Additionally, monitoring systems can be updated and expanded as IoT technologies evolve to support new devices, protocols, and applications, ensuring scalability and future-proofing the organization's IoT infrastructure.

What Is the Value Proposition of IoT Monitoring?

The value proposition of IoT monitoring lies in its ability to enhance operational efficiency, improve security, reduce costs, ensure compliance, enhance user experience, optimize resource utilization, enable data-driven decision-making, foster innovation, and support future growth. By providing real-time insights into device performance, network health, and data integrity, IoT monitoring allows organizations to maximize the benefits of IoT deployments while mitigating risks and overcoming challenges.

For organizations, the value proposition of IoT monitoring includes

- Operational Efficiency: IoT monitoring helps organizations detect and address issues proactively, minimizing downtime and optimizing resource allocation. This translates to an increase in productivity and operational efficiency.

- Improved Security: IoT monitoring systems identify security threats in real-time by continuously monitoring device behavior and network traffic, enabling organizations to protect their assets and data immediately.

- Cost Savings: By preventing equipment failures, optimizing maintenance schedules, and reducing resource wastage, IoT monitoring helps organizations reduce operational costs and improve profitability.

- Compliance Assurance: Organizations can demonstrate compliance with regulatory requirements and industry standards by monitoring IoT logs, reports, and audit trails, preventing legal penalties and protecting their reputation.

- Enhanced User Experience: IoT monitoring enhances user satisfaction and engagement, increasing loyalty and retention by ensuring IoT devices and services operate smoothly and reliably.

- Optimized Resource Utilization: By tracking resource consumption and identifying inefficiencies, IoT monitoring helps organizations maximize resource usage, reduce waste, and improve sustainability.

- Data-Driven Decision-Making: By analyzing data collected from IoT devices, organizations gain valuable insights that inform strategic decision-making, enabling them to identify opportunities for improvement and innovation.

Overall, the value proposition of IoT monitoring lies in its ability to help organizations maximize the benefits of IoT deployments while minimizing risks and overcoming challenges, ultimately driving business success and growth.

IoT and SIEM

As a comprehensive security solution, SIEM (security information and event management) monitors and analyzes security events within an organization's IT infrastructure in real-time, centralized, and real-time. SIEM's role has become increasingly critical in IoT (Internet of Things) due to the massive volume and type of data generated by countless interconnected devices. To detect potential security threats and anomalies, these devices generate considerable log data, including everything from basic sensors to complex machinery.

IoT devices often have limited processing power and security features, making them vulnerable to cyber-attacks. SIEM systems address these vulnerabilities by aggregating log data from all connected devices and correlating this information to identify patterns indicative of malicious activity. This correlation is vital in detecting sophisticated multi-vector attacks that might go unnoticed if each device were monitored in isolation. By providing a holistic view of the IoT ecosystem, SIEM not only enhances the security posture but also plays a crucial role in maintaining the integrity and confidentiality of the data transmitted and processed by IoT devices.

Furthermore, SIEM systems enable organizations to comply with industry-specific regulatory requirements by maintaining detailed logs and providing comprehensive reporting capabilities. This is particularly important in healthcare, finance, and critical infrastructure, where protecting sensitive information is paramount. SIEM helps organizations meet their regulatory obligations and protect against data breaches and other cyber threats by ensuring that all IoT devices and their communications are continuously monitored and logged.

CHAPTER 5 DESIGN AND DEPLOY AZURE IOT MONITORING AND MANAGEMENT

Why SIEM Is Required in IoT Cybersecurity?

The requirement for SIEM in IoT cybersecurity primarily arises from the unique challenges IoT environments pose. IoT devices often lack robust security controls, making them prime targets for cyberattackers. These devices can be easily compromised, and once an attacker gains access, they can use the device as a foothold to infiltrate the broader network. SIEM helps mitigate this risk by providing continuous monitoring and real-time analysis of security events across all connected devices, ensuring that any suspicious activity is promptly detected and addressed.

Another critical reason for implementing SIEM in IoT environments is the need for comprehensive visibility and control. IoT networks can be vast and complex, comprising numerous devices with varying functionalities and communication protocols. A centralized system for collecting and analyzing data makes effective oversight and managing security incidents possible. SIEM consolidates data from multiple sources, enabling organizations to gain a unified view of their IoT infrastructure. This consolidated view is essential for identifying and responding to threats that may go unnoticed.

In addition to security and visibility, regulatory compliance is a significant driver for adopting SIEM in IoT. Many industries are held to tough data protection and privacy rules requiring continuous monitoring, logging, and reporting of security events. SIEM systems provide the necessary tools to meet these regulatory requirements by ensuring that all security-relevant data is captured, stored, and made available for audits and investigations. This capability helps organizations avoid costly fines and legal repercussions and enhances their security posture by ensuring continuous compliance with industry standards.

Value Proposition for Leadership Team

Implementing SIEM in IoT cybersecurity offers several strategic advantages for the leadership team. First and foremost, it provides a robust defense strategy to combat the ever-changing topography of cyber threats. SIEM reduces the likelihood of successful cyberattacks by ensuring continuous monitoring and real-time analysis of security events, thereby protecting the organization's critical assets and sensitive information. This proactive method of security creates confidence in the leadership team, knowing they have a reliable system to detect and promptly respond to threats.

Moreover, SIEM supports the organization's risk management strategy by providing detailed insights into potential vulnerabilities and threats within the IoT ecosystem. By identifying and mitigating these risks in real time, SIEM reduces the organization's overall risk exposure and helps avoid significant financial and reputational damage from security breaches. This translates into lower operational risks and enhanced business continuity for the leadership team, ensuring the organization can keep its leading edge in the market.

Additionally, SIEM enhances decision-making capabilities by offering comprehensive reporting and analytics. With detailed dashboards and reports, the leadership team can gain valuable insights into the organization's security posture, identify trends and patterns, and make informed decisions about future security technologies and process investments. This data-driven approach optimizes resource allocation and aligns security initiatives with the organization's broader strategic goals, driving continuous improvement and innovation in IoT cybersecurity.

Value Proposition for SOC Team

SIEM is more than just a tool for the security operations center (SOC) team. It's a strategic asset significantly enhancing their capacity to detect, analyze, and reply to security incidents. Data from multiple sources aggregates and correlates in SIEM, providing a comprehensive view of security risks. SOC teams can improve their situational awareness by pinpointing patterns and anomalies that may indicate potential threats, thereby more accurately detecting possible security incidents.

SIEM also automates routine and repetitive tasks, such as log collection, normalization, and initial event correlation. By automating these tasks, SIEM frees up crucial time for SOC analysts to concentrate on more complex and high-priority issues. This not only improves the efficiency and effectiveness of the SOC team but also enhances their ability to respond to incidents promptly and accurately. Additionally, advanced SIEM solutions like Microsoft Azure Sentinel utilize machine learning to deliver predictive insights and automated responses, further augmenting the capabilities of the SOC team.

SIEM facilitates better incident response by providing detailed forensic data and historical logs. SOC analysts can rely on this data to understand a security incident's root cause and develop effective response strategies. Forensic capabilities are essential for minimizing the impact of security breaches and preventing them in the future. By providing the SOC team with the tools and information they need to respond to incidents effectively, SIEM helps ensure that the organization's IoT environment stays secure and protected against cyber threats.

Key Points to Focus on Designing and Deployment of SIEM in IoT Cybersecurity

When designing and deploying SIEM for IoT cybersecurity, scalability is a crucial factor to consider. IoT environments are dynamic and can expand rapidly as new devices are added. The chosen SIEM solution must be capable of scaling to handle increasing data volumes without degrading performance. Solutions like Microsoft Azure Sentinel are designed with scalability in mind, offering a cloud-native architecture that can grow

CHAPTER 5   DESIGN AND DEPLOY AZURE IOT MONITORING AND MANAGEMENT

alongside the organization's IoT deployment. This ensures that the SIEM system remains effective even as the number of connected devices increases.

Integration capabilities are critical in the design and deployment of SIEM in IoT cybersecurity. IoT environments often mix various manufacturers' devices, each with unique communication protocols and data formats. A SIEM solution must seamlessly integrate with these diverse devices to provide comprehensive visibility and monitoring. Azure Sentinel offers extensive integration options with Microsoft and third-party products. This broad compatibility ensures that all relevant data is captured and analyzed, providing a comprehensive view of the security landscape.

Scalability: Scalability is crucial in designing and deploying an SIEM system for IoT cybersecurity. The number of connected IoT devices can increase, and an SIEM solution must be able to handle growing data volumes without performance degradation. This means the system should be able to scale horizontally and vertically to accommodate the influx of data from new devices. Cloud-native solutions like Microsoft Azure Sentinel offer inherent scalability, enabling organizations to expand their security monitoring capabilities seamlessly. Azure Sentinel leverages the cloud's elasticity to scale up resources as needed, ensuring continuous and efficient monitoring without needing constant manual adjustments.

Ensuring that data ingestion rates do not overwhelm the system in a scalable SIEM deployment is essential. The architecture should support high-throughput data collection and processing to maintain real-time threat detection and analysis. Additionally, the system must be designed to handle peak loads, such as during security incidents when data volumes can spike significantly. Properly architected scalability ensures that the SIEM solution will remain effective and efficient, regardless of the size and complexity of the IoT environment.

CHAPTER 5   DESIGN AND DEPLOY AZURE IOT MONITORING AND MANAGEMENT

Integration Capabilities: Integration capabilities are vital for an SIEM solution in IoT cybersecurity due to the diverse nature of IoT ecosystems. IoT environments often include various devices from different manufacturers, each using multiple communication protocols and data formats. A robust SIEM system must integrate seamlessly with these heterogeneous devices to provide comprehensive visibility and monitoring. This includes supporting standard protocols like MQTT, CoAP, HTTP, and proprietary protocols used by specific devices.

Microsoft Azure Sentinel excels in integration, offering extensive support for Microsoft and third-party products. It provides connectors and APIs that facilitate easy integration with various data sources, ensuring that all relevant security data is captured and analyzed. Effective integration ensures the SIEM system can aggregate data from all devices, creating a unified security posture that gives you a sense of control and security. This comprehensive data collection is essential for identifying correlations and patterns that may indicate potential security threats.

Security Analytics and Threat Intelligence: Advanced security analytics and threat intelligence are critical components of an effective SIEM solution for IoT cybersecurity. IoT environments generate vast amount of data, making identifying and responding to threats challenging without sophisticated analytics. The SIEM system should incorporate advanced analytics capabilities, including ML to detect anomalies and potential threats in real time. These technologies can analyze large datasets, identify patterns, and provide predictive insights that enhance threat detection and response.

Azure Sentinel, a beacon of hope in the cybersecurity landscape, harnesses the power of AI and ML to offer advanced threat detection abilities. It can sift through data from diverse sources, spotting unusual behavior that could signal a security breach. The integration of threat intelligence feeds further fortifies the system, keeping it abreast of the latest attack vectors and emerging threats. This proactive stance instills a sense of reassurance, helping organizations anticipate and neutralize threats before they can wreak havoc. The effective use of security analytics and threat intelligence ensures that the SIEM system, primarily when powered by Azure Sentinel, remains a robust fortress against sophisticated cyber threats.

Data Management and Retention: Effective data management and retention policies are essential in an SIEM deployment for IoT cybersecurity. IoT devices create enormous volumes of data, and the SIEM system must be able to handle this data efficiently. This involves collecting and analyzing data in real-time and storing and long-term retaining logs for forensic analysis and compliance purposes. The system should support scalable storage solutions that accommodate growing data volumes while ensuring quick historical data retrieval when needed.

Azure Sentinel offers flexible data storage options, allowing organizations to store security data cost-effectively. It supports long-term retention integration with Azure Data Lake, providing a centralized repository for all security logs and events. Proper data management ensures that the SIEM system can maintain performance while adhering to regulatory requirements for data retention. Additionally, efficient data storage and retrieval capabilities are crucial for conducting thorough investigations and audits, helping organizations maintain a strong security posture.

Automation and Orchestration: Automation and orchestration are vital features that enhance the effectiveness of an SIEM system in IoT cybersecurity. Given the high volume of data and potential security incidents in IoT environments, manual processes can quickly become overwhelming for security teams. Automation helps streamline routine tasks such as log collection, normalization, and initial event correlation, allowing security analysts to focus on more complex and high-priority issues. Orchestration enables the integration of various security tools and processes, creating a cohesive and efficient incident response workflow.

CHAPTER 5   DESIGN AND DEPLOY AZURE IOT MONITORING AND MANAGEMENT

Azure Sentinel provides robust automation and orchestration capabilities through its playbooks, which use Azure Logic Apps to automate responses to specific security events. These playbooks can be customized to trigger automated actions based on predefined rules, such as isolating compromised device or alerting security personnel. Automation and orchestration improve the efficiency of security operations and ensure a faster and more consistent response to security incidents. This reduces the mean time to detect (MTTD) and mean time to respond (MTTR), minimizing the potential impact of security breaches.

User and Entity Behavior Analytics (UEBA): Incorporating user and entity behavior analytics (UEBA) into the SIEM system is crucial for detecting insider threats and compromised devices within an IoT environment. UEBA uses ML to define a baseline of normal behavior for users and devices and then monitors for deviations from this baseline. These deviations can indicate potential security issues, such as unauthorized access or compromised devices. By focusing on behavioral patterns, UEBA can identify threats that traditional signature-based detection methods might miss.

Azure Sentinel integrates UEBA capabilities to enhance its threat detection and response. It continuously and in real-time analyzes user and device behavior, looking for anomalies that could signify a security breach. For example, if an ordinarily static IoT device suddenly starts transmitting large volumes of data to an unfamiliar destination, the system would flag this as suspicious. Incorporating UEBA into the SIEM system provides an additional layer of security, helping to identify and mitigate threats more effectively.

Compliance and Reporting: Ensuring compliance with industry standards and regulations is critical to SIEM deployment in IoT cybersecurity. Many industries, such as healthcare, finance, and critical infrastructure, are subject to stringent regulatory requirements that mandate continuous monitoring, logging, and reporting of security events. A SIEM system must provide robust logging and reporting capabilities to help organizations meet these compliance requirements. This includes generating detailed reports for audits and maintaining records of security incidents and responses.

Azure Sentinel offers comprehensive reporting and compliance features, assembling it more convenient for organizations to stick to regulatory standards. It provides predefined compliance templates and highly adaptable reporting options that allow security teams to generate reports tailored to specific regulatory requirements. These data insights can be applied for internal audits and regulatory submissions and to demonstrate the organization's adherence to maintaining a strong security posture. Effective compliance and reporting capabilities help avoid regulatory fines and penalties and enhance the organization's reputation and trustworthiness.

IoT and SOAR

The Internet of Things (IoT) is a concept that opens up a world of possibilities. It pertains to the interconnected network of physical devices that exchange information and share data over the Internet. These devices, from simple household items like smart thermostats and wearables to complex industrial machinery and smart city infrastructures, are part of a vast, interconnected web. IoT devices are outfitted with sensors, software, and other tools that enable them to collect and transmit data, allowing for automation, remote monitoring, and control. The proliferation of IoT devices has significantly expanded the digital landscape, introducing new opportunities and challenges in terms of security.

Security Orchestration, Automation, and Response (SOAR) is a category of security solutions designed to improve an organization's security operations and incident response capabilities. SOAR platforms integrate various security tools and technologies, automate repetitive tasks, and orchestrate workflows to streamline and enhance security operations. By leveraging automation and orchestration, SOAR solutions help security teams manage and respond to the growing number of alerts and incidents more efficiently and effectively. Microsoft Azure Sentinel, for instance, incorporates SOAR capabilities to offer a single platform for overseeing security operations.

In the context of IoT, SOAR plays a critical role in addressing the unique security challenges posed by the vast and diverse array of connected devices. IoT environments generate massive data and alerts, making it difficult for security teams to manually manage and respond to incidents. SOAR solutions help by automating the detection, analysis, and response to security events, ensuring that threats are identified and mitigated promptly. This strengthens the general security posture of the IoT ecosystem and improves the efficiency and effectiveness of security operations.

What Role Does SOAR Play in IoT Cybersecurity?

In IoT cybersecurity, SOAR plays a pivotal role by integrating and automating various security processes to manage the complexity and scale of IoT environments. IoT devices often have a lack of processing power and security features, making them susceptible to attacks. SOAR platforms enhance the security of these devices by providing a centralized system for monitoring, detecting, and responding to security threats. By automating routine tasks and orchestrating workflows, SOAR helps ensure that security incidents are addressed swiftly and efficiently, reducing the risk of widespread impact.

One of the primary roles of SOAR in IoT cybersecurity is to aggregate and correlate data from diverse sources, including IoT devices, network infrastructure, and security tools. This comprehensive data collection enables security teams to gain a holistic view of the IoT environment, making identifying patterns and anomalies indicative of potential threats easier. With its integration capabilities, Azure Sentinel excels at capturing and analyzing information from a wide range of sources, providing valuable insights that enhance threat detection and response.

Additionally, SOAR platforms facilitate the automation of incident response processes, enabling security teams to adapt to threats in real time. In an IoT environment, where the sheer volume of alerts can be overwhelming, automation is essential for managing incidents efficiently. SOAR solutions can automatically trigger predefined response actions, such as isolating a compromised device or blocking malicious traffic, based on the severity and nature of the threat. This immediate response capability helps contain and mitigate threats before they can cause significant damage.

Why Is SOAR Required in IoT Cybersecurity?

The necessity of SOAR in IoT cybersecurity arises from the inherent challenges of managing and securing a vast network of interconnected devices. IoT environments generate a tremendous amount of data, and manual processes must be improved to handle the scale and complexity of security operations required to protect these environments. SOAR solutions address this challenge by automating data collection, analysis, and response, enabling security teams to manage the high volume of alerts and incidents more effectively.

One critical reason for implementing SOAR in IoT cybersecurity is to enhance the efficiency of security operations. IoT devices often lack robust security features and can be easily targeted by attackers. With the automation capabilities of SOAR, organizations can quickly recognize and respond to threats, reducing the risk of successful attacks. Azure Sentinel's automation features, for example, allow for the creation of automated playbooks that can execute predefined actions in response to specific threats, significantly reducing the time and effort required to manage incidents.

Comprehensive visibility and control are crucial in IoT cybersecurity, given the heterogeneous nature of IoT environments. These environments comprise devices with different functionalities and communication protocols. A centralized system to monitor and manage security events is essential for maintaining effective oversight and control. SOAR solutions provide this unified platform, aggregating and correlating data from all IoT devices. This ensures that security teams have a complete view of the environment and can respond to threats more effectively.

Value Proposition for Leadership Team

For the leadership team, SOAR's value proposition in IoT cybersecurity is multifaceted. First, SOAR provides a robust defense mechanism against cyber threats' complex and evolving landscape targeting IoT devices. By automating detection and response processes, SOAR ensures that security incidents are addressed promptly, minimizing the risk of data breaches and further cyberattacks. This proactive method to security instills confidence in the leadership team, knowing that the organization has a reliable system to protect its critical assets and sensitive information.

Second, SOAR enhances the organization's risk management strategy by providing detailed insights into potential vulnerabilities and threats within the IoT environment. By identifying and mitigating these risks in real time, SOAR reduces the organization's overall risk exposure and helps avoid significant financial and reputational damage from security incidents. This translates into lower operational risks and enhanced business continuity for the leadership team, ensuring the organization can keep its competitive edge in the market.

Furthermore, SOAR supports strategic decision-making by offering comprehensive reporting and analytics. With detailed dashboards and reports, the leadership team can gain valuable insights into the organization's security posture, identify trends and patterns, and make informed decisions about future security technologies and process investments. With its advanced analytics capabilities, Azure Sentinel provides actionable intelligence that helps leaders optimize resource allocation and align security initiatives with the organization's broader strategic goals.

Value Proposition for SOC Team

SOAR is an invaluable tool for security operations centers (SOCs) that helps them detect, analyze, and respond to security incidents. SOAR's core value lies in its ability to automate routine tasks and orchestrate complex workflows, allowing analysts to focus on more strategic and high-priority issues. This improves the SOC team's efficiency and effectiveness, enabling them to manage more alerts and incidents with greater accuracy and speed.

A SOAR platform streamlines workflows and enhances collaboration by combining a number of tools and technologies to manage security operations. Using Azure Sentinel's integration capabilities, SOC teams can collect and correlate data from multiple sources, providing a comprehensive view of security risks. Analysts can detect security incidents more accurately and timely using this holistic approach to identify patterns and anomalies that may indicate potential threats.

Moreover, SOAR enhances incident response by providing detailed forensic data and historical logs. In the aftermath of a cyber incident, SOC analysts can use this data to conduct thorough investigations, understand the incident's root cause, and develop effective response strategies. The automation capabilities of SOAR also enable the execution of predefined response actions, such as isolating compromised devices or blocking malicious traffic, reducing the time required to mitigate threats. This improves the organization's overall security posture and enhances the SOC team's ability to respond to incidents effectively and efficiently.

Key Points to Focus on Designing and Deployment of SOAR in IoT Cybersecurity

Scalability is a paramount consideration when designing and deploying SOAR for IoT cybersecurity. The rapid expansion of IoT environments, driven by the continuous addition of new devices, necessitates a SOAR

CHAPTER 5   DESIGN AND DEPLOY AZURE IOT MONITORING AND MANAGEMENT

solution that can flexibly scale to accommodate this growth. It's imperative to ensure that the platform can endure the increasing data volumes and alert frequencies without performance degradation. Cloud-native solutions like Azure Sentinel, with their inherent scalability, enable organizations to seamlessly expand their security operations as their IoT environment evolves.

Integration capabilities are crucial to playing a crucial role in the effective deployment of SOAR in IoT cybersecurity. The diversity of IoT ecosystems, with their devices having varying functionalities and communication protocols, necessitates a robust SOAR solution that can seamlessly integrate with these heterogeneous devices. This integration is crucial for providing comprehensive visibility and monitoring. Azure Sentinel stands out in integration, offering connectors and APIs that facilitate easy integration with a wide range of data sources and security tools. This ensures that all relevant data is captured and analyzed, providing a comprehensive view of the IoT environment.

Automation and orchestration are pivotal features to consider when designing a SOAR solution for IoT cybersecurity. The high volume of data and alerts generated by IoT devices makes manual processes impractical. Automation helps streamline routine tasks such as log collection, normalization, and initial event correlation, freeing up security professionals to focus on important, complex, and high-priority issues. Orchestration enables the integration of various security tools and processes, creating a cohesive and efficient incident response workflow. Azure Sentinel's automation capabilities, for instance, enable the creation of playbooks that automate response actions based on predefined rules, enhancing the efficiency and effectiveness of security operations.

Security analytics and threat intelligence are essential components of a SOAR solution for IoT cybersecurity. Advanced analytics abilities, including ML, are necessary to detect sophisticated threats and anomalies in real-time. Integrating threat intelligence feeds ensures that the SOAR

CHAPTER 5   DESIGN AND DEPLOY AZURE IOT MONITORING AND MANAGEMENT

solution remains updated on the latest attack vectors and emerging threats. Azure Sentinel utilizes ML to offer advanced threat detection tools, allowing companies to identify and respond to threats more effectively.

Effective data management and retention policies are essential in designing and deploying SOAR for IoT cybersecurity. IoT devices produce large amounts of data, and the SOAR solution must be able to handle this data efficiently. This involves collecting and analyzing data in real-time and storing and long-term retaining logs for forensic analysis and compliance purposes. Azure Sentinel offers flexible data storage options, allowing organizations to store security data cost-effectively and ensuring that the SOAR system can maintain performance while adhering to regulatory requirements.

User and entity behavior analytics (UEBA) should be incorporated into the SOAR solution to enhance threat detection capabilities. UEBA uses ML to select a baseline of normal behavior for users and devices and then monitors for deviations from this baseline. These deviations can indicate potential security issues, such as unauthorized access or compromised devices. Azure Sentinel integrates UEBA capabilities to continuously analyze user and device behavior, providing an additional layer of security that helps identify and mitigate threats more effectively.

Finally, ensuring compliance with industry standards and regulations is critical to SOAR deployment in IoT cybersecurity. Many industries are subject to rigorous regulatory requirements that mandate continuous monitoring, logging, and reporting security events. A SOAR solution must provide robust logging and reporting capabilities to help organizations meet these compliance requirements. Azure Sentinel offers comprehensive reporting and compliance features, making it possible for organizations to stay compliant to regulatory standards and generate detailed reports for audits and investigations. Effective compliance and reporting capabilities help avoid regulatory fines and penalties and enhance the organization's reputation and trustworthiness.

CHAPTER 5 DESIGN AND DEPLOY AZURE IOT MONITORING AND MANAGEMENT

IoT and NDR

The Internet of Things (IoT) is a global network of physical devices, vehicles, appliances, and other items embedded with sensors, software, and connectivity, enabling them to collect and exchange data. In addition to household appliances such as smart refrigerators and fitness trackers, complex industrial machinery and intelligent city infrastructures are included in this category. The proliferation of IoT devices has revolutionized various sectors, enhancing automation, improving efficiency, and enabling new services and capabilities. IoT integration introduces significant security challenges as connected devices can also act as entry points for cyber threats.

Network detection and response (NDR) is a cybersecurity approach focused on monitoring, detecting, and responding to anomalous or malicious activities within a network. Traditional security measures might miss threats uncovered by NDR solutions, which use advanced technologies like machine learning, behavioral analytics, and threat intelligence. Unlike conventional security tools that rely on predefined signatures, NDR systems analyze network traffic patterns to detect deviations indicative of potential threats. By providing continuous monitoring and automated response capabilities, NDR enhances an organization's ability to defend against sophisticated cyberattacks.

In the context of IoT, NDR plays a vital role in solving the unique security challenges posed by the extensive and diverse array of connected devices. IoT devices often lack robust security features and can be easily compromised, making them attractive targets for cybercriminals. NDR solutions help protect IoT environments by providing real-time visibility into network activities, detecting suspicious behaviors, and automating response actions to mitigate threats. By focusing on network traffic patterns and leveraging advanced analytics, NDR solutions ensure comprehensive security coverage for IoT ecosystems.

What Role Does NDR Play in IoT Cybersecurity?

In order to secure the vast and diverse network of IoT devices, NDR provides real-time visibility and detection capabilities that are essential to securing them. Using traditional security measures, it can be difficult to monitor and secure IoT devices because they communicate using various protocols and are located in different parts of the network. To detect unusual patterns and actions that might indicate a security breach, NDR solutions continuously monitor network traffic. NDR provides a layer of security that does not depend on the security capabilities of individual IoT devices since it focuses on network-level activities.

One of the primary roles of NDR in IoT cybersecurity is to detect and respond to threats that take advantage of the flaws of IoT devices. Many IoT devices have insufficient CPU power and storage capacity, making implementing comprehensive security measures directly tricky. NDR solutions address this challenge by analyzing network traffic to detect anomalies and potential threats, such as unauthorized access attempts, unusual data transfers, or communication with known malicious IP addresses. This network-centric approach ensures that even devices with minimal security features are protected.

Additionally, NDR solutions enhance incident response by delivering comprehensive insights into the nature and scope of detected threats. When a potential threat is identified, the NDR system can automatically trigger predefined response actions, such as isolating affected devices or blocking malicious traffic. This automated response capability is crucial in IoT environments, where numerous devices and alerts can overwhelm security teams. By automating threat detection and response, NDR solutions reduce the risk of security incidents impacting the organization by ensuring timely and effective mitigation.

Why Is NDR Required in IoT Cybersecurity?

NDR is required in IoT cybersecurity due to the inherent challenges of securing a vast and heterogeneous network of connected devices. IoT devices often lack built-in security features, making them vulnerable to cyber threats. Typical security tools, such as network firewalls and antivirus software, are insufficient to protect IoT environments, as they rely on predefined signatures and rules that sophisticated attackers can easily bypass. NDR solutions address this gap by providing continuous monitoring and advanced threat detection capabilities for securing IoT networks.

One of the critical reasons for implementing NDR in IoT cybersecurity is the need for real-time visibility into network activities. IoT environments generate a massive volume of data, and monitoring this data is essential to continuously identify potential threats. NDR solutions provide real-time insights into network traffic, empowering security teams to recognize and respond to threats as they occur. In addition to preventing breaches, NDR solutions minimize the impact of successful attacks. By utilizing advanced analytics and machine learning, NDR solutions can detect subtle anomalies that might indicate a security threat.

NDR is necessary in IoT cybersecurity is the increasing sophistication of cyberattacks. Cybercriminals are constantly coming up with new methods to exploit vulnerabilities in IoT devices and networks. NDR solutions use behavioral analytics and threat intelligence to identify and respond to these evolving threats. By continuously analyzing network traffic and comparing it to known attack patterns, NDR systems can detect and mitigate threats that traditional security measures might miss. This adaptive and intelligence-driven approach is essential for defending against IoT environments' complex and dynamic threat landscape.

Value Proposition for Leadership Team

NDR's value proposition in IoT cybersecurity is significant for the leadership team. First, NDR provides a robust defense mechanism against the complex and evolving landscape of cyber threats targeting IoT devices. By continuously monitoring network traffic and using advanced analytics to detect and respond to anomalies, NDR ensures that incoming threats are detected and mitigated promptly. This proactive method of security instills confidence in the leadership team, knowing that the organization has a reliable system to protect its critical assets and sensitive information.

Second, NDR enhances the organization's risk management strategy by providing detailed insights into potential vulnerabilities and threats within the IoT environment. By identifying and mitigating these risks in real-time, NDR reduces the organization's overall risk exposure and helps avoid significant financial and reputational damage from security incidents. This translates into lower operational risks and enhanced business continuity for the leadership team, ensuring the organization can keep its market edge. Demonstrating robust cybersecurity measures also improves the organization's reputation and trustworthiness among customers, partners, and regulators.

Furthermore, NDR supports strategic decision-making by offering comprehensive reporting and analytics. With detailed dashboards and reports, the leadership team can gain valuable insights into the organization's security posture, identify trends and patterns, and make informed decisions about future security technologies and process investments. This visibility into the organization's cybersecurity landscape helps leaders allocate resources more effectively, prioritize security initiatives, and ensure that their security strategy aligns with their overall business objectives. By leveraging the advanced analytics capabilities of NDR solutions, the leadership team can optimize their cybersecurity investments and enhance the organization's resilience against cyber threats.

CHAPTER 5   DESIGN AND DEPLOY AZURE IOT MONITORING AND MANAGEMENT

Value Proposition for SOC Team

For the security operations center (SOC) team, NDR is an indispensable tool that significantly enhances their capacity to identify, investigate, and reply to security incidents. The core value of NDR for the SOC team lies in its ability to provide real-time visibility into network activities and detect potential threats that might bypass traditional security measures. By continuously monitoring network traffic and using advanced analytics to identify anomalies, NDR enables SOC analysts to identify and reply to threats more rapidly and efficiently.

NDR solutions provide a unified interface for managing security operations, integrating various tools and technologies to streamline workflows and enhance collaboration. This integration capability is crucial in IoT environments, where devices and data sources are diverse and often use different communication protocols. By combining and connecting data from numerous sources, NDR solutions provide a comprehensive view of the security landscape, helping SOC analysts identify patterns and anomalies that might indicate potential threats. This holistic approach to security enhances the SOC team's ability to identify and reply to incidents promptly.

Moreover, NDR enhances incident response by providing detailed forensic data and historical logs. In the case of a cybersecurity incident, SOC analysts can use this data to conduct thorough investigations, understand the incident's root cause, and develop effective response strategies. The automation capabilities of NDR also enable the execution of predefined response actions, such as isolating compromised devices or blocking malicious traffic, reducing the time required to mitigate threats. This improves the organization's overall security posture and enhances the SOC team's ability to respond to incidents effectively and efficiently. The ability to automate routine tasks and orchestrate complex workflows allows SOC analysts to focus on more strategic and high-priority issues, improving the efficiency and effectiveness of security operations.

CHAPTER 5 DESIGN AND DEPLOY AZURE IOT MONITORING AND MANAGEMENT

Key Points to Focus on Designing and Deployment of NDR in IoT Cybersecurity

NDR for IoT cybersecurity must be scalable from design to operational use. IoT environments can expand rapidly as new devices are added, and the NDR solution must be capable of scaling to accommodate this growth. This implies guaranteeing that the platform can manage increasing data volumes and alert frequencies without performance degradation. Cloud-native solutions offer inherent scalability, allowing organizations to expand their security operations as their IoT environment grows seamlessly. Properly architected scalability ensures that the NDR solution continues to be reliable and scalable, regardless of the size and complexity of the IoT environment.

Integration capabilities are also crucial for effectively deploying NDR in IoT cybersecurity. IoT ecosystems are diverse, comprising devices with varying functionalities and communication protocols. A robust NDR solution must integrate seamlessly with these heterogeneous devices to provide comprehensive visibility and monitoring. This includes supporting standard protocols and enabling the aggregation and correlation of data from various sources. Effective integration ensures that all relevant data is captured and analyzed, providing a holistic view of the IoT environment and enhancing threat detection and response.

Automation and orchestration are not just features but critical components when designing an NDR solution for IoT cybersecurity. The sheer quantity of data and alerts produced by IoT devices makes manual processes impractical. Automation helps streamline routine tasks such as log collection, normalization, and initial event correlation, allowing security professionals to concentrate on high-priority issues. Orchestration enables the integration of various security tools and processes, creating a cohesive and efficient incident response workflow. By automating detection and response processes, NDR solutions ensure timely and effective mitigation of security incidents, reducing the potential impact on the organization.

CHAPTER 5   DESIGN AND DEPLOY AZURE IOT MONITORING AND MANAGEMENT

Security analytics and threat intelligence are essential components of an NDR solution for IoT cybersecurity. Advanced analytics techniques, including ML, are necessary to detect sophisticated threats and anomalies in real time. Integrating threat intelligence feeds ensures that the NDR solution remains updated on the latest attack vectors and emerging threats. This combination of analytics and intelligence enhances the capabilities to detect and respond to cybersecurity problems, providing a robust defense against IoT environments' complex and evolving cyber threat landscape.

Effective data management and retention policies are essential in designing and deploying NDR for IoT cybersecurity. IoT devices constantly produce expansive amounts of data, and the NDR solution must handle this data efficiently. This involves the collection and real-time analysis of data and the storage and long-term retention of logs for forensic analysis and compliance purposes. Flexible data storage options ensure that the NDR system can maintain performance while adhering to regulatory requirements. Proper data management practices help ensure that critical security data is available when needed for investigations and compliance audits.

User and entity behavior analytics (UEBA) should be incorporated into the NDR solution to enhance threat detection capabilities. UEBA uses ML to define a standard of expected behavior for users and devices and then monitors for deviations from this baseline. These deviations can indicate potential security issues, such as unauthorized access or compromised devices. Continuous analysis of user and device behavior provides an additional layer of security that helps identify and mitigate threats more effectively. Integrating UEBA capabilities into the NDR solution enhances the comprehensive security posture of the IoT domain.

Finally, ensuring compliance with industry standards and regulations is not just a consideration, but a critical aspect of NDR deployment in IoT cybersecurity. Many organizations are obligated to stringent regulatory requirements that mandate continuous monitoring, logging, and reporting security events. A robust NDR solution must provide comprehensive logging and reporting capabilities to help organizations meet these compliance requirements. Detailed reports and compliance features make it easier for organizations to adhere to regulatory standards and generate necessary documentation for audits and investigations. Effective compliance and reporting capabilities help avoid regulatory fines and penalties and enhance the organization's reputation and trustworthiness.

IoT and XDR

A transformative cybersecurity approach, extended detection and response (XDR), is more than just an advanced cybersecurity solution. Security products are integrated into a unified platform to comprehensively recognize, assess, and react to threats. By incorporating data from multiple security layers, including networks, endpoints, servers, and cloud environments, XDR goes beyond traditional endpoint detection and response (EDR). This holistic approach empowers XDR solutions to offer enhanced, comprehensive, and compelling retorts to cybersecurity problems, leveraging automation, machine learning, and advanced analytics to detect and mitigate sophisticated attacks.

In the realm of IoT, XDR assumes a unique and indispensable role by tackling the distinct security challenges presented by the vast and diverse network of interconnected devices. IoT environments generate copious amounts of data, posing a challenge for conventional security tools. XDR solutions rise to this challenge by integrating and analyzing data from all connected devices, providing a unified perspective of the IoT ecosystem. This comprehensive view enables more precise threat detection, swifter incident response, and enhanced security posture, ensuring that IoT networks are shielded against a broad spectrum of cyber threats.

What Role Does XDR Play in IoT Cybersecurity?

XDR plays a pivotal role in IoT cybersecurity by providing comprehensive visibility and detection capabilities across the entire network of connected devices. IoT devices often run in diverse domains and use diverse communication protocols, making them difficult to monitor and secure using traditional security tools. XDR solutions address this challenge by integrating data from multiple sources, including endpoints, networks, and cloud services, to provide a holistic view of the IoT environment. This unified approach allows for more effective monitoring and detection of potential threats.

One of the primary roles of XDR in IoT cybersecurity is to enhance threat detection and response. Traditional security tools may be unable to detect advanced threats that exploit vulnerabilities in IoT devices. XDR solutions leverage advanced analytics, machine learning, and behavioral analysis to identify real-time anomalies and potential threats. By fusing data from multiple origins, XDR can detect sophisticated attack patterns that might go unnoticed by standalone security products. This improved detection capability ensures that threats are recognized and addressed before they can cause substantial deterioration.

Additionally, XDR enhances incident response by automating and orchestrating response actions across the IoT ecosystem. When a potential threat is detected, XDR solutions can automatically trigger predefined response actions, such as isolating compromised devices, blocking malicious traffic, or initiating further investigations. This automated response capability is crucial in IoT environments, where numerous devices and alerts can overwhelm security teams. By automating repetitive tasks and orchestrating complicated workflows, XDR ensures that incidents are addressed promptly and effectively.

Furthermore, XDR provides detailed insights into the nature and scope of detected threats, enabling security teams to conduct thorough investigations and develop effective response strategies. The ability to meld data from considerable origins helps security analysts understand the full context of an incident, including how the threat entered the network, which devices were affected, and what actions were taken. This comprehensive view is essential for developing targeted and effective remediation plans, ensuring that security incidents are resolved efficiently and thoroughly.

Why Is XDR Required in IoT Cybersecurity?

The unique features of XDR solutions make them a necessity in IoT cybersecurity. The inherent complexities and challenges of securing a vast and diverse network of connected devices, which typically contain minimal computational power and security elements due to their small nature, make them vulnerable to various cyber threats. Traditional security tools are not designed to handle the scale and diversity of IoT environments, resulting in gaps in visibility and protection. XDR solutions, with their unified platform that integrates and correlates data from all connected devices, address these gaps and enable more effective threat detection and response.

One of the critical reasons for implementing XDR in IoT cybersecurity is its proactive nature. IoT devices construct large volumes of data; monitoring this data is essential to identify potential threats continuously. XDR solutions provide real-time visibility into network traffic, device behavior, and security events, enabling security teams to detect and respond to threats as they occur. This proactive approach to security instills confidence, helping prevent breaches and minimize the impact of successful attacks. By leveraging advanced analytics and machine learning, XDR solutions can detect subtle anomalies that might indicate a security threat.

Another compelling reason for the necessity of XDR in IoT cybersecurity is the relentless advancement of cyberattacks. Cybercriminals are constantly coming up with new processes to influence vulnerabilities in IoT ecosystem. XDR solutions employ behavioral analytics and threat intelligence to identify and respond to these evolving threats. By continuously analyzing data from various sources and comparing it to known attack patterns, XDR systems can detect and mitigate threats that traditional security measures might overlook. This adaptive and intelligence-driven approach is pivotal for defending against IoT environments' intricate and ever-changing threat landscape.

XDR is essential for managing the sheer volume of alerts and data IoT devices generate. The high number of devices and continuous data streams can quickly overwhelm traditional security systems, leading to alert fatigue and missed threats. XDR's capability to handle this volume is crucial for maintaining an efficient and effective security posture in large-scale IoT environments.

Additionally, deploying XDR in IoT cybersecurity ensures better compliance with industry standards and regulations. Many industries that use IoT devices, such as healthcare, finance, and manufacturing, are subject to stringent regulatory requirements. XDR solutions provide robust logging, reporting, and auditing capabilities that help organizations meet these compliance requirements. By maintaining detailed records of security events and responses, XDR ensures that organizations can demonstrate their adherence to regulatory standards, avoiding potential fines and penalties.

Finally, XDR enhances the overall resilience of IoT environments by providing continuous monitoring and adaptive response capabilities. Cyber threats constantly evolve, and security solutions must adapt to emerging threats. XDR systems use ML and threat intelligence to stay updated on the most recent attack types and techniques, ensuring the organization's defenses remain effective. This continuous adaptation is crucial for maintaining an effective security posture in a continuously evolving threat terrain.

Value Proposition for Leadership Team

XDR's value proposition in IoT cybersecurity is substantial for the leadership team. First, XDR provides a robust defense mechanism against the dynamic and rapidly changing environment of cyber threats targeting IoT devices. By constantly observing and reckoning information from diverse sources, XDR ensures that potential threats are swiftly identified and addressed. This proactive security strategy fosters confidence among the leadership team, assuring them that the organization has a dependable system to safeguard its critical assets and sensitive information.

Second, XDR enhances the organization's risk management strategy by providing detailed insights into potential vulnerabilities and threats within the IoT environment. By identifying and mitigating these risks in real-time, XDR significantly reduces the organization's overall risk exposure. This reduction in operational risks and enhanced business continuity ensures the business can maintain its competitive advantage in the market. Demonstrating robust cybersecurity measures enhances the organization's reputation and trustworthiness among customers, partners, and regulators.

Furthermore, XDR supports strategic decision-making by offering comprehensive reporting and analytics. With detailed dashboards and reports, the leadership team can gain valuable insights into the organization's security posture, identify trends and patterns, and make informed decisions about future security technologies and process investments. This visibility into the organization's cybersecurity landscape helps leaders allocate resources more effectively, prioritize security initiatives, and ensure that their security strategy aligns with their overall business objectives. By leveraging the advanced analytics capabilities of XDR solutions, the leadership team can optimize their cybersecurity investments and enhance the organization's resilience against cyber threats.

Additionally, XDR provides a clear return on investment (ROI) by reducing the cost and complexity of managing multiple security tools. Traditional security approaches often require deploying and maintaining numerous standalone products, each with its management interface and operational overhead. XDR consolidates these functions into a single platform, simplifying management and reducing operational costs. This consolidation reduces costs and enhances the efficiency of security operations, allowing the organization to achieve better protection with fewer resources.

Moreover, XDR enhances the organization's ability to respond to security incidents quickly and effectively. XDR solutions' automation and orchestration capabilities reduce the time required to detect, assess, and react to cybersecurity problems, minimizing the potential impact of security incidents. For the leadership team, this improved incident response capability translates into reduced downtime, lower recovery costs, and less disruption to business operations. By ensuring that security incidents are addressed promptly and effectively, XDR helps maintain the organization's operational continuity and stability.

Finally, deploying XDR demonstrates the organization's commitment to cybersecurity excellence. In today's digital age, strong cybersecurity measures are a crucial selling point and a critical factor in maintaining customer trust and loyalty. By investing in advanced security technologies like XDR, the leadership team signals to customers, partners, and stakeholders that the organization is serious about protecting its assets and data. This commitment to cybersecurity can enhance the organization's brand reputation, attract new customers, and foster long-term business relationships.

Value Proposition for SOC Team

For the security operations center (SOC) team, XDR stands out as a must-have platform, delivering a unique value in its ability to provide real-time visibility into network activities. This proactive feature allows it to detect potential threats that might bypass traditional security measures, significantly enhancing cybersecurity operations. XDR enables SOC analysts to detect and respond to threats more effectively and efficiently.

XDR solutions provide a unified interface for managing security operations, integrating various tools and technologies to streamline workflows and enhance collaboration. This integration capability is crucial in IoT environments, where devices and data sources are diverse and often use different communication protocols.

Moreover, XDR enhances incident response by providing detailed forensic data and historical logs. In case of a cybersecurity problem, SOC analysts can use this data to conduct thorough investigations, understand the incident's root cause, and develop effective response strategies. The automation capabilities of XDR also enable the execution of predefined response actions, such as isolating compromised devices or blocking malicious traffic, reducing the time required to mitigate threats. This improves the organization's security posture and enhances the SOC team's ability to respond to incidents effectively and efficiently.

Additionally, XDR plays a crucial role in reducing the burden of alert fatigue on the SOC team. In IoT environments, where high alerts are generated, traditional security tools often struggle to prioritize and manage these alerts effectively. XDR solutions, with their advanced correlation and prioritization techniques, excel in filtering out false positives and highlighting the most critical threats. This ensures that SOC analysts can concentrate their efforts on the most pressing issues, thereby improving the efficiency and effectiveness of security operations.

Furthermore, XDR is a strong supporter of continuous improvement in security operations. By providing detailed analytics and reporting, it equips SOC teams with the insights they need to identify trends, evaluate the effectiveness of their security measures, and make informed decisions about future security initiatives. This data-driven approach to security operations enables SOC teams to adapt to evolving threats and continuously enhance their detection and response capabilities.

The integration capabilities of XDR also facilitate better collaboration between different security teams and stakeholders. XDR enables SOC teams to collaborate more effectively with IT, compliance, and risk management teams by providing a unified platform for managing security operations. This collaboration is essential for developing comprehensive security strategies and ensuring security measures align with the organization's overall business objectives. By fostering better collaboration and communication, XDR enhances the organization's ability to respond to security incidents and mitigate risks.

Finally, XDR empowers SOC teams with an advanced platform to stay on top of emerging cybersecurity problems. Cyber threats constantly evolve, and SOC teams need access to the latest platform to detect and respond to these threats. XDR solutions leverage machine learning, threat intelligence, and advanced analytics to provide SOC teams with the capabilities to defend against sophisticated attacks. By equipping SOC teams with the latest technologies and insights, XDR ensures they are well prepared to protect the organization's IoT environment from a wide range of cyber threats.

Key Points to Focus on Designing and Deployment of XDR in IoT Cybersecurity

When designing and deploying XDR for IoT cybersecurity, scalability is a crucial consideration and security advantage. As IoT environments can expand rapidly with the addition of new devices, the XDR solution's ability

CHAPTER 5   DESIGN AND DEPLOY AZURE IOT MONITORING AND MANAGEMENT

to scale is vital. This means ensuring the platform can handle increasing data volumes and alert frequencies without performance degradation. With their inherent scalability, cloud-native solutions allow organizations to expand their security operations as their IoT environment grows seamlessly. Ensuring an adequately architected scalable solution ensures that the XDR solution remains effective and responsive, independent of the size of the IoT environment, providing a sense of security in the face of rapid expansion.

Integration with already available security platforms and infrastructure is not just another aspect but a critical one in designing and deploying XDR for IoT cybersecurity. Organizations often have diverse security tools and systems in place, and the XDR solution needs to integrate seamlessly with these tools. This integration enables the XDR platform to integrate, collect, and visualize data from multiple sources, providing a unified view of the security landscape and enhancing the efficiency of security operations by leveraging the capabilities of existing investments. This reassures the audience that their security investments are well spent but effectively utilized in a cohesive security strategy.

Effective data stewardship is compulsory for the triumph of XDR deployments in IoT environments. IoT devices accumulate large sets of data, and the XDR solution must be capable of handling this data efficiently. This involves collecting and analyzing data in real-time and storing and long-term retaining logs for forensic analysis and compliance purposes. Flexible data storage options, including cloud-based solutions, can help manage the data effectively while maintaining performance and compliance. Proper data management practices ensure that critical security data is available when needed for investigations and audits.

User and entity behavior analytics (UEBA) should be integrated into the XDR solution to enhance threat detection capabilities. UEBA uses machine learning to establish baselines of normal behavior for users and devices and then monitors for deviations from these baselines. These deviations can indicate potential security issues, such as compromised

CHAPTER 5 DESIGN AND DEPLOY AZURE IOT MONITORING AND MANAGEMENT

devices or unauthorized access. By continuously analyzing user and device behavior, UEBA delivers an auxiliary layer of security that helps identify and mitigate threats more effectively. Incorporating UEBA capabilities into the XDR solution enhances the general security posture of the IoT ecosystem.

Automation and orchestration are essential for an effective XDR solution for IoT cybersecurity. Given the scale and complexity of IoT environments, manual intervention in response to security incidents could be more practical. XDR solutions should include robust automation capabilities to execute predefined response actions, such as isolating compromised devices or blocking malicious traffic. Orchestration capabilities enable the coordination of response actions across multiple security tools and systems, ensuring a swift and effective response to incidents. Automation and orchestration improve the efficiency of security ops and lessen the prospect of human falsehood.

Compliance with industry regulations is not only another consideration but a critical one when designing and deploying XDR for IoT cybersecurity. Many industries that use IoT devices are subject to stringent regulatory requirements, and the XDR solution needs to provide comprehensive logging, reporting, and auditing capabilities. These features help organizations meet their compliance obligations by maintaining detailed records of security events and responses. This not only ensures compliance but also gives a sense of security and confidence in the face of regulatory scrutiny. Ensuring compliance helps avoid regulatory fines and penalties and enhances the organization's reputation and trustworthiness among customers and partners.

Finally, ongoing monitoring and continuous improvement are not just good practices but vital for the success of XDR deployments in IoT environments. Cyber threats constantly evolve, and the XDR solution must adapt to new and emerging threats. Continuous monitoring ensures that the XDR platform effectively detects and mitigates threats, while regular reviews and updates to the system help address any gaps or weaknesses.

CHAPTER 5   DESIGN AND DEPLOY AZURE IOT MONITORING AND MANAGEMENT

By fostering a spirit of continuous improvement, associations can ensure that their XDR solution remains robust and resilient, providing adequate protection for their IoT environments over the long term. This proactive approach helps the audience feel controlled and prepared for future threats.

Design Microsoft Azure-Based IoT Monitoring and Management

Designing a Microsoft Azure-based IoT monitoring and management system for network and security is critical in today's increasingly connected world. With the growing number in the implementation of IoT devices across various industries, ensuring robust and comprehensive monitoring and management of these devices is essential. The complexity and diversity of IoT environments and the sensitive nature of the data they handle necessitate a sophisticated approach to network and security management. Microsoft Azure provides a powerful platform to address these challenges, offering tools and services to enhance IoT ecosystems' security and operational efficiency.

Azure's IoT monitoring and management capabilities enable organizations to gain real-time visibility into their IoT environments. This visibility is crucial for detecting and mitigating potential security threats, ensuring that devices operate as intended, and maintaining the network's overall health. By leveraging Azure's advanced analytics and machine learning capabilities, organizations can proactively identify anomalies and potential issues before they escalate into significant problems. This proactive approach enhances security and improves the reliability and performance of IoT devices.

Azure provides a robust security framework that protects IoT devices and the data they generate and instills a sense of peace of mind. This includes IAM (identity and access management), data encryption, and continuous security assessments.

489

CHAPTER 5   DESIGN AND DEPLOY AZURE IOT MONITORING AND MANAGEMENT

One key advantage of using Azure for IoT monitoring and management is its scalability. IoT environments can snowball, with new devices being added frequently. Azure's cloud-based infrastructure allows organizations to scale their monitoring and management capabilities seamlessly without significant upfront investments in hardware. This flexibility ensures that the IoT management system can evolve with the expanding network, maintaining optimal performance and security.

Moreover, Azure offers comprehensive management tools that streamline the administration of IoT devices. These tools provide centralized control over device configurations, firmware updates, and policy enforcement, all in a user-friendly interface. This streamlines the administration approach and diminishes the operational burden on IT teams.

Integrating Azure IoT monitoring and management with existing enterprise systems further enhances its value. Organizations can leverage Azure's extensive ecosystem of services and partners to build customized solutions that address their specific needs. This integration capability allows for seamless data flow between IoT devices and other business applications and sparks the potential for real-time decision-making and operational efficiency. Organizations can unlock new growth prospects and competitive benefits by designating a unified IoT management framework.

In conclusion, designing a Microsoft Azure-based IoT monitoring and management system for network and security is a critical responsibility for businesses examining to harness the full potential of IoT platforms. Azure's comprehensive tool suite provides the foundation for building a secure, scalable, and efficient IoT ecosystem. By leveraging Azure's capabilities, organizations can enhance their security posture, improve device performance, and drive innovation, positioning their organizations for success in the dynamically expanding digital landscape.

Microsoft Recommendation

When embarking on the design and architecture of an IoT solution, it's paramount to grasp the potential threats and incorporate the proper defenses. Understanding how an attacker could compromise the system is critical to ensuring the necessary mitigations are in place. This proactive security approach is especially crucial in IoT environments, where the multitude and intricacy of devices can lead to numerous vulnerabilities. By employing a comprehensive threat modeling process, organizations can methodically identify and address these threats, thereby bolstering the overall security of their IoT infrastructure.

Microsoft strongly advocates including a threat modeling process as a fundamental part of your IoT solution design. This process entails identifying potential threats to each component of the IoT system and devising appropriate security measures to mitigate these threats. This structured approach empowers organizations to anticipate and counteract possible attack vectors, thereby fortifying the security posture of their IoT environment.

Dividing the IoT architecture into several distinct zones can significantly enhance the threat modeling process. Each zone typically has data, authentication, and authorization requirements, which must be carefully managed to ensure robust security. These zones include the device zone, field gateway zone, cloud gateway zone, and services zone. By isolating each zone, organizations can contain potential security breaches and minimize the impact of compromised low-trust zones on higher-trust zones.

Each zone in the IoT architecture is separated by a trust boundary, representing the data transition from one zone to another. This transition point is critical, as data can be most vulnerable to threats. Organizations can use the STRIDE methodology to effectively model these threats, which helps identify and mitigate potential vulnerabilities across the IoT

CHAPTER 5   DESIGN AND DEPLOY AZURE IOT MONITORING AND MANAGEMENT

architecture. By applying STRIDE to each component within each zone, organizations can develop comprehensive security strategies that address a wide range of possible threats.

Aspect	Description
STRIDE model overview	The STRIDE model is used in computer security and threat modeling to categorize and analyze potential threats and vulnerabilities associated with software systems and applications. STRIDE stands for spoofing, tampering, repudiation, information disclosure, denial of service, and elevation of privilege.
Spoofing	Spoofing involves attackers assuming false identities to gain unauthorized access to a system or resource. This can include impersonating a legitimate user, device, or component.
Tampering	Tampering threats involve unauthorized alterations or modifications to data, software, or hardware components. Attackers may tamper with data integrity, software code, or system configurations.
Repudiation	Repudiation threats deal with entities (users, devices, etc.) denying that they performed a particular action or transaction. These threats are especially relevant for non-repudiation requirements, such as maintaining a reliable audit trail.
Information disclosure	This threat encompasses the unauthorized exposure of sensitive information, which can occur through data leaks, eavesdropping, or other means, leading to the disclosure of confidential or personal data.
Denial of service (DoS)	Denial of Service threats aim to disrupt or degrade the availability and functionality of a system. Attackers often flood a target system with excessive traffic or requests, rendering it inaccessible or unusable.
Elevation of privilege	Privilege threats involve attackers gaining unauthorized access to higher system privileges or rights, allowing them to perform actions or access resources that are typically restricted.

CHAPTER 5   DESIGN AND DEPLOY AZURE IOT MONITORING AND MANAGEMENT

The device zone encompasses the environment around each IoT device, where both physical and local network digital access is feasible. This includes any short-range wireless technologies that enable peer-to-peer communication between devices. Ensuring the security of the device zone involves protecting devices from physical tampering and unauthorized network access. This can be achieved through secure boot processes, encryption, and robust access control mechanisms. By securing the device environment, organizations can prevent attackers from gaining physical access or exploiting local network vulnerabilities to compromise IoT devices.

The field gateway zone includes the field gateway itself and all connected devices. A field gateway is a communication hub and often performs data processing and control functions. Securing the field gateway zone involves protecting the gateway from physical intrusion and cyberattacks, as it represents a critical point of entry into the IoT network. Measures such as hardware security modules, secure communication protocols, and regular firmware updates can help protect the field gateway from compromise. The field gateway should also be designed to operate with limited redundancy, ensuring that potential disruptions do not significantly impact the IoT system.

The cloud gateway zone facilitates remote communication with devices and field gateways deployed across multiple sites. It enables cloud-based control and data analysis systems, making it a crucial component of the IoT architecture. Securing the cloud gateway zone involves implementing robust access controls, encryption, and monitoring to prevent unauthorized access and data breaches. The cloud gateway should also be integrated with network virtualization technologies to isolate it from other network traffic, enhancing its security. By ensuring the protection of the cloud gateway, organizations can maintain the CIA triad of the data flowing through the IoT ecosystem.

The services zone comprises software components or modules that interface with devices through field or cloud gateways. These services collect data, issue commands, and expose information and control capabilities to authorized users. Ensuring the security of the services zone involves:

- Implementing strong authentication and authorization mechanisms

- Encrypting data in transit and at rest

- Regularly auditing and monitoring service interactions

By securing the services zone, organizations can prevent unauthorized access to critical IoT functions and data, thereby maintaining the integrity and reliability of their IoT operations.

In conclusion, designing and implementing an IoT solution with robust security requires a thorough understanding of potential threats and the application of appropriate defenses. Microsoft Azure provides a comprehensive IoT monitoring and management platform. Microsoft offers platforms, tools, and services that assist businesses in securing their IoT ecosystem by using a structured threat modeling process and dividing the IoT architecture into distinct zones.

STRIDE Model

In IoT cybersecurity, ensuring the security and integrity of systems involves a comprehensive approach that covers multiple facets of the architecture. Three critical areas that require meticulous attention are processes, communication, and storage. Each of these elements represents distinct aspects of the IoT infrastructure that, if compromised, can lead to significant security breaches and operational disruptions. Understanding and securing these components are essential for building a robust and resilient IoT environment.

Processes in an IoT system encompass the various operations and activities performed by devices, gateways, and applications. These processes include data collection, processing, and control actions IoT devices execute. Given their diversity and complexity, these processes are susceptible to various threats, including spoofing, tampering, and denial-of-service attacks. Ensuring the security of these processes involves implementing stringent access controls, secure coding practices, and regular audits to detect and mitigate vulnerabilities.

Core Elements of Threat Model	Description
Processes	Threats are classified according to the STRIDE model.
Spoofing	An attacker gains access to cryptographic keys, either through software or hardware exploitation, and uses these keys to impersonate the original device from a different physical or virtual device.
Denial of service	This threat involves rendering a device non-functional or disrupting its communication by interfering with radio frequencies or physically tampering with it.
Tampering	An attacker may replace a device's software, compromising its cryptographic keys and allowing unauthorized access, or manipulate the device to provide false information.
Information disclosure	Devices running manipulated software may leak data to unauthorized parties, or attackers with access to cryptographic keys can inject code into the communication path to intercept sensitive information.
Elevation of privilege	An attacker manipulates a device to perform unintended actions, such as tricking a valve programmed to open halfway into opening fully.
Repudiation	Attackers can anonymously manipulate a device's state using inadequately secured consumer remote controls, leading to potential spoofing, tampering, and repudiation threats.

CHAPTER 5   DESIGN AND DEPLOY AZURE IOT MONITORING AND MANAGEMENT

Communication in IoT, which refers to data exchange between devices, gateways, and cloud services, is a critical point of vulnerability. The urgency of securing communication channels cannot be overstated. Implementing adequate security measures can prevent unauthorized access, data interception, and tampering. These include using encryption, secure communication protocols, and robust authentication mechanisms to ensure that data passed over the network stays clandestine and untouched.

Communication Threats	Description
Denial of service	Constrained devices are susceptible to DoS threats when actively listening for inbound connections or unsolicited datagrams on a network. Attackers can open numerous links in parallel, either not servicing them or doing so slowly, or flood the device with unsolicited traffic.
Spoofing, information disclosure	Constrained and specialized devices often rely on simplistic security measures like passwords or PINs. If the network's shared key is compromised, an attacker could take control of the device or intercept the data it transmits.
Spoofing	Attackers may intercept or partially override broadcast signals and impersonate the legitimate source.
Tampering	Attackers may intercept or partially override broadcast signals and transmit false information.
Information disclosure	Attackers may eavesdrop on broadcast communications and obtain information without proper authorization.
Denial of service	Attackers may jam the broadcast signal, preventing the distribution of information.

Storage in IoT systems involves retaining and managing data collected and processed by devices and gateways. This data can include sensitive information such as telemetry data, command and control instructions, and configuration settings. Ensuring the security of stored data is paramount to prevent unauthorized access and tampering. Implementing strong encryption, access control lists, and regular backups are essential to protecting data at rest. Additionally, ensuring the integrity of the operating system and software components through measures like signed OS images and read-only partitions helps safeguard against malicious alterations.

Storage Threats	Description
Device storage	Implementing encryption and log signing helps mitigate the risks associated with reading data, tampering with telemetry data, or altering cached command control data.
Device OS image	The primary concern is tampering with or replacing OS components. Measures like a read-only OS partition, a signed OS image, and encryption are recommended.
Field gateway storage	Data queuing benefits from storage encryption and log signing to protect against unauthorized data access and tampering. Implementing BitLocker is an effective solution.
Field gateway OS image	The focus is on preventing tampering or replacing OS components, achieved through a read-only OS partition, a signed OS image, and encryption.

Each area – processes, communication, and storage – presents unique challenges and requires specific security strategies. By understanding the threats associated with each component and implementing targeted security measures, you can significantly improve the comprehensive security posture of IoT ecosystems. This multi-layered approach, which protects individual devices and data and ensures the resilience and reliability of the entire IoT infrastructure, is necessary in today's complex threat landscape.

Securing processes, communication, and storage in IoT systems is fundamental to maintaining their integrity and functionality. As IoT deployments continue to grow and become more complex, the importance of a holistic security strategy that addresses these critical areas cannot be overstated. Organizations can build robust defenses against cyber threats by focusing on these elements, ensuring their IoT solutions remain secure and operational.

Azure IoT Central

Azure IoT Central is a highly scalable IoT application platform that simplifies IoT solutions' development, deployment, and management. It provides a ready-made environment where developers can quickly connect, monitor, and manage a fleet of IoT devices. This platform abstracts much of the complexity of IoT solution deployment, allowing organizations to stay focused on their primary business operations instead of getting mired down by technical fragments.

Azure IoT Central offers substantial value propositions from a monitoring and management standpoint. The platform allows for comprehensive device management, which includes the ability to control device connectivity, authenticate devices, and manage them through device templates. These templates define device types, enabling consistent and streamlined device interactions. Users can set properties or execute commands on connected devices individually via a web UI or in bulk through scheduled jobs. This facilitates efficient management of device metadata, such as customer information or service dates, ensuring up-to-date records.

Azure IoT Central provides robust capabilities for data viewing and analysis. Users can transform complex telemetry data into structured formats using mapping tools. Device templates also support custom views for specific device types, making it easy to monitor and analyze data such as temperature trends for thermostats or the location of delivery trucks. Built-in analytics allow for the aggregation and visualization of data across multiple devices, which can be used to derive insights like occupancy rates across retail stores. Custom dashboards enhance data management by integrating maps, tiles, and charts to present device telemetry intuitively.

Security in Azure IoT Central is managed across several fronts. User, device, and programmatic access to applications is configurable, ensuring only authorized entities can interact with the system. Additionally, audit logs provide a trail of activity within the application, enhancing traceability and accountability.

Devices in an IoT Central application act as the primary data collectors, transmitting telemetry from sensors. These devices report their state through properties and can also be controlled via commands issued by the application. This bidirectional communication ensures that devices can be managed dynamically by updating firmware or adjusting operational parameters in real time. The defined device capabilities are encapsulated in device templates, and device interactions and IoT Central application interactions are standardized.

For scenarios where direct device connectivity is challenging, gateways serve as intermediaries. These local gateway devices aggregate sensor data, reduce the data sent to the cloud, and respond faster to local anomalies. Azure IoT Edge can be used to implement these gateways, leveraging its robust processing capabilities to perform local computations and actions.

Azure IoT Central's data export functionalities allow seamless integration with external services and applications. Data can be transformed before export to fit the requirements of different destinations. This feature supports long-term storage and comprehensive analysis using external tools, facilitating business automation through rule-triggered actions and enabling additional computations necessary for further data enrichment.

CHAPTER 5   DESIGN AND DEPLOY AZURE IOT MONITORING AND MANAGEMENT

Finally, the platform's extensibility is demonstrated through its REST API, which allows for deeper integrations. Other applications and services can programmatically manage the IoT Central application, ensuring that the solution can scale and adapt to evolving business needs by integrating with external systems and automating device management tasks.

Azure IoT Central provides a robust, user-friendly environment for developing and managing IoT solutions, with extensive device management, data analysis, security, and extensibility capabilities.

Key Design Elements and Best Practices

The critical design elements and best practices for Azure IoT Central encompass a range of considerations essential for building robust, scalable, and secure IoT solutions. These elements include device management, data handling and analytics, security, scalability, integration capabilities, user interface design, and operational efficiency.

Device management is central to any IoT solution, and in IoT Central, it involves defining device templates that standardize how devices interact with the application. A best practice is carefully designing these templates to include all necessary telemetry, properties, and commands. This ensures consistency and simplifies device onboarding and management. Implementing robust authentication mechanisms for devices to connect securely is also crucial. Using certificates or hardware security modules (HSMs) can enhance security. Moreover, devices should support over-the-air (OTA) updates to facilitate seamless firmware upgrades, ensuring all devices can get the latest functions and security patches without manual intervention.

Data Handling and Analytics are critical for deriving insights from the vast amounts of data IoT devices generate. A best practice is to utilize IoT Central's built-in analytics tools to monitor and analyze device data in real time. This includes setting up custom dashboards that visually represent data trends and anomalies. Implementing data transformations

CHAPTER 5   DESIGN AND DEPLOY AZURE IOT MONITORING AND MANAGEMENT

to structure complex telemetry data is essential for making it usable. Moreover, aggregating data from multiple devices can provide a holistic view of system performance and health. Using these analytics capabilities, organizations can make well-informed decisions and react swiftly to issues.

Security is paramount in IoT solutions, given the potential risks associated with connected devices. IoT Central provides various security features, such as role-based access control (RBAC), which restricts access to the application based on user roles. Best practices include regularly auditing access permissions and using strong, unique passwords for all accounts. Device security should also be prioritized, with secure communication protocols like MQTT or AMQP with TLS encryption. Additionally, enabling audit logs to track user and device activities helps identify and mitigate potential security threats. Implementing these security measures ensures the integrity and confidentiality of data within the IoT system.

Scalability is crucial for IoT solutions to handle growing numbers of devices and increasing data volumes. Designing IoT solutions with scalability in mind involves using Azure IoT Central's capabilities to manage and scale device fleets efficiently. This includes setting up automated device provisioning and leveraging IoT Hub's capabilities to handle high-throughput data ingestion. Best practices also involve monitoring resource usage and performance metrics to anticipate and address any bottlenecks. Employing horizontal scaling strategies, such as adding more IoT Hubs or leveraging cloud-native services, ensures the system can grow without compromising performance.

Integration capabilities allow IoT Central to interact with other systems and services, enhancing its functionality. Using REST APIs to integrate IoT Central with external applications enables programmatic device management and data synchronization. Best practices include designing robust and well-documented APIs to facilitate smooth integration. Azure Logic Apps or Microsoft Power Automate can also automate workflows based on IoT data, such as sending alerts or triggering business processes. Integrating IoT Central with external analytics platforms can enhance data analysis capabilities, providing deeper insights into device performance and operational trends.

User interface design in IoT Central involves creating intuitive and informative dashboards that present data clearly and effectively. Best practices include using a mix of charts, maps, and tiles to display key metrics and trends. Customizing dashboards for different user roles ensures relevant information is easily accessible to each user type. Implementing interactive elements like drill-down capabilities allows users to explore data in greater detail. Ensuring the UI is responsive and accessible on various devices, including tablets and smartphones, enhances user experience and enables on-the-go monitoring and management of IoT solutions.

Operational efficiency in managing an IoT solution is achieved through automation and proactive maintenance. Best practices include setting up rules and alerts within IoT Central to automatically respond to certain conditions, such as sending notifications if a device exceeds temperature thresholds. Reviewing device logs and telemetry data can help identify and address issues before they escalate. Utilizing IoT Central's job scheduling capabilities to perform routine tasks, such as device reboots or configuration updates, reduces manual intervention and streamlines operations. Additionally, implementing robust incident management processes ensures swift resolution of any operational issues, maintaining the reliability and uptime of the IoT system.

In summary, designing an effective IoT solution with Azure IoT Central requires careful consideration of device management, data handling, security, scalability, integration, user interface design, and operational efficiency. By adhering to best practices in these areas, businesses can create IoT solutions that are robust, secure, and capable of delivering valuable insights and operational improvements.

CHAPTER 5   DESIGN AND DEPLOY AZURE IOT MONITORING AND MANAGEMENT

Azure Monitor

Azure Monitor for IoT is a comprehensive suite of monitoring services designed to help organizations manage and secure their IoT deployments effectively. As part of the broader Azure IoT suite, Azure Monitor for IoT provides real-time insights into the performance, security, and operational health of IoT devices and applications. This service is not just a tool but a peace of mind, ensuring the reliability and security of IoT environments by promptly identifying and addressing any potential issues.

Azure Monitor for IoT's proactive ability to collect and analyze telemetry data from a wide range of IoT devices is a key feature that empowers organizations. This data, including device performance, connectivity status, and operational health metrics, is aggregated to detect anomalies, diagnose issues, and optimize device performance. This forward-thinking method not only aids to thwart downtime but also positions the control of IoT devices' efficiency and effectiveness in the hands of the organizations, making them feel in control and empowered.

IoT Monitor for Azure isn't simply a monitoring platform but a comprehensive security solution. In addition to providing advanced security monitoring capabilities, it continuously monitors IoT devices and networks for possible cybersecurity problems, such as malicious access attempts, unusual behavior patterns, and potential breaches. By integrating with Azure Security Center, Azure Monitor for IoT offers comprehensive security insights and recommendations, providing a shield of protection to organizations' IoT security posture. This integration ensures that security teams can respond quickly to potential threats, mitigating risks before they escalate and giving the audience a sense of reassurance and protection.

Azure Monitor for IoT's scalability and flexibility is another significant advantage. It can handle large volumes of data from thousands of devices, making it suitable for small-scale and large-scale IoT deployments. Organizations can customize monitoring rules and alerts to fit their

CHAPTER 5 DESIGN AND DEPLOY AZURE IOT MONITORING AND MANAGEMENT

needs, ensuring they receive relevant and actionable insights. This level of customization allows businesses to focus on the most critical aspects of their IoT operations, making the audience feel that their unique needs are met.

Azure Monitor for IoT also integrates seamlessly with other Azure services, such as Azure IoT Hub and Azure Time Series Insights. This integration provides

- A unified view of IoT operations
- Combining device data
- Analytics
- Monitoring in a single platform

By leveraging these integrated services, organizations can gain deeper insights into their IoT environments, streamline operations, and enhance decision-making processes.

Additionally, Azure Monitor for IoT supports the creation of custom dashboards and reports. These tools enable organizations to visualize their IoT data meaningfully, track key performance indicators, and share insights with stakeholders. Custom dashboards can be tailored to specific roles within the organization, ensuring everyone, from engineers to executives, can access the information they need to make informed decisions.

In conclusion, Azure Monitor for IoT is a powerful tool that provides comprehensive monitoring, security, and analytics capabilities for IoT deployments. Its ability to collect and analyze telemetry data, monitor security threats, and integrate with other Azure services makes it an essential component of any IoT strategy. By leveraging Azure Monitor for IoT, organizations can ensure their IoT operations' reliability, security, and efficiency, driving better business outcomes and enhancing their competitive edge in the market.

Designing and implementing Azure Monitor for IoT involves carefully considering elements and best practices to ensure effective monitoring, security, and operational efficiency. These elements and practices help organizations harness Azure Monitor for IoT's full potential while maintaining robust security and performance.

Key Design Elements for Azure Monitor

Telemetry Data Collection: The cornerstone of Azure Monitor for IoT is its ability to collect telemetry data from various IoT devices. This involves setting up Azure IoT Hub as the central message broker that receives device data. Devices should be configured to send critical performance metrics, status updates, and event logs to the IoT Hub. This data is then routed to Azure Monitor for analysis and visualization.

Data Ingestion and Storage: Designing an efficient data ingestion pipeline is crucial. Data from the IoT Hub should be ingested into Azure Stream Analytics or Azure Functions for real-time processing. Depending on the retention and query requirements, the processed data can be stored in Azure Data Lake, Azure Blob Storage, or Azure SQL Database. This setup ensures that historical data is available for trend analysis and reporting.

Monitoring and Alerting Configuration: Configuring monitoring rules and alerts is essential for proactive management. Azure Monitor allows custom alerts to be created based on specific metrics or log data. These alerts can trigger notifications via email, SMS, or integration with ITSM tools like ServiceNow. Setting up threshold-based alerts ensures that deviations from normal operations are immediately flagged.

Visualization and Dashboards: Custom dashboards in Azure Monitor are a powerful tool for data visualization. These dashboards should present key performance indicators (KPIs) and metrics most relevant to the organization, empowering you with the information you need. Power BI integration can further enhance data visualization, providing interactive reports and insights that can be shared across the organization.

Integration with Azure Security Center: Security is critical to any IoT deployment. Integrating Azure Monitor with Azure Security Center provides a comprehensive security overview, giving you a sense of security and protection. Security Center continuously assesses the security posture of IoT devices and provides recommendations to mitigate risks. This integration ensures that security alerts are included in the overall monitoring strategy.

Scalability and Performance: IoT deployments can scale from a few devices to millions. Azure Monitor for IoT should be designed to handle this scale. This involves configuring Azure IoT Hub to support auto-scaling, ensuring that data ingestion services like Azure Stream Analytics can scale out to handle increased data volumes, and optimizing storage solutions to manage large datasets efficiently.

Compliance and Data Governance: Ensuring compliance with regulatory requirements is not just important, it's vital. Data governance policies should be configured to control data access and ensure privacy. Azure Policy and Azure Blueprints can be used to enforce compliance policies, and data encryption should be employed both in transit and at rest. This commitment to compliance is a key part of your role in managing an IoT deployment.

Key Best Practices for Azure Monitor

To effectively utilize Azure Monitor Logs, you need to set up at least one Log Analytics workspace. This workspace is essential for collecting various types of data, including logs from Azure resources and guest operating systems of Azure Virtual Machines. It also serves as a foundational requirement for enabling most Azure Monitor insights. Additionally, services like Microsoft Sentinel and Microsoft Defender for Cloud can utilize the same Log Analytics workspace used for Azure Monitor, streamlining data management and analysis.

CHAPTER 5   DESIGN AND DEPLOY AZURE IOT MONITORING AND MANAGEMENT

Creating a Log Analytics workspace is a cost-effective choice, as it incurs no initial cost. Charges may apply once you start configuring data collection into it, but detailed pricing information for log data can be easily found in Azure Monitor Logs pricing details. You can create and manage Log Analytics workspaces directly from the Azure portal, ensuring access management is configured appropriately. While you can deploy Log Analytics workspaces using scalable methods such as Resource Manager templates, it's often unnecessary initially as most environments typically require only a minimal number of workspaces.

Start with a single workspace to support initial monitoring needs for optimal monitoring efficiency. Analytics workspace configurations determine when multiple workspaces are necessary and how to set them up appropriately for your specific requirements.

Following is the list of key best practices to consider:

Device Configuration and Management: Devices should be securely configured and managed. This includes implementing secure boot processes, regularly updating firmware, and using robust authentication methods such as X.509 certificates. Azure Device Provisioning Service (DPS) can be used to automate the provisioning and management of IoT devices securely.

Efficient Data Processing: Use Azure Stream Analytics or Azure Functions for real-time data processing. These services enable real-time insights and actions on incoming data, such as triggering alerts or executing automated workflows based on predefined conditions. Ensure that data processing rules are optimized to minimize latency and maximize throughput.

Robust Security Practices: Security should be embedded into every layer of the IoT architecture. Implement security controls, such as Azure Virtual Network and Network Security Groups (NSGs), to restrict access to critical resources. Use Azure Key Vault to manage and secure cryptographic keys and other secrets.

Custom Alerts and Notifications: Concerning Alerts and Notifications, following are the key elements:

1. Define custom alerts that align with operational thresholds and business requirements.

2. Utilize dynamic thresholds that adapt to changing patterns in device behavior.

3. Integrate alerts with incident management systems to promptly address any issues.

Comprehensive Logging and Auditing: Enable comprehensive logging to capture detailed information about device operations and user activities. Azure Log Analytics can collect and analyze log data, providing insights into system behavior and helping detect and investigate anomalies.

Continuous Monitoring and Improvement: Concerning monitoring and improvement, following are the key elements:

- Review and update monitoring rules and configurations regularly to adapt to changing environments and new threat landscapes.

- Execute regular security assessments and penetration testing to identify and mitigate vulnerabilities.

- Use insights from monitoring to continuously improve the overall IoT infrastructure.

Documentation and Training: Maintain comprehensive information about the monitoring and management setup. Ensure that all stakeholders, including IT and security teams, are adequately trained on using Azure Monitor for IoT. Regular training sessions and updates can help teams stay up-to-date about new functions and best practices.

CHAPTER 5 DESIGN AND DEPLOY AZURE IOT MONITORING AND MANAGEMENT

Designing and implementing Azure Monitor for IoT requires a holistic approach that considers data collection, processing, security, scalability, and compliance. By following these design elements and best practices, organizations can build a robust monitoring and management system that ensures their IoT deployments' reliability, security, and efficiency. This proactive approach enhances operational performance and mitigates risks, providing a secure and resilient IoT ecosystem.

Deploy Microsoft Azure-Based IoT Monitoring and Management

Deployment in the context of Azure IoT Central and Azure Monitor comprises two essential components that together form a robust framework for managing and monitoring IoT solutions. Azure IoT Central is a comprehensive platform for deploying and managing IoT applications at scale, offering streamlined device provisioning, data visualization, and operational insights. It simplifies the complexities of IoT deployment by providing pre-built templates and intuitive tools for device management, making it accessible even to users without extensive programming knowledge.

Azure Monitor, working in tandem with Azure IoT Central, provides powerful monitoring and analytics capabilities. It enables real-time monitoring of IoT device health, performance metrics, and operational data across diverse environments. What's noteworthy is its integration with Log Analytics, which provides deep insights into IoT infrastructure. This integration facilitates proactive management and rapid response to emerging issues, ensuring you are always one step ahead. With its customizable dashboards and alerts, Azure Monitor gives you the confidence that your IoT operations are in good hands.

Let us get started with Azure IoT Central for management and monitoring.

CHAPTER 5   DESIGN AND DEPLOY AZURE IOT MONITORING AND MANAGEMENT

Azure IoT Central

Deploying Azure IoT Central is straightforward and allows businesses to connect, monitor, and manage their IoT devices rapidly. First, you create an Azure IoT Central application through the Azure portal. This step involves selecting an appropriate template that matches your industry requirements or opting for a custom template if specific configurations are needed. Once the application is developed and deployed, you can browse to it from the Azure portal, where you will have access to various tools for device management, data analytics, and application security.

The next step in deployment is to register your devices with the IoT Central application. This registration process provides the necessary connection information to assure secure contact between your devices and the application. With devices registered, you can then proceed to connect them and begin sending telemetry data. IoT Central's intuitive interface allows for real-time monitoring and control of connected devices, enabling you to view telemetry data, issue commands, and manage device properties directly from the application dashboard.

In a QuickStart scenario, you can create an Azure IoT Central application and connect your first device using a smartphone app. This method accelerates the setup process by using your phone as a stand-in for an IoT device. The app sends telemetry, reports properties, and responds to commands, providing a hands-on experience that will engage you with IoT Central's capabilities.

To begin, create an IoT Central application and register a new device within the application. You can then connect your smartphone to the application and view the telemetry it sends. This setup lets you control the device from the application interface, offering a practical demonstration of device management.

CHAPTER 5   DESIGN AND DEPLOY AZURE IOT MONITORING AND MANAGEMENT

Microsoft Azure login account with an active subscription is mandatory, and you should have at least Contributor access to your Azure subscription. Rest assured, an Android or iOS smartphone is also needed to install the free app from the official stores, which should be readily available.

Stage 1: To create an application

In stage 1, navigate to the Azure portal's Create IoT Central Application page and sign in with your Azure account.

Please fill in all the required details, such as Microsoft Azure, subscription, resource group, resource name, application URL, template, region, and pricing plan.

Once these details are entered, select Review + Create and then Create. You can access the app from the Azure portal when it is ready.

Next, to register a device, navigate to the Devices page in IoT Central and select Add a device. Accept the defaults and create the device on the Create a new device page. Click on the device name in the list of devices, select Connect, and then QR Code. This QR code contains the necessary connection information for your device.

Install the IoT Plug and Play smartphone app from the app store to connect your device. Open the app, select Scan QR code, and point your smartphone's camera at the QR code. The communication is to be initiated, and you can view the telemetry data the app sends to IoT Central. On the telemetry page in the app, data sent to IoT Central is displayed, and logs show the device's connection status and initialization messages.

To access the telemetry from the mobile app offered by Azure IoT Central, navigate to the Devices page, click on the device name, and select Overview. The overview page displays telemetry plots, providing insights into the data sent by your device.

Manage and control your IoT devices efficiently with IoT Central. Select the Commands view for your device, and use the available commands to interact with the smartphone app. For example, to make the light on your smartphone flash, use the LightOn command with specified parameters and select Run. The light will flash accordingly, and you can view the acknowledgment from the smartphone app in the command history. This process underscores the interactive capabilities of IoT Central, allowing you to manage and control IoT devices with maximum productivity.

Stage 2: Configure rules and actions

In stage 2, you will configure an IoT Central rule. IoT Central rules enable you to automate actions based on specific conditions. This example uses accelerometer telemetry from a smartphone to trigger a rule when the phone is turned over.

To get started, you will create a rule that detects when a telemetry value exceeds a threshold, configure the rule to send an email notification, and test the rule using the smartphone app.

To proceed, ensure you have an Azure account with an active subscription and have completed the initial quickstart to create an Azure IoT Central application.

The smartphone app sends telemetry, including values from the accelerometer sensor, which behaves differently on Android and iOS devices. When the mobile phone is flat on its back, the z value is higher than 9; when it is on its front, the z value is less than −9.

Creating a telemetry-based rule is a straightforward process. Simply navigate to the Rules section in the left pane of your IoT Central application, select "Create a rule," and enter "Phone turned over" as the rule name.

Against the Target devices section, choose "IoT Plug and Play mobile" as the Device template. This filters the devices the rule applies to by device template type. Additional filter criteria can be added by selecting "+ Filter."

In the Conditions section, define the trigger for your rule using the following information to set up a condition based on the accelerometer's z-axis telemetry. Every five minutes, you'll receive one email notification for each device based on aggregation:

CHAPTER 5   DESIGN AND DEPLOY AZURE IOT MONITORING AND MANAGEMENT

- Time aggregation: On, 5 minutes
- Telemetry: Acceleration / Z
- Operator: Is less than
- Aggregation: Minimum
- Value: −9

Next, add an email action to run when the rule triggers. In the Actions section, select "+ Email" and use the following information to define your action:

- Display name: Your phone moved
- To: Your email address

Notes: Your phone is face down!

To receive an email notification, the specified email address must be a user ID in the application, and the user must have signed in to the application at least once.

Select "Save." Your rule is now listed on the Rules page.

To test the rule, ensure the smartphone app actively sends data, then place the phone face down. After five minutes, IoT Central will send an email notification indicating your smartphone is face down.

Once testing is complete, turn off the rule to stop receiving notification emails.

Stage 3: Export data

In stage 3, you will configure your IoT Central application to export data to Azure Data Explorer. Azure Data Explorer enables you to store, query, and process telemetry from devices like the IoT Plug and Play smartphone app. You will use the data export feature in IoT Central to send telemetry from the smartphone app to an Azure Data Explorer database. Then, you will use Azure Data Explorer to run queries on the telemetry data. Your Azure account will incur a small charge for the Azure Data Explorer instance, but your IoT Central application will be free for the first two devices.

CHAPTER 5   DESIGN AND DEPLOY AZURE IOT MONITORING AND MANAGEMENT

Before embarking on this journey, ensure you have an active Azure account subscription and have completed the initial quickstart to create an Azure IoT Central application. The second quickstart, which involves configuring rules and actions for your device, is optional. You will need the IoT Central application URL prefix chosen during the initial setup and access to the Bash environment in Microsoft Azure Cloud Shell. Azure CLI can be installed locally to run CLI reference commands. To access the Azure CLI locally, run az login and follow the authentication steps displayed in your terminal. Make sure your Azure CLI is current by running az upgrade.

You must first set up an Azure Data Explorer cluster and database to export data from your IoT Central application. Configure them by running a bash script in Azure Cloud Shell. In this script, you sign in to Azure, create an Azure Data Explorer cluster and database, generate a managed identity for IoT Central, configure it with the appropriate permissions, and add a table to the database for storing incoming telemetry from IoT Central. To download and run the script, run the following commands:

```
wget https://raw.githubusercontent.com/Azure-Samples/iot-central-docs-samples/main/quickstart-cde/createADX.sh
chmod u+x createADX.sh
./createADX.sh CLUSTER_NAME CENTRAL_URL_PREFIX
```

When replacing CLUSTER_NAME with a unique name for your Azure Data Explorer cluster and CENTRAL_URL_PREFIX with the URL prefix of your IoT Central application, it's crucial to note the Azure Data Explorer URL results via script. This URL is vital for completing this quickstart and should be used later in the process. Please note that the script may take 20 to 30 minutes to complete.

Navigating to the Data export page in your IoT Central application is essential when configuring the data export destination from IoT Central. Choose the Destinations tab and, respectively, Add a destination.

CHAPTER 5   DESIGN AND DEPLOY AZURE IOT MONITORING AND MANAGEMENT

It's crucial to enter "Azure Data Explorer" as the destination name and select Azure Data Explorer as the destination type. This ensures the data is exported to the correct location and prevents potential loss. Enter the Azure Data Explorer URL in the Cluster URL you noted earlier. In the Database name, enter "phone data." In the field name, enter "acceleration." For Authorization, select System-assigned managed identity and then save the settings.

Next, to configure the data export, go to the Exports tab on the Data export page and select Add an Export. Enter "Phone accelerometer" as the export name and choose Telemetry as the type of data to export. Add the following filters:

- Name: Device template, Operator: Equals, Value: IoT Plug and Play mobile

- Name: Sensors/Acceleration/X, Operator: Exists

Ensure the option to export the data is selected if all conditions are proper. Add Azure Data Explorer as the destination and define a data transformation query as follows:

```
import "iotc" as iotc;
{
  Device: .device.id,
  EnqueuedTime: .enqueuedTime,
  X: .telemetry | iotc::find(.name == "accelerometer").value.a
  Y: .telemetry | iotc::find(.name == "accelerometer").value.b,
  Z: .telemetry | iotc::find(.name == "accelerometer").value.z
C
```

CHAPTER 5 DESIGN AND DEPLOY AZURE IOT MONITORING AND MANAGEMENT

To test the transformation, use the following sample telemetry message:

```
{
 "messageProperties": {},
 "device": {
  "id": "8hlsasa7n ",
  "properties": {
   "reported": []
  },
  "approved": true,
  "types": [],
  "name": "8hlsasa7n",
  "simulated": false,
  "provisioned": true,
  "modules": [],
  "templateId": "urn:modelDefinition:vlcd3zvzdm:y425jkkpqzeu",
  "templateName": "IoT Plug and Play mobile",
  "organizations": [],
  "cloudProperties": [],
  "blocked": false
 },
 "component": "sensors",
 "applicationId": "40b77c91-50cc-88f0-9f73-71387713facc",
 "messageSource": "telemetry",
 "telemetry": [
  {
   "id": "dtmi:azureiot:PhoneSensors:__accelerometer;1",
   "name": "accelerometer",
   "value": {
```

(continued)

```
    "x": 0.09960123446598816,
    "y": 0.0954132205426025,
    "z": 9.902221600952148
   }
  }
 ],
 "enqueuedTime": "2021-11-12T10:01:30.588Z",
 "enrichments": {}
}
```

It's crucial to save the transformation and the data export definition. This step is critical to ensuring the integrity of your data. Wait until the export status shows Healthy, indicating your data is ready for further analysis.

To query the exported telemetry, navigate to your Azure Data Explorer environment using the URL from the script. Expand the cluster node and select the "phone data" database. Open a new tab and paste the following Kusto query to plot the accelerometer telemetry:

```
['acceleration']
  | project EnqueuedTime, Device, A B,CZ
  | render timechart
```

Wait for several minutes to collect enough data. Change the orientation of your phone to see the telemetry values update.

Azure Monitor

Let us move forward with Azure Monitor.

Starting with Azure Monitor from an IoT standpoint involves setting up a comprehensive monitoring solution that captures and analyzes telemetry data from your IoT devices. The first step is integrating Azure

CHAPTER 5 DESIGN AND DEPLOY AZURE IOT MONITORING AND MANAGEMENT

Monitor with your IoT Central application, which involves configuring diagnostic settings to collect telemetry data, logs, and metrics from your devices. This setup ensures that all relevant data is streamed into Azure Monitor for further analysis. One of the key benefits of this setup is the ability to proactively manage your IoT ecosystems by creating alerts based on specific conditions. For example, you can set alerts for device anomalies, such as unexpected spikes in temperature or humidity, ensuring that you are notified immediately when critical thresholds are breached. This proactive approach gives you a sense of security and control over potential issues.

By leveraging Azure Monitor's integration with other Azure services, such as Azure Data Explorer and Power BI, you can enhance your monitoring capabilities and gain a deeper understanding of your IoT operations. This integration empowers you to explore in-depth data and create rich visual dashboards for real-time insights. With Application Insights within Azure Monitor, you can also gain visibility into the performance and reliability of your IoT applications, tracking key metrics such as response times, error rates, and throughput. This holistic approach to monitoring puts you in control, helping you maintain the health and efficiency of your IoT infrastructure and make data-driven decisions.

Artificial Intelligence for IT Operations (AIOps) offers powerful ways to improve service quality and reliability. It uses machine learning to process and automatically act on data collected from IoT devices and resources integrated into Azure Monitor.

Azure Monitor's built-in AIOps capabilities provide insights that help troubleshoot issues and automate data-driven tasks specific to IoT environments. These tasks include predicting device usage and autoscaling resources, identifying and analyzing device performance issues, and detecting anomalous behaviors in IoT devices and connected systems. These features enhance your IoT monitoring and operations, enabling efficient management without requiring extensive machine learning knowledge or additional investment.

CHAPTER 5   DESIGN AND DEPLOY AZURE IOT MONITORING AND MANAGEMENT

Azure Monitor also provides the tools to create custom machine-learning pipelines. These pipelines introduce new analysis and response capabilities, enabling you to act on data in Azure Monitor Logs. Due to this flexibility, IoT ecosystems can be customized to meet their unique monitoring and response needs. This level of control empowers you to ensure optimal performance and reliability, putting you in the driver's seat of your IoT infrastructure.

Azure Monitor becomes available when you create an Azure subscription, with specific features activated immediately. For instance, the activity log starts collecting events about subscription activity immediately, platform metrics are automatically gathered for any Azure resources you create, and Metrics Explorer is ready to use for data analysis straight out of the box.

Azure Monitor offers a rich set of features and empowers you to fine-tune your monitoring and alerting to your unique requirements. Diagnostic settings, for example, allow you to collect detailed information from your resources, and alerts will enable you to receive notifications of critical events. This high level of customization ensures a monitoring and alerting system precisely tailored to your needs, providing you with the adaptability and flexibility you require.

Accessing Azure Monitor is straightforward and can be done through multiple methods. You can access all Azure Monitor features and data from the Monitor menu in the Azure portal. Each Azure service menu also includes a Monitoring section that provides Azure Monitor tools with data filtered for that specific resource. You can also access and manage Azure Monitor data for more advanced scenarios with the Azure CLI, PowerShell, and REST API.

Let's use the Azure IoT Edge to monitor the use case here.

Azure Monitor Workbooks provide essential tools and visualizations to monitor Azure IoT Edge deployments effectively. Following stages of prodecure explain you through deploying and configuring the metrics collector module on IoT Edge devices, enabling you to monitor device health and performance metrics.

519

CHAPTER 5 DESIGN AND DEPLOY AZURE IOT MONITORING AND MANAGEMENT

Stage 1: Deploy a Log Analytics workspace
To access the Azure portal

1. Sign in to your Azure account.

2. Navigate to Log Analytics workspaces by searching for it.

3. Click on "Create" and follow the instructions to set up a new workspace.

4. Once created, click "Go to resource" for your newly created workspace.

5. In the main menu, go to Settings and select "Agents management."

6. Copy the Workspace ID and Primary key provided. These will be used later to configure the metrics collector module for sending metrics to this workspace.

Next, IoT Edge devices generate metrics through runtime modules like the IoT Edge agent and hub, which monitor module lifecycle and communication. These metrics include CPU usage, memory usage, and module execution times. To simplify monitoring without custom solutions, Microsoft offers the reliable azureiotedge-metrics-collector module. This module efficiently gathers metrics from runtime modules and optionally from other modules for cloud transmission.

Stage 2: Deploy metrics collector

1. Sign in to the Azure portal and go to your IoT hub.

2. In the left menu, go to Devices under Device management.

3. Select the device ID of your IoT Edge device to open its details page.

CHAPTER 5   DESIGN AND DEPLOY AZURE IOT MONITORING AND MANAGEMENT

4. On the top menu, click Set Modules.

5. If "SimulatedTemperatureSensor" is not listed under IoT Edge modules, add it:

   a. Click Add, then choose IoT Edge Module.

   b. Enter the following module settings:

      i. IoT Module name: SimulatedTemperatureSensor

      ii. Image URI: mcr.microsoft.com/azureiotedge-simulated-temperature-sensor

      iii. Restart policy: always

      iv. Desired status: running

   c. Click Next: Routes to configure routes.

6. Add a route to send messages from the simulated temperature module to IoT Hub:

   a. Name: SimulatedTemperatureSensorToIoTHub

   b. Value: FROM /messages/modules/SimulatedTemperatureSensor/* INTO $upstream

7. Add and configure the metrics collector module:

   a. Click Add, then choose IoT Edge Module.

   b. Search for and select IoT Edge Metrics Collector.

   c. Enter the following module settings:

      i. IoT Module name: IoTEdgeMetricsCollector

      ii. Image URI: mcr.microsoft.com/azureiotedge-metrics-collector

      iii. Restart policy: always

      iv. Desired status: running

d. Navigate to the Environment Variables tab.

e. Add the following environment variables:

  i. Name: ResourceId, Value: Your IoT hub resource ID

  ii. Name: UploadTarget, Value: AzureMonitor

  iii. Name: LogAnalyticsWorkspaceId, Value: Your Log Analytics workspace ID

  iv. Name: LogAnalyticsSharedKey, Value: Your Log Analytics key

8. Click Apply to save your changes.

9. Review your module configurations and click Review + create.

10. Finally, click Create to deploy the modules.

This process sets up your IoT Edge device to collect and send metrics directly to Log Analytics in Azure Monitor.

Afterward, ensure you have an IoT Edge device with the simulated temperature sensor module deployed. If not, follow the steps to deploy a virtual Linux device with this module. Metrics collected by the azureiotedge-metrics-collector module can be securely sent directly to Log Analytics, leveraging a Log Analytics workspace created beforehand. With its robust security measures, this workspace is the repository for IoT Edge metrics, facilitating easy visualization and analysis through Azure Monitor Workbooks.

Once your Log Analytics workspace is set up, retrieve the workspace ID and primary key. Similarly, obtain the Azure Resource Manager resource ID for your IoT hub. These IDs are crucial for configuring the metrics collector module. Deploying the module involves setting its environment variables with these IDs and specifying AzureMonitor as the upload target.

After deployment, metrics flow to Log Analytics, where Azure Monitor Workbooks provides curated visualizations. These include Fleet View for overall device health across multiple IoT resources, Device Details for detailed metrics on messaging, module performance, and host device information, and Alerts View for monitoring device alerts.

Azure Monitor allows individual module logs to be viewed directly from the Azure portal for troubleshooting, providing real-time insights and support. This comprehensive approach using Azure Monitor Workbooks ensures efficient monitoring and troubleshooting of Azure IoT Edge deployments, enhancing operational visibility and reliability.

Summary

This chapter begins by laying a solid IoT monitoring and management basics foundation. It covers the critical need for robust monitoring solutions to ensure IoT deployments' optimal performance, security, and reliability. Key concepts such as device telemetry, event processing, and alerting are introduced. Gathering, assessing, and refining data from connected devices to gain actionable insights are emphasized, along with discussions on common challenges faced in IoT ecosystems, such as scalability, latency, and data integrity. This section sets the stage for understanding how Azure's comprehensive suite of tools addresses these challenges.

Design Microsoft Azure-Based IoT Monitoring and Management

Moving into the design phase, the chapter delves into the architectural considerations for implementing an IoT monitoring and management solution using Microsoft Azure. It explores Azure services like Azure IoT Hub, Azure Monitor, Azure Time Series Insights, and Azure Log Analytics.

CHAPTER 5   DESIGN AND DEPLOY AZURE IOT MONITORING AND MANAGEMENT

Detailed guidance is provided on designing a scalable and resilient architecture that can handle large volumes of data generated by IoT devices. Best data ingestion, storage, processing practices, and strategies for ensuring data security and compliance are discussed. This section also highlights the importance of creating intuitive dashboards and reports for adequate visualization and decision-making.

Deploy Microsoft Azure-Based IoT Monitoring and Management

The final section of the chapter is a practical guide to deploying an IoT monitoring and management solution on Azure. It provides a clear roadmap with step-by-step instructions for setting up and configuring the necessary Azure services. This includes provisioning IoT Hub for device connectivity, setting up Azure Monitor for comprehensive monitoring, and configuring Log Analytics for advanced data analysis. The deployment process also covers creating and deploying IoT Edge modules, setting up alerting mechanisms, and integrating with other Azure services for enhanced functionality. Real-world scenarios and use cases are presented to illustrate the deployment process, ensuring readers can confidently apply the knowledge in their own IoT projects.

Through these sections, the chapter provides a comprehensive understanding of how to design and deploy an efficient IoT monitoring and management solution using Microsoft Azure. The book offers readers with the insight and platforms they need to manage IoT ecosystems successfully so they can confidently tackle the challenges of IoT projects.

Glossary

Actuators
Devices that take an action or produce an effect in response to input from sensors.

Analytics
The process of interpreting data collected from IoT devices to extract useful insights.

Application Gateway
A load balancer that helps IoT devices interact securely with web services.

Authentication
The process of verifying the identity of an IoT device or user.

Authorization
Ensuring that an authenticated entity has permission to access certain resources in the IoT system.

Azure Active Directory (AAD)
Microsoft's identity and access management service that helps secure IoT resources.

Azure Bastion
A service that provides secure access to IoT virtual machines without using a public IP.

Azure Digital Twins
A service that enables the creation of digital models of physical environments to manage IoT devices.

GLOSSARY

Azure DNS
A service to manage domain names and enable IoT devices to connect through specific IPs.

Azure IoT Central
A managed app platform for building IoT applications without deep cloud development skills.

Azure IoT Edge
A service that extends cloud intelligence to local devices to process data closer to where it is generated.

Azure IoT Hub
A managed service that facilitates secure and reliable communication between IoT devices and the cloud.

Azure Key Vault
A service for securely storing and accessing encryption keys, secrets, and certificates used by IoT systems.

Azure Load Balancer
A service that distributes incoming network traffic across multiple IoT servers.

Azure Sphere
A security solution for IoT devices with built-in hardware, software, and cloud security.

Azure Time Series Insights
A fully managed analytics, storage, and visualization service for IoT data.

Big Data
Large volumes of data generated by IoT devices, often characterized by their complexity.

Bluetooth
A short-range wireless communication technology used for IoT device connectivity.

GLOSSARY

Cloud Computing
Storing and processing data from IoT devices over the internet rather than locally.

Cloud-to-Device Messaging
The ability to send commands from the cloud to IoT devices using Azure IoT Hub.

Conditional Access
Policies that enforce multi-factor authentication and restrict access based on user or device conditions.

Connectivity
The ability of IoT devices to communicate with each other and external systems.

Cyber-Physical Systems
Integrations of computation, networking, and physical processes through IoT.

Data Encryption
The method of converting data into a secure format to prevent unauthorized access during transmission.

Data Loss Prevention (DLP)
Techniques used to protect sensitive IoT data from unauthorized access and accidental exposure.

Defender for IoT
A comprehensive security solution that protects IoT devices and systems against cyber threats.

Device Fingerprinting
Identifying devices based on their unique attributes to secure an IoT network.

Device Provisioning Service (DPS)
A service that helps automate the secure provisioning of IoT devices to Azure IoT Hub.

GLOSSARY

Digital Twin
A virtual model of a physical device that reflects real-time data from the IoT-connected object.

Edge Computing
Processing data closer to where it is generated (at the edge) rather than in a central cloud.

Endpoint Protection
Security software designed to detect and block cyber threats targeting IoT devices.

Ethernet
A wired network technology often used to connect IoT devices to local networks.

ExpressRoute
A service that creates a private connection between IoT networks and the Azure cloud.

Firewall Rules
Rules in Azure Network Security Groups that block or allow specific network traffic to IoT systems.

Firewall
A security system that controls incoming and outgoing network traffic based on predetermined rules.

Firmware
Software embedded into IoT devices that can be updated to improve security.

Front Door
An Azure service that ensures IoT applications are available and perform well globally.

Gateway
A device that connects IoT devices to the internet or other networks, often facilitating protocol translation.

Identity Management
Systems and processes that manage the identities and permissions of IoT devices.

Interoperability
The ability of different IoT devices, systems, or platforms to work together seamlessly.

Intrusion Detection Systems (IDS)
Tools that monitor network traffic for suspicious activities or policy violations.

Intrusion Prevention System (IPS)
Technology that detects and prevents identified threats from affecting IoT systems.

IoT Plug and Play
A feature that simplifies the device-to-cloud integration by offering pre-validated device templates.

IoT SDKs
Software development kits provided by Azure to help developers connect devices to Azure IoT services.

Key Management
The process of handling cryptographic keys for encryption and authentication purposes.

Latency
The time it takes for data to travel between an IoT device and a server or system.

GLOSSARY

LoRaWAN
A low-power, wide-area network protocol designed specifically for IoT applications.

Machine Learning
An AI technology that allows IoT systems to improve their operations by learning from data.

Malware
Malicious software that targets IoT devices and networks, potentially compromising security.

Mesh Network
A network structure where IoT devices (or nodes) connect directly to multiple other devices, enhancing network reliability.

Message Routing
A feature in Azure IoT Hub that allows filtering and routing of messages to various endpoints.

Middleware
Software that connects IoT devices to applications, often facilitating communication and data management.

Module Identity
A security identity assigned to IoT Edge modules, ensuring secure communication between them.

MQTT (Message Queuing Telemetry Transport)
A lightweight messaging protocol for IoT device communication.

Multi-Factor Authentication (MFA)
A security process that requires two or more forms of verification for access to IoT systems.

NB-IoT (Narrowband IoT)
A low-power wide-area network technology designed for IoT applications.

GLOSSARY

Network Security Groups (NSGs)
Rules that control inbound and outbound traffic to IoT resources on Azure virtual networks.

Network Segmentation
Dividing a network into multiple segments to contain security breaches within isolated sections.

Network Topology
The arrangement and structure of a network and how IoT devices are connected.

Patch Management
Regular updates to IoT devices and software to fix vulnerabilities and improve security.

Platform
The software infrastructure that allows developers to build, deploy, and manage IoT applications.

Private Link
A service that enables private, secure connections to Azure IoT services without exposing traffic over the internet.

Privileged Identity Management (PIM)
A service that manages, monitors, and controls privileged access to IoT resources.

Protocols
Standardized rules that dictate how data is transferred between IoT devices.

Public IP
An IP address assigned to IoT resources that can be accessed via the internet.

GLOSSARY

Public Key Infrastructure (PKI)
A framework for managing digital certificates and encryption keys in IoT systems.

Radio Frequency Identification (RFID)
A technology that uses electromagnetic fields to identify and track IoT devices.

Role-Based Access Control (RBAC)
Azure's mechanism for restricting IoT users' access to resources based on roles.

Route Tables
Rules used in Azure to direct traffic from IoT devices through specific network paths.

Secure Boot
A process that ensures an IoT device boots using only trusted software.

Security Baselines
Predefined security settings that apply best practices for securing IoT resources.

Sensors
Devices that detect and measure physical properties like temperature, light, or motion.

Service Endpoints
A feature that provides secure access to Azure services from IoT virtual networks.

Sigfox
A global IoT network operator that provides low-power, wide-area network (LPWAN) connectivity.

Static IP
An IP address that doesn't change, often used for securing IoT devices or servers.

GLOSSARY

Thread
An IPv6-based networking protocol designed for low-power, mesh-networked IoT devices.

Threat Detection
Monitoring IoT systems for suspicious activity or threats in real-time.

Traffic Manager
A tool that routes network traffic to the most optimal endpoint for IoT applications.

Twin Properties
A JSON document in Azure IoT that stores metadata and state information about devices.

Virtual Network Peering
The linking of IoT virtual networks for secure communication without passing traffic over the internet.

Virtual Networks (VNet)
Private networks in Azure that allow IoT devices to communicate securely.

Virtual Private Network (VPN)
Encrypted network connections used to secure communication between IoT devices and Azure.

VPN Gateway
A service that enables secure communication between IoT networks and Azure over public internet.

Wi-Fi
A wireless network technology widely used to connect IoT devices to the internet.

X.509 Certificates
Digital certificates used for device authentication and encryption in Azure IoT solutions.

GLOSSARY

Z-Wave

Another wireless communication protocol designed for low-power IoT devices, commonly used in home automation.

Zero Trust Architecture

A security model that assumes no device or user can be trusted without verification, even within the network.

Zero-Day Vulnerability

A security flaw in IoT software or hardware that is exploited by attackers before a patch is available.

Zigbee

A wireless protocol for low-power, low-data-rate IoT networks, often used in smart homes.

Index

A

ABAC, *see* Attribute-Based Access Control (ABAC)
Access Control Lists (ACLs), 344, 371
ACK, *see* Acknowledgment (ACK)
Acknowledgment (ACK), 125, 126, 132, 152
ACLs, *see* Access Control Lists (ACLs)
Actuators, 14, 18, 19, 70
ADAS, *see* Advanced driver assistance systems (ADAS)
A2DP, *see* Advanced Audio Distribution Profile (A2DP)
Advanced Audio Distribution Profile (A2DP), 191
Advanced driver assistance systems (ADAS), 37
Advanced encryption techniques, 62, 66, 326
Advanced Manufacturing Solutions (AMS), 23–29
Advanced Message Queuing Protocol (AMQP), 21, 22, 109, 112, 207, 208, 215, 273, 501

AI, *see* Artificial intelligence (AI)
AIOps, *see* Artificial Intelligence for IT Operations (AIOps)
AM, *see* Amplitude modulation (AM)
Amplitude modulation (AM), 103
AMS, *see* Advanced Manufacturing Solutions (AMS)
AMS use case
   IIoT implementation, 24
      asset tracking and inventory management processes, 26
      chain management optimization, 27, 28
      energy management and sustainability, 27
      predictive maintenance, 24, 25
      quality control and process optimization, 25
   medium-sized manufacturing company, 24
   network connectivity, 28, 29
   security, 29

INDEX

Application layer
  CoAP (*see* Constrained Application Protocol (CoAP))
  communication and interoperability, 122
  end-user applications and services, 120
  end-users and IoT network, 122
  industries, IoT applications, 124
  in managing data, 122
  mediator, 123
  MQTT (*see* Message queuing telemetry transport)
  role in managing security, 123
  scalability, 123
  smart home application, 122
  user interaction, 122
  user interface design, 123
Artificial intelligence (AI), 324, 365
  IoT security, 324
  Sentinel, 398
  threat detection capabilities, 388
Artificial Intelligence for IT Operations (AIOps), 518
ASCII (American Standard Code for Information Interchange), 103–105
Asset tracking and inventory management, 31
Attribute-Based Access Control (ABAC), 321, 362, 380, 383
Attribute Protocol (ATT), 192

Authentication and authorization, 360
  users and devices, 361
  verification, 361
Automated HVAC, 32
Automated patch management, 435
Automotive industry, 36, 37
Autonomous network
  architecture, 227
  artificial intelligence, 263
  automation tool, 263
  benefits, 264
  challenges, 264
  future, network management, 264
  machine learning algorithms, 263
  modern, complex network environments, 262
  network elements, 262
  orchestration tools, 263
  self-managing networks, 262
  traditional network management approaches, 263
  use of, 262
Autonomous networks, 227, 230
Azure Application Gateway, 271
Azure App Service, 85, 86
Azure Bastion, 268
Azure CDN, 271
Azure Cosmos DB, 82–84
Azure Data Explorer, 513–515, 517, 518
Azure Data Lake, 463, 505

INDEX

Azure DDoS Protection, 267
Azure Defender for IoT, 91, 92
Azure Digital Twins, 93, 94, 225
Azure DNS, 271
Azure ExpressRoute, 269, 286, 298, 300
Azure Firewall, 268, 298, 316
Azure Firewall Manager, 268
Azure Front Door, 271, 296, 304, 307
Azure Functions, 76, 77, 86, 87, 280
Azure IoT Central, 79, 498–500
Azure IoT Edge
  analytical power of cloud, 203
  architecture and topology, 213, 214
  authentication, 209
    symmetric key attestation, 212
    TPM attestation, 212
    X.509 certificate attestation, 211
  best practices, 218–220
  compliance and regulatory requirements
    AI and analytics workloads on IoT Edge, 217
    data privacy, 216
    deployment and management using containers, 217
    near real-time response to local changes, 217
    offline or intermittent mode operation, 217
    optimize data costs, 218
    privacy for IoT Edge deployments, 218
    regulatory standards, 216
    security for iot edge deployments, 217
  components, 78
  containerized deployment, 201
  cost-effective data management, 202
  cost management, 216
  data storage, 215
  definition, 78
  device management, 215
  distributed AI and analytics, 202
  edge computing potential, 79
  edge computing scenarios, advantages, 79
  edge device management, 201
  enhanced security, 202
  IoT Edge Cloud Interface, 205
  IoT Edge modules, 204, 205
  IoT Edge runtime, 206–210
  leverage existing skills and code, 202
  Linux Containers
    on Linux, 210
    on Windows, 210
  local data processing, 215
  machine learning, 212
  managing cloud services, 78
  modules, 78
  monitoring and diagnostics, 216

INDEX

Azure IoT Edge (*cont.*)
   near real-time local
      response, 201
   network topology, 215
   offline capabilities, 215
   platform layer, 79
   platform options, 210
   privacy protection, 202
   protocol gateway
      functionality, 203
   provisioning, 209
   provisioning IoT Edge
      devices, 211
   reliability, 214
   reliable offline operation, 202
   scalability, 214
   scalable and flexible, 79
   secure and certified
      hardware, 201
   security, 214
   software lifecycle, 212, 213
   third-party modules, 203
   Windows containers on
      windows, 211
Azure IoT Edge deployments, 519
Azure IoT Hub
   Azure Security Center, 80
   bi-directional
      communication, 80
   central messaging hub, 76
   comprehensive and versatile
      service, 78
   critical role, 77
   definition, 76
   device management
      capabilities, 76
   edge layer, 78
   integrating Azure services, 81
   integration, 77
   key characteristics, 77
   message encryption, 77
   Microsoft Azure ecosystem, 80
   monitoring and diagnostic
      tools, 77
   regulatory requirements, 77
   robust device management
      capabilities, 80
   scalable and reliable, 77
   security, 80
Azure Key Vault, 87–90, 371, 507
Azure Load Balancer, 267, 296
Azure Logic Apps, 87, 88, 408
Azure Monitor for IoT, 503
   custom dashboards and
      reports, 504
   elements and best practices, 505
   integration, 504
   key best practices, 507
      comprehensive logging and
         auditing, 508
      concern monitoring and
         improvement, 508
      custom alerts and
         notifications, 508
      device configuration and
         management, 507
      documentation and
         training, 508

INDEX

efficient data processing, 507
robust security practices, 507
key design elements
  compliance and data governance, 506
  data ingestion and storage, 505
  integration with Azure Security Center, 506
  monitor and alert configuration, 505
  scalability and performance, 506
  telemetry data collection, 505
  visualization and dashboards, 505
Log Analytics workspace, 507
proactive ability, 503
scalability and flexibility, 503
security monitoring capabilities, 503
Azure NAT Gateway, 272
Azure network connectivity
  Azure Firewall, 298
  design considerations, 299, 300
  design recommendation, 300, 301
  ExpressRoute, 298
  Network Peering, 299
  organizations, 296, 299
  outbound/inbound connectivity design consideration, 302, 303
  design recommendation, 305
  VNets, 297
  VPN Gateway, 297
Azure Network Function Manager, 269
Azure networks, IOT
  IoT devices, connection patterns, 273
  IoT use cases, 267
Azure Operator 5G Core, 272
Azure Pricing Calculator, 279
Azure Private 5G Core, 270
Azure Private Link, 268
Azure Programmable Connectivity, 272
Azure Public MEC, Azure Private MEC, 270
Azure Resource Manager (ARM), 317
Azure Security Center, 80, 88, 89, 91, 216, 320, 370, 371, 395, 407, 503, 506
Azure security services, 417
Azure services, 76, 85, 204
Azure Stream Analytics, 77, 81, 82, 204, 205
Azure Synapse Analytics, 84, 85
Azure Virtual WAN, 270, 280, 281, 284, 290
Azure VPN Gateway, 270, 293, 297
Azure Web Application Firewall, 271

539

INDEX

Azure well-architected framework
   architectural tasks, 275
   Azure network connectivity (*see* Azure network connectivity)
   cost optimization tools, 279
   digital disruption, 275
   Internet of Things, 275, 276
   IoT design process, 275
   IoT solution, 275
   manageability, 277
   network topology (*see* Network topology)
   performance efficiency, 280
   principles, 276
   reliability, 277
   security, 277, 278

B

Behavioral analysis, 324, 480
Binary digit, 102
Bits, 102, 103, 105, 106
BLE, *see* Bluetooth Low Energy (BLE)
Bluetooth, 184
   A2DP, 191
   advantages, 188–190
   architecture, 190
   attacks, 185
   audio profiles, 187
   authentication and encryption mechanisms, 187
   BLE, 186
   communication channels, 186
   convenience and flexibility, 185
   features, 186–188
   HCI, 191
   HFP, 191
   HID, 191
   Host Controller Interface (HCI), 191
   interoperability, 187
   in IoT networks, 185
   L2CAP, 191
   LMP, 190
   mesh networking, 187
   proliferation, 186
   radio and baseband, 190
   SDP, 191
   security challenges, 186
   security mechanisms, 192
   security protocols, 187
   smart home appliances, 185
   standards, 188
   tampering/cloning, 185
   versatility, 187
   vulnerabilities, 185
Bluetooth Low Energy (BLE), 7, 11, 15, 186, 187, 195, 198, 420
Business-related systems, 312
Bus topology, 227, 236
   advantages, 238, 239
   central cable, 235
   coaxial cables, 240
   data collisions, 239
   data packets, 239
   disadvantages, 239

INDEX

IoT/IIoT networks, 236, 237
key features, 237, 238
maintenance, 240
reliability, 239
single central cable, 239
troubleshooting, 240
Bytes, 105

C

Cellular connectivity, 7, 8
Cellular networks, 7, 71, 103, 194, 199
Central hub, 232, 234, 235
Checksums, 101, 147, 149, 153, 155, 161, 162, 391
CGMs, *see* Continuous glucose monitors (CGMs)
CIA principles, 390
CI/CD, *see* Continuous integration and deployment (CI/CD)
Cloud-connected sensors, 402
Cloud services, 22, 55, 71
CoAP, *see* Constrained Application Protocol (CoAP)
Communication, 4
　in IoT, 496
　protocols, 21, 22, 70, 71
Compliance monitoring, 91, 434, 447
Configuration management tools, 389
Configuring devices, 393
Confirmable (CON), 125, 126

Constrained Application Protocol (CoAP), 22, 71, 109, 114, 121, 156, 165
　advantages, 127–129
　architecture, 129
　asynchronous communication, 127
　built-in support for multicast, 127
　client-server model, 124
　DTLS, 125
　IoT applications, 129
　layers
　　application, 131
　　message, 131
　　observation, 132
　　proxying and caching, 132
　　transport, 131
　lightweight and efficient, 125
　message formats
　　ACK (Acknowledgment), 132
　　CON (Confirmable), 132
　　NON (Non-Confirmable), 132
　　RST (Reset), 132
　messages, 125
　message types and reliability, 126
　multicast support, 130
　observation mechanism, 130
　proxying and caching, 131
　request-response communication model, 129
　request/response model, 126
　resource discovery and URI-based addressing, 126

541

INDEX

Constrained Application Protocol (CoAP) (*cont.*)
   RESTful architecture, 124
   role of methods
      DELETE, 133
      GET, 133
      POST, 133
      PUT, 133
      type of interaction, 133
   tokenization and message ID, 130
   UDP, 124
   UDP-Based Transport, 126
   use of UDP, 130
Continuous glucose monitors (CGMs), 30
Continuous integration and deployment (CI/CD), 86, 220, 337
Continuous monitoring, 347, 361, 374, 377, 387
   secure IoT strategy, 349
   traditional monitoring, 349
Coordinated vulnerability disclosure (CVD) programs, 323
Cost optimization tools, 279
CRC, *see* Cyclic Redundancy Check (CRC)
CRM, *see* Customer relationship management (CRM)
CVD, *see* Coordinated vulnerability disclosure (CVD) programs

Cyclic Redundancy Check (CRC), 101
Cryptography, 64, 66, 353
Customer relationship management (CRM), 73–75
Cyberattacks, 113, 156, 264, 322, 328–330, 352, 366, 369, 375, 379, 383, 421, 422, 459, 468, 481
Cybersecurity
   Azure IoT security, 395
   confidence, 392
   confidentiality, 390
   data and systems, 392
   designing, 392
   design principles, 394
   integrity, 391
   obscurity, 394
   robust security, 392
Cyber threats, 367

D

Data center network, 274
Data center network architecture, 274
Data collisions, 237–239, 252
Data encryption, 278, 321, 325, 373, 375, 380, 419, 428, 437, 439, 506
Data exchange, 4, 5, 168, 169
Data flow design, 427
Datagrams, 106, 155, 160

INDEX

Datagram Transport Layer Security (DTLS), 114, 125, 165
Data integrity and provenance, 324
Data management phase, IoT network and security lifecycle
  data encryption, 437
    data at rest, 438
    end-to-end encryption, 438
    key management, 438
    transit, 438
  data privacy, 439
    access controls, 440
    anonymization, 439
    consent management, 439
    data minimization, 439
    policies, 440
    pseudonymization, 439
  data retention, 440
    archive solutions, 441
    automated retention management, 440
    compliance audits, 441
    effective management, 441
    policies, 440
    secure disposal, 441
  organizations, 441
Data packets, 106, 115, 121, 151, 239
Data processing and analytics, 22–23, 215
Data protection and privacy, 380, 386
Data stream, 71, 106, 146
Data transmission, 100, 102
Data wiping, 442, 444
DDS, 97, 109, 112
Decommissioning phase, IoT network and security lifecycle, 442
  adherence, 445
  review and learn
    process, 443
    feedback loop, 444
    post-mortem analysis, 443
    security incident review, 444
    training and awareness, 444
    update policies and procedures, 444
  secure decommissioning, 442
    configuration removal, 442
    data wiping, 442
    device removal from network, 443
    documentation, 443
    physical destruction, 442
  secure practices, 445
  supply chain security, 445
  threat modeling, 445
  training and awareness programs, 445
Defense-in-depth strategies, 338
  ACLs, 344
  continuous monitoring, 341
  elements, 340
  encryption, 342

INDEX

Defense-in-depth strategies (*cont.*)
    IAM, 341, 344
    network
        segmentation, 341, 342
    OT/IoT/IIoT security, 339
    patch management, 341
    proactive measures, 339
    reactive security, 339
    secure coding practices, 341
Defense-in-depth strategy,
    338–340, 342, 358
Demilitarized Zones (DMZs), 343
Denial-of-service (DoS) attacks,
    153, 157, 328, 492, 495, 496
Deploy Azure IoT networks
    access layer, 309
    basics tab
        inputs, 314
        key settings, 314
    core layer, 308
    distribution layer, 309
    endpoint devices, 308
    IP configuration
        inputs, 314
        key settings, 314
    NSG configuration
        inputs, 315
        key settings, 315
    OT/IoT networks integration,
        309, 310
    overview, 312–317
    Purdue Networking
        Model, 310–312
Deploying Azure IoT Edge

installing and starting IoT Edge
    runtime, 220, 221, 223
IoT Hub, 220
module deployment,
    221, 223–225
and registering, 221
registering, 222
setting up IoT Hub, 221, 222
Design Azure IoT network, 273, 274
Development, Security, and
    Operations
    (DevSecOps), 336–338
Device authentication
    mechanisms, 77, 80
Device management, 72, 344
DevSecOps, *see* Development,
    Security, and Operations
    (DevSecOps)
Digital communication systems, 103
Digital disruption, 275
Digital twin, 15, 277
Direct Sequence Spread Spectrum
    (DSSS), 181, 183
Disaster recovery (DR), 83, 93, 94,
    277, 388, 389
DMZs, *see* Demilitarized
    Zones (DMZs)
DoS, *see* Denial-of-service
    (DoS) attacks
DR, *see* Disaster recovery (DR)
DSSS, *see* Direct Sequence Spread
    Spectrum (DSSS)
DTLS, *see* Datagram Transport
    Layer Security (DTLS)

E

ECC, *see* Elliptic Curve Cryptography (ECC)
Edge computing, 8, 63, 79, 95, 324, 365
Edge devices/gateways, 19, 20, 71
Edge network, 274
EHR, *see* Electronic health records (EHR)
Electric actuators, 19
Electronic health records (EHR), 33
Electronic signals, 102
Elevation of privilege, 492, 495
Elliptic Curve Cryptography (ECC), 357
Enabling Business Continuity and Growth, 330
Encoding and decoding process, 103
Encryption, 358, 376, 384
    authentication and authorization, 356
    battery-powered devices, 357
    data transmit, 356
    encryption and decryption, 356
    landscape, 358
    management practices, 357
    penetration testing and vulnerability assessments, 358
    protocols, 357
    public keys, 356
    security strength, 357

End-to-end deployment cycle, 213
End-to-end encryption, 29, 165, 438
Enterprise resource planning (ERP), 74, 75, 312
Enterprise-wide business planning and management systems, 312
Ephemeral connections, 273
ERP, *see* Enterprise resource planning (ERP)
Error correction, 101, 144, 163, 183, 190
Error detection, 101, 144, 153, 159
Ethernet, 7
    connection, 6
    networks, 102
ExpressRoute, 269, 274, 281, 287–289, 298, 300
Extended detection and response (XDR), 479
    designing and deployment, IoT cybersecurity
        automation, 488
        compliance, 488
        continuous monitoring, 488
        cyber threats, 488
        data stewardship, 487
        integration, 487
        orchestration, 488
        scalability, 486
        UEBA, 487, 488
    requirements in IoT cybersecurity, 481, 482

INDEX

Extended detection and response (XDR) *(cont.)*
  role in IoT cybersecurity, 480, 481
  value proposition in IoT cybersecurity
    for leadership team, 483, 484
    for security operations center (SOC) team, 485, 486
Extensible Messaging and Presence Protocol (XMPP), 22, 119, 124, 199

F

Fault tolerance, 77, 250–252, 254, 255, 257, 259, 261
FEC, *see* Forward Error Correction (FEC)
FHSS, *see* Frequency Hopping Spread Spectrum (FHSS)
Fiber optic networks, 103
Field-programmable gate arrays (FPGAs), 201
Finance industry, 35, 36
FM, *see* Frequency modulation (FM)
Forward Error Correction (FEC), 183
4G LTE, 7, 9, 116
FPGAs, *see* Field-programmable gate arrays (FPGAs)

Frequency Hopping Spread Spectrum (FHSS), 183
Frequency modulation (FM), 103
Frequency Shift Keying (FSK), 183
FSK, *see* Frequency Shift Keying (FSK)
Fundamentals, IoT monitoring and management
  anomaly detection, 421
  automation, 422
  compliance, 422
  data collection and storage, 421
  device management, 420
  IAM frameworks, 421
  monitoring and analytics, 421
  network connectivity, 420
  network segmentation, 422
  security threats, 421

G

Gateways, 71
GDPR, *see* General Data Protection Regulation (GDPR)
General Data Protection Regulation (GDPR), 329, 373, 424
Global System for Mobile communications (GSM), 114
GSM, *see* Global System for Mobile communications (GSM)

H

HA, *see* High availability (HA)
Hands-Free Profile (HFP), 191
Hannover01, 205
Hardware security modules (HSMs), 90, 211, 379, 384, 500
Healthcare industry, 34
HealthTech Solutions (HTS), 30–32
HFP, *see* Hands-Free Profile (HFP)
HID, *see* Human Interface Device Profile (HID)
High availability (HA), 77, 83, 86, 93, 94, 214, 268, 269, 277
HSMs, *see* Hardware security modules (HSMs)
HTS use case
    IIoT implementation
        asset tracking and inventory management, 31
        environmental monitoring and control, 32
        predictive maintenance, 31, 32
        remote patient monitoring, 30, 31
        workflow optimization and patient flow management, 33
        network connectivity and security, 33, 34
HTTP, *see* Hypertext Transfer Protocol (HTTP)
Human Interface Device Profile (HID), 191
Hybrid networks, 8, 241, 244, 403
Hybrid topology, 227, 229
Hypertext Transfer Protocol (HTTP), 21, 114, 121

I

IAM, *see* Identity and access management (IAM)
Identity and access management (IAM), 344, 345, 387, 421, 489
    authentication, 345
    authorization, 345
    benefits, 345
    foundation, 345
    implementing, 346
IEEE 802.15.4, 174–182
IETF, *see* Internet Engineering Task Force (IETF)
Incident response, 381, 435–437
Industrial Control System (ICS) security, 310
Industrial Internet of Things (IIoT), 267, 330, 339, 340, 451
Industrial, Scientific, and Medical (ISM) bands, 182
Industry 4.0 initiatives, 39
Information disclosure, 492, 495, 496
Intelligent building systems, 37
Intelligent connected sensors, 4

INDEX

Internet, 102
Internet Analyzer, 272
Internet Engineering Task Force
    (IETF), 115, 173
Internet of Things (IoT), 102, 231,
    345, 358, 367, 370, 394
  architecture, 107 (*see also* IoT
    architecture)
  cloud and application
    security, 386
  cloud environments, 390
  communication methods
    evolution, 5
  conventional computing
    devices, 3
  critical aspects, 4
  cybersecurity, 370, 372
  data harnessing, 3
  defense-in-depth elements, 340
  defense-in-depth strategy, 340
  definition, 2, 4, 14, 17
  deployments, 107
  devices, 36, 37
  device security, 368, 375
  ecosystem, 375, 382
  -enabled connected car
    services, 37
  -enabled devices, 35
  -enabled educational tools, 37
  -enabled predictive
    maintenance systems, 38
  -enabled sensors, 38
  -enabled smart grid
    technologies, 38
  -enabled telematics systems, 36
  enabling IoT, 5
  environments, 108
  growth, 3
  homes and businesses, 5
  Hub, 280, 316
  interconnected smart devices
    and sensors, 3
  network connection, 6, 7
  Patch Management, 351
  platforms, 22
  -powered predictive
    maintenance solutions, 35
  proliferation, 358
  technological advancement, 2
  technologies and protocols, 8
  terminologies, 14, 17
  traditional security models, 359
  types, 4
Internet of Things (IoT) security,
    107, 417
  boot processes, 323
  burgeoning, 338
  component, 319
  crucial security strategy, 322
  CVD programs, 323
  device authentication, 320
  ecosystem, 322
  edge computing, 324
  environments, 322
  firmware, 323
  fundamentals, 319, 321
  manufacturers, 321
  network, 320

INDEX

physical security, 322
PoLP, 324
safety and privacy, 325
stakeholders, 325
supply chain, 323
TEEs, 323
Internet Protocol Security (IPsec), 167, 169, 170, 172
Interoperability standards and protocols, 72
Intrusion Detection and Prevention Systems (IDPS), 384
IoT application industries
  automotive, 36, 37
  education, 37
  energy and utilities, 38
  finance, 35, 36
  healthcare, 34, 35
  manufacturing, 38, 39
  retail, 36
IoT applications architecture
  actions, 93
  Azure PaaS components, 93
  considerations, 93
  devices, 93
  insights, 93
  manageability, 94
  reliability, 94
  security, 94
IoT architecture
  application layer
    applications and services, 73
    facilities, 74
    flexibility and scalability, 74
    IoT use cases implementation, 74
    key aspect, 73
    user interfaces, 73
  business layer
    facilities, 75
    IoT deployment's strategic and operational aspects, 74
    key aspect, 75
    logic and rules, 74
    monetization and business models, 75
    primary functions, 75
    ROI development strategies, 75
    use cases, 75
  cloud services, 68
  device layer, 67
  edge layer, 68
  integration and interoperability, 76
  interconnected layers, 67
  layers, 68
  middleware layer
    description, 72
    device management, 72
    external systems and services integration, 73
    higher-level application and business layers, 72
    primary functions, 72
    protocol translation, 72

INDEX

IoT architecture (cont.)
  network layer
    communication protocols, 71
    device connectivity, 70
    gateways, 71
    scalability and interoperability, 71
  perception layer
    actuators, 70
    challenges, 70
    data acquisition, accurate and reliable, 69
    data collection, 69
    IoT device connectivity, 70
    link provisioning, 69
    physical devices, 69
    sensors types, 69
  reference architecture (*see* Microsoft's IoT reference architecture)
  security, 75
  security measures, 68
IoT cybersecurity strategy, 325
  awareness and education, 327
  data protection, 326
  element, 326
  landscape, 327
  monitoring and threat detection, 326
  robust security, 326
IoT developers
  network architecture (*see* IoT network architecture)

network protocols (*see* IoT network protocols)
IoT Edge Agent, 206, 207, 223
IoT Edge Cloud Interface, 205
IoT Edge hub, 78, 79, 206–209, 223
IoT Edge modules
  Azure services, 204
  module identities, 205
  module identity, 204
  module image, 204, 205
  module instance, 204, 205
  module twins, 204, 205
IoT Edge runtime
  components, 206
  and downstream devices, 206
  functions, 206
  IoT Edge Agent, 206, 207
  IoT Edge hub, 207–209
  responsibilities, 206
IoT gateways, 368, 382
  devices and users, 380
  hardware security, 379
  protocols, 380
IoT/IIoT building blocks
  cloud services, 22
  communication protocols, 21, 22
  data processing and analytics, 22
  edge devices/gateways, 19, 20
  IoT platforms, 22
  monitoring and management, 23
  network connectivity, 20, 21
  security measures, 23

sensors and actuators, 18, 19
use case and
   requirements, 17, 18
IoT/IIoT networks
  bus topology, 236, 237
  mesh topology, 253, 254
  network types, 9
  point-to-point topology, 240,
    241, 243, 244
  ring topology, 248, 249
  security, 232
  star topology, 231, 232
  tree topology, 258, 259
IoT monitoring
  aspects, 448
  benefits, designing and
    deployment, 452
    cost savings, 453
    data-driven decision-
      making, 454
    data quality and integrity, 453
    industry standards, 454
    innovation and future
      growth, 455
    operational efficiency, 453
    proactive security, 453
    regulatory requirements, 454
    resource utilization and
      sustainability, 454
    strategic planning, 454
    user experience, 454
  continuous monitoring, 445
    adaptive security
      measures, 446
    incident response, 446
    network segmentation and
      isolation, 447
    privacy and integrity, 447
    real-time threat
      detection, 446
    vulnerability
      management, 446
  definition, 448
  effective monitoring, 448
  industrial IoT, 448
  industries and applications, 451
    in agriculture, 451
    in healthcare, 451
    IIoT devices, 451
    in residential
      applications, 452
    retails, 452
    in smart city
      deployments, 451
    smart meters, 452
  and NDR (*see* Network
    detection and
    response (NDR))
  requirements, 449, 450
  scope, 448
  security, 449
  and SIEM (*see* Security
    information and event
    management (SIEM)
  and SOAR (*see* Security
    orchestration, automation
    and response (SOAR)
  tools, 449

INDEX

IoT monitoring (*cont.*)
  value proposition, 455, 456
    compliance assurance, 456
    cost savings, 456
    data-driven decision-making, 456
    enhanced user experience, 456
    improved security, 455
    operational efficiency, 455
    optimized resource utilization, 456
  and XDR (*see* Extended detection and response (XDR))
IoT network and security lifecycle, 425, 426
  data management phase (*see* Data management phase, IoT network and security lifecycle)
  decommissioning phase (*see* Decommissioning phase, IoT network and security lifecycle)
  deployment phase, 429, 432
    access control, 431–433
    device configuration, 429, 430
    network configuration, 430, 431
  operation and maintenance phases, 433
    incident response, 435–437
    monitoring and logging, 433, 434
    patch management, 434, 435
  phases, 425
  planning and design phase, 426, 427
    architecture design, 427
    requirement assessment, 427
    risk assessment, 427
    security policies, 428
IoT network architecture
  application layer, 119, 120, 122–143
  communication and data exchange, 119
  data processing, 120
  design scalable and reliable systems, 107
  network layer, 119, 121, 163–182
  physical layer, 119, 121, 122, 182–200
  structure, 120
  transport layer, 119, 121, 143–163
IOT networking
  deployment models with IoT protocol mapping, 194–196
  LANs, 192, 194
  PANs, 192–194
  WANs, 192–194
IoT network protocols
  AMQP, 109
  characteristics, 111, 113
  CoAP, 109, 114

INDEX

communication, 108
communication and data exchange, 102
communication medium, 100
computer networks, 98, 99
connection establishment, 100
cost savings, 110
customer experiences, 110
data transmission and management, 100, 102, 109
DDS, 109
decision-making, 110
DTLS, 114
efficiency, 112
efficiency and automation, 109
environmental sustainability, 111
error correction, 101
error detection, 101
flexibility and adaptability, 113
GSM, 114
HTTP, 114
IEEE, 115
IETF, 115
innovation and new business models, 110
interoperability, 107, 111
IP, 115
IP address, 99
LLN, 115
LPWAN, 116
LTE, 116
MQTT, 109, 116
network security, 101
packet delivery, 101
packets, 99, 100
performance, 102
QoS, 116
reliability, 112
REST, 117
routing and forwarding, 101
RPL, 117
rules and conventions for data exchange, 106
rules and standards, 108
safety and security, 110
scalability, 102, 112
security, 113
security features, 107
SSL, 117
TCP, 118
TCP/IP, 98
TLS, 118
UDP, 118
URI, 119
URL, 118
XMPP, 119
IoT networks and security
    future opportunities, 62, 63
    importance, 39, 40
    key challenges, 44–46
IoT network types
    cellular networks, 7
    Edge computing networks, 8
    hybrid networks, 8
    satellite networks, 8
    wired networks, 7
    wireless networks, 7

553

INDEX

IoT user security, 372
    MFA, 372
    RBAC, 372
IoT Zero Trust, 366
IP address management (IPAM) tools, 296
IPsec, *see* Internet Protocol Security (IPsec)
IPv6, 165, 166
    adoption, 296
    advantages, 170, 171
    architecture, 171–173
    32-bit addresses, 172
    128-bit address scheme, 166
    components, 171–173
    connectivity and interoperability, 167
    DHCPv6, 172
    end-to-end security, 168
    features, 167–170
    hexadecimal notation, 172
    IPsec, 168, 172
    multicast communication, 167
    multimedia applications, 172
    operates, 167
    QoS, 172
    secure overlay networks, 168
    security, 167

J

Just-in-Time Access, 89, 362

K

KPIs, *see* Key performance indicators (KPIs)
Key performance indicators (KPIs), 74, 333

L

LANs, *see* Local area networks (LANs)
Lasers, 103
Last will and testament (LWT), 137
L2CAP, *see* Logical Link Control and Adaptation Protocol (L2CAP)
Least privilege, 277, 320, 324, 353, 361
LEDs, *see* Light-emitting diodes (LEDs)
Legacy OT systems, 331, 339
Light-emitting diodes (LEDs), 19, 103
Light pulses, 103
Link Manager Protocol (LMP), 190, 191
LMP, *see* Link Manager Protocol (LMP)
Local area networks (LANs), 4, 6, 192, 194, 198
Location-based tracking technologies, 33
Logging, 322, 432, 434, 458, 464, 471, 478, 482, 488, 508
Logical Link Control and Adaptation Protocol (L2CAP), 191

INDEX

Log Management Tools, 348
Log Retention Policies, 409
Long-Term Evolution protocol (LTE), 116
LoRaWAN, 7, 184, 198
6LoWPAN, 165, 166
   adaptation layer, 179
      header compression, 179
      packet fragmentation and reassembly, 179
   advantages, 177, 178
   architecture, 174, 179, 182
   development, 173
   features, 175
   fragmentation and reassembly, 174
   header compression, 175
   interoperability with IPv6, 177
   link layer
      error detection and correction, 180
      functions, 180
      MAC, 180
   low-bandwidth wireless networks, 173
   low power consumption, 176
   mesh networking, 174, 176
   mesh topology, 181
   network layer, 180
      addressing, 180
      routing, 180
   packet fragmentation and reassembly, 176
   physical layer
      defines, 181
      frequency bands, 181
      modulation techniques, 181
   scalability and flexibility, 176
   security, 174
   security mechanisms, 177
      link-layer security, 182
      network-layer security, 182
   star topology, 181
   WSNs, 173
Low Power and Lossy Network (LLN), 115
Low-power wide area networks (LPWANs), 5, 116
Low-rate wireless personal area networks (LR-WPANs), 174
LR-WPANs, *see* Low-rate wireless personal area networks (LR-WPANs)
LPWANs, *see* Low-power wide area networks (LPWANs)
LWT, *see* Last will and testament (LWT)

M

Machine learning (ML), 324, 365
   autonomous network architecture, 262
   Azure Security Center, 89
   IoT security, 324
   threat detection and response, 395

INDEX

Maintaining customer trust, 329
Managed security service providers (MSSPs), 410
Maximum transmission unit (MTU), 174, 179
Media Access Control (MAC) addresses, 101, 174, 176–179, 403
Mesh networking, 174, 176
Mesh topology, 181, 227, 252, 253
   advantages, 255, 256
   disadvantages, 256
   IoT/IIoT networks, 253, 254
   key features, 254, 255
   works, 256, 257
Message encryption and TLS/SSL protocols, 80
Message Queuing Telemetry Transport (MQTT), 21, 71, 109, 116, 121, 165, 207
   access control, 137
   advantages, 138–140
   architecture and components, 140
      client, 141
      messages, 140
      server/broker, 141, 142
      topics, 142, 143
   authentication, 136
   efficiency, 133
   features, 134
   lightweight and efficient, 136
   LWT, 137
   persistent sessions, 137
   publish-subscribe model, 133, 135
   QoS, 134–136
   real-time monitoring and control applications, 134
   retained messages, 137
   scalability and flexibility, 137
   security features, 136, 137
   small code footprint, 138
   TLS, 134, 136
MFA, *see* Multi-factor authentication (MFA)
Microsoft Defender, 395, 400
   analytics engines, 402
   Azure portal, 403
   components, 401
   deployment perspective, 404
   for IoT, 395, 400
   IoT device, 404
   IoT sensors, 405
   landscape, 395
   network segmentation, 396
   OT/ICS security, 406
   threat detection and response, 395
   vulnerabilities, 396
Microsoft Defender XDR, 396
   behavioral analytics, 397
   contextualization, 397
   investigate and remediate threats, 397

INDEX

Microsoft 365 and Azure services, 398
threat detection and response, 397
Microsoft Sentinel, 398, 406–408, 410, 413
  architecture, 410
  auditing and health monitoring, 415
  data, 411
  data sources, 415
  features, 398, 399
  health and audit feature, 414
  workspace, 412
  workspace design, 413
Microsoft services, 93, 401
Microsoft's IoT reference architecture, 92
  Azure Cosmos DB, 82–84
  Azure Defender for IoT, 91, 92
  Azure Functions, 86, 87
  Azure IoT Edge, 78–80
  Azure IoT Hub, 77, 78
  Azure Key Vault, 90
  Azure Logic Apps, 87, 88
  Azure Security Center, 88, 89
  Azure Stream Analytics, 81, 82
  Azure Synapse Analytics, 84–86
  comprehensive framework, 76
  IoT devices and cloud communication, 76
Mitigating Financial Risks, 329
ML, *see* Machine learning (ML)
Monetization and business models, 75
Monitoring and management, Azure's IoT, 445
  automation power, 424
  build, trust and transparency, 424
  challenges, 422
  complexity at scale, 423
  data flood, 423
  compliance and data privacy, 424
  deploy Azure IoT Central, 510
    configure rules and actions, 512, 513
    create application, 511, 512
    export data, 513–517
    in QuickStart scenario, 510
  deploy Azure Monitor, 517
    AIOps, 518
    Azure Data Explorer and Power BI, 518
    custom machine-learning pipelines, 519
    diagnostic settings, 519
    Log Analytics workspace, 520–522
    metrics collector, 520–522
    Workbooks, 519
  deployment, 509, 510, 524
  design elements and best practices for Azure IoT Central, 500

557

INDEX

Monitoring and management, Azure's IoT (*cont.*)
    data handling and analytics, 500
    device management, 500
    integration capabilities, 501
    operational efficiency, 502
    scalability, 501
    security, 501
    user interface design, 502
    designing, 489, 523
        Azure IoT Central, 498–500
        Azure Monitor, 503–505
        cloud gateway zone, 493
        field gateway, 493
        integration capability, 490
        proactive security approach, 491
        scalability, 490
        services zone, 494
        streamlines, 490
        STRIDE model, 492, 494–498
        zones, 491
    fundamentals (*see* Fundamentals, IoT monitoring and management)
    future-proofing, investment, 424
    lifecycle, IoT network and security (*see* IoT network and security lifecycle)
    optimize performance, 424
    proactive problem solving, 423
    unlock true potential, IoT, 425
    vulnerable landscape, 423
        See also IoT monitoring

Motion sensors, 18, 69

MQTT, *see* Message Queuing Telemetry Transport (MQTT)

MQTT brokers
    message routing, 141
    QoS handling, 142
    retained messages, 142
    security, 142
    session management, 142

MQTT client
    control packets, 141
    publishers, 141
    subscribers, 141

MQTT messages
    header, 140
    message identifier, 140
    payload, 140
    topic name, 140

MQTT topics
    hierarchical structure, 142
    retained messages, 143
    wildcard subscriptions, 143

MSSPs, *see* Managed security service providers (MSSPs)

MTU, *see* Maximum transmission unit (MTU)

Multicast communication, 130, 167–171

Multi-factor authentication (MFA), 361, 368, 372, 384, 387, 431

INDEX

N

NAT Gateway, 316
NDR, *see* Network detection and response (NDR)
Network connectivity and security, 20, 21, 29
Network detection and response (NDR), 472
    designing and deployment, IoT cybersecurity
        automation, 477
        compliance requirements, 478
        data management, 478
        integration capabilities, 477
        orchestration, 477
        retention policies, 478
        scalability, 477
        security analytics, 478
        threat intelligence, 478
        UEBA, 478
    requirements in IoT cybersecurity, 474
    role, in IoT cybersecurity, 473
    security challenges, 472
    traditional security measures, 472
    value proposition in IoT cybersecurity
        for leadership team, 475
        for security operations center (SOC) team, 476

Network layer
    bandwidth and resources, 164
    challenges, 164
    deployment models (*see* IOT networking deployment models)
    DTLS, 165
    edge computing, 164
    fog computing, 164
    IoT deployments, 165
    IoT ecosystems, 163
    in IoT networks, 164
    IPv4 and IPv6 protocols, 121
    IPv6, 165–173
    6LoWPAN, 165, 166, 173–182
    security and privacy, 165
    wireless connectivity technologies, 164
Network of networks, 6
Network Peering, 299
Network security, 76, 101
Network security groups (NSGs), 291, 315, 318
Network segmentation, 381, 430
    critical defense strategy, 342
    and isolation, 383
    secure IoT deployments, 344
    series of fortified walls, 341
Network topology, 227
    bus topology, 235–240
    design, 229
    devices, 227, 230

559

INDEX

Network topology (*cont.*)
  IoT applications, 229
  IoT deployments, 229
  IoT IP planning
    Azure, 292
      design consideration, 293
      design recommendation, 294
    Ipv6 planning
      deployment consideration, 296
      design consideration, 295
  mesh topology, 252–257
  point-to-point topology, 229, 240 (*see also* Point-to-point topology)
  ring topology, 247–252
  star topology, 229, 231 (*see also* Star topology)
  traditional network topology, 285, 288
  tree topology, 257–262
  Virtual Network Manager, 290–292
  Virtual WAN, 281–283
Network Traffic Analysis (NTA) tools, 348
Network Watcher, 269, 318
NON, *see* Non-Confirmable (NON)
Non-Confirmable (NON), 125, 126
Non-critical transmissions, 125
NSGs, *see* Network security groups (NSGs)

O

OBEX (Object Exchange), 192
Operational technology (OT), 401
Optical communication systems, 103
Optical signals, 103
OT/IoT networks integration, 309
  access layer, 310
  core layer, 310
  distribution layer, 310

P

Packet delivery, 101
Packets, 99–101
PAN, *see* Personal area networks (PANs)
Partial mesh topology, 257
Patching IoT devices, 350
Patch management, 349, 350, 352
Persistent connections, 273
Personal area networks (PANs), 192–194, 198
Personal health information (PHI), 328
Pervasive/ubiquitous computing, 265
Phase Shift Keying (PSK), 183
Photodetectors, 103
PHI, *see* Personal health information (PHI)
Physical layer
  bluetooth, 184–192
  efficiency and robustness, 122

electrical, mechanical, and procedural specifications, 182
encryption and authentication, 184
energy efficiency, 183
FEC, 183
frequency band, 183
hardware components and physical transmission media, 121
innovations, 184
interference, 183
IoT networking and challenges
  bandwidth, 197–199
  data transfer, 197
  intermittent connectivity, 197, 199
  interoperability, 197, 200
  power usage, 199
  range, 197, 198
  security, 197, 200
in IoT networks, 184
ISM bands, 182
LoRaWAN, 184
modulation and coding techniques, 183
in power consumption, 183
PUFs, 184
transmitting and receiving raw data, 182
Physical security, 42, 48, 67, 278, 322, 377–379
Physical unclonable functions (PUFs), 184
PoE, *see* Power over Ethernet (PoE)
Point-to-point topology, 227, 229, 240
  advantages, 241, 242, 245, 246
  communication channel, 242
  disadvantages, 242, 246
  IoT/IIoT networks, 240, 241, 243, 244
  key features, 244, 245
  works, 242, 243, 246, 247
PoLP, *see* Principle of least privilege (PoLP)
Power over Ethernet (PoE), 7, 10, 20
Predictive maintenance, 31, 32
Principle of least privilege (PoLP), 324
Privacy, 264, 373, 380
Proactive defense strategies, 362
Proactive threat mitigation, 63, 65, 339, 340
Protecting sensitive data, 177, 254, 328, 390, 424, 446
PSK, *see* Phase Shift Keying (PSK)
Protocol translation, 14, 72
Publish-subscribe model, 133, 135, 137, 138
PUFs, *see* Physical unclonable functions (PUFs)
Purdue Networking Model, 310–312

INDEX

Q

QAM, *see* Quadrature Amplitude Modulation (QAM)
QoS, *see* Quality of service (QoS)
Quadrature Amplitude Modulation (QAM), 183
Quality of service (QoS), 116, 134–136, 172, 190, 309
Quantum key distribution, 62, 67

R

Radio Frequency Communication (RFCOMM), 192
Radio signals, 103
RBAC, *see* Role-based access control (RBAC)
Real-time alert systems, 433
Real-time threat detection, 50, 381, 446, 447, 461
Remote patient monitoring, 30, 31, 34, 75, 451
Representational State Transfer (REST), 117, 500, 501
Repudiation, 492, 495
Request-response communication model, 129
Request/response model, 126
Requirement assessment, 427
Reset (RST), 125, 126
Resource-constrained devices, 22, 139, 140, 177, 346, 350, 356, 357
REST, *see* Representational State Transfer (REST)
RESTful architecture, 124
Retail industry, 36
Retained messages, 137, 142, 143
Return on investment (ROI), 75, 484
RFCOMM, *see* Radio Frequency Communication (RFCOMM)
RFID technology, 36
Ring topology, 227, 248
   advantages, 251
   disadvantages, 251
   IoT/IIoT networks, 248, 249
   key features, 249, 250
   works, 251, 252
Risk assessment, 402, 426, 427
Robust access control, 321, 383, 493
ROI, *see* Return on investment (ROI)
Role-based access control (RBAC), 361, 372, 409, 428, 431, 440, 501
Routes, 209, 224, 261
Routing and forwarding, 101, 169, 171
Routing over Low power and Lossy networks (RPL), 117
Routing preference, 270
Runtime modules, 206, 520

S

SaaS applications, 88
Safeguarding Intellectual Property, 329
Satellite communication, 8, 194, 196
Scalability, 107, 344
Scalable network architectures, 71
SCM, *see* Supply chain management (SCM)
SDP, *see* Service Discovery Protocol (SDP)
Secure application development, 387
Secure coding
    benefits, 354
    data privacy, 356
    data tampering, 355
    IoT devices, 352, 355
    knowledge and training, 354
    memory management, 353
    practices, 354
Secure communication protocols, 431
Secure Device Design, 375
Secure hardware design, 62, 66, 379, 382
Secure Sockets Layer (SSL), 86, 117, 118, 438
Securing communication channels, 321, 374, 496
Securing IoT devices, 368, 376–378, 399
Securing IoT networks, 41, 42, 45, 318, 383, 386, 474
Security, 29, 232, 242, 254, 264, 277, 278
    administrator rules, 292
    measures, 23, 34
    mechanisms, 192
Security information and event management (SIEM), 333, 334, 348, 412, 457
    designing and deployment, IoT cybersecurity, 460
    automation and orchestration, 463, 464
    data management and retention policies, 463
    integration capabilities, 461, 462
    scalability, 461
    security analytics and threat intelligence, 462, 463
    UEBA, 464
    requirement, in IoT cybersecurity, 458
    value proposition in IoT cybersecurity
        for leadership team, 459
        for security operations center (SOC) team, 459, 460

INDEX

Security operations centers (SOCs), 330, 332, 412
    awareness and training, 335
    building block, 332
    collaboration and communication, 335
    containment and recovery, 336
    and DevSecOps, 338
    framework, 332
    functions
        intelligence gathering, 334
        monitoring, 334
    in IoT cybersecurity, 336
    operates, 334
    operations, 334, 335
    roles, 333
    security tools and software, 333
    threat intelligence and proactive defense, 336
Security orchestration, automation and response (SOAR)
    automation and orchestration, 465
    designing and deployment, IoT cybersecurity
        automation, 470
        compliance requirements, 471
        data management and retention policies, 471
        integration capabilities, 470
        orchestration, 470
        scalability, 469
        security analytics, 470
        threat intelligence, 470
        UEBA, 471
    requirements in IoT cybersecurity, 467, 468
    role in IoT cybersecurity, 466, 467
    security challenges, 466
    security solutions, 465
    security tools, 465
    value proposition in IoT cybersecurity
        for leadership team, 468
        for security operations centers (SOCs) team, 469
Security teams, 347, 349, 399
Segments, 153, 422
Sensors, 6, 18–20, 67, 69, 401
Service Discovery Protocol (SDP), 191
Shift-Left Security, 337
SIEM, *see* Security information and event management (SIEM)
SLAAC, *see* Stateless autoconfiguration (SLAAC)
Smart meters, 38
SOAR, *see* Security orchestration, automation and response (SOAR)
SOCs, *see* Security operations centers (SOCs)
Spoofing, 156, 157, 492, 495, 496
Spread spectrum, 183, 184
SSL, *see* Secure Sockets Layer (SSL)
Standard actuators, 19

Standard transport
   protocols, 121
Star topology, 181, 227, 231
  advantage, 233, 234
  central hub, 234
  central hub/switch, 231
  disadvantages, 234
  IoT/IIoT networks, 231, 232
  key features, 232, 233
  works, 234, 235
Stateless autoconfiguration
   (SLAAC), 172
Storage
  in IoT systems, 497
Stream Analytics, 93, 280
STRIDE model, 492
Supply chain management
   (SCM), 74, 75
Symmetric key attestation, 212

T

Tampering, 492, 495–497
TCP, *see* Transmission Control
   Protocol (TCP)
TCP/IP, *see* Transmission Control
   Protocol/Internet Protocol
   (TCP/IP)
TEE, *see* Trusted execution
   environment (TEE)
Temperature sensors, 18, 23, 69, 70,
   141, 224, 522
Threat Intelligence and
   Monitoring, 385

TLS, *see* Transport Layer
   Security (TLS)
TPMs, *see* Trusted platform
   modules (TPMs)
Traditional hub-and-spoke
   deployment, 291
Traditional network management
   approaches, 263
Traditional network topology
  critical factors, 286
  design network architecture, 288
  IoT networks
    deployment
      recommendations, 288
    design considerations, 286
  organization, 285
Traditional software development
   methodologies, 352
Traffic Manager, 269
Transmission Control Protocol
   (TCP), 101, 118, 144, 146
  advantages, 151
  architecture and
    components, 152
  congestion
    management, 153
  connection
    establishment, 152
  data integrity and
    security, 151
  error detection and
    recovery, 153
  flow control, 153
  HTTP protocol, 152

565

INDEX

Transmission Control Protocol
(TCP) (*cont.*)
  interoperability and compatibility, 154
  IP layer, 152
  resource optimization, 154, 155
  security enhancements, 154
  segmentation and reassembly, 153
compatibility with network infrastructure, 150
data integrity, 147
encryption for confidentiality, 148
error detection and correction, 149
error recovery mechanisms, 150
establish and maintain reliable connections, 149
flow control, 147, 149
interoperability, 150
in IoT environments, 145
mitigating threats through authentication, 147
optimizes performance, 147, 149
regulating access through firewalls and proxies, 148
reliable connections, 147
resilience against network failures, 148
scalability, 150
secure authentication and encryption, 149

Transmission Control Protocol/
Internet Protocol (TCP/IP), 98, 115, 146, 246, 247
Transparency, 374, 375, 424
Transport layer, 121
  characteristics, 144
  data integrity, 121
  end-to-end communication, 143
  flow control and control mechanisms, 145
  in IoT networks, 145
  reliability, 146
  reliability of data transmission, 144
  remote monitoring and control systems, 144
  security, 145
  standard transport protocols, 121
  TCP, 144, 146
  UDP, 144, 146, 155–163
Transport Layer Security (TLS), 118, 134, 136, 142, 145, 149, 154
Tree topology, 227, 258
  advantages, 260
  disadvantages, 261
  IoT/IIoT networks, 258, 259
  key features, 259, 260
  nodes, 257
  works, 261, 262
Trusted execution environment (TEE), 323
Trusted platform modules (TPMs), 209, 212, 375, 379

INDEX

U

Ubiquitous network architecture
    benefits, 266
    embedding computing capabilities, 266
    fundamental principles, 265
    goal, 265
    smart homes, 266
    technologies, 265
    transformative future vision, 266
UDP, *see* User Datagram Protocol (UDP)
Uniform Resource Locator (URL), 118, 511, 514
URL, *see* Uniform Resource Locator (URL)
User and entity behavior analytics (UEBA)
    and NDR solution, 478
    and SIEM system, 464
    and SOAR solution, 471
    and XDR solution, 487, 488
User Datagram Protocol (UDP), 118, 124, 130, 144, 146
    advantages, 158, 159, 163
    architecture, 160, 163
    communication, 161, 162
    components, 161–163
    datagrams, 155
    datagram structure, 160, 161
    flexibility, 157
    IoT applications, 156
    in IoT landscape, 155
    low latency, 155, 157
    protocol compatibility, 158
    resource efficiency, 157
    robust performance, 158
    scalability, 157
    security considerations, 157
    simplicity and speed, 155
    trade-offs, 163
    transport, 126
User interfaces, 73, 74, 85, 121, 123, 349, 500, 502

V

Vehicle-to-everything (V2X), 37
Vehicle-to-vehicle (V2V), 37
Virtual Local Area Networks (VLANs), 342, 343, 381, 383, 431
Virtual Network Manager, 290–292
Virtual Networks (VNets), 267, 297, 312, 313, 318
Virtual WAN network topology
    connectivity strategies, 281
    IoT networks
        design considerations, 282
        design recommendations, 283, 284
    Microsoft-managed service, 281
    optimal network architecture, design, 283
    organizations planning, 281
VLANs, *see* Virtual Local Area Networks (VLANs)

INDEX

VOCs, *see* Volatile organic compounds (VOCs)
Volatile organic compounds (VOCs), 32
VNets, *see* Virtual Networks (VNets)
VPN Gateway, 297
Vulnerability management, 333, 348, 396, 404, 434, 446, 447
V2V, *see* Vehicle-to-vehicle (V2V)
V2X, *see* Vehicle-to-everything (V2X)

W

WANs198, *see* Wide area networks (WANs)
Web-based dashboards, 73, 121
Wide area networks (WANs), 5, 192–194, 198, 274
Wi-Fi, 7, 11, 20, 70, 100, 103, 121, 164, 193, 194, 198, 200, 247, 257, 262, 374, 420
Wired communication systems, 102
Wired networks, 7, 100
Wired protocols, 71
Wireless communication systems, 103
Wireless mesh networks, 255, 257
Wireless networks, 3, 7, 13, 17, 53, 60, 100, 166, 173, 175, 178, 182, 183, 199, 247
Wireless sensor networks (WSNs), 173
Wireless technologies, 20
WSNs, *see* Wireless sensor networks (WSNs)

X, Y

X.509 certificate attestation, 211
XMPP, *see* Extensible Messaging and Presence Protocol (XMPP)
XDR, *see* Extended detection and response (XDR)

Z

Zero trust, 94, 277, 278, 366, 370, 393
 in IoT networks, 364, 367
 policies, 365
 principles, 359, 360, 363, 366

GPSR Compliance

The European Union's (EU) General Product Safety Regulation (GPSR) is a set of rules that requires consumer products to be safe and our obligations to ensure this.

If you have any concerns about our products, you can contact us on

ProductSafety@springernature.com

In case Publisher is established outside the EU, the EU authorized representative is:

Springer Nature Customer Service Center GmbH
Europaplatz 3
69115 Heidelberg, Germany